The Humane Vision of Wendell Berry

# The Humane Vision
# of Wendell Berry

Edited by
Mark T. Mitchell and Nathan Schlueter

Wilmington, Delaware

Library of Congress Cataloging-in-Publication Data

The humane vision of Wendell Berry / edited by Mark T. Mitchell and Nathan Schlueter.
    p. cm.
    Includes bibliographical references and index.
    ISBN 978-1-61017-001-7
1.  Berry, Wendell, 1934– —Criticism and interpretation.  I. Mitchell, Mark T.
    II. Schlueter, Nathan W.

    PS3552.E75Z73 2011
    818'.5409—dc23                    2011021519

Published in the United States by:

ISI Books
Intercollegiate Studies Institute
3901 Centerville Road
Wilmington, Delaware 19807-1938
www.isibooks.org

*We dedicate this book to our children, Seth, Noah, and Scott Mitchell, and Leo, Helen, Emil, Karol, Mary, and William Schlueter, for keeping alive our hope, beyond expectation.*

# Contents

Introduction ix

Chapter 1: Wendell Berry, a Placed Person 1
    Wallace Stegner

Chapter 2: Marriage in the Membership 7
    Anne Husted Burleigh

Chapter 3: Not Safe, nor Private, nor Free: Wendell Berry on 19
Sexual Love and Procreation
    Allan Carlson

Chapter 4: An Education for Membership: Wendell Berry on 28
Schools and Communities
    Richard Gamble

Chapter 5: And for This Food, We Give Thanks 40
    Matt Bonzo

Chapter 6: The Third Landscape: Wendell Berry and 50
American Conservation
    Jason Peters

Chapter 7: Wendell Berry and Democratic Self-Governance 65
    Patrick J. Deneen

Chapter 8: First They Came for the Horses: Wendell Berry 89
and a Technology of Wholeness
    Caleb Stegall

Chapter 9: Living Peace in the Shadow of War: 106
Wendell Berry's Dogged Pacifism
    Michael R. Stevens

Chapter 10: Wendell Berry's Unlikely Case for 124
Conservative Christianity
    D. G. Hart

Chapter 11: The Rediscovery of *Oikonomia* 147
    Mark Shiffman

Chapter 12: Wendell Berry's Defense of a Truly Free Market 167
    Mark T. Mitchell

Chapter 13: The Restoration of Propriety: Wendell Berry 190
and the British Distributists
    William Edmund Fahey

Chapter 14: The Integral Imagination of Wendell Berry 210
    Nathan Schlueter

Chapter 15: Earth and Flesh Sing Together:
The Place of Wendell Berry's Poetry in His Vision of the Human 234
    Luke Schlueter

Chapter 16: If Dante Were a Kentucky Barber 255
    Anthony Esolen

Chapter 17: Wendell Berry: A Latter-Day St. Benedict 275
    Rod Dreher

Acknowledgments 288

Notes 289

The Works of Wendell Berry: A Selected Bibliography 319

About the Authors 322

Index 325

# Introduction

*Mark T. Mitchell and Nathan Schlueter*

On a warm Sunday afternoon in the summer of 2006, we drove down a winding country road to Lane's Landing Farm in Henry County, Kentucky. We had arranged to visit Wendell Berry, whose hillside farm lies just outside the tiny village of Port Royal. We were greeted by Tanya, Wendell's wife of more than fifty years. Wendell soon joined us, and we spent the afternoon on the porch talking and laughing. The man was as delightful in person as we had hoped.

The bare facts of his biography suggest something of the man. Born in 1934 in Henry County, Kentucky, Berry attended the University of Kentucky, where in 1956 he earned a B.A. in English followed by an M.A. in English in 1957. He and Tanya were married in 1957, and they soon embarked on several years of travel away from Kentucky. Berry attended Stanford University as a Wallace Stegner Fellow and then lived in Italy for a year on a Guggenheim Fellowship, after which he secured a teaching job at New York University. But after two years, and against the professional advice of most of his friends and acquaintances, Berry returned home to his native Kentucky, purchasing a farm overlooking the Kentucky River and adjacent to the favorite haunt of his youth, the "Camp." According to Berry, this fateful decision was not merely the result of personal preference; it was emblematic of his deeper commitment to being a "placed person," a theme that pervades nearly all of his writings. After returning to Kentucky, Berry taught creative writing at the University of Kentucky until he left academia altogether. For more than fifty years, Berry has been a prolific writer. At last count, he is the author of fourteen works of fiction, twenty-three collections of essays, and twenty-two books of poetry, in addition to many other uncollected essays, short stories, and poems.

Although Berry is often associated with the political Left, it is our conviction that his work is profoundly conservative and that, as a consequence, conservatives should attend carefully to what he writes. As evidence of his conservatism, one might cite his position on any number of issues a conservative would recognize: his defense of decentralization and the relative autonomy of local communities; his healthy suspicion of government power and support for a robust civil society; his hostility to the welfare state and defense of private property; his opposition to abortion, promiscuity, and divorce; his respect for tradition and distrust of leveling abstractions such as scientism. At the same time, Berry also holds positions that would make many American conservatives uncomfortable, including his pacifism, conservationism, and opposition to corporate capitalism.

Berry, however, is more than the sum of his positions on the issues. We agree with Anne Husted Burleigh that he is "too gifted and universal to be claimed by any one movement or literary tradition," whether it be liberalism or conservatism.[1] Berry himself resists such labels, although he will occasionally describe himself as an agrarian in the Jeffersonian tradition. This seems an intriguing and revealing self-description, for it points to that salutary tension in the thought of both Jefferson and Berry between Enlightenment concerns for individual liberty and limited government on the one hand, and classical republican concerns for virtue and the common good on the other, both of which played a decisive role in the founding of America.

The agrarianism of Jefferson and Berry is grounded in an appreciation of the moral and political value of culture and agriculture, and centers on what Berry has called "the democratic ownership of the land."[2] In the words of Jefferson, whom Berry quotes, "it is not too soon to provide by every possible means that as few as possible shall be without a little portion of land. The small landholders are the most precious part of a state."[3]

It is important to point out that Berry is not simply yearning for a lost agrarian past. He is not suggesting that the cities be summarily abandoned for the farm. He is, however, suggesting that the industrial mind is fundamentally different from a mind formed by agrarian values, for industrialism and agrarianism represent essential dispositions and not merely two forms of labor. Berry writes:

> I believe that this contest between industrialism and agrarianism now defines the most fundamental human difference, for it divides not just two nearly opposite concepts of agriculture and land use, but also two nearly opposite ways of understanding ourselves, our fellow creatures, and our world.[4]

While at one level, Jeffersonian agrarianism seems to capture something of Berry's humane vision, the description is incomplete. For example, one could never imagine Jefferson writing something like the following:

> I take literally the statement in the Gospel of John that God loves the world. I believe the world was created and approved by love, that it subsists, coheres, and endures by love, and that, insofar as it is redeemable, it can be redeemed only by love. I believe that divine love, incarnate and indwelling in the world, summons the world always toward wholeness, which ultimately is reconciliation and atonement with God.[5]

This passage brings one much closer to the central thread of Berry's thought. In scope and sentiment it is redolent of Dante, one of Berry's favorite poets, and expresses his confidence in the ultimate goodness of God and the harmony of Creation. Again like Dante's vision, Berry's humane vision points to an integral whole, which refuses to dissolve particulars into the universal (as transcendentalism and scientism do) or to reduce the universal to its particulars (as romanticism often does). In doing justice to both the universal and the particulars, his humane vision can be described as both analogical and sacramental. Once more like Dante, Berry seeks to grasp the whole but is not afraid to admit of mystery, a fact that explains much of the surprising freshness one discovers in his writings.

Berry frequently refers to the natural world as a "creation." Creation implies that nature is an ordered whole established by an intelligent and loving Creator. While Berry's precise understanding of that Creator is open to dispute (some of our essays treat this problem), Berry falls firmly within the biblical tradition when he points to the peculiar place of human beings within the created order. Neither beasts nor gods, human beings participate in both material and spiritual reality. They are neither wholly autonomous nor wholly determined by the natural world. This means that although they are intelligent and free, they are so in a particularly human or limited way. They are more like actors who find themselves in a drama they did not create, whose part is to discover, acknowledge, and act a particular role with propriety and grace upon the stage where they have been placed.

In this, Berry is no more of a romantic or utopian than Dante. He is perfectly aware of the pervasive and enduring obstacles to wholeness in the created order. He writes:

> This is also a fallen world. It involves error and disease, ignorance and partiality, sin and death. If this world is a place where we may learn of our involvement in immortal love, as I believe it is, still such learning is only possible here because that love involves us so inescapably in the limits, sufferings and sorrows of mortality.[6]

Moreover, not all human limits are the result of man's fallen condition. Some follow from the simple fact that man is not God and that his achievable wholeness involves the free and responsible participation in an order he did not make. Like St. Augustine, Berry affirms that human beings can have only an imperfect knowledge of the whole and so must learn to act with respect for what they do not know. Following T. S. Eliot, Berry calls this recognition "the way of ignorance."[7] The way of ignorance is the way of humility in the face of what we do not and cannot know about the past, the present, and the future. It is born of wonder, expressed in reverence, and rooted in faith.

Far from being a utopian, then, Berry offers the only real antidote to utopianism. For utopianism is ultimately grounded in the Gnostic conviction that nature is fundamentally hostile to human flourishing and must therefore be subjugated by human power. It is the mad Machiavellian quest to gain complete control over fortune for the relief of man's estate and therefore is a refusal to accept and recognize the goodness in the limits of the created order.

Americans ordinarily associate utopianism with the speculative and totalitarian systems of twentieth-century communism and fascism, and therefore rest in the complacent belief that we are free of its influence. Yet utopianism is seductive and manifests itself in guises quite palatable to the liberal soul. Berry stands against all *isms* that would reduce the whole to one of its parts or dissolve all of the parts into one universal whole. He is for piety against pietism, intellect against intellectualism, individuality against individualism, community against communitarianism, liberty against libertarianism.

It is one of Berry's most important achievements, then, to reveal with singular eloquence the implicit utopianism that often lurks at the very heart of liberal society, a utopianism all the more dangerous because it is hidden from our view. Fortunately, through his poetry and fiction, Berry's mythopoeic medicine provides the moral imagination with a powerful inoculation against the false promises of utopianism in all its forms.

As with that other man for all seasons, Thomas More, Berry's work grows naturally from a fixed center of intellectual and moral character that constitutes his humane vision. And also like More, Berry couched his moral seriousness in good humor. Few people enjoy a good joke as much as Berry, and if you happen to visit him, you are bound to hear a few, delivered with the ease of a practiced storyteller, spoken in a soft Kentucky drawl, and concluded with a hearty and contagious laugh. This cheer in the midst of care is a reflection of Berry's abiding hope, a testament to his sanity, and an example of his eager desire to do justice to the whole of reality.

Hope, humor, sanity—and not the shrill voice of talk radio and cable television—are the marks of any conservatism worthy of the name. Berry offers us the possibility of a conservatism informed by a humane vision open to all of reality. It is sustained by a recognition of the ultimate giftedness of the created order, and it responds with gratitude. These gifts include not only the natural world but also our cultural inheritance, our political institutions, our local communities, our families, and indeed our very selves. He makes us aware of the various ways we are all dependent—on one another, on the natural world, and ultimately on God. He calls his readers to live lives of gratitude, responsibility, friendship, and love. These notions, we contend, should be at the heart of a thoughtful and coherent conservatism.

We begin our collection of essays with a reprint of an open letter written to Berry by his friend and mentor, novelist Wallace Stegner. We take no position on where Stegner falls on the liberal/conservative continuum, but we include the letter here because it expresses so well the integrity of Wendell Berry not only as a writer but also as a human being. The remaining essays were written by individuals who, despite their differences, write as social conservatives. Each has learned much from Berry and finds a deep kinship with his work. Yet for all that, the essays are not merely appreciative summations of Berry's ideas. This collection attempts to engage critically Berry's ideas and to situate them within the larger context of conservative thought. Each essay, therefore, is itself a contribution to the conversation that is conservatism.

As we were leaving the farm on that summer day in 2006, Berry remarked that, curiously, liberals publish him but conservatives come to visit. We took the remark as a compliment as well as a challenge. This book is our response. By it we intend to express our gratitude to a man who has taught us much. By it we also hope to introduce conservatives to the richness, beauty, and wisdom of Berry's work. Ultimately, we hope to encourage a fruitful intellectual engagement between Berry, conservatives, and thoughtful people of all political persuasions.

# I

# Wendell Berry, a Placed Person

## *Wallace Stegner*

*In the 1958–59 academic year, Berry received a fellowship to study creative writing at Stanford University under the American novelist and essayist Wallace Stegner. This open letter from Stegner to Berry, written in 1990, captures well the integrity of Berry the artist and Berry the man.*

Greensboro, Vermont
July 25, 1990

Dear Wendell,

It has taken me a long time to write you about your latest book [*What Are People For?*], and I know exactly why. I want to praise not only the book but the man who wrote it, and it embarrasses my post-Protestant sensibilities to tell a man to his face that I admire him. If I know you, what I want to say will embarrass you too, but we will both have to stand it.

Obviously I have not got through a long life without praising people—their houses, their gardens, their wives, their children, their political opinions, quite often their writing. But though I have liked a lot of people and loved a few, I have never been much good at telling them so, or telling them why. The more my admiration goes out to a man or woman personally, and not to some performance or accomplishment, the harder it is for

I

me to express. The closer I come to fundamental values and beliefs, the closer I come to reticence. It is a more naked act for me to tell someone I am impressed by his principles and his integrity than to say that I like his book or his necktie.

Nevertheless, though I admire this book as I have admired all of yours since you read the last chapters of *Nathan Coulter* in my Stanford classroom more than thirty years ago, and though I am touched by the inclusion of a friendly essay on myself, I want to say something further, whether it embarrasses us both or not. I acknowledge you as a splendid poet, novelist, and short story writer, and as one of the most provocative and thoughtful essayists alive, and I am not unaware that as a writer you make me, one of your "teachers," look good. My problem is that I can't look upon your books simply as books, literary artifacts. Without your ever intending it, without the slightest taint of self-promotion, they are substantial chunks of yourself, the expression of qualities and beliefs that are fundamental, profound, and rare, things that not even your gift of words can out-dazzle.

That gift, as Conrad says somewhere, is not such great matter: a man is not a hunter or warrior just because he owns a gun. When I quote you, as I often do, I am paying tribute to your verbal felicity, which is always there, but I am really quoting you for qualities of thoughtfulness, character, integrity, and responsibility to which I respond, and to which I would probably respond if they were expressed in pidgin.

Those qualities inform every page of *What Are People For?* They are fleshed out in the people you approve, such as Nate Shaw, Harry Caudill, and Ed Abbey. They are documented in your stout preference for the natural over the artificial or industrial, the simple over the complex, the labor-intensive over the labor-saving, a team of Belgians over a tractor, manure over chemical fertilizers, natural variety over man-managed monocultures. You reaffirm, in "Writer and Region," the respect for place that was evident in *A Place on Earth*, *The Unsettling of America*, *A Continuous Harmony*, *The Long-Legged House*, and other books. In humorously repudiating the speed and ease of the word processor you repeat your lifelong distaste for technical innovations that elevate the mechanical and reduce the human. In "The Pleasures of Eating" you carry your belief in natural wholesomeness from the production to the consumption of foods, and emphasize your sense of the relatedness of the agricultural and the cultural.

Some people have compared you with Thoreau, probably because you use your own head to think with and because you have a reverence for the natural earth. I am not sure the comparison can be carried too far, though it is meant to be flattering. Thoreau seems to me a far colder article than you have ever been or could ever be. He was a triumphant and somewhat chilly consummation of New England intellectualism and Emersonian self-reliance. Emerson himself said he would as like take hold of an oak limb as Henry's arm. You are something else. The nature you love is not wild but humanized, disciplined to the support of human families but not overused, not exploited. Your province is not the wilderness, where the individual makes contact with the universe, but the farm, the neighborhood, the community, the town, the memory of the past, and the hope of the future—everything that is subsumed for you under the word "place." Your "ruminations," as you call them, most often deal with matters that did not engage Thoreau's mind: human relations, love, marriage, parenthood, neighborliness, shared pleasures, shared sorrow, shared work and responsibility. Your natural move is not inward toward transcendental consciousness, but outward toward membership, toward family and community and human cohesion. Though you share with Thoreau a delight in the natural world and the pleasures of thought, I think you do not share his austerity, and I doubt that you will end, as he did, as a surveyor of town lots.

What has always struck me as remarkable about you, and hence about your writing, is how little you have been influenced either by the fads of *Tendenzliteratur* or by the haunted and self-destructive examples of many contemporary writers. You may well have learned from the Delmore Schwartzes, the John Berrymans, the Randall Jarrells, the Sylvia Plaths, but I can't conceive of a time, even in your most erratic youth, when you were in danger of following them down. . . . You never had a drinking problem or a drug problem; you have been as apparently immune to the *Angst* of your times as you have been indifferent to contemporary hedonism and the lust for kicks.

By every stereotypical rule of the twentieth century you should be dull, and I suppose there are some people, especially people who have not read you, who think you are. By upbringing and by choice you are a countryman, and therefore a sort of anachronism. The lives you write about are not lives that challenge or defy the universe, or despair of it, but lives that accept it and make the best of it and are in sober ways fulfilled.

We have grown used to the image of the artist as a person more notable for his sensibility than his balance. We might go to that artist for the flash of insight, often achieved at terrible cost to himself, but not for sober wisdom. I don't disparage those Dionysian writers; they have lighted dark corners for all of us, and will continue to. But I find your example comforting because it restores a lost balance—one doesn't *have* to be crazy, or alcoholic, or suicidal, or manic, to be a legitimate spokesman to the world, and there is more to literature, as there clearly is to life, than aberration and sadomasochism. Your books *seem* conservative. They are actually profoundly revolutionary, and I have watched them gain you an increasingly devoted following over the years. Readers respond to them as lost dogs in hope of rescue turn toward some friendly stranger. The thought in your essays is so clear and unrattled that it reassures us. Your stories and poems are good like bread.

I say that your books are revolutionary. They are. They fly in the face of accepted opinion and approved fashion. They reassert values so commonly forgotten or repudiated that, reasserted, they have the force of novelty. In *What Are People For?* you quote some correspondents who are dumbstruck at your refusal to use a word processor, and your explanation of your refusal is as revolutionary as it is sane: you don't *want* the speed and ease of a word processor. You already, you say, write too fast and too easily. (You don't, but that is partly because you understand that a degree of difficulty is as necessary to prose as a scythe stone is to a scythe.) You don't want very many of the speed-and-ease facilitators of industrial life. You want, as many others of us do, to be able to work even if the power is down. You understand such things as word processors as the fences and walls that can collectively imprison us. You prefer to be free and at large, with your pad and pencil. But you want to be free in the place you have chosen, in the society of which you are a voluntary member.

From the time when you first appeared as a Fellow in the writing program at Stanford in 1958, I recognized you as one who knew where he was from and who he was. Your career since has given not only me but a large public the spectacle of an entirely principled literary life, a life not merely observant and thoughtful and eloquent but highly responsible, a life in which aesthetics and ethics do not have to be kept apart to prevent their quarreling, but live together in harmony. During the thirty-two years since we first met, plenty of people have consciously or unconsciously tried to influence the direction of your life. You tried the wider world for a few years, at Stanford, in New York, on a year's Guggenheim in Italy, and eventually you concluded that you belonged back in Kentucky, where you had come from.

That was a move as radical as Thoreau's retreat to Walden, and much more permanent. I am sure that people told you you were burying yourself, that you couldn't come into the literary world with manure on your barn boots and expect to be welcomed, that you owed it to yourself and your gift to stay out where the action was. I was myself guilty of trying to persuade you against your decision, for some time in the 1960s I alighted at your Kentucky River farm and tried to talk you into coming to Stanford on some permanent basis. Fortunately, I got nowhere. And you and I both know of a more dramatic instance when you refused an opportunity that many writers would sell their souls for. You refused it because you felt that it might obligate you or impede your freedom of mind. Some might have called you stubborn, or perhaps too timid to risk yourself in deep water. I learned to think of you as simply steadfast.

It has been a robust satisfaction to me that, incongruous as you are in post–World War II America, little as you reflect the homogenized and hyperventilated lives of termite Americans, stoutly as you rebuff the blandishments of technology and progress and the efforts to make life effortless, you have won a large and respectful audience. You have established yourself as a major figure in the environmental movement, even though the environmentalism you promote is really stewardship in land use, and has less popular appeal than the preservation of wilderness, parks, and recreational land. You look upon the earth not mystically but practically, as a responsible husbandman, but your very practicality has made you one of the strongest voices against land abuse.

Those who read you devoutly—and this letter is an indication that I am one of them—find something else in you that their world too much lacks: the value, the real physical and spiritual satisfaction, of hard human work. We respond to your pages as victims of pellagra or scurvy respond to vitamins. You may lack readers among agribusinessmen and among those whose computers have already made unnecessary both the multiplication tables and the brains that once learned them, but you are a hero among those who have been wounded and offended by industrial living and yearn for a simpler and more natural and more feeling relation to the natural world.

And you give us all this with such directness and grace. "Grace" is a word that in fact I borrow from you, and it is the only word that fits. In an essay you comment on two fishing stories, Hemingway's "Big Two-Hearted River" and Norman Maclean's "A River Runs Through It," the one "a feat of style" that deals with mystery and complication by refusing to deal with it, the other a work of art that ultimately "subjects itself to its subject." I like that distinction, for it helps to clarify your own performance. None of your writings that I know, and I think I must know almost all, can be dismissed as a feat of style. Everything you write subjects itself to its subject, grapples with the difficult and perhaps inexpressible, confronts mystery, conveys real and observed and felt life, and does so modestly and with grace. In the best sense of the word, your writing is a by-product of your living.

I should add that you wouldn't be as good a man as you are if you were not a member of Tanya, and she of you.

Yours,
Wallace Stegner

# 2

# Marriage in the Membership

*Anne Husted Burleigh*

In the year 2007, on May 29, Wendell and Tanya Berry marked their fiftieth wedding anniversary. Wendell protested against a party, but, as Tanya said, their children announced they were having one anyway—and a fine party it was, hosted at the Smith-Berry Vineyard and Winery on a beautiful evening in June.

It was a joy to congratulate Wendell and Tanya, my friends and Kentucky neighbors, on their fifty years of marriage. A half century of marriage is a great accomplishment for any couple—but in the case of Wendell and Tanya, it meant even more. Tanya is the reason, Wendell undoubtedly would say, that he has been able to write what he has written. Without Tanya, Wendell would have written things, but they would be different from and less than the essays, stories, and poems he has given us.

The theme of marriage is utterly central to Wendell Berry's work. Whether we address Berry's fiction, his poetry, or his essays, the same theme is pivotal and fundamental: the mysterious love and life of a man and woman in marriage.

Because Wendell Berry respects the profound mystery that both absorbs and transcends a man and woman in marriage, he treats marriage with delicacy and reverence. He also treats it as the foundation stone of community, the means by which we become members of a community and stewards of the place where we are, the place we are given.

In the order of the gifts of Creation bestowed upon Adam and Eve, marriage is basic in its capacity to unite man and woman in friendship, in membership. To begin human life in right order is to begin with marriage—and so, consequently, in the order of Berry's novels, stories, essays, and poetry, to begin at the beginning is to begin with marriage.

Marriage is also to acknowledge that we are looking at a connection between two people that is not private. This relationship that begins with a mere glance in one another's direction or an unseen flutter of the heart, this relationship that one assumed was a private bond between two people, turns out to be a vastly open connection that impacts the children who come from it, the community that both arises from it and supports it, the country that builds upon it, and the civilization that springs from it. Even as a marriage appears to be mostly a private affair, it has ramifications that are political, economic, and cultural. Although marriage is a domestic relationship, it is also an institution that is distinctly civil and, as such, is ratified and witnessed by the community. In Berry's writing, there is no such thing as a marriage that is solely private; it always is related to the community; it always is responsible to the community, just as the community is responsible to it. The reader who seeks a pair of romantic lovers who hold themselves apart from or above responsibility to the community will almost never find them in Wendell Berry's fiction. The enduring romantic pair in Berry's stories are sure to be loyal to the commonwealth. Appropriately for a writer who lives in the Commonwealth of Kentucky, Berry often uses this rich medieval term *commonwealth*, by which he means a community united for the purpose of the common good.

Whether he is writing a story, a poem, or an essay, Wendell Berry addresses three elements of marriage: fidelity, incarnation, and memory.

The first of these themes is crucial to the other two—that is, marriage is based on fidelity, and fidelity is the foundation of all relationships, civil and domestic. Fidelity is the foundation of order, order in the soul, order in the family, order in the community. Fidelity is the foundation of all law, moral law and civil law. Even more, fidelity is the signature, the guarantor, the seal, the very essence of love. Fidelity is the word of love, the promise that enables love to last, to stretch across time and distance and between generations. Fidelity makes us better, nobler, greater, wiser, stronger than we are or could be without it. Fidelity is the word of love without which none of us would find life worth living.

As Andy Catlett says in Berry's story "Pray Without Ceasing," "You work your way down, or not so much down as within, into the interior of the present, until finally you come to that beginning in which all things, the world and the light itself, at a word welled up into being out of their absence."[1] Andy is talking about God's word, which, once given, wells up into life itself. God's word when uttered becomes the very reality that God speaks. We can give our word because God first gives his. His faithfulness to us is the reality of which our fidelity—to him and to each other—is the reflection. God's word, which is faithfulness itself, stands behind our words and makes possible both our capacity and our duty to stand by our words.

It is significant that one of Berry's most important books of essays bears the apt title *Standing by Words*. In Berry's writing, words are serious business, serious because they relate to reality itself, to the reality of God's word. Berry is a careful writer who uses words with great reverence and economy. In his view, how we stand by our words, doing what we say we will, being who we say we are, is the very measure of our fidelity to those we love and to the community. Berry's loyalty to the truth of the words he uses, the extreme care he takes with his words, is a key to the power of his writing. Like his best characters of the Port William membership, such as Mat Feltner, Burley Coulter, Wheeler Catlett, and Andy Catlett, Wendell Berry is a faithful man. He is also a faithful writer.

Fidelity, standing by one's words, is the standing in place, staying in place and not leaving, that is requisite to marriage. The faithfulness of marriage is fidelity to the word, the vow one has given, the word one chooses to give and gives over and over.

One bright Sunday afternoon, Wendell and I sat talking at his kitchen table.

"That question of whether or not people stand by their word and take it seriously is a real issue," Wendell said. "I think the fundamental fact of a marriage is that you've given your word." Continuing the conversation, he went on:

Marriage for me has great power as a metaphor or analogue of other relationships. In an intact community, the marriage vows are given *before* the membership. The couple doesn't just exchange them with one another. The vows are given *before* witnesses, who are there partly because they are party to the contract. This young couple is pledging from now on to be to a certain extent predictable in their behavior. It's a terrible thing to say those vows. Something like that *ought* to be witnessed by people who will acknowledge that it happened and that these awe-full things were said. And in my own experience the sense of having loved ones' expectations directed toward me has been very influential, and it still is.[2]

The requirement to stand by one's words, to remain faithful to the promise one has made to another, to *be* there, in place, and not to leave holds true whether in a marriage or in the larger membership of the community. Says Berry in one of his "Sabbath" poems:

Whatever happens,
those who have learned
to love one another
have made their way
to the lasting world
and will not leave,
whatever happens.[3]

Yet the very choice to be faithful, no matter what, sets up the possibility of disappointment and suffering. Choosing to give oneself in a marriage opens the chance that love will not be returned, or it will be returned inadequately, or external circumstances may derail the best laid plans of the couple.

Berry's character Jayber Crow says,

Just as a good man would not coerce the love of his wife, God does not coerce the love of His human creatures, not for Himself, or for the world or for one another. To allow that love to exist fully and freely, He must allow it not to exist at all. His love is suffering. It is our freedom and His sorrow. To love the world as much even as I could love it would be suffering also, for I would fail. And yet all the good I know is in this, that a man might so love this world that it would break his heart.[4]

The temptation, especially where no community exists to protect, insulate, and hold accountable the two spouses, is sometimes for the troubled husband or wife—or both—to run away.

As Wendell said about marriage on that Sunday afternoon:

> What marriage says is to stay and find out. It doesn't say what you are going to find out. When you think this is it, we are at a complete dead end here, the marriage says to you: wait, stay and find out. Always you find out more. The thing is too great to be belittled by any decision that you can make about it. This is the same for your relation to the community or anything else.[5]

Marriage, in which the giving of the spouses to each other is both so powerful and so vulnerable that it must be protected by the membership of the community, is the natural ally of the community. Marriage and community, depending "absolutely on trust," as Berry puts it in his essay "Sex, Economy, Freedom, and Community," cannot do without each other.[6] Thus faithful husbands and wives are faithful members of the community.

Faithful couples drive the Port William membership at the same time that they are supported by it: Marce and Dorie Catlett, Mat and Margaret Feltner, Wheeler and Bess Catlett, Elton and Mary Penn, Danny and Lyda Branch, Andy and Flora Catlett, Hannah and Virgil Feltner, and then, after Virgil's death in World War II, Hannah and Nathan Coulter. Even Burley Coulter, who admitted he learned things too late, took responsibility for his might-as-well-be wife, Kate Helen Branch. Jayber Crow, a lifelong bachelor, in a heroic vow of faithful love known only to himself, made himself the spiritual husband of Mattie Keith, whose own husband, Troy, was unfaithful to her. The way Jayber saw it, "My marriage to Mattie was validated in a way by Troy's invalidation of his marriage to her."[7] All those years Jayber never let on to Mattie or to anyone else that he had taken a marriage vow to her.

"All I can say is," Jayber explained, "that I did love her all my life— from the time before I ever saw her, it seems, and until she died. I do love her all her life, and still, and always."[8]

Wendell Berry's stories are anchored in fidelity. The aberrations of modern culture that sometimes are touted as marriage have no place in

Berry's work. Not until one of his most recent novels, *Hannah Coulter*, does Berry address the modern pestilence of divorce. It is an ugly topic that Berry has put off until lately—no doubt because, despite some unhappy marriages among its members, the Port William membership cannot survive divorce, at least not more than an occasional case. The shattering fact of a series of divorces is death to the membership. When a spouse departs from a marriage, he leaves not only his wife and children; he also leaves the membership. A disloyal spouse is unfaithful on two counts: to the betrayed spouse and children and to the membership.

The Tuesday that Hannah Coulter heard her daughter Margaret's car come over the hill, slow down, and turn into the lane, Hannah sensed something was wrong. Greeting Margaret in the backyard, Hannah asked, "Where's Marcus?"

"She could manage only one word, 'Gone,' and then," Hannah said, "I was holding my daughter all in pieces in my arms."

As Hannah tells the story, Marcus's reasons were the usual ones—absurd and trivial. He "had fallen in love with another woman," a younger woman. "It had happened, Marcus said, because 'it wanted to happen.' Not because he wanted it to happen, of course. He had rented an apartment, and that day had moved out of the house. He had asked for a divorce."[9] And so, Marcus was gone—gone out of the membership, gone by his own choice.

And what of daughter Margaret? Nathan Coulter, her stepfather since she was a tiny girl, sat her down at the kitchen table. "He took her hand. He said, 'Margaret, my good Margaret, we're going to live right on.'"[10] Margaret, though abandoned, is still in the membership, where she remains, enfolded.

Virgie, her son, suffers the grief of a betrayed child. Nurtured by his grandparents, he nonetheless eventually breaks—turns to drugs and runs away. The pull of the membership and the memory of his place in it, however, bring him back to his grandmother Hannah, where the novel ends, with our hope that Virgie, strengthened by the care of those who are faithful to him, will stay. We know that if he stays in this place, his life will come back to him.

Fidelity, standing by our words, our vows, is the first point of reflection on Wendell Berry's theme of marriage. The second point is incarnation.

"I begin with the Christian idea of the Incarnate Word," says Berry, "the Word entering the soul as flesh, and inevitably therefore as action. . . ."[11] He likewise writes of the Incarnation in a short poem:

The incarnate Word is with us,
is still speaking, is present
always, yet leaves no sign
but everything that is.[12]

Incarnation, patterned after God's Incarnation, his embodiment in his Son, Jesus Christ, becomes in marriage the concrete realization of the couple's love for each other. Sexual love is so vibrant and powerful that it can become embodied in life itself—a baby. In no other institution but marriage does love concretize so dramatically, becoming so utterly concrete that it becomes another human life. Just as God speaks and becomes God dwelling among us, so can a man and a woman speak with the language, the gift, of their bodies, and their speaking can become enfleshed in a child. In choosing each other, a man and a woman freely become a gift to the other, and a baby may turn out to be the gift that is returned to them.

This powerful, concrete expression of love incarnated in the sexual act within marriage is the glue of community, the bond around which the community builds a protective web of social, religious, and legal conventions. Without these community restraints, sex becomes a wild, untamed, even vicious force that destroys the very families it created in the first place.

As Berry says in his essay "Sex, Economy, Freedom, and Community":

The sexuality of community life, whatever its inevitable vagaries, is centered on marriage, which joins two living souls as closely as, in this world, they can be joined. This joining of two who know, love, and trust one another brings them in the same breath into the freedom of sexual consent and into the fullest earthly realization of the image of God.[13]

He continues:

From their joining other living souls come into being, and with them great responsibilities that are unending, fearful, and joyful.

The marriage of two lovers joins them to one another, to forebears, to descendants, to the community, to Heaven and earth. It
is the fundamental connection without which nothing holds, and
trust is its necessity.[14]

Again, then, we circle back to the fidelity of married love as the cen-
terpiece of family and community and as the vehicle through which people move through history.

The beauty of marriage is that by way of its fidelity and incarnation,
it moves people away from the egoism of abstraction and allows them to
meet the world in all its concrete goodness. Married people dare not dally
in abstractions and individualistic dreams about freedom from responsibility. The very nature of their life requires giving and sacrifice. It requires
that they take and make their place, that they tend it and send down roots
in the place of their giving. Rootlessness and family life do not mix; but
permanence, place, and family life do. Marriage does not unfold in thin
air; rather, it requires the protection of a particular incarnated place in
which to thrive.

The concrete, particular, enfleshed, daily reality of marriage and family life, embedded in love and work and sacrifice and lived out in a particular place, reveals what the Incarnation of God's Word—that is, God
himself enfleshed and dwelling among us as a man—means to the world.
It means that the created world is suffused with God's imprint. The invisible is present in the visible. The work of God's hand, the things of earth,
are valuable and indeed sacred. The material world is good. It is blessed,
a theme that Berry repeats over and over. A man, a woman, a child, soil,
grass, books, barns, fields are good. Things—concrete, touchable, know-
able, mysterious things—are good, and they are a gift. They are given to
us to love, to care for, to reverence. Even though we may make a mess of
things, we do not destroy the goodness that pervades the things of this
world. In one of his poems, Berry writes,

There are no unsacred places;
there are only sacred places
and desecrated places.[15]

When Hannah Coulter's young husband Virgil died in World War II, leaving her a young widow with an infant daughter, it was the simple beauty of the world that drew her back into life,

> ordinary pleasures in ordinary things: the baby, sunlight, breezes, animals and birds, daily work, rest when I was tired, food, strands of fog in the hollows early in the morning, butterflies, flowers. The flowers didn't have to be dahlias and roses either, but just the weeds blooming in the fields, the daisies and the yarrow. I began to trust the world again. . . .[16]

Hannah understood that the one thing necessary is to be in the world, to love it, and to rejoice and give thanks for it. Ingratitude is a vice that Wendell Berry does not tolerate in his characters. Hannah, like Mat Feltner, Andy Catlett, and other Port William characters, utters the statement of highest self-knowledge, "I am blessed."

Berry looks at the world with a sacramental imagination. In other words, the world itself—created and given—is a sign to us that we are loved and chosen, that what we are given we did not make but merely cultivate and care for. What we are given in this world, though sometimes pierced with grief and sadness, is nonetheless drenched with the very love of God that will sanctify and redeem it. Any tears we have must finally be tears not of despair but of hope and joy.

Fidelity and incarnation are essential links in Berry's theme of marriage. So, too, is the third link: memory. Because of the couple's memory of their forebears and their children's memory of them, marriage is more than one generation deep. It attaches to the community not only horizontally or sideways but also backward from the couple to the generations behind them and forward from the couple to the generations in front of them. Thus the couple are responsible to the cloud of witnesses that made possible their coming into history at all and are likewise responsible to the children coming after them. Marriage, therefore, is the fulcrum on which the community rests. It is, moreover, the engine by which the community extends through history. The couple is always historical. As Andy Catlett puts it in the novel *Remembering*, they are in "a place of history—a place, in part, the result of history. . . ."[17] A man and woman cannot escape their place in time. They are located in time—yet they are bonded with those who have gone beyond them into eternity. Theirs is the commonwealth of the living, the dead, and those to come. Membership in this commonwealth, which is knit together through memory, is one of the strongest elements of Berry's work. It is essential to Berry that his characters know themselves to be members of the commonwealth of living, dead, and those to come. That understanding requires memory; it requires remembering.

Wheeler Catlett, Andy's father and one of the strongest, noblest men of the Port William membership, understands that we do not simply drift into the membership. Rather, we were chosen generations before we came to be, chosen by our Creator, chosen by the great-great grandparents who married and gave us the gift of life generations before they knew we would be, and gave us the gift of their work, their stewardship, long before we were here to accept their gift.

Ultimately, this gift of love and life and labor and land is a friendship, as Wheeler explains to the young farmer Elton Penn, who is being offered a piece of land that once belonged to a stalwart of the Port William membership, the late Jack Beechum:

> "The way you got in it," Wheeler says, "was by being chosen. The way you stay in it is by choice." Jack Beechum chose Elton and his wife Mary to take the farm.
>
> "He chose you and Mary," Wheeler says. "He thought you two were a good match, and that mattered to him. . . . You could say he chose you. But there's more to it. He chose you, we'd have to say too, because he'd been chosen. The line is long, and not straight."[18]
>
> "I mean," Wheeler says, "you're indebted to a dead man. So am I. So was he. That's the story of it. Back of you is Jack Beechum. Back of him was Ben Feltner. Back of him was, I think, his own daddy. And back of him somebody else, and on back that way who knows how far? And I'm back of you because Jack Beechum is, and because he's back of me, along with some others."[19]

Underlying the gift that Beechum bestowed upon a worthy young married couple is the corresponding obligation of Elton and Mary to remember Jack, to hold him in memory and in gratitude. They are to remember another thing: there is no such thing as independence. Someone has always come before. Someone has always prepared the way. And someone will always come after. We live only as dependents, in relationship to others and in relationship to our Creator. We live entrusted one to another. Elton and Mary, entrusted to each other in marriage, are another couple in the long line of gifting and entrusting, for whom it is a duty to remember the old ones and for whom it will be a gift one day to be themselves remembered by those who come after them.

Andy Catlett, who suffers bitter anger over the loss of his hand in a farm accident, is actually healed of his spiritual anguish by his redemptive remembering of the love of his grandparents and others of the Port William membership and finally of his wife.

" 'Out of the depths have I cried unto thee, O Lord,' " Andy grieves, and the words come to him in his grandmother's voice.[20] His healing comes as the result of a long series of remembrances that bring him back to himself; memories in which he imagines himself seeing the world through the eyes and mind and heart of his ancestors.

He imagines, for example, his grandfather Mat Feltner coming home from college to marry his love, Margaret Finley, and planning to settle on his father's farm at Port William.

It is a sunny day, early in June of 1906, when Mat, aboard the little Kentucky River steamboat *The Blue Wing*, impatiently waits for his landing stop.

> At last he sees forming ahead of them, still blue with distance, the shape of the Port William hill, and then one of his father's open ridgetops, and then the steeple pointing up over the trees, and then the old elm at the landing. As the boat sidles in out of the current, he looks up and sees standing on the porch of the store above the road Margaret, who has loved him all his life until then, and will love him all the rest of it. She has heard the whistle and walked down to meet him. He waves. She smiles and waves back, and an old longing, the size of himself, opens within him.[21]

Just as he is ready to step onto the plank, an old man hooks him with his cane and asks him if he is Ben Feltner's boy. When Mat acknowledges that he is, the old man asks, "'Well, you'll be going away now, I reckon, to make something of yourself.'" Mat, stepping free then, says, " 'No sir,

I reckon not.'" He sees ahead of him the compass of his life: "Margaret is coming down the bank to meet him, her long skirt gathered in one hand to keep it out of the dew."[22]

Years later, when Mat and Margaret have grown old together in love, and Mat sees that the end of his life is near, he thinks tenderly of Margaret "and of all that his plighting with her has led to."[23] All these years of their fidelity, of their cleaving to each other and to their membership; all these years in which they could have lived their marriage any number of ways but they chose this particular incarnation of it, in this place, in this membership, on this farm, with these children; all these years in which they held in memory their grandparents, who came to Kentucky when the land was thick with great virgin forest and giant canebrakes and every species of wild game—all this faithfulness to each other, to their particular incarnated place and to the remembering of the gift they have been given, has created a work of art. This garden of marriage that they have tilled, tending their plot as stewards, holding it in trust, in answer to a direct commission from Genesis to be fruitful and multiply, is a work of art— not a production of technology, but rather a work of art.

Their marriage is bigger than the two of them individually; yet it is not the sum of the two of them. It transcends them; it is a new thing altogether, a new creation, an expansion of reality, a third thing. As their daughter-in-law Hannah says, it is "a room of love."

In the end, Wendell Berry's works are hymns of fidelity, fidelity in marriage and in all other ways, fidelity that can only be the result of God's faithfulness to us. Finally, then, Wendell Berry's heroes and heroines are above all thankful for what they have been given, echoing the canticle of Isaiah,

> The living, the living give you thanks,
> as I do today,
> Fathers declare to their sons,
> O God, your faithfulness. (Isa. 38:19)

# 3

## Not Safe, nor Private, nor Free: Wendell Berry on Sexual Love and Procreation

### Allan Carlson

A modest political-cultural tragedy occurred in summer 2007, without attracting much attention among the usual pundits: the announcement that *Weekly World News* would cease print publication. This periodical, you will recall, was the tabloid faithfully found at the supermarket checkout line. It courageously pursued the truth. For example, it was the first publication to report that "Saddam Hussein Has Arsenal of Giant Slingshots and Dinosaurs" and also the memorable "60 Members of U.S. Senate Are Space Aliens." (I note in passing that that second article does stand as an excellent explanation for recent behavior in the U.S. Senate.)

Like all good tabloids, *Weekly World News* also featured advice columns. A few years ago, one caught my eye: "Improve Your Sex Life Tonight— The Amish Way." The article quotes Dr. Milton Ayres of the Society for the Cross-Cultural Study of Sexuality: "The best sex starts with getting down to the basics—and there are few societies on Earth more basic than the Amish." For reasons of prudence, which is the supreme conservative virtue, I do not want to dwell on many of the article's details. However, I would like to note some of Dr. Ayres's more specific advice to couples.

- "Turn off all the lights in your house. The Amish have no electricity, which means every sexual encounter takes place by romantic candlelight."

- "Wear plain modest clothing, which covers up most of your body. All the more to intensify the feeling of discovery when. . . ."
- "Purchase some farm animals to keep around your yard. The Amish are constantly around farm animals that are reproducing. This reinforces the fact that sex is natural."
- "Turn off all radios and TVs . . . so there's no comparison between the 'perfect' media fantasy people and your own romantic partner."
- And "[r]egularly read the Bible, a book which encourages a healthy sex life between husband and wife."[1]

Now, it is true that the sex-advice column is not a literary genre commonly associated with Wendell Berry. All the same, I suspect he would agree with most of these recommendations, notably: turning off the electricity and lighting candles; throwing out the radio and TV; viewing the procreative barnyard as the best and most natural form of sex education, for all ages; understanding that modesty is the surest prelude to sexual joy; and holding the Bible to be the most reliable sex manual.

Still, with the exception of the last point, these "basic" guides to agrarian reproductive behavior *are* fairly superficial. Fortunately, Mr. Berry does discuss sexual love and procreation with more depth and with some frequency in his fiction, nonfiction, and poetry. Recently, in fact, he has addressed sexual questions in two essays that some might call quixotic.

The first of these possibly quixotic endeavors is entitled "Rugged Individualism." It initially appeared in *Playboy*. Mr. Berry's intent, it seems, was to reach out to that almost mythical body of subscribers who actually do acquire the magazine to read the articles. His essay contrasts the "rugged individualism" of the political Right with that of the Left. On the Right, the author says, the focus is on private property and "the presumptive 'right' of individuals to do [with it] as they please, as if there were no God, no legitimate government, no community, no neighbors, and no posterity." Mr. Berry adds that this form of absolute individualism became worse as the great corporations received the status of "persons," also leaving them free "to do whatever they please with their property."

The rugged individualism of the Left focuses on the human body. As Mr. Berry elaborates, this approach holds that "the owners of bodies may, by right, use them as they please, [also] as if there were no God, no legitimate government, no community, no neighbors, and no posterity." He finds this "supposed right . . . manifested in the democratizing of 'sexual liberation.'"

"The comedy begins," Mr. Berry goes on, when these extreme forms of individualism meet. The rugged individualism of the Right celebrates "family values" and condemns "lust" but has nothing to say about the profits gained through advertising that exploits lust and the other six deadly sins. The individualism of the Left, meanwhile, casts sin as a private matter and defends the environment. However, Mr. Berry explains, the Left's notion of "environment" excludes "the economic landscapes of agriculture and forestry" and their human communities, their children and families. This environmentalism also excludes "the privately-owned bodies of other people," all of which seem to have been turned over "in fee simple to the corporate individualists." The common agenda of both "rugged individualisms," he says, is a claim to be "free" to grab as much as they can of whatever they want while ignoring the duties of kindness, caretaking, faithfulness, neighborliness, or peace.[2]

The second seemingly quixotic essay is a "Letter to Daniel Kemmis." Mr. Kemmis is a former minority leader and Speaker of Montana's House of Representatives, and a Democrat. Mr. Berry's goal was to salvage a Democratic Party held hostage to sexual radicalism, among other recent obsessions. "Why not just give up on the Democratic Party?" he asks himself, and answers: "Well, because of its name." On social matters, the author blasts "the moral timidity or incompetence of the Democrats" in allowing Republicans to confine the "values" issues to evolution, abortion, and homosexuality.

All the same, regarding the second of these issues—abortion—Mr. Berry is forthright in asserting "that I am opposed to abortion except as a last resort to save a pregnant woman's life." He continues: "The crucial question raised by this practice is: What is killed? The answer can only be: A human being." He wrestles with the language of a "woman's right to choose" and concludes that if this is a right, it is a very problematic and peculiar one. In contrast, Mr. Berry finds the "right to life" embedded in the U.S. Declaration of Independence and in "a 'reverence for life' to which we are called by much instruction." This means that his opposition to abortion is parallel to, or consistent with, his opposition to capital punishment and to war, "especially the killing of innocent women, children, and old people."

Concerning the third "values" issue, Mr. Berry concludes that the Democrats have been "further weakened by mishandling the issue of homosexuality." He blasts the knee-jerk liberalism that gives "categorical approval" to any group that once faced broad disapproval. "[T]his is nonsense," he declares, for some people in minority groups—just as some people in majority groups—behave in ways that should always face disapproval. Regarding cries for same-sex marriage, he becomes something of a libertarian, arguing that state "approval of anybody's sexual behavior is as inappropriate and as offensive to freedom as governmental *dis*approval." After endorsing equal "domestic partnership" benefits for all adults living in households—be they heterosexual, homosexual, widowed sisters, bachelor brothers, or friends—Mr. Berry abandons the state's regulation of marriage: "Let sacraments such as marriage be the business of religion and communities."[3] This devolution of authority assumes—perhaps incorrectly—that modern churches and small communities have the ability to regulate and enforce marital vows.

Summoning *Playboy* readers to social and sexual responsibility, and calling on the twenty-first-century Democratic Party to reclaim the mantle of family protector, which it once proudly held, are most worthy—if possibly futile—endeavors. Beyond them, though, Mr. Berry's work carries rich insights into the nature and meaning of sexual love and procreation. Importantly, he rejects three assertions common to our era: sex can be safe; sex is a private matter; and sex should be free.

Mr. Berry responds: First, sex is not safe. As he writes in the splendid essay "Sex, Economy, Freedom, and Community": "Sex was never safe, and it is less safe now than it has ever been."[4] Community customs, arrangements, and laws had existed "in part, to reduce the volatility and the danger of sex." These controls would "preserve its energy, its beauty, and its pleasure" so that the sexual act would in turn bond husbands to wives, "parents to children, families to the community, [and] the community to nature."[5] Whenever sex becomes "autonomous," freed from communal restraints, and valued solely for its own sake, it also becomes "frivolous" and "destructive—even of itself."[6]

Mr. Berry considers modern sex education in the schools, and concludes: "What we are actually teaching the young is an illusion of . . .

purchasable safety, which encourages them to tamper prematurely, disrespectfully, and dangerously with a great power."[7] Similar delusions, he contends, are found among adults. Men eagerly flock to the vasectomy clinics, convinced that the procedure is "simple" and "harmless." For their part, infertile women desperately submit their bodies to doses of chemicals and other intrusions, oblivious to the risks involved while accepting their dangerous new status as "productive machines."[8]

Second, sex is not private. Mr. Berry rejects the U.S. Supreme Court's concept of a "right to sexual privacy." He writes: "It is wrong to assume that sex carries us into a personal privacy that separates us from everything else. On the contrary, sex joins us to the world."[9] As the foundation of the household, as the source of children, and as the primal social unit, the sexual bond of man and woman bears powerful and necessary communal obligations. The conjugal vows, for example, are said "to the community as much as to one another," and the community comes to listen and wish the couple well, "on their behalf and on its own." In return, the community's task is to see that these lovers "die" into their union with one another, becoming one flesh through a "momentous giving." Mr. Berry adds: "If the community cannot protect this giving, it can protect nothing—and our time is proving that this is so." The consequence is the squandering of "moral capital built up by centuries of community life."[10]

The unacknowledged victims of "sexual privacy" are children. He writes in *Another Turn of the Crank*:

> I know of nothing that so strongly calls into question our ability to care for the world as our present abuse of our own reproductivity. How can we take care of other creatures, all born like ourselves from *the world's miraculous fecundity*, if we have forsaken the qualities of culture and character that inform the nurture of children?[11]

Mr. Berry muses that this indifference toward human children might be a by-product of the modern regard for productivity, since children are not very productive. Or it might be the fault of an economy that now commonly requires both parents to work outside the home. Or it might be a consequence of the broad commodification of family bonds. "Whatever the reason," he continues, "it is a fact that we are now conducting a sort of general warfare against children, who are being aborted or abandoned, abused, drugged, bombed, neglected, poorly raised, poorly taught, and poorly disciplined."[12]

Mr. Berry also qualifies the claims of privacy relative to the body. While acknowledging the obvious "right of any person to control his or her own body," he focuses on the limits of this right. Referring specifically to abortion, he states: "If you can control your own body only by destroying another person's body, then control has come much too late." On the same issue, he acknowledges the argument that the fetus is not a child until it can live outside the womb, yet responds: "Every creature is surrounded by such questions of dependence and viability all its life. If we are unworthy to live as long as we are dependent on life-supporting conditions, then none of us has any rights."[13]

More broadly, Mr. Berry concludes: "In dealing with our own fertility and its consequences, we are not just carrying on personal or private 'relationships.' We are establishing one of the fundamental terms of our humanity and our connection to the world."[14]

And third, sex is never free. "Sexual liberation is as much a fraud and as great a failure as the 'peaceful atom,'" Mr. Berry declares.[15] He is equally dismissive of the idea of sex as "recreation," or more properly "re-creation"; he writes: "Thinking to claim for [sex] 'a new place,'" advocates "only acknowledge its displacement from Creation."[16] Free and recreational sex actually feed into the matrix of the industrial economy, where the result is superficiality. As Mr. Berry notes in a recent essay: "This is an economy, and in fact a culture, of the one-night stand. 'I had a good time,' says the industrial [just as the recreational] lover, 'but don't ask me my last name.'"[17]

Rather than freedom, the disintegration of the household through "sexual liberation" has produced a novel form of bondage. The new overlords, Mr. Berry says, are the sexual specialists—sex clinicians and pornographers—"[b]oth of whom subsist on the increasing possibility of sex between people who neither know nor care about each other" and who also "subsist on our failure to see any purpose or virtue in sexual discipline." American culture grants to these "technologists of fertility" the "powers of gods and the social function of priests," despite their scorn for community ties and cultural responsibilities.[18]

Mr. Berry's work highlights other themes that explore sexual love and procreation. Notably, he stresses the close bond between human and agricultural fertility. An early poem, "The Broken Ground," tells of the fertility initiated by the plow in the soil:

> The opening out and out,
> Body yielding body:
> the breaking
> through which the new
> comes, perching
> above its shadow. . . .
> bud opening to flower
> opening to fruit opening
> to the sweet marrow
> of the seed.[19]

Mr. Berry underscores that physical love is not enough to sustain an intimate relationship. In order to last, human sexual life "must enflesh itself in the materiality of the world—produce food, shelter, warmth or shade, surround itself with careful acts, well made things." True sexual love also binds these lovers into "the cycles of fertility and the seasons," into "life and death," where they find the "deepest solemnity" and the "highest joy." More broadly, just as "agricultural fertility is . . . the survival of natural process in human order," natural human procreativity finds its ordered setting on the small, function-rich farm.[20]

Sexual love, Mr. Berry adds, also expresses the wild side of human nature. Sex is "part of the world's wilderness; it is part of our wildness. To say that we must be careful of it is not to say that we must make it tame, but rather that we must not damage it or ourselves by ignorance or foolishness." Put another way, this physical wildness of humans needs to be recognized, channeled, and cherished as part of our being.[21]

Another remarkable aspect of Mr. Berry's work is the critical attention he gives to birth control, rare among non-Catholic writers. He calls modern contraceptive practices "horrifying" not only because "we are relying so exclusively on a technology of birth control that is still experimental" but also because "we are using it casually, in utter cultural nakedness, unceremoniously, without sufficient understanding, and as a substitute for cultural solutions." In this culture of contraception, women must submit to "a technology of chemicals" found in "the pill." Meanwhile, men turn to sterilization, which he calls the most troubling form of birth control, for "to give up fertility is a major change, as important as birth, puberty, marriage, or death."

Mr. Berry denies any affection for the "self-hating, self-congratulatory Victorian self-restraint" of decades or centuries past. Instead, he praises inherited cultural mechanisms of sexual self-control. In one essay, Mr. Berry points specifically to the Hunza people of northern Pakistan, where the women left their husbands' beds until each new child was weaned, so spacing their children about four years apart. He directly praises breast-feeding as a natural method of child spacing (while speculating that this durable form of home production became unfashionable in America precisely because the corporations could find "no way . . . to persuade a woman to purchase her own milk").[22]

On the broad question of human fecundity, Mr. Berry rejects the charge that "there are too many people." Contemplating the "unsettled," depopulated American countryside, he is sure that overpopulation does not afflict the United States. Moreover, he fears the implication of the term "overpopulation," for it implicitly summons a dangerous calculation of "who are the surplus." The real environmental problems, he asserts, are those "technological multipliers" that artificially increase the negative footprints of some peoples on the world. The obvious response for them is to live simpler lives.[23]

Finally, Mr. Berry does provide positive visions of procreative sexual love. For the man, it means recovering the tasks of husbandry, "the work of a domestic man, a man who has accepted a bondage to the household." This husbanding man is "both careful and humble." He is ready "to keep, to save, to make last, to conserve" and to suborn his personality to his home, to his wife, and to his children. He must become in this way a home-maker.[24] In the novel *Hannah Coulter*, Mr. Berry gives expression to this natural urge:

> The possibility that among the world's wars and sufferings two people could love each other for a long time, until death and beyond, and could make a place for each other that would be a part of their love, as their love for each other would be a way of loving their place.[25]

Mr. Berry raises up several of the farm women in his fiction as models of sexual fulfillment. For example, he describes young Hannah Coulter on a walk: "She feels good. She feels full of the goodness, the competency, of her body that can love a man and bear his children, that can raise and prepare food, keep the house, work in the field."[26] Mr. Berry also offers as example Minnie Branch: "a large, muscular, humorous" woman who could butcher hogs, shoot a fox, split firewood, and wring a hen's neck and who "conceived and birthed as faithfully as a good brood cow, welcomed each newcomer without fuss, prepared without complaint for the next."[27] And, in my favorite of Mr. Berry's short stories, "A Jonquil for Mary Penn," he provides the example of Mary and Elton Penn:

> That she was his half, she had no doubt at all. He needed her. At times she knew with a joyous ache that she completed him, just as she knew with the same joy that she needed him and he completed her. How beautiful a thing it was, she thought, to be a half, to be completed by such another half! When had there even been such a yearning of halves toward each other, such a longing, even in quarrels, to be whole? And sometimes they would be whole. Their wholeness came upon them as a rush of light, around them and within them, so that she felt they must be shining in the dark.[28]

Or, as *Weekly World News* would have phrased the same point: "You really haven't lived 'til you've tried sex [agrarian style]."[29]

# 4

# An Education for Membership:
# Wendell Berry on Schools
# and Communities

## *Richard Gamble*

If future generations find the grace and imagination to recover the scattered remnants of our civilization, they may well come to understand the midpoint of Wendell Berry's *Remembering* as a sign of that recovery. Among Berry's shortest novels, *Remembering* tells the story of Andy Catlett's journey from self-pity and ingratitude to forgiveness. It tells of his homecoming. His return home began in the 1960s, when he quit his upwardly mobile career as a journalist in Chicago. He and his wife, Flora, left the city and bought a dilapidated but salvageable farm in Port William, Kentucky. There, for the past dozen years or so, they have made a home for themselves and their children. But recently, Andy lost his right hand to a piece of farm machinery and with it all the knowledge of the world that had belonged to that hand. Now, shrunken into bitterness and resentment, Andy finds himself alone in a dark hotel room in San Francisco, a stranger to himself. Waking him hours before sunrise, his restless mind leaps from memory to memory, from the farming accident that severed his hand, to the argument with his wife the morning he left home, to the inane babbling of agricultural "experts" at an academic conference he had just escaped, and to his own embarrassing anger when he addressed the same audience. Unable to sleep, he walks the predawn city, impelled toward the "verge and immensity of the continent's meeting with the sea."[1] Reaching the end of the fishing pier that arcs out into the bay from Aquatic Park, with the voices of his ancestors in his head, Andy realizes that his home—not someplace else, but his home—is the only place that can give him wholeness. There is where redemption lies. Berry describes Andy as physically turning around and stepping away from the parapet. But much more happens at that moment and place. "A history turns around in his mind," Berry writes, "as if some old westward migrant, who had reached the edge at last and seen the blue uninterruptible water reaching out around the far side of the world, had turned in his tracks and started eastward again."[2]

Andy's return home fits within "a pattern of a succession of such returns," Berry writes.[3] Berry has most immediately in mind the pattern of returns that runs through Andy's own family history. He frames Andy's recognition of what kind of man he is and ought to be by the stories of his grandfather's and father's homecomings, stories that Andy has heard his family tell over the years and that have become part of his own memories and inheritance. Back in 1906, Mat Feltner, Andy's maternal grandfather, returned home to Port William after two years at the state college in Lexington, Kentucky. As he was about to step off the steamboat that brought him back to Port William, an old man stopped him abruptly and began a friendly interrogation:

"You been up there to that college, my boy?"
"Yessir."
"Well, you'll be going away now, I reckon, to make something out of yourself."
. . ."Nosir, I reckon not."[4]

Berry uses this old man's questions to challenge two modern assumptions about education: that it is normal for children to leave their hometowns after their schooling and that these children ought not to be content with who they are.

In the next generation, Mat's future son-in-law and Andy's father, Wheeler Catlett, returned home to practice law. He graduated from college and then finished law school while working for a congressman in Washington, D.C. Destined next for a successful career in Chicago, he deliberated over life in the city and life on the land he knew. In his mind's eye, he saw "what he could be. He saw it all. A man with a law degree did not have to go to Chicago to practice. He could practice wherever in the whole nation there was a courthouse. He could practice in Hargrave. He could be with his own."[5] Guided by a properly constrained imagination, the gift of his upbringing, Wheeler pictured himself returning to his people, to the place of his birth, and to the way of life unique to that place. He realized, like his father-in-law before him, that a truly educated man does not have to live someplace other than home or to become somebody other than who his family and neighbors raised him to be. And so he brought what he learned at college back to his community, for the good of his community.

Beautifully unfolded, this intricate "pattern of a succession of such returns" works its way through the memory and experience of three generations, converging in Andy's life and reminding him just in time who he is. Part of that self-knowledge had come to him years before on the day he quit his job in Chicago. "He was a throwback," he then realized, "to that hope and dream of membership that had held together his lineage of friends and kin. . . ."[6] The self can be truly and adequately known only in the context of other lives. In deliberate and striking contrast to the romantic hero, Andy rejects the seductive image of himself as a loose individual, ends his quest at the farthest edge of the frontier, and answers the call of fidelity to return to his marriage, to the soil that made him, and to his ancestral memory. He rejects the modern world's standard of success, and that act of resistance bears within it a sort of quiet and dignified heroism all its own. As he is about to head from his San Francisco hotel to the airport for his flight back to Kentucky, Andy realizes how much his education had been to blame for the destructive yearnings within him. Berry writes of Andy, "Years ago, he resigned himself to living in cities. That was what his education was for, as his teachers all advised and he believed. Its purpose was to get him away from home, out of the country, to someplace where he could live up to his abilities. He needed an education, and the purpose of an education was to take him away."[7]

While Andy's homecoming in *Remembering* merges with the stories of Mat and Wheeler, becoming almost one simultaneous experience with theirs, these returns also fit within a larger pattern of return in Berry's work that emerges prominently in two later novels, *Jayber Crow* and *Hannah Coulter*. During the Great Depression, Jayber decides to leave the University of Kentucky after only a semester there and makes a home for himself in Port William. His decision to head back surprises him, he discovers, because "not a one of my teachers had ever suggested such a possibility."[8] His decision never does bring him power or wealth or any of the other trappings of worldly success as the town's bachelor barber, but it did enable him to find and make a home. For Nathan Coulter, the Second World War provided its own brutal kind of education. But he, too, returned from his education to the place he knew and loved. "Nathan plainly wasn't trying to make it big in the 'postwar world,'" his widow Hannah recalled years later. "He wasn't *going* anywhere. He had come back home after the war because he wanted to. He was where he wanted to be. As I too was by then, he was a member of Port William. Members of Port William aren't trying to 'get someplace.' They think they *are* someplace."[9] Sadly, however, Hannah and Nathan discovered with their own children that "the way of education leads away from home."[10] The dislocations of the modern world prove too powerful for Port William's membership.

That membership had been consciously sustained over generations by one act of homecoming and homemaking after another. The community did not flourish because of some wise policy emanating from Washington, D.C. It flourished because of simple acts of devotion to a place, to a people, and to a way of life. Several of Berry's essays suggest that he envisions the stories of Mat Feltner, Wheeler Catlett, Andy, Jayber Crow, and Nathan and Hannah Coulter within an even longer succession of returns found in what he simply calls "our literature"—the ancient stories that form our inheritance and to which we belong. In "The Work of Local Culture," an essay written about the same time as *Remembering*, Berry points out a few of the landmarks in this once-continuous sequence of returns, broken only in the past two hundred years or so with the birth of the industrial age and of romantic individualism. He understands these stories of return, such as the prodigal son's, as part of what he calls the "old norm." For thousands of years, civilization had honored as normal the return home and the longing to be surrounded by one's children and grandchildren. The wanderer in exile desired to see his home and family once again. Berry hears the unmistakable voice of the "old norm" in a verse from Psalm 128: "Thou shalt see thy children's children, and peace upon Israel." The Old Testament patriarch Jacob, prefiguring the prodigal son, "errs, wanders, returns, is forgiven, and takes his place in the family lineage"—words that in turn perfectly describe Andy Catlett's own journey of redemption. Berry hears the old norm speaking again in Homer's depiction of Odysseus, a wanderer reunited with his son who longs to return to his father and his wife, his household and his kingdom. Two thousand years later, the poet Dante, embellishing the tale of Odysseus, damns him to an eternity among the Evil Counselors for sailing off with his crew on a new adventure. In the old norm, persisting over millennia, the endlessly questing adventurer threatens to sever every tie that makes life in a community possible.[11]

Berry finds the old norm enduring down to the year 1800 in William Wordsworth's poem "Michael," the story of a shepherd and his wife who send their son to the city to work in order to clear a claim against their land. The son is meant to return and inherit his ancestral land. For Wordsworth, Berry writes, that "return is still understood as the norm." But in this case, it never happens. The longing is still there, but the economic reality of the industrial age has torn the family apart. Berry calls this poem "a sort of cultural watershed. It carries on the theme of return that goes back to the beginning of Western culture, but that return now is only a desire and a memory; in the poem it fails to happen."[12] Tennyson's poem "Ulysses" takes the next step by subverting the desire and helping to obliterate the memory. Here, Berry writes later in *Life Is a Miracle*, a new longing takes over as the dominant cultural norm. Where Dante once condemned Odysseus (Ulysses) for his restlessness, Tennyson launches a self-indulgent, impulsive Ulysses on a romantic quest toward an ever-receding horizon.[13] This new Ulysses appeals to the perpetual adolescence of the new age. He knows no boundaries, no limits to his appetite, and sacrifices home and family and peace and order for the sake of a future that never arrives. The anxiety once possible in a poem such as "Michael," by its contrast to modernity's endless pioneering, startles us, with Berry's help, into the recognition of what we have lost. "And by now the transformation of the ancient story is nearly complete. Our society, on the whole, has forgotten or repudiated the theme of return. Young people still grow up in rural families and go off to the cities, not to return. But now it is felt that this is what they *should* do. Now the norm is to leave and not return."[14]

The Port William membership struggles generation after generation to keep the pattern of succession alive. Any break in the succession damages the community, whether that break is brought on by mobilization for global war or by industrialization or by advertisers promising a better life somewhere else. Through the membership's stories, Berry makes the old norm visible again to a distracted America that knows only mobility, transience, and the most superficial sort of material progress. His characters never find "authenticity" and shallow self-fulfillment by leaving their spouses, families, homes, and communities. They come to know who they are by remaining faithful to things larger and older and more important than themselves. They live their lives according to the "logic of vocation" and not according to the "logic of success."[15] They heed the call of family and place. Berry manages to make goodness and simplicity and ordinary life attractive in these characters. And he does so without ever idealizing Port William. Suffering and death, disappointment and despair, are real and ever present in his world. Port William knows fire and flood, suicide and murder. Berry is sensitive to loss and widens the horizon of that loss. Indeed, his ability to make loss visible may be one of his greatest gifts as an artist. The costs of world wars, economic consolidation, mass media, and faceless bureaucracy haunt his novels. But to these more obvious culprits, he adds another institution that few at first would expect: the whole modern educational establishment from grade school to graduate school. War may carry off young men. Agribusiness may radically reduce the need for farm laborers. But modern schools uproot children in their own more subtle ways, and from the inside out. "The child is not educated to return home and be of use to the place and community," Berry writes; "he or she is educated to *leave* home and earn money in a provisional future that has nothing to do with place or community."[16]

The Port William membership experiences for itself the damage that schools, when run according to the logic of business efficiency and to the dictates of an alien agenda, inflict on their Kentucky neighbors, on their own families, and on their way of life. Jayber Crow, recalling the days before school consolidation, said he "liked best the school as it was when I first knew it, when it served only the town and immediate neighborhood, when the students got there on foot."[17] The school belonged to the town. But "experts" shut down the school in 1964 and began busing the children to Hargrave. The school board had adopted the language and logic of business and now talked of "efficiency, economy of scale, and volume." "Closing the school just knocked the breath out of the community," Jayber recalls. "It did worse than that. It gave the community a never-healing wound." Jayber admits the old school's shortcomings, but something more fundamental than success had been at stake: the bond between the school and the community. "Some of the teachers, of course, had been bad and some good," he acknowledges. "But how good or bad they were Port William knew, and knew without delay. Whether the parents interfered for good or ill, the school was right there in sight and they at least could interfere. The school was in the town and it was in the town's talk."[18]

Busing and school consolidation, Berry writes in an autobiographical section of *The Hidden Wound*, had done these very things to his own children, taking them "well beyond the range of close or easy parental involvement." And this experience leads him to reflect on the costs of these policies for any community:

> There can be no greater blow to the integrity of a community than the loss of its school or loss of control of its school—which always means loss of control of its children. The breakdown of discipline and academic standards in the schools can only originate in, and can only cause, the breakdown of community life. The public school, separated from the community by busing (for whatever reason), government control, consolidation, and other 'advances,' has become a no-man's-land, a place existing in reference only to itself and to a theoretical "tomorrow's world."[19]

Likewise, Jayber understands that his own college and university had attempted to function precisely as this sort of "no-man's-land." The University of Kentucky had become a "floating or a flying island," not belonging to anybody or to any place, and serenely disconnected from the consequences of anything it taught. "Every one of the educational institutions that I had been in," he complains, "had been hard at work trying to be a world unto itself." Some tried to be the "world of the past." Some tried to be the "world of the future." But "what was missing was the world of the present, where every body was living its small, short, surprising, miserable, wonderful, blessed, damaged, only life."[20] Inevitably, these institutions turned out graduates who know any number of things about the world except "where they were." An example of this ignorance presents itself to Jayber in the form of the young preachers who fill the pulpit week by week in Port William. Even those who might move to Port William never "stayed long enough to know where they were." But knowledge of a place and of a people and of a way of life had never been the point of their education. "They were not going to school to learn where they were, let alone the pleasures and the pains of being there, or what ought to be said there. You couldn't learn those things in a school. They went to school, apparently, to learn to say over and over again, regardless of where they were, what had already been said too often."[21] Jayber, who had once felt "called" to the ministry, spent all of his adult life becoming part of the Port William membership. But these preachers had no such intention and made no such effort.

Education for membership, or the loss of that purpose for education, pulses through Berry's essays and through his own memory. In *Life Is a Miracle*, in which he unmasks the pretensions of scientific materialism and its agenda for remaking man and his world, Berry ponders the sad paradox between the technical expert's precise and vast knowledge of physical nature and his ignorance of real places on earth. "There are scientists, one must suppose, who know all about atoms or molecules or genes, or galaxies or planets or stars, but who do not know where they are geographically, historically, or ecologically. Our schools are turning out millions of graduates who do not know, in this sense, where they are."[22] In contrast, Berry's own father saw to it that he was educated for membership. "My father was the first, and the most passionate and comprehensive, of my teachers," he writes. "Too much occupied in town to teach me himself everything he wanted me to know, he saw that I found other teachers. He more or less turned me loose in a landscape populated by teachers: my grandfather and [his hired hand] Nick, and many others. He set me free to know a place and a way of life and a kind of people outside the direction, perhaps beyond the scope, and certainly beyond the respect, of the mainstream of the society. Though I am sure he has had to tolerate rather than admire some of the results, it was a great gift."[23] Free to know a place and a way of life and a kind of people—this is the freedom denied to Jayber's young preachers, denied to the trained specialists mass-produced by the research university, and denied to nearly every other graduate of America's school system.

Late in life, the twice-widowed Hannah Coulter comes to understand the damage placeless educational institutions have done to her children.

Both she and her second husband, Nathan, had wanted their children to go to college. They believed they "owed it to them." But a painful lesson awaited these parents. "It just never occurred to either one of us that we would lose them that way. The way of education leads away from home. That is what we learned from our children's education." This insight led Hannah immediately into a sweeping indictment of modern education. "The big idea of education, from first to last, is the idea of a better place. Not a better place where you are, because you want it to be better and have been to school and learned to make it better, but a better place somewhere else. In order to move up, you have got to move on. I didn't see this at first. And for a while after I knew it, I pretended I didn't. I didn't want it to be true."[24]

But the college was not solely to blame. Hannah faces the possibility that she herself had planted the wrong longings and assumptions in her children's hearts and minds. Along the way, Nathan had tried to teach her about contentment. He had tried to teach her to live a life of gratitude. He had shown her that "you musn't wish for another life. You musn't want to be somebody else." And that thought, Hannah says, "passed through everything I know and changed it all." But another thought still nags at her. She fears that she and Nathan had told the stories of their own lives to their children in such a way as to make them discontent, that the schools had only completed the destructive work that she had begun. She told the right stories, because they were *her* stories. "But did we tell the stories right?" she wonders. It is possible to tell the right stories but not to tell the stories right, and that makes all the difference for the shape of the child's imagination. The question haunts her: "But did we tell the stories in such a way as to suggest that we had needed a better chance or a better life or a better place than we had?"[25]

The eventual return of Hannah's wayward grandson and the reordering of life that comes to him as farm work takes him into its rhythm and into its discipline gives Hannah reason for hope. "When you have gone too far, as I think he did," she decides, "the only mending is to come home."[26] And that mending, when it comes, will be in no small part due to her love for him and for Port William. The defense of family and community and a way of life demands love. It also demands resistance to everything that opposes these things, including the modern university and its specialized education. Resistance takes effort. Berry told the 2007 graduating class at Bellarmine University that "if you love your family, your neighbors, your community, and your place, you are going to have to resist." Berry often quotes Wes Jackson's book *Becoming Native to This Place* in this regard. "The universities now offer only one serious major: upward mobility," Jackson writes. "Little attention is paid to educating the young to return home, or to go some other place, and dig in. There is no such thing as a 'homecoming' major. But what if the universities were to ask seriously what it would mean to have as our national goal becoming native to this place, this continent?"27 These words and sentiments could not be closer to Berry's own. He affirms them throughout the body of his work. But he also senses that something more will be required of us. If children are to come home after college or to stay home after high school, they must have homes. Countless Americans coming of age in the twenty-first century have no home to return to. Therefore, Berry adds, "part of the sense of 'homecoming' must be home*making*, for we now must begin sometimes with remnants, sometimes with ruins."28

Cherishing the remnants and ruins, Wendell Berry labors to recover the wisdom that once knew as a matter of course that schools and communities must belong to each other. That wisdom emerged not from a "philosophy of education" but instead from a way of life. It would be a mistake to distill anything so abstract as a "philosophy of education" from the stories of the Port William membership. Berry himself urges his readers not to try to "explain" his work. Citing Mark Twain's famous threat at the beginning of *Huckleberry Finn* to bring all sorts of harm upon those who try to figure out his book, Berry warns that the meaning of a work of art is to be found in the whole, not in its analyzed parts. The meaning of a story is in the telling.29 Likewise, at the beginning of *Jayber Crow*, Berry threatens vengeance on anyone who tries to find a "subtext" or even a "text" in the novel. But no attentive reader could fail to see Berry's indictment of modern education throughout his stories. That indictment is as plain and persistent as his judgment against modern agribusiness, the interstate highway system, and total war. Berry is a faithful teacher, much like his characters who prepare the young to see what they need to see about their world in order to live well within it. He gathers up the pieces of a way of life few modern Americans have ever known.

Despite our collective amnesia, the memory of that life seems to be woven into the very fabric of who we are. Berry revives that memory. He helps us to love what we ought to love. He helps us to see that education is the task of the whole community—the task of parents and grandparents, of aunts and uncles and neighbors. Andy Catlett sees this truth when he recalls one of his grandfather Feltner's stories. Uncle Jack Beechum had attached a board to the plowbeam for the talkative youngster Mat Feltner to sit on. Jack answered Mat's eager questions. He taught him as they plowed together. "Was that a school?" Andy asks himself. "It was a school," comes the answer. "Andy thought of his own children, who had descended, in part, from that school on the plowboard and did not know it."[30] We have all descended from teachers and schools far beyond the formal classroom. And even with the help of so many teachers, much of what we need to know can be learned only from the experience of life itself, and even a lifetime will not be long enough for all we need to learn.[31]

Berry never intends his stories to offer a prescription for educational reform. He leaves that effort to the homeless progressives and other experts who aspire to remake the world. Institutions certainly matter, whether they be educational, political, economic, or religious. But a preoccupation with institutional change can mislead us into thinking of these structural innovations as another kind of technological quick fix for an ailing world. How our schools are funded, where they are located, whose agenda they serve, the curriculum and teaching methods they use—all these things matter. But even the most civic-minded charter school, the most "conservative" home school, or the most "traditional" private college will have done nothing to address Berry's concerns if it fails to restore the old norm, if it fails to tell the "right stories" the right way. Any type of school can become an unaccountable "floating island." Any type of school can raise a generation of alienated individuals content to be connected to "virtual" communities via phone lines and fiber-optic cables but caring nothing about their neighbors.

Renewal, Berry writes, must come "from the inside by the ancient rule of neighborliness, by the love of precious things, and by the wish to be at home."[32] Teachers of all kinds can leave no greater gift to the rising generation than this ancient rule, this love, and this wish. Parents and families and neighbors must first live by the "old norm" themselves and then dare to plant these subversive ideas and habits in the rising generation. They must help "boomers" long to become "stickers."[33] And this inward turn depends on us telling the stories of homecoming once again. Telling them not as cultural artifacts, as curiosities of a benighted and bygone era, and certainly not as texts to be deconstructed, but rather as a living legacy. Doing so demands something more from us than professional expertise. It demands an openness to being shaped by the old norm, to having our communities and way of life reordered by the stories of homecoming. It demands that each of us, like Andy Catlett, turn around and make a home and a life for ourselves and our children.

# 5

# And for This Food, We Give Thanks

## *Matt Bonzo*

Food is everywhere these days. Perhaps it would be more precise to say that talk about food is everywhere. From cooking shows and gourmet magazines to books and movies about food production and consumption, to warnings about the impending worldwide food crisis, the how, what, and why of eating has become the topic du jour. On a recent summer day, as my son and I moved on to weed the next fifty-foot row of tomatoes in our garden, my thoughts turned to some of these issues as I wondered how our work would be understood by someone unacquainted with the taste of vine-ripened tomatoes, consumer-supported agriculture, or farm life in general. I suppose the easiest way to understand our growing of vegetables is to frame it as a way of making money amid the current concerns for organic, local, and farm-fresh produce. But such a utilitarian understanding would mistake our farm for an agribusiness. While we certainly do not grow food for free, money is not our primary motivation. If you do try to interpret our efforts that way, the long hours; the inefficient, meaningful conversations in the field; and the sometimes less than ideal results do not make much sense, especially in an age shaped by efficiency and high productivity.

We also do not look at our garden as a complete escape from the people, the market, or the powers around us. Rather, I think Wendell Berry captures our primary motivation in his poem "The Satisfaction of the Mad Farmer." We farm, in our small way, because of the satisfaction produced in our customers, our land, our animals, and, most of all, in ourselves. So much of the conversation about food today has to do with negative reactions. Some people worry about pesticides in their food, some people are angered by the damage done to the soil by current agribusiness practices, some people are perturbed by rising food prices, and some people are frustrated by the various critiques offered against mainstream food production. I don't deny the reality behind these feelings, but I simply affirm that there is something more than a reaction against certain practices that leads us to do what we do. The satisfaction my family and I feel is rooted in a deeper reality, and, we hope, all of our work begins in the gratitude that emerges with our awareness of this reality.

Berry can speak so truthfully of satisfaction because at the heart of his work is an understanding of the given-ness of our world. The land, the soil, life itself, are not realities that we either bring into existence or whose continued existence totally relies upon us. While the understanding of Creation as gift is ubiquitous in his work, Berry's essay "The Gift of Good Land" helps us to see the important connections between land, soil, and food that are simply the givens of any practice worthy of being called agriculture. Berry uses the biblical account of the Promised Land to provide a lens through which we can properly see land as "a gift because the people who are to possess it did not create it."[1] As a gift, the land comes with a set of obligations.[2] As given, the land issues forth a call regarding how it is to be treated and used. In recognizing this notion of obligation, Berry observes that the land is "not a free or a deserved gift, but a gift given upon certain rigorous conditions."[3] In relationship to farming, the recognition of the rigorous conditions begins with an awareness of the ultimate mysteries of the field: How does soil bring forth life? How does a "dead" seed resurrect? How does a plant use sunlight to grow? By starting with an acknowledgment of the limits of humanity's ability to comprehend the ways of nature, Berry reminds us to think about food with a sympathetic knowledge of the land and soil of a given place.[4] The understanding of land and soil as a gift means recognizing the given norms for how we plant, grow, harvest, and deliver our food. Such norms are not abstract universals that present themselves at the end of some hypothetical exercise. Rather, the conditions attached to the gift of land, soil, or food are particulars, and the mind that discerns the conditions is "local, almost absolutely placed, little attracted to mobility either upward or lateral, it is not provincial; it is too taken up and fascinated by its work to feel inferior to any other mind in any other place."[5]

The work of growing food consists of more than strong-backed people throwing manure in early spring or people in sweat-soaked shirts weeding and picking under a blazing July sun. Farming also entails the intellectual work of discerning what animals and plants will prosper on your land and in your soil and under what conditions they will flourish. No test for pH levels can tell you once and for all what your soil is like. No state agricultural manual can tell you what animals belong on your land. The task of cultivating a healthy farm is ongoing as you learn more about the givenness of your land, which also includes knowing the history of its successes and failures. The land has a story. This story guides those willing to listen and to learn to farm within the ultimately mysterious limits of the place. In this way, the farm will judge.[6]

And when the soil does give forth "raspberries ripe and heavy amid their foliage,"[7] the appropriate response is to give thanks because you have not so much manipulated or controlled the land for your purposes as learned to cooperate with the land in the bearing of the gift that it intended to give all along. The satisfaction of producing a good-tasting tomato is not the price it will get at the market. Nor is it merely the nod of approval at the end of the row that has been weeded so that the plants receive adequate moisture and nutrition. These factors contribute to the feeling, but it is more. It is a sense of belonging to a place that under your nurture yields a harvest of fruit and vegetables. And in the seeing, feeling, and tasting of the harvest there is a fulfillment as the connections between soil and seed, seed and chick, chick and farmer, farmer and soil, become clear as you stand in the cool of a summer evening looking out over your land. As plant, animal, and human mature toward their appropriate ends, a heart filled with gratitude accepts and gives with open hands.

But as Berry reminds us, this sense of satisfaction and gratitude associated with food is not confined to the farmer. While the farmer stands in a unique relationship to the land and its produce, we all eat. And the fact that all people eat provides an important set of connections for Berry. In eating there is a direct link between humanity and the land. The economy of food is part of a bigger economy, and the way we eat reveals much about how we participate in the greater economy. At a certain point, Berry, following Wes Jackson, calls this comprehensive economy "the Kingdom of God."[8] The truism "you are what you eat" has been heard often enough, but for Berry, the way a people obtain and consume their food shows where their treasure is. That is to say, the way in which you buy, prepare, and eat your food reveals your fundamental attitudes toward life, God, other people, and the land both near and far.[9] So Berry responds to non-farm dwellers who wonder what they can do about the plight of farms and farmers: "Eat responsibly." Rather than understanding themselves as passive consumers, people need to realize that they are playing an important role in the economy of food. Instead of being, at most, concerned with the grocery bill, Berry suggests that a set of questions regarding their food needs to be asked:

> How fresh is it? How pure or clean is it, how free of dangerous chemicals? How far was it transported, and what did transportation add to the cost? How did manufacturing or packaging or advertising add to the cost? When the food product has been manufactured or "processed" or "precooked," how has that affected its quality or price or nutritional value?[10]

In these questions the buyer, the preparer, and the eater bump up against the "rigorous conditions" of food. Parallel to the farmer's intellectual work is the partaker's work of selecting, cooking, and eating her food. In what Berry calls "the human economy,"[11] where value is supposed to originate in human choice, convenience and efficiency may be characteristic of both farm and table. These characteristics, however, are not the hallmarks of a responsible understanding of food production or preparation. We become blinded to the deeper connections evident in the greater economy when our relationship with food consists of slapping down five dollars on the counter and in return receiving a highly processed food item wrapped in cardboard. As the deeper connections sink beneath the surface, gratitude becomes a much more difficult task. Saying grace in a fast food restaurant verges on the sacrilegious. In the practices surrounding this understanding of food, we have given value to "that [which] is first abstract and then false, tyrannical, and destructive of real value."[12]

When our understanding of food is pushed in the direction of false value, a more extreme violation of the nature of food can emerge. Here food can quickly be transformed from its life-giving and life-affirming role in the Great Economy into something more dangerous. One example of the way in which food can become threatening is the historically prevalent view of food as weapon.[13] For nearly as long as agriculture has been around, food has been used as a means of violence to coerce, incorporate, or kill the residents of villages and empires. In his book *Guns, Germs, and Steel*,[14] Jared Diamond explains that two early results of the development of agricultural systems were the ability to harvest more food than was immediately needed and the ability to store the excess food. Production beyond immediate need and the capacity to store and transport food helped smaller local populations grow in numbers and expand in territory. But beyond that reality, developments in agriculture allowed for military campaigns that were carried out over years and vastly expanded the geographic reach of such campaigns. An army can do battle only as long as it is being fed.[15] Keeping the attacking soldiers fed while laying siege to a city and withholding food from the denizens of the besieged city make for a relatively one-sided battle. With stockpiles of food and flowing supply lines, military forces could stretch the boundaries of empires. Diamond maintains that certain ancient civilizations expanded and became dominant in their time because of their ability to incorporate food into the military structure. In this way, food became a weapon, and, as Berry writes, "to think of food as a weapon, or of a weapon as food, may give an illusory security and wealth to a few, but it strikes directly at the life of all."[16]

Of course, understanding food as a weapon is not merely an ancient practice of war. Food continues to be a means whereby power is exercised over individuals, small groups of people, and even nations. Many, if not all, of the cases of mass starvation in the world currently have more to do with political powers withholding food or the forced removal of people from their land than with lands that cannot produce an adequate crop.[17] The promise of food along with other of life's basic needs can easily make people pliable to the will of others. Likewise, the withholding of sustenance from people can lead to their submission to those powers that control access to food. In this way, food again becomes connected with violence. The receiving of food under such conditions does not result in gratitude but serves as a constant reminder of one's servitude. As numerous narratives recount, going to bed hungry because someone wishes to control or exterminate you can quickly push you beyond normal behavior.

The food offered under enslavement or the food withheld during besiegement dehumanizes because false conditions are placed on your reception of that which physically sustains you. Food under such strictures ceases to be a gift and instead becomes a symbol of the curse. When food is used violently, a person is not invited freely to the table. Instead the diseased restrictions resulting when food is used as a weapon breaks relationships and enforces false values. Neither the person using food as a weapon nor the person against whom it is being used can experience the goodness of being human.

While the development from hunter-gatherers into makers of agriculture has made life much easier for most, it does have the negative by-product of possibly being manipulated by those who control some aspect of the growing and delivery of food to our table. The curse of weeds that must be pulled in order for the crop to flourish pales in comparison to the curse of wicked human hearts that transpose the abundance of the soil into a scarcity constructed by ideology. Understanding food as a weapon does not merely make victims of individuals, but such an attitude, as Berry explains, "foster(s) a mentality willing to use it as such" and it "is to prepare, in the human character and community, the destruction of the sources of food."[18] In North America, there has been no specific military or police campaign to remove farmers from their farms as there has been in Zimbabwe. Nevertheless, as Berry points out, "the concept of food-as-weapon is not surprisingly the doctrine of a Department of Agriculture that is being used as an instrument of foreign political and economic speculation."[19] The result of this policy is the "mechanization and chemicalization of farming"[20] that simultaneously diminishes the land while making farming too expensive for the small farmer. The tendency of this understanding of food production is "to complete the deliverance of American agriculture into the hands of corporations."[21] While not as direct as the practices of ancient military regimes, in the end people are still displaced by abstract visions of political and economic success.

Thinkers from Heidegger to Berry have articulated the difference between house and home.[22] More recently the idea of homelessness has been used to describe cultural and social displacement. To be homeless is different from simply being without shelter. Homelessness designates experiences of being displaced, dislocated, or not belonging. Emotional and existential damage can be expected when men and women, or even communities, have been uprooted from their home as their world ceases to cohere because they are no longer placed and can only hope to belong.[23]

Berry's concern for the future of the small farm is not nostalgic; rather it is an attempt to conserve an important connection between human beings and the earth upon which they trod. Our attitude toward food is a linchpin keeping us from being uprooted from our earthy home. In thinking of our food as having its origin in the aisle of a grocery store, in thinking that our food must look like its virtual image in advertisements, or in thinking of our food as cheap and easy, a kind of cultural amnesia overtakes us as we become forgetful of our place. Our attitude toward food, in its most reductionist form, is that food is only a carrier of nutrition. For industrial agriculture, the real issue is processing food in such a way that efficiency is increased, in part by using the few crops best produced by agribusiness. According to some surveys, corn and/or soybean derivatives show up in some 80 percent of food in the average grocery store food product. In the name of efficiency to meet desire, we have turned to petrochemical fertilizers and pesticides to produce more. In so doing, we have in many instances deadened the soil. The soil's natural nutrients and water-holding ability have been weakened as agricultural practices have come to view the soil as an inert medium through which we build our food. Vegetables in the soil seem as little at home in the dirt as families do on the farm in an age of massive agribusinesses.

Likewise, we treat farm animals as future processed meat products. We raise and slaughter animals in meat factories. In massive barns, dairy cows never graze in a field, rather their diet and activity is precisely controlled in order to produce milk at an unnatural rate. In other massive barns, chickens are so cramped together that air must be forced in to maintain life. In our current economic climate, the excessive desire for meat, a desire that is being replicated in "developing" countries, has led to the displacing of animals for efficiency's sake. Increasingly, meat producers must yield more in less time at less cost in order to supply an ample amount of meat at a low enough cost to feed this appetite. The idyllic sight of small herds of cattle in a field or chickens in a barnyard coop is easily dismissed as nostalgic in light of the increasing demand. But, again, as Berry suggests, we must appeal to the agrarian standard that "requires bringing local nature, local people, local economy, and local culture into a practical and enduring harmony."[24]

The subtle ways in which this industrial food attitude is extended keeps us from easily recognizing the way in which our society has pushed its understanding of food as a weapon to the extreme. Once we have acknowledged the result of consuming high-calorie, high-sugar, high-fat food products, we respond by turning to a further technological manipulation of food. While still attempting to meet the need to eat in an efficient way, we also attempt to prevent the delivery of calories by food. The minds that direct industrial agriculture have created diet food to be "nothing" in order to create stylized virtual bodies. What we typically view as food is replaced by even more processed products whose function is to appease the guilt of being hungry. Food is now not merely something that needs to be improved by processing; it has become a necessary evil. In a Gnostic sort of move, bodily pleasure has been separated from the act of eating. Taste, smell, and look are subsumed under the workings of a rational mind that is nowhere "perfectly embodied."[25] By contrast, the lettuce from our field has taste. It is not the bland green transporter of dressing. And the fact that it does taste is sometimes offensive to taste buds shaped by the bland vegetables contrived by industrial agriculture. If food delivers no aesthetic stimulus, then it makes perfect sense to move beyond it and simply deliver the necessary nutrition through energy bars, drinks, and powders.

The cycling between high-calorie, high-sugar, high-fat food and dieting tells more about us than we may want to admit. Such a contradiction is yet another example of the schizophrenia of our age. It seems that at this point we are more at home in a space capsule or a laboratory than in a kitchen. The uprooting of families from the land where our fruit and vegetables are grown and where our meat is raised has not only uprooted farm families it has also displaced all of us who eat. In being shaped by cultural forces to view food as a weapon, we have consented to governmental and corporate policies that challenge our humanity and our place in creation. In acquiescing to current governmental and corporate policy about food, we cease to view food in its appropriate context. In our increasingly technological interactions with food, we have uprooted our food from its place. Hence, we are willing to sacrifice the small family farm because our food can come from any place or no place at all. Berry's critical insight here is that we are quickly becoming farmless, and in becoming farmless the disorientation of being homeless deepens.

In the face of these powers, despair would be a reasonable response, except that cracks are already evident in the structures of industrial agriculture. For Berry, the choice is clear, as he lays out in *The Way of Ignorance*: "If we cannot establish an enduring or even a humanly bearable economy by our attempt to defeat nature, then we will have to try living in harmony and cooperation with her."[26] The basis for hope is the goodness of creation and our ability to recognize it. Hope does not come from constructing another system to counter the one in which we find ourselves as, according to Berry, "arrogance cannot be cured by greater arrogance, or ignorance by greater ignorance."[27] Our current situation demands humility as we begin by submitting to the limits that define our place. In returning to an understanding of creation and its goodness as gift, we find our place again within the boundaries that allow for health. We begin with the givens: "land, plants, animals, weather, hunger, and the birthright knowledge of agriculture."[28] We are no longer trapped in the rhetoric of competition, scarcity, and absolute control of nature. Instead, we view the world through the language of faith, hope, and love and see the mutuality, provision, and nurture of the Great Economy.

As a gift, the soil calls forth our cultivation of it. In the Great Economy, food is far from a weapon or a necessary evil. Food is a good gift of the soil that still demands the work of the field, the market, and the kitchen in an economy of use, but food is also part of an economy of return where we become worthy of the gift through our "praise, gratitude, responsibility, good use, good care, and a proper regard for future generations," as Berry wrote in *Citizenship Papers*.[29] The link that food provides between farm and home is vital in helping to create and maintain households, neighborhoods, and communities rooted in gratitude, and which are able to extend invitations far and wide to the shared table. A neighbor farmer replied when asked if he would be willing to lease his land for wind towers, "No, I promised my dad that I would give the land to my children in the same condition he gave it to me." I can only hope to weed my tomatoes in such a way that I can give such good gifts to my son and to my community.

Berry captures this understanding of food in his description of mealtime in various places throughout his fiction. For instance, in *Andy Catlett: Early Travels*, Berry describes the cooking of meals by his two grandmothers as acts full of love and care. Likewise, in *The Memory of Old Jack*, the noon meal served by the Feltners for the laborers and Old Jack shows the hospitality that is at the core of the membership. The work of preparing a meal together is not portrayed as a burdensome task, though it is a work that demands attention to detail. In preparing and eating the meal, there is a bringing together of the household. Perhaps in Berry's stories the people of Port William are most placed when they gather around the table sharing the bounty of the farm. As we look into the dining room of the Catletts or the Feltners, the membership congregates for the communion of being at home; out of the fullness of this gift arises Berry's doxology: "May my brain be bright with praise / of what I eat, in the brief blaze / of motion and of thought. / May I be worthy of my meat."[30]

6

# The Third Landscape:
# Wendell Berry and
# American Conservation

*Jason Peters*

Wendell Berry calls himself a conservationist and is generally considered an environmentalist, but he hasn't exactly been inclined to think of membership in institutional terms. He doesn't cut the figure of a joiner or a committee member, and certainly not a company man. Distrustful of movements and organizations, Berry has tended to go his own way, often preferring to keep counsel with himself.

Or that, it seems, is the popular perception, a perception not entirely without merit. But anyone who has bothered to pay attention knows the fuller story: Berry is careful to acknowledge his teachers past and present and has a public record of cooperating with those who fight for causes he himself fights for and believes in. He has opposed, for example, state-sponsored strip-mining and mountaintop removal in Kentucky as vigorously and visibly as he has opposed federally sponsored industrial farming. That is, he has opposed the war-faring tactics of the extractive economy, whether its absentee captains have lusted after coal or corn. He has gone so far as to extend this opposition to the prevailing tendencies in higher education, which has become an extractive enterprise that mines local talent and sends it off to be burned up elsewhere. Back of all this stands Berry's impressive record of opposing the war-faring tactics of an empire that is as necessarily extractive as it is indifferent to the consequences of extraction.

But it is nevertheless true that Berry is fairly adept at remaining unaffiliated. He is as successful at eluding the card-carrying Planet Savers who would claim him as their own as he is at outrunning recruiters from the political Left and Right desperate for someone to articulate their thick-tongued inebriate notions of the good life. As early as *The Unsettling of America* (1977), he was skeptical of an organization's ability to define "our relationship to the world . . . except in general terms," a problem that the "conservation movement has never resolved" because it is "divided between its intentional protection of some places . . . and its inadvertent destruction of others." This was a mild criticism compared with the accusation that the conservation movement "is variously either vacation-oriented or crisis-oriented."[1] Twelve years later, he showed no signs of relenting: "Public movements of thought quickly produce a language that works as a code, useless to the extent that it is abstract."[2] A decade after that, he said, "People in movements too readily learn to deny to others the rights and privileges they demand for themselves"; they become "unable to mean their own language"; they are "too specialized, as if they cannot help taking refuge in the pinhole vision of the industrial intellectuals." Ultimately, he said, they deal "in effects rather than causes,"[3] and so he doubted that "the conservation organizations alone will ever make us a conserving society."[4] And then a couple of years into the new millennium, as unaffiliated as ever, at least with respect to the available camps and *isms*, he criticized the conservation movement for having "no economic program," for being "exterior to daily life, surviving by emergency, like an ambulance service."[5] At about the same time, he issued a declaration of independence: "I decided not long ago that I would not endorse any more wilderness preservation projects."[6]

But this announcement was born of the usual subtlety; it came with an important stipulation: he would not endorse such projects *unless* they could demonstrate an attempt "to improve the health of the surrounding economic landscapes and human communities."[7] This contingency is crucial, and I want to suggest that if there is a sine qua non of all that Berry says about conservation, this is it. It provides the one good reason—and it *is* a good one—for taking any interest at all in Berry's somewhat embattled relation to the conservation movement.

As for the announcement itself, it certainly reaffirmed Berry's distrust of movements and his preference for being unaffiliated. No doubt it also irritated the certified environmentalists who read about it over their morning lattes. And yet the poet who says "what I stand for is what I stand on"[8] is probably the most situated conservationist in America. It will be the final task of this essay to explain and justify that claim.

But before proceeding any further, I want to provide at least some readers with a reason to stop. Two fairly obvious options immediately present themselves here. One would be to reproduce Berry's argument in the most obviously pertinent of his essays, "Conservation Is Good Work," in which he says that there are "three kinds of conservation currently operating," all of which are "inadequate, both separately and together."[9] The other would to place Berry in some kind of genealogy of conservationists. Neither option seems to me to be a useful exercise at all. Anyone who wants to can go read Berry on the inadequacies of the three kinds of conservation—and would certainly be better for doing so. And although there are certainly good reasons to attend to the lineage of writers Berry himself has attended to, anyone well-versed in his work could sketch the ancestry easily enough and see that back of Berry, or alongside him, stand Henry David Thoreau, John Muir, Ananda Coomaraswamy, E. F. Schumacher, Aldo Leopold, Wallace Stegner, Guy Davenport, Harry Caudill, Gary Nabhan, Philip Sherrard, Donald Worster, Edward Abbey, and Harlan Hubbard, among several others.[10] But, with the exception perhaps of the Southern Agrarians, who provided Berry with the terms that would frame much of his thinking—I mean especially John Crowe Ransom's paradigmatic use of "agrarian" and "industrial" in the "Statement of Principles" that introduced *I'll Take My Stand*[11]—Berry has made no more use of these "conservationists" than of several others in an older and more far-reaching tradition, a tradition in which nature is the

> final judge, lawgiver, and pattern-maker of and for the human use of the earth. We can trace the lineage of this thought in the West through the writings of Virgil, Spenser, Shakespeare, Pope, Jefferson, and on into the work of the twentieth-century agriculturalists and scientists J. Russell Smith, Liberty Hyde Bailey, Albert Howard, Wes Jackson, John Todd, and others. The idea is variously stated: We should not work until we have looked and seen where we are.[12]

And this list still does not include all those mute inglorious farmers, laid to rest in the Port Royal cemetery, whom Berry often mentions as his equally important, if unofficial, teachers. Berry has the tradition of conservation in his blood, to be sure, and he has been a very active conservationist. But, as the foregoing quotation makes clear, he has been careful not to lock himself into an identifiable lineage any younger than the agrarian record descending to us from the ancients. Moreover, he has consistently resisted the prevailing tendency among environmentalists to use scientific or technological definitions of who we are and what our place in the world is.[13] Instead of this, he has put together from all the various sources, at home and abroad, a version of conservation not readily available otherwise—and certainly not in such clear and forceful prose. Discussing this version—a version implicit at least as far back as *The Unsettling of America*—seems to me a far more useful exercise than summarizing a perfectly clear primary document or tricking out the details of influence and points of departure. At any rate, it is the task I have proposed for myself here.[14] Readers looking for something else needn't turn another page.

At the heart of Berry's dissent from the available movements is a long-held conviction that they are not comprehensive enough. This is a shortcoming evident now in the language such movements employ. "Environment," for example, suggests something that *surrounds* us, a thing *separate from* us, and so confers upon us a certain permission to stand at several removes from it. "We tend to think," Berry told an interviewer in 1991, "that there can be a distinction between people and the air they breathe, for instance, or people and the food they eat, or people and the water they drink." He called this an "absurd distinction":

> there is no line that you can draw between people and the elements they depend on. That is why the term "environment" is so bothersome to me. "Environment" is based on that dualism, the idea that you can separate the human interests from the interests of everything else. You *cannot* do it. We eat the environment. It passes through our bodies every day.[15]

This failure of language is no less problematic if we substitute the word *conservation*, for sooner or later conservationists, always sophisticated and progressive, are going to have to admit, much to their embarrassment, that they are "conservatives"—just as our current "conservatives" are going to have to admit that they are nothing of the sort so long as they are hell-bent on not conserving anything. It simply won't do, Berry says, to be selectively interested in conservation:

> If we want to use the world with care, we cannot exempt ourselves from our cultural inheritance, our tradition. This is a delicate subject at present because our cultural tradition happens to be Western, and there is now a fashion of disfavor toward the Western tradition. But most of us are in the Western tradition somewhat as we are in the world: we are in it because we were born in it. We can't get out of it . . . [a]nd perhaps we would not like to get out of it if that meant giving up, as we would have to do, our language and its literature, our hereditary belief that all people matter individually, our heritage of democracy, liberty, civic responsibility, stewardship, and so on.[16]

Which is to say that "in order to preserve the health of nature, we must preserve ourselves as human beings; as creatures who possess humanity not just as a collection of physical attributes but also as the cultural imperative to be caretakers, good neighbors to one another and to the other creatures."[17]

The problem here for anyone who has paid attention to the official noisemakers in the environmental and conservation movements is obvious: it strikes at the heart of a cherished prejudice against the past. How, for example, can we preserve ourselves as "caretakers" *and* continue blaming our Western, specifically Judeo-Christian, heritage for the ecological offenses we wish to absolve ourselves of?[18] How can we be good stewards of our local places and neighborhoods and therefore of the earth itself while supposing that we can go outside our tradition for culture-borne instructions on how to be good stewards?

We can no more think of the "environment" as something that surrounds us than regard conservation as a forward-thinking Parks and Recreation program, for just as the "environment" (which is actually the world) "surpasses mere connection and verges on identity,"[19] so also conservation requires attention to all that a conserving impulse entails, including an imperative to defend "an authentic (which is to say a land-based) multiculturalism," as Berry asserts in *Another Turn of the Crank*.[20] Sooner or later, the environmentalists are going to have to abandon the cool detachment from the weather that they enjoy as they sit at their computers, just as progressive sophisticates are going to have to get over their embarrassment at finding "husbandry" a useful and necessary word.

The failure of language, Berry suggests, is an intentional evasion. In 1990 he told the *Progressive* that we can't take environmental awareness seriously "until people begin to talk seriously about lowering the standard of living. When people begin to see affluence, economic growth, unrestrained economic behavior, as the enemies of the environment, then we can take it seriously. But people are saying, 'Give us everything we want *and* a clean environment,' and that isn't a possibility."[21] This was a way of saying, as Berry has in fact said, that American conservation is at worst a "sham" and at best "embarrassingly incomplete."[22] It is a sham, Berry says, because it does not wish to rid itself of what it opposes. Forget, for example, that many environmentalists want governments and *other* people to do something about greenhouse gas emissions.[23] Forget that many environmentalists want to continue to get energy from food they expend no energy to produce. Forget all that. Too many environmentalists have no real interest in getting serious about their economic lives or reducing their standards of living. In the late 1980s, as rising tides were putatively lifting all boats but actually sinking most of them, Berry quoted Orwell's essay on Kipling: "All left-wing parties in the highly industrialized countries are at bottom a sham, because they make it their business to fight against something which they do not really wish to destroy." Their "internationalist aims" are at odds with the standard of living they struggle to maintain. "We all live by robbing Asiatic coolies," Orwell said, "and those of us who are 'enlightened' all maintain that those coolies ought to be set free; but our standard of living, and hence our 'enlightenment,' demands that the robbery shall continue."[24] This remark, Berry said, has never lost its timeliness. "The religion and environmentalism of the highly industrialized countries are at bottom a sham," he said, because they have no real desire—especially in the age of "permanent" globalization—to abolish what they rail against. "We all live by robbing nature, but our standard of living demands that the robbery shall continue."[25]

To call the movement a sham is perhaps the least charitable way of looking at it; in its most favorable light, it is incomplete. It proceeds on the assumption that "parts of the world can be preserved while others are abused or destroyed," as if it were enough to "save a series of islands of pristine and uninhabited wilderness in an otherwise exploited, damaged, and polluted land."[26] "So far," says Berry,

> [t]he moral landscape of the conservation movement has tended to be a landscape of extremes, which you can see pictured in any number of expensive books of what I suppose must be called "conservation photography." On the one hand we have the unspoiled wilderness, and on the other hand we have scenes of utter devastation—strip mines, clear-cuts, industrially polluted wastelands, and so on.[27]

This picture is "embarrassingly incomplete" because it presents the world "as either deserted landscape or desertified landscape." But "if we are to have an accurate picture of the world, even in its present diseased condition, we must interpose between the unused landscape and the misused landscape a landscape that humans have used well"—that is, a third landscape.[28]

This is one instance among many in which Berry—mindful of the opposing interests of hikers and developers, or of preservationists and conservationists, or of wilderness advocates and ranchers, or of the defenders of wildness and domesticity broadly conceived—has framed the problem of the human relation to nature. He has framed it, that is, in such a way as to interpose between the feuding families an *agrarian* standard. This is crucial. If we fail to understand it, we will fail to understand what Berry means when he calls himself a conservationist. We will also fail to understand what conservationists and environmentalists must do if they wish to live, as they must, in the inescapable and uncompromising paradox of nature's inexhaustible limits.[29]

The landscape Berry has in mind can of course be found almost anywhere people thrive. But ultimately what he has in mind is the well-made small-scale farm, a place farmed well by people who are equal to their own needs, conscious of their own and the place's limitations, and willingly governed by an exacting agrarian—as opposed to an industrial—standard. These people willingly live on and from the farm by nature's economic principle of return; their concern, certainly, is to live well by the place, but they also wish to ensure its enduring fertility and health. They refuse to extract from the place what cannot be returned as fertility. They are conscious, that is, of their own and the world's necessary participation in the inescapable cycle of death and resurrection, of life's dying into the ground and being reborn and then living and dying and living again. They understand both the economic and ecological value of plant and animal diversity. They run the farm on energy that comes primarily from contemporary rather than ancient sunlight, which is to say they prefer animal and hand labor to petroleum-powered machinery.[30] Their eyes-to-acre ratio, as Wes Jackson says, implies a scale that makes intimate care of the place possible. The bookkeeping on the place is as comprehensive as it can be, which is to say it is honest.[31] There prevails, in other words, a respect for the inescapable and uncompromising paradox of nature's inexhaustible limits.

So when Berry says, "I am a conservationist and a farmer, wilderness advocate and an agrarian," he is interposing between the sometimes warring parties an agrarian standard that recognizes its own enduring paradox, a standard that attends not only to unused and misused landscapes but also—and especially—to well-used landscapes. He wants "to preserve the natural health and integrity of the world's economic landscapes" and to ensure that the "world's farmers, ranchers, and foresters . . . live in stable, locally adapted, resource-preserving communities."[32]

And so I come now to that important stipulation I mentioned at the start: it is in *this* context—it is with the interposed third landscape on his mind, the landscape used well—that Berry says he has decided not to endorse any more wilderness-preservation projects *unless* they "seek also to improve the health of the surrounding economic landscapes and human communities." He doesn't believe "we can preserve either wildness or wilderness areas if we can't preserve the economic landscapes and the people who use them."[33]

This conviction is born of Berry's dissatisfaction with the assumptions, noted above, of the American conservation and environmental movements. So long as we give ourselves easy permission to live, as Berry put it, on the "far side of a broken connection"[34]—that is to say, at several removes from the fundamental processes that sustain us—we will perpetuate two errors: (1) the notion that some places of the world can be safely abused so long as others are set aside,[35] and (2) the notion that the environment can therefore be thought of as something that surrounds rather than passes through us. Nothing good can come of these fundamental errors, except that the second will eventually betray the first: the "environment," which is to say both the unused and the abused landscapes alike, will inevitably pass through us—perhaps instructively and probably unpleasantly. Whether we are witnessing a significant change in our governing delusion—that we can have a clean "environment" *and* a high standard of living (the principal consequence of which is garbage)—is beside the point as long as the robbery continues. As Berry says in *Home Economics*, "[T]he wildernesses we are trying to preserve are standing squarely in the way of our present economy," and "the wildernesses cannot survive if our economy does not change."[36]

Case in point: the essay for which Berry has perhaps been most traduced—"Why I am Not Going to Buy a Computer"—elicited from the environmental technorati this predictable response: "Computers can be an invaluable tool in the fight to protect our environment. In addition to helping me write, my personal computer gives me access to up-to-the-minute reports on the workings of the EPA and nuclear industry."[37] Almost twenty years prior to this, Berry had written, "If you are worried about the damming of wilderness rivers, join the Sierra Club, write to the government, but turn off the lights you're not using, don't install an air conditioner, don't be a sucker for electrical gadgets, don't waste water. In other words, if you are fearful of the destruction of the environment, then learn to quit being an environmental parasite."[38]

Note that the dissenter has asked purchasable goods (that is, he has asked the extractive economy) to tell him what his own eyes and his own sense of beauty—were it not dulled—could tell him: that destructiveness and ugliness are everywhere. But because the testimony of the senses is free, it does nothing for that cherished and unassailable standard of living—or what Edward Abbey called the Grossest National Product[39]—that the hybrid-driving environmentalists do not really wish to see lowered. It doesn't continue to liberate them from Adam's curse, which is a liberation they apparently will have at all costs. This is why we're witnessing a push for wind to run our electronic gadgets, as if these gadgets don't exist by the grace of limited resources and don't eventually become poisons, or as if the solemn slavelike churning of wind turbines doesn't offend the eye and despoil the landscape. This is why we are enlisting corn to run our hybrid vehicles. This is why we have an ethanol drug trade to support our automobile addiction.

What Berry argues for is a kind of responsibility that would reduce the economic abstractions that lead to abuse, abstractions that implicate all of us whenever we spend our money with the wrong kinds of producers. His patience with those who want a clean environment *and* wish to exempt themselves from production—specifically food production—has worn pretty thin: "Urban conservationists," for example, "may feel entitled to be unconcerned about food production because they are not farmers. But they can't be let off so easily, for they all are farming by proxy. They can eat only if land is farmed on their behalf by somebody somewhere in some fashion." What would happen if conservationists attempted "to resume responsibility for their need to eat"? What if they supported and assigned proper economic value to the kind of land use and farming described above? They would be "led back fairly directly to all their previous concerns for the welfare of nature."[40]

I acknowledge that I am in some danger of being reductive in the manner of the moral simpleton who would reduce all effects to a single cause, so I will say plainly that food production is one area among *many* in which conservationists must resume responsibility for their needs. But if we want to get Berry right, we must understand that the issue of food—the question of how we shall eat—has been at the heart of things from the start. It informs almost everything he says about environmental degradation, and there is no use trying to make sense of his work if we are going to ignore this central feature.[41] With every new recruit to the absentee food economy, another part of the world will be used poorly; but each time a defector returns to—and comes to terms with his dependence on—the soil, another part of the world is likely to be used well. Indeed, *The Unsettling of America* was a sustained attempt to explain the inevitable dangers awaiting those who would be delivered from the "drudgery" of growing their own food. It was also an attempt to show that "[o]nly by restoring the broken connection can we be healed. . . . We lose our health—and create profitable diseases and dependences—by failing to see the direct connections between living and eating, eating and working, working and loving."[42]

So in several subsequent works, Berry has said that we should stop acting as if the only way to meet our needs is by shopping. Grow some food, he says. Prepare some food. "Odd as I am sure it will appear to some," he said in the early 1970s (before the publication of *The Unsettling of America*),

> I can think of no better form of personal involvement in the cure of the environment than that of gardening. A person who is growing a garden, if he is growing it organically, is improving a piece of the world. He is producing something to eat, which makes him somewhat independent of the grocery business, but he is also enlarging, for himself, the meaning of food and the pleasure of eating. The food he grows will be fresher, more nutritious, less contaminated by poisons and preservatives and dyes than what he can buy at a store. He is reducing the trash problem; a garden is not a disposable container, and it will digest and reuse its own wastes. If he enjoys working in his garden, then he is less dependent on an automobile or a merchant for his pleasure. He is involving himself directly in the work of feeding people.[43]

That is, he is availing himself of "a new kind of life—harder, more laborious, poorer in luxuries and gadgets, but also, I am certain, richer in meaning and more abundant in real pleasure."[44] This person cultivating a garden may even learn that in gardening "one works with the body to feed the body," that the "work, if it is knowledgeable, makes for excellent food," that "it makes one hungry," and that it "keeps the eater from getting fat and weak." And this, says Berry, "is health, wholeness, a source of delight. And such a solution, unlike the typical industrial solution, does not cause new problems."[45]

What is Berry's hope for the conservation movement if fewer urban conservationists farm by proxy and begin to take an interest in the well-used landscape and the environment that passes through rather than surrounds them?

His hope is not that everyone will start farming.[46] His hope, simply, is that conservationists will get serious about farming; that they will spend their money with their allies rather than with their enemies; that they will begin to eat conscionably and in full consciousness. For if

> conservationists merely eat what the supermarket provides and the government allows, they are giving economic support to all-

out industrial food production: to animal factories, to the depletion of soil, rivers, and aquifers; to crop monocultures and the consequent losses of biological and genetic diversity; to the pollution, toxicity, and overmedication that are the inevitable accompaniments of all-out industrial food production. . . .

And so on and so forth.[47] That is, they are consenting to that most dangerous of ideas: that so long as some places are either managed or left alone, others can be used poorly, and that the environment, true to the current permissible sentiments, can continue to surround rather than pass through us.

On this point, Berry has been unambiguous: if we persist in the delusion that the environment merely surrounds us, then when it passes through us, as it inevitably will, it will poison us, and catastrophes will force us to make the changes we ought to have been good enough and smart enough to make in advance of their arrival.

But if conservationists are going to get serious about farming, farmers must likewise become serious about conservation. They must learn and be willing to farm well—or else continue "to increase the ecological deficit that is being charged to the future."[48] What we need, Berry says, are farmers who conserve their knowledge, ways, and skills but who also conserve the wildness of the world that alone can remind them of "their inescapable dependence on nature."[49]

In fine, Berry is trying to "define a congruity or community of interest between farmers and conservationists who are not farmers."[50] The site of this congruity is not the "environment." It is not unused or misused land. It is land that is used well, land that is governed by a true agrarian standard mutually upheld and equally understood by both producers and consumers alike.

Often at odds with farmers, conservationists must pay better attention to the consequences of farming-by-proxy and become better acquainted with the cultural, economic, and political adversities that good farmers face. Often at odds with conservationists, farmers must not lose sight of "their own economy's basis in nature."[51] Bad farmers have assumed that "land can be subordinated to the capability of technology, and that conservation could safely be left to conservationists." Conservationists, on the other hand, have assumed "that the integrity of the natural world could be preserved mainly by preserving tracts of wilderness." Both sides are "clinging to a common error." Conservationists must "know and deal competently with the methods and economics of land use"; farmers must "recognize the urgency, even the economic urgency, of the requirements of conservation."[52] And both must quit buying whatever is for sale simply because it is for sale.

Berry once said that a convocation of environmentalists is a gathering not of the innocent but of the guilty.[53] One can easily imagine the opening dinner of such a gathering: there, in the conference-center dining room, everyone eats in utter ignorance, and no one eating has done any of the work. This is absurd. This is one among many incoherencies to which we have reconciled ourselves.

I have quoted liberally from the essay "Conservationist and Agrarian." I want to say something now about the temporal context of this essay and of another that bears the title "The Agrarian Standard."

Both essays belong to the same general period (2001–2) that saw *The Unsettling of America* turn twenty-five, "The Agrarian Standard" having in fact been written for a conference organized specifically to mark the anniversary of the book's publication.[54] If both essays suggest that *The Unsettling* was on Berry's mind during its silver year, and they do, they also clearly resuscitate some of its salient concerns.[55] They remind us that although Berry was obviously at pains in that book to oppose industrial farming methods and the federal policies that inaugurated, sanctioned, and supported them, he was also attempting to restore to conservation this third landscape, to enlarge conservation and honor its complexity by adding to it what ought to have been its most pressing concern: the agrarian standard, the possibility of land used well that makes eating possible not just for us but for our children and grandchildren as well.[56]

In light of the aforementioned essays, *The Unsettling* reasserts itself for its unwillingness to treat of conservation and ecology without also treating of agriculture.[57] The question of our relation to nature, Berry said then, whatever else that question is, is always an agricultural question, "for no matter how urban our life, our bodies live by farming; we come from the earth and return to it, and so we live in agriculture as we live in flesh."[58] It is hard to be a member of a movement or an organization, Berry seemed to be saying, if the land cannot feed you long enough for you to sign on and pay your annual fees.

And what did Berry say, even then, about the word *environment*?

The concept of country, homeland, dwelling place becomes simplified as "the environment"—that is, what surrounds us. Once
we see our place, our part of the world, as *surrounding* us, we have
already made a profound division between it and ourselves. We
have given up the understanding—dropped it out of our language
and so out of our thought—that we and our country create one
another, depend on one another, are literally part of one another;
that our land passes in and out of our bodies just as our bodies
pass in and out of our land; that as we and our land are part of
one another, so all who are living as neighbors here, human and
plant and animal, are part of one another, and so cannot possibly
flourish alone.[59]

The unused, poorly used, and well-used landscapes alike all pass in
and out of our bodies. This observation is a distinctly agrarian contribution to conservation. If environmentalists and conservationists wish to
keep this present to their minds and so rebuild a life of integrity and substance, they are going to have to learn to eat responsibly, to use land well,
to understand that a coherent and comprehensive relationship to nature is
inescapably economic, to understand that *any* economy is ultimately land-
based, whether its high priests know this or not. The land must therefore
be used knowledgeably and gratefully, with restraint and awe. Above all,
land use must accord with the natural principle of return that governs
nature's economy and that alone can preserve the life and health of the
world. To use land thus is to begin to recover the third landscape.

When he went to work on *The Unsettling of America*, Berry was insti-
tutionally affiliated enough to have been chairman of the Sierra Club's
Cumberland chapter. He was a conservationist asking his fellow conservationists to take agriculture seriously and to think about a third kind of
landscape. Thirteen years prior to its publication, Berry had returned at
the age of twenty-nine to his native Kentucky county to farm the land
he still farms today. If today he is unaffiliated among the available movements and *isms* in contemporary conservation and environmentalism, he
is not for that reason unsituated. On the contrary: he is as placed as any
conservationist now living—and nearly as placed as those who are dead.

And the run-down hillside farm he bought in 1964, the place he not only stands *for* but stands *on*, is a healthier third landscape today because a conservationist has lived *on* and *from* it and farmed it according to the agrarian standard. "Maybe the finest sources of hope," he suggests, "are the people for whom the effort of conservation has ceased to be a separate activity and has come to be at one with their ways of making their living." Such people "have not achieved perfection, of course, but they have achieved a kind of unity of vision and work. For them, land health is not something added to their economy but is at once their economy's basis and result."[60]

# 7

# Wendell Berry and
# Democratic Self-Governance

*Patrick J. Deneen*

## The False Anthropology of Liberal Democracy

In today's common parlance, *democracy* means in most instances "liberal democracy." While the term is often used unreflectively as descriptive of a modern form of government, the two terms at best coexist in uneasy juxtaposition. To the extent that liberal democracy is democratic—that is, to the extent that it rests upon government by popular rule—its popular dimension is achieved mainly through two mechanisms. First, liberalism aspires to legitimacy through a theory of popular consent, namely consent to the rules by which government is established and operates. Secondly, there is the ongoing democratic practice of periodic elections, which at once serves the function of continuous legitimation and the expression of the popular will.

Most citizens have come to accept these two functions as key features of a democratic system, but in its most essential aspects, liberal democracy is more fundamentally liberal in its anthropology than it is democratic. At base, its anthropology is first and foremost about the "liberation" of individuals from constitutive bonds and cultural ties and only secondarily about the core value of democracy, that is, self-government within shared acknowledgment of constraint and limits. Liberalism's anthropology is drawn from depictions of human nature in the early modern period, particularly articulated in the political philosophies of Thomas Hobbes and John Locke, the scientific theory of Francis Bacon, the theological-political writings of Baruch Spinoza, and the epistemological reflections of Rene Descartes. It is liberal, that is, in a specific way: it argues on behalf of institutional, political, and social arrangements that result in the liberation of humankind from arbitrary constraints on the human will. In the political realm—advanced by the social-contract theories of Hobbes and Locke—it delegitimizes the claims of the ancestral or traditional in favor of consent and that which is freely chosen. In the scientific realm, it calls for the conquest of nature, the overcoming of what once were regarded as natural limits or constraints upon human exercise of will. Nature is treated—in Bacon's reckoning—as a "prisoner" who must be forced to divulge its secrets, through "torture" if necessary. In the epistemological domain, as formulated by Descartes, it rejects the counsel of history, experience, and tradition in favor of the ratiocination of the incorporeal human mind, the knowledge of reality solely through the process of thought experimentation.

Liberal anthropology is based upon an abstract and arguably fictive form of liberty: it begins by imagining that human beings in their natural state are placeless, historyless, timeless, loveless and without governance. They are, by nature, creatures without a past, and a future that can only include a rapacious desire to acquire and increase possessions and power. They possess insatiable desires and calculating reason. Anything short of thorough dominion by individuals is an imposition upon our nature.

Liberalism's anthropology stresses, above all, the reality of only two fundamental motivations that drive human behavior: fear and desire. Humans are understood to be bundles of unlimited appetite and fear, at once desirous of limitless satisfactions but also fearful of obstacles that may prevent such satiation. Our nature as appetitive creatures was aptly summarized by Thomas Hobbes, who wrote that humanity is that creature that seeks "power after power that ceaseth only in death." As Hobbes portrays the human creature, we are defined above all by our incapacity to be content or to acknowledge satiation within a world we recognize to be bounded by laws and limits. Even those, he writes, who might "otherwise be glad to be at ease within modest bounds, should [they] not by invasion increase their power, they would not be able, long time, by standing only on their defense, to subsist."[1] Given the basic assumption that human nature is essentially the effort for "power after power" and that personal restraint of this impulse is always imperfect, even otherwise modest humans have no choice but to engage in the effort to accumulate power.

Hobbes and Locke both describe the natural expression of the human scramble for power as that presocial condition known as the state of nature. Through the contrivance of the social contract, individuals agree to put themselves under the command of a Sovereign power that reduces the need for individuals to accumulate power as a matter of personal survival. However, the social contract exists not only out of *fear* for one's life in the natural state but also in order to secure the fulfillment of the human *desires* that are so central in the accumulation of "power after power." Thus, Hobbes concludes his famous chapter "Of Man" by observing that "the passions that incline men to peace" are not only "feare of death" but also the "desire of such things as are necessary to commodious living. . . ."[2] Similarly, John Locke averred in *A Letter Concerning Toleration* that matters of "civil interest" concern "life, liberty, health and *indolency of the body*; and possessions of outward things, such as money, lands, houses, furniture and the like."[3] And, along these lines, Francis Bacon argued in *The Advancement of Learning* that the aim of the New Science directed at the conquest of nature is "relief of the human estate." In short, philosophical developments in the early-modern period that formed the basis of liberal democracy placed as the primary end of human life the satisfactions of the body, to be secured by the extension of human power over a recalcitrant and often niggardly nature.

Liberal democracy at base defined the human creature as a being of will and appetite, the obstacle to fulfillment of which lies in the current arrangements as well as the niggardliness of the natural order. It called for the creation of political, social, scientific, and economic arrangements that would increase human power over that natural order, extracting from nature the goods necessary for "indolency of the body" and reshaping nature if need be to increase "commodious living." Liberal democracy—now often simply called democracy—was and is still today based upon the liberation of individuals from the limits of nature, of time, and of place. To the extent possible, we theoretically agree to the existence of polities to the extent that they permit us some approximation of the condition we left behind in the state of nature—bereft of the burden of history, the constraints of culture, the limits of place, and the obstacles to our desires imposed by nature. The existence of the state is agreeable to the extent that it increases our collective and individual power, and in so doing, necessarily increases its own scope and dominion. While we may exercise exceedingly little control over the activities of the state, we assent to its ongoing and expansive activities so long as human power and dominion over nature—and our own nature—is extended and perfected. This condition of ever more perfect mastery—and submission—is called, by most moderns, the state of democracy.

## Another Democracy: Ruling and Being Ruled

This largely implicit, if widely accepted, contemporary understanding of democracy—a form of political organization that results in maximum human autonomy, premised upon the dominion of nature—does not, however, exhaust the range of possible understandings of democracy. Centuries ago, Plato and Aristotle formulated definitions of democracy that in some instances map well onto our contemporary understanding (the close identification in Plato's thought between Sophists—willing to do whatever it takes to gain power—and democracy is a case in point) but also others that present a radically distinct understanding at odds with widespread contemporary definitions.

Particularly revealing are two definitions of democracy offered by Aristotle in the *Politics*. In book 6, Aristotle argues that democracy is a regime that has its basis in freedom and that freedom can take two forms. The first sort, he argues, consists of citizens "ruling and being ruled in turn." This definition of democracy accords with his earlier and more comprehensive definition of citizenship, which suggests that the most perfectly realized form of citizenship—the basis of the city—is a properly constituted democracy. In book 3, Aristotle provides a concrete example of "ruling and being ruled in turn," namely, the cultivation of discipline and martial order that is learned in the cavalry.

> This rule we call political rule, and the ruler must learn it by being ruled, just as one learns to be a cavalry commander by serving under a cavalry commander, or to be a general over an army

by serving under a general and commanding a regiment and a company. Hence it was nobly said that one cannot rule well without having been ruled. And while virtue in these cases is different, the good citizen must learn and be able both to be ruled and to rule. This is, in fact, the virtue of a citizen, to know rule over the free from both sides.[4]

Democracy, by this definition, is a learned discipline, requiring first the acquisition of the habit and ability to be ruled before assuming the mantle of ruling. We must first learn to be subject to the governance of others in positions of command—positions that they similarly achieved first by being ruled by their superiors—before advancing to positions of governance. Only in being ruled under the compulsion of the demands of the common good does one acquire the discipline of the citizen: the capacity to be governed by law, not to automatically or instinctively bridle against authority or limitations upon our individual freedom. Remarkably, this definition of citizenship is evoked again when speaking of democracy as a regime based upon freedom. The freedom of citizens in a democracy, according to Aristotle, consists first and perhaps foremost in learning to be ruled.

This first definition radically departs from the definition of freedom among early modern authors for whom freedom is most fully realized when the most desires are fulfilled and the human will expands to its greatest extent. Yet, this version of democratic freedom was not unknown to Aristotle—it constitutes the other basic self-definition of democracy: democracy that is organized around the principle of freedom *from* rule. This second form of democracy, he states, consists in the freedom of the individual "to do as one likes, for they say this is the work of freedom since to live as one does not like is characteristic of the slave. From it has come the feature of not being ruled by anyone at all but preferably, failing that, of being ruled in turns."[5]

This form of democracy has the appearance of "being ruled in turns"—on the surface it might be mistaken for that form of citizenship that consists of "ruling and being ruled in turn"—but this first impression is mistaken inasmuch as this form of democratic governance is accepted due to the inability to realize the preferred form of freedom: "the freedom to do as one likes." Failing to exert one's will freely—as would also be the case in a Hobbesian State of Nature—citizens of this debased form of democracy agree to rule and be ruled in turn, but only grudgingly and at least in their hearts harboring the ambition and desires of a tyrant. Political society is thus understood to be an unnatural imposition upon our natural urges and at best as a necessary evil. This form of democracy is thus a collection of frustrated tyrants, untutored in truer forms of self-government, grudgingly subject to shared rule but only toward the end of at least partially fulfilling otherwise unlimited desires. The organization of society is to be directed toward the end of increasing human mastery over the natural world, thereby achieving through the devices of society what was impossible before its institution, namely the overcoming of limits that had previously frustrated countless human desires.

Because humans under liberalism are conceived as self-interested and driven toward goals of acquisition and comfort, and government is a contractual artifice that aims to limit our self-destructive self-seeking and unleash more productive forms of self-interest, citizens (or "consumers") under liberal democracy are to be extensively freed from the burdens and responsibilities of self-government. Their involvement in the affairs of the public—*res publica*—are to be minimized, allowing them the liberty to pursue and succeed in the private realm and leaving the sphere of politics to elected leaders. Political leaders are charged with the responsibility of enacting policy that increases the human dominion of nature and enlarges the opportunities for individual comfort and material acquisition.

Citizenship, Aristotle argues, consists of ruling and being ruled in turn, which—extended most widely—results in democratic self-rule. Citizenship is not defined as the satisfaction of private interests but rather as the discipline of being ruled and ruling over those who have acquired similar dispositions and capacities of discipline. "Being ruled" means to be subject to a higher standard than mere private interest. As the example of the cavalry commander suggests, one is ruled and subsequently exercises rule on behalf of the public good—a good that may at times require restraint of individual appetite. The necessary civic discipline of being ruled is above all an education in learning to discern a good that transcends individual interest.

For Aristotle, the human good, above all, consisted in the realization of human nature. Human nature itself was fundamentally political, directed at the good of the city as a whole that superseded the private satisfactions of individuals. The good of the polis allowed for the flourishing of individuals within the city, centrally if not exclusively, in the exercise of citizenship as part of the well-lived life in which we strive to come to a closer understanding of "the whole." Further, the city is noteworthy for its self-sufficiency, its capacity to provide for itself across time. The city is a generational undertaking, a form of organized education in the ways of self-rule of one generation to the next. The polis is a culture of moderation and self-restraint, devoted to the education and enactment of self-government. Any such education in self-governance—in human virtue—begins at the earliest age, even before the pupils are conscious of the necessary conditions for virtue. The education of each new generation for lives of moderate self-governance is achieved through habituation—the lived experience of self-rule that is initially imposed as the discipline of being ruled. Only after learning self-rule, and thereby having come to understand the antecedent good of the polis, is a young adult permitted to engage in the active role as ruler of others.

For Aristotle, therefore, economic considerations are subject to the ruling standard of the common good. While some individuals might be disposed to pursue their own good at the expense of the public good, a properly constituted polity will restrain any such proclivity by limiting the extent of private economic pursuit. At base, this restraint is informed by the view that economic pursuits serve potentially limitless desires. Only by restraining the limitless desire of humans can a human appropriately be considered to be free. To be subject to the burning ambition to fulfill limitless desires is, in fact, to be a slave to one's ungoverned appetite. Thus, for Aristotle, economic pursuits are appropriate, in due measure, to provide for "the good life," but any effort to acquire excessive material possessions should be regarded as a form of "money-making" and subject to restraint. Ideally such restraint is born of the well-ordered and self-governing soul, but such individual virtue is to be reinforced by custom and law (*nomos*). The city does not exist in the market; rather, the market exists as a central but not dominant part of the city.

Thus we discern a critical distinction between Aristotelian citizenship and citizenship as conceived within liberal democracy. For liberal democracy, citizenship is at best the periodic attentiveness to public matters, but public matters are ultimately directed by their service to private satisfactions. Citizenship under liberal democracy is essentially a private condition, and the occasional thoughtfulness required of such "citizens" is to assess whether "public" figures have advanced opportunities for private satisfaction. By contrast, under Aristotle's understanding, citizenship is directed at a concern for public matters. Citizenship begins as a habituation in "being ruled" and eventually involves ruling not in pursuit of private goods but rather in accordance with public weal. Citizenship thus involves an exercise of comprehensive concerns—an attentiveness to the goods of the community as a whole, as difficult as that attainment must always be in practice. Moreover, its concerns extend to the comprehensive conditions of the polity, adjudging even private matters as concerns of the public weal (to the extent that even so-called private matters will always effect the broader polity). Moreover, because the polis is fundamentally a community that cultivates successive generations in the arts of self-governance, its concerns are temporally expansive, taking into account lessons from the past and obligations to the future.

In our own time, we live decisively with the consequences of a decision to make democratic commitments secondary to those of liberalism. In the politics of modern America, the public sphere increasingly has come to serve private interest, and the performance of public servants is judged based upon their ability to increase—or fail to increase—widespread private satisfaction. The role of the citizen has come to be that of a periodic judge of the effectiveness of public functionaries. In particular, it has come to be the special role of the public realm to increase the power and dominion of the economic realm, one that is to provide ever-increasing opportunities for private satisfaction. The performance and standing of the nation has come to be judged by reference to the performance of the market. Meanwhile, citizenship has been reduced to the exercise of that periodic assessment—via elections—in which candidates for public office attempt to demonstrate their greater capacity to satisfy the private satisfactions of the citizenry. (It follows that elections are increasingly understood in terms of economic choice, and the study of elections is dominated by theories derived from economic- choice theory.) Citizenship has been reduced to a near-empty formalism in which almost every public question is reduced to this: does the particular policy increase or decrease private satisfactions? Citizens are relieved of any burden to consider whether and how their private satisfactions may contribute to—or, more important, detract from—the common weal, while the very idea of the "common weal" comes to be defined as the aggregation of increasing private satisfactions. Politics thus comes to be defined by the goal of expanding the human dominion over nature and the increase of individual liberty resulting from the removal of any natural or arbitrary obstacles.

Ironically, then, in liberal democracy, "politics" is reduced to a concern for private matters before the public body of the nation's representatives, whose aim increasingly becomes the expansion of opportunities for private satisfactions. By contrast, according to an Aristotelian definition of democracy, "politics" has among its central concerns activities and conditions that might otherwise be regarded under a liberal regime as "private" but that—in considering the common weal in more comprehensive terms—are necessarily public. Liberal democracy shrinks politics to the actions of political actors (acting on behalf of the private interests of citizens); Aristotelian democracy expands politics to consider the broadest array of human activities of all citizens, including the role of families, the activity of the economic realm, the education of future generations, and the tending of tradition. By extension, for liberal democracy, *democracy* consists of the periodic action of voting and is otherwise invoked as a system of government that promotes maximum individual freedom. By contrast, Aristotelian democracy involves the comprehensive activities of the citizenry, demanding self-governance in all aspects of life.

## Wendell Berry: Democracy as Living with Nature, Living through Time, and Living in Place

Wendell Berry is not typically considered a political thinker, much less a theorist of democracy, in the wider sense of the term. His essays have often spoken to contemporary political issues—ranging from concerns over mining practices and farm policy to military interventionism and economic policies that lead to concentrations of size and power—but one would be hard-pressed to find a comprehensive statement of Berry's broader political views throughout his corpus. He has often written in criticism of the partisan alignment of contemporary politics (e.g., his criticisms of the ethic of "rugged individualism" that informs both parties) and has argued that the proper stance of one seeking fundamental change is to eschew inevitably narrowing involvement in specific movements.[6]

Berry is ultimately mistrustful of narrowly conceived political "solutions" to problems that he understands to transcend the normal approaches of politics. As he writes in the essay "In Distrust of Movements," "I am dissatisfied with such efforts [e.g., movements for clean air or sustainable agriculture] because they are too specialized, they are not comprehensive enough, they virtually predict their own failure by implying that we can remedy or control effects while leaving the causes in place."[7] His interests have thus been more broadly focused on "big questions," particularly the conditions of society and culture that sustain a people in a place over a long period of time.

Viewed through the lens of contemporary assumptions about the nature of democracy—a narrow concern with politics and policy at the national level that advances national interests—Berry is decidedly outside the scope of what passes for political writing. Considered in light of the more fundamental divide between liberal and Aristotelian democracy, however, Berry is perhaps our clearest and most profound thinker about an alternative understanding to the prevailing commitments of liberal democracy today. His large corpus of writing evinces a broad concern for all of the dimensions of shared civic life, including and especially those areas that would typically be considered "private." When he addresses economic, cultural, and communal issues, he emphasizes a theme that goes to the heart of Aristotelian democracy: cultivating the capacity for self-governance. Seen broadly, this capacity translates equally into private and public spheres, as well as the individual, communal, and national, making possible a competing conception of democracy that challenges the deepest presuppositions of contemporary liberal democracy.

Wendell Berry has described America as a nation with two fundamental "tendencies" that map well onto the two competing understandings of democracy discussed above. These two tendencies, he has argued, were set in motion by the earliest European settlers in America and continue to define the fundamental political alternatives for America and, increasingly, the modern world. The "dominant tendency" was manifested as a proclivity toward mobility and restlessness that aimed at maximum extraction of resources and accumulation of profits from the bounty of the new continent. Berry acknowledges that this worldview was dominant because it was "organized" at the very inception of the settlement of America. Berry, however, also recognizes "another tendency" that characterized a great many other settlers: this "weaker" tradition was marked by "the tendency to stay put, to say 'No farther. This is the place.'"[8]

In effect, at the most basic level of analysis of America's competing tendencies, Berry has effectively depicted and traced the grand debate of both antiquity and modernity about the nature of democracy itself as it has unfolded in America. Taking those basic "tendencies" as embodiments of certain philosophical traditions that contended for supremacy at the time of the American founding and that remain deeply embedded in the American tradition, one can point to the early modern liberal tradition as a primary source for the "dominant" tradition of colonization *qua* exploitation, and a contending republican or communitarian tradition that had its deepest sources in ancient philosophy and the biblical tradition. To some—one thinks of Louis Hartz—the dominant liberal tradition has been the *only* tradition in American political history.[9] Berry rejects this monolithic view of American political history, instead joining a number of defenders of the view that the "alternative" tradition, drawn especially from classical and biblical sources, has been present throughout American political history, though in a subdominant tone—one ever less audible— to its rival.[10]

Much of Berry's writings have sought to articulate a proper understanding of the relationship of humanity with nature—a vexed subject on which much of modern theories of power and mastery rest. Berry's analysis has been devoted to the idea, or ideal, that human creatures thrive only when they live with, not against, nature. Berry acknowledges that this is a difficult state to achieve and maintain: human beings by necessity— even by nature—are creatures who, to survive, must manipulate and alter the natural world. As a farmer, Berry recognizes that humans must, and indeed should, alter the world around them to allow the continuation of life, home, and community, and indeed that, properly speaking, there is no condition known as "nature" that doesn't include the actions of biological creatures upon that condition. Beavers change the course of streams; birds spread seeds to different places; carnivores thin herds, and so on. Yet, in doing so, he argues, nature's creatures do not, as a rule, actively destroy the places from which they derive the goods of life. They live under both the dictates of instinct and the exigencies of natural limits, both of which exert limits upon the kinds and extent of activities that allow them to change the conditions of nature as they find them. Human beings, by contrast, have increasingly transcended what had once seemed to be hard limits of nature and increasingly alter at will its basic conditions—whether in the external world or through the manipulation of the basic materials of the human creature itself. In doing so, however, Berry argues that the laws of nature have not been suspended, only delayed, and that their reassertion will be, as a result of the delay, harsh and exacting. Berry seeks to engage in the hard discipline and imperfect "science" of line-drawing by discerning what practices allow humans to live in harmony with nature. This must be accomplished without falling into either extreme represented by the modern hostility toward nature: seeing it solely as a dead resource for use, or the pantheistic and antihuman belief that humans should cease having any effect on nature, which is tantamount to saying that humans should cease to exist. Berry calls instead for hard work and conscious reflection upon the kinds of actions that allow humans to live well while simultaneously maintaining the health of the world on which we rely for the continuation of human life.

In the first instance, this calls for the forthright rejection of the modern project—at the heart of liberalism—of the conquest of nature. Berry has argued that the effort to master nature has turned out to be, ultimately, damaging to ourselves.

> At about [Edmund] Spenser's time or a little after, we set forth in our "war against nature" with the purpose of conquering her and wringing her power and lucrative secrets from her by various forms of "tortious Injurie." This we have thought of as our "enlightenment" and our "progress." But in the event this war, like most wars, has turned out to be a trickier business than we expected. We must now face two shocking surprises. The first surprise is that if we say and believe that we are at war with nature, then we are in the fullest sense at war; that is, we are both opposing and being opposed, and the costs to both sides are extremely high.
>
> The second surprise is that we are not winning. On the evidence now available, we have to conclude that we are losing—and, moreover, that there was never a chance that we could win.[11]

Berry challenges the idea that we can disconnect the consequences of the effort to conquer nature from the benefits. He argues that we engage in bad accounting practices when we do not add in the cost of every great and small retribution from nature. "Many of the occurrences that we call 'acts of God' or 'accidents of nature' are simply forthright natural responses to human provocations. . . . If we see the industrial economy in terms of the Great Economy, then we begin to see industrial wastes and losses not as 'trade-offs' or 'necessary risks' but as costs that, like all costs, are chargeable to somebody, someday."[12]

This does not mean, however, that there is some easily discernible condition in which we live in a state of instinctual harmony with nature. Humans must uniquely negotiate between the condition of wildness and artifice. Arguing on behalf of a "roomy and bewildering" middle course, Berry has insisted, in *Home Economics*, that we can assume neither a "division or divisibility" between humanity and nature nor "that there is no difference between the natural and the human. . . . Our problem, exactly, is that the human and the natural are indivisible, and yet are different."[13] The difficulty of discovering where one has appropriately lived in that "roomy and bewildering" middle between transgressing nature and inhumane submission to it requires a difficult, even perilous effort at drawing lines. Berry writes, "I am not sure where the line ought to be drawn, or how to draw it. But it is an intelligent question, worth losing some sleep over."[14]

This negotiation between nature and humanity—which according to Berry takes place in the domain of culture—requires a supremely democratic virtue, namely a kind of charity toward one's interlocutors. Contemporary forms of liberal democracy valorize "deliberation" while ignoring the extent to which the basis of liberalism is based upon a dictatorial and even totalitarian relationship toward nature. The modern industrial economy—built upon the premises of the liberal anthropology—

> has dealt with nature, including human nature, in the manner of a monologist or an orator. It has not asked for anything or waited to hear any response. It has told nature what it wanted, and in various clever ways has taken what it wanted. And since it proposed no limit upon its wants, exhaustion has been its inevitable and foreseeable result. This, clearly, is a dictatorial or totalitarian form of behavior, and it is totalitarian in its use of people as it is in its use of nature.[15]

Berry argues instead that the proper relationship with nature is within the idiom of a conversation. We would ask of a place what it can offer and what we can offer in return, and listen even as we express our wants.

> The conversation itself would thus assume a creaturely life, binding the place and its inhabitants together, changing and growing to no end, no final accomplishment, that can be conceived or foreseen. . . . And if you honor the other party to the conversation, if you honor the *otherness* of the other party, you understand that you must not expect always to receive a reply that you foresee or that you would like. A conversation is immitigably two-sided and always to some degree mysterious; it requires faith.[16]

Berry insists that any such conversation that takes place between humanity and nature—negotiating the appropriate relationship that acknowledges both dependence and freedom—would necessarily also inform the relationship between human beings as well. Further, absent such a conversational relationship with nature, the tendency will be, over time, to treat humans as objects of personal satisfaction in just the way we tend to treat the natural world.

Culture is the medium in which such conversations take place. It is the space in which responsibility of our freedom and constraint within limits is learned. It is, according to Berry (like Aristotle before him), the locus where we become fully human:

> Humans differ most from other creatures in the extent to which they must be *made* what they are—that is, to the extent that they are artifacts of their culture. . . . To take a creature who is biologically human and make him or her fully human is a task that requires many years (some of us sometimes fear that it requires more than a lifetime), and this long effort of human making is necessary, I think, because of our power. . . . And so it is more important than ever that we should have cultures capable of making us into humans—creatures capable of prudence, justice, fortitude, temperance, and the other virtues. For our history reveals that, stripped of the restraints, disciplines and ameliorations of culture, humans are not "natural," not "thinking animals," or

"naked apes," but monsters—indiscriminate and insatiable killers and destroyers.[17]

In contrast to liberal anthropology, humans cannot be conceived as preculturally human in any real sense: there is no humanness in a "state of nature." As such, we are by nature social, cultural and political animals—creatures that attain the completeness of our humanity through self-governance, responsibility, and virtue. To be a human is to be part of a whole—a whole that we know only imperfectly, whose delineation is the result of prudence and negotiation, and whose vast interconnections we can only partially perceive. To be human demands attentiveness and care, not simple or narrow concentration upon the fulfillment of appetite and satisfactions. It calls us toward participation in a community of fellow creatures who are for the most part close to us, as well as those who are physically absent by dint of time but present by dint of memory and anticipation.

Berry thus forcefully rejects a basic feature of liberal anthropology that conceives of humans as *choosers* who are largely liberated from obligations and considerations of the past and the future. Liberal anthropology portrays a humanity driven by choices made in the present that, moreover, throws suspicion upon the inherited or traditional as an arbitrary imposition upon the liberty of individuals. For Berry, we are always at least partially governed by the past as we are also partially governed by nature. Indeed, the past is best understood as the accumulation of best practices of how to live well with nature. Tradition is not arbitrary but the purposive, if largely unreflective, preservation of memory and generational connection; and thus culture is the effort to transmit these best practices from the past, through the present, into the future.

> The experience of many people over a long time is traditional knowledge. This is the common knowledge of a culture, which it seems that few of us any longer have. To have a culture, mostly the same people have to live mostly in the same place for a long time. Traditional knowledge is knowledge that has been remembered or recorded, handed down, pondered, corrected, practiced, and refined over a long time.[18]

Culture is invariably the collection of the past and future into the present, a living and ongoing embodiment of human memory and gratitude toward the past and obligation and responsibility toward the future. For Berry, "a good local culture, in one of its most important functions, is a collection of memories, ways and skills necessary for the observance, within the bounds of domesticity, of this natural law."[19]

Culture is thus rightly a form of education that draws each new generation into an inheritance and birthright. Education is thus concrete, a habituation not only in certain forms of knowledge but also the underlying virtue that is needed to live within the limits of what nature and human culture can responsibly afford. Education within a culture prepares each new generation for a life in that place, and for responsible stewardship of practices and inheritance so that they can be conveyed to subsequent generations. Such education is stunningly egalitarian: whether aimed to cultivate the life of a community's leaders or its handworkers, all are prepared alike for the responsibilities of life in place and within the limits that are dictated by nature, place, and history. Equality is not an abstract legal construction but instead equal subjection to the laws of nature and place. Such an education is not to be experienced as a burden or constraint but rather as a preparation for freedom within the bounds of responsible stewardship.

One can starkly contrast Berry's understanding of education within a culture—one that weds land and memory—with a modern form of education that aims to liberate young people from place and from history, and to relieve them of burdensome obligations to the past or the future. (A key feature of what is currently conceived of as a "democratic" form of education, namely a "meritocracy," is today equally supported by the Left and the Right alike.) This modern form of meritocratic education stresses "upward mobility," deracinated forms of critical thinking that detach its students from particular places and prepare them for a work in what Berry has called an "absentee" economic system populated by a "powerful class of itinerant professional vandals." Young people are formed to be

the purest sort of careerists—"upwardly mobile" transients who will permit no stay or place to interrupt their personal advance. They must have no local allegiances; they must not have a local point of view. In order to be able to desecrate, endanger, or

destroy a *place*, after all, one must be able to leave it and forget it.
. . . Unlike a life at home, which makes ever more particular and
precious the places and creatures of this world, the careerist's life
generalizes the world, reducing its abundant and comely diversity
to "raw material."[20]

He notes that this training brings no capacity to assess the value of
locality in terms other than profit and growth. Such people, above all, lack
the capacity to assess the nonmonetary value of localities because they
have been raised and educated both to avoid any such local commitments
and even to disdain them as untoward forms of limitation.

These modern elites—mobile, homeless cosmopolitans—are the product of a particular system of education that induces particular preferences
and produces particular outcomes. Not simply or reductively the product
of a neutral "market," the "market" is itself the product of a certain culture—in this case, a culture against culture. Berry is particularly critical
of modern universities for their betrayal of an earlier mandate to educate
young men and women of particular localities (particularly at land-grant
institutions) so they might gratefully contribute to the very communities
that sponsored their course of study. Classically understood, education "is,
literally, 'to bring up,' to bring young people to a responsible maturity, to
help them be good caretakers of what they have been given, to help them
to be charitable toward fellow creatures." By contrast, according the practices of modern universities, education that orients people to leave home
becomes a "commodity"—"something to be bought in order to make
money. . . . To make a commodity of education, then, is inevitably to
make a kind of weapon of it because, when it is dissociated from the sense
of obligation, it can be put directly in the service of greed."[21] A university
education becomes yet one more portable commodity, a ticket into the
exploiting class.[22]

For Berry, there are two economies and, correspondingly, two kinds
of education. The first kind of economy is that which we currently have:
oriented toward the short term in pursuit of quickly won wealth, it is an
exploitative economy that hollows out traditional and communal forms of
life and thereby induces amnesia about how to sustain and work in concert with nature's limited bounty. One is less "educated" than "trained" in
this first economic context. The second kind of economy, and the values

correspondingly inculcated through such an education, takes into account the economic whole—not only the "bottom line," with the presumption that growth and increase of human power and comfort are the aim, but also an economy that accounts for both moral and physical ecology, that considers its effects upon future generations, that hews more closely to the wisdom of past tradition and eschews the easy assumption that new always implies progress and "better." The first economy is based upon the control of nature that permits unrestrained human greed; the second economy is based upon the self-control of properly educated human beings.

Because of the importance of particular knowledge and experience, Berry, like Aristotle, stresses the central importance of place and scale, that is, an embodied and real set of relationships of particular people in particular and relatively delineated and exclusive places. Berry is an unapologetic defender of community. For Berry, community is a rich and varied set of personal relationships, a complex of practices and traditions drawn from a store of common memory and tradition, and a set of bonds forged between a people and a place that—because of this situatedness—is not portable, mobile, fungible, or transferable. Community is more than a mere collection of self-interested individuals brought together to seek personal advancement together. Rather, community "lives and acts by the common virtues of trust, goodwill, forbearance, self-restraint, compassion, and forgiveness."[23]

Berry does not shy away from the conclusion, nor is he embarrassed to acknowledge, that community is a place of constraint and limits. Indeed, in this simple fact lies its great attraction. Community, properly conceived, is the appropriate setting for flourishing human life—flourishing that requires culture, discipline, constraint, and forms. At the most elemental level (again, echoing Aristotle, if unconsciously), community is both derived from and in turn makes possible healthful family life. Absent the supports of communal life, family life is hard-pressed to flourish. This is because family life is premised, in Berry's view, upon the suppression of otherwise individualistic tendencies toward narrow self-fulfillment, particularly those erotic in nature. Berry commends

> arrangements [that] include marriage, family structure, divisions
> of work and authority, and responsibility for the instruction of
> children and young people. These arrangements exist, in part, to
> reduce the volatility and dangers of sex—to preserve its energy, its

beauty, and its pleasure; to preserve and clarify its power to join not just husband and wife to one another but parents to children, families to the community, the community to nature; to ensure, so far as possible, that the inheritors of sexuality, as they come of age, will be worthy of it.[24]

Communities maintain standards and patterns of life that encourage responsible and communally sanctioned forms of erotic bonds, particularly with an aim toward fostering strong family ties and commitments that are the backbone of communal health and the conduit for the transmission of culture and tradition. Communities thus supersede the absolutist claims of "rights bearers." For instance, Berry insists that communities are justified in maintaining internally derived standards of decency in order to foster and maintain a certain desired moral ecology. He explicitly defends the communal prerogative in the field of education to demand certain books be removed from the curriculum; to insist upon the introduction of the Bible into the classroom as "the word of God"; and even suggests that "the future of community life in this country may depend on private schools and home schooling."[25] Family is the wellspring of the cultural habits and practices that foster practical wisdom, judgment, and local forms of knowledge by which humans can flourish and thrive in common and rightly claim the primary role in the education and upbringing of a given community's children.

The priority of community begins with the family but extends outward to incorporate an appropriate locus of the common good. For Berry, the common good can only be achieved in small, local settings. These dimensions cannot be precisely drawn, but Berry seems to endorse, at a minimum, the town as the most basic locus of commonweal and, at the utmost, and mainly in the economic and not interpersonal realm, the region. Berry is not hostile toward a conception of national, or even international, common good but recognizes that the greater scope of these latter large units tends toward abstraction and hence come always at the expense of the former, namely, at the expense of the flourishing of real human lives. Units larger than the locality or the region can flourish in the proper sense only when the constitutive parts flourish. Modern liberalism, by contrast, insists upon the priority of the largest unit over the smallest and seeks everywhere to create a homogenous standard to be imposed upon a world of particularity and diversity. One sees this tendency across the board in modern liberal society, from education to court decisions that effectively "nationalize" sexual morality, from economic standardization to minute and exacting regulatory regimes.[26] The tendency of modern politics—born of a philosophy that endorses above all the expansion of human power and control—is toward massification, the subjection of all particularities to the logic of market dynamics, the resulting exploitation of local resources, and an active hostility toward the diversity of local customs and traditions in the name of progress and rationalism.

Modern politics, as Berry has pointed out, is impatient with local variety, particularly forms of life that do not accept the modern embrace of progress, and most especially *material* progress in the form of economic growth and personal liberation from all forms of work that are elemental or forestall mobility and efficiency. Berry is a strong critic of the homogenization that modern states and modern economic assumptions enforce upon the variety of local forms. He is a defender of "common" or "traditional" sense, that sense of the commons that in many respects can prove to be resistant to the logic of economic and liberal development and progress. Such "common knowledge" is the result of practice and experience, the accumulated common store of wisdom born of trials and corrections of people who have lived, suffered, and flourished in a particular setting. Rules and practices cannot be imposed based on a preconceived notion of right, absent the prudential consideration and respect toward common sense. This is not to suggest that traditions cannot be changed or altered, but, much as in Burke's understanding, traditions must be allowed to change internally and thus with the understanding and assent of people who have developed lives and communities based upon those practices. There is then, in Berry's thought, a considerable respect for the dignity of "common sense," a non-expert way of understanding the world that comes through experience, memory, and tradition, and is the source of much democratic opinion that liberalism typically dismisses and actively seeks to eviscerate.

## Democracy Rightly Understood

Among the most degraded words of our time is *democracy*, a word that implies self-governance but instead has come to mean unbridled liberty and unrestrained consumption. A more accurate rendering of our current political choices would be distilled as the choice between liberalism (the autonomous, rights-bearing chooser) and democracy (as individual and political self-governance). Democracy, beginning with a strong tendency to self-restraint, results in the liberty of self-governance, particularly the liberty that accompanies living within limits. Liberalism, by contrast— beginning with a strong tendency to self-interest and pursuit of limitless fulfillment of desire—appears to enlarge the sphere of liberty but ironically results in liberty's loss, as the impetus to fulfill unlimited desires results in personal forms of slavishness and a shrinking of actual political liberty. This irony tends to be lost on most contemporary "democrats" for whom personal autonomy is tantamount to the definition of democracy and hence who tend to overlook or ignore the extent to which such notional autonomy is in fact contradicted by political and economic impotence.

Democracy, in fact, must always encourage a high degree of public-spiritedness. Such public-spiritedness cannot be abstract or theoretical only but must derive from felt and sensible sources of common interests and a sense of a shared common fate. As such, thinkers from Aristotle to the American Anti-Federalists to Wendell Berry have argued on behalf of small-scale and local arrangements. While our humanity can and ought to be understood to be common, its manifestations will be as various as the many ecosystems in which humanity finds itself. Only through long experience with a given place and a familiar set of family, neighbors, and fellow citizens is there a high degree of likelihood that a strong sense of care, affection, and even love will manifest itself in our civic lives and our attentiveness to nature, land, and place. Investment in a people and a place derives from lived experience and practice and exhibits gratitude to the past and a sense of obligation to the future. Eschewing the abstraction of a social contract that binds people only insofar as they achieve personal satisfactions, a truer social contract was that articulated by Edmund Burke, one that binds generations in a shared space: "a partnership not only between those who are living, but between those who are living, those who are dead, and those who are to be born."[27] Respecting the wisdom of tradition and the experience of common sense, such democracy is respectful of the sense of the community, hesitant and mistrustful of significant departures from past practice, cautious of innovation, yet open to the slow and tentative expressions of trial and alteration.

Democracy is a locus of equal concern, less vigorous in its defense of equality of opportunity or equality of outcome than the equality of shared fate and lives characterized by "great austerity, sacrifice, and selfless discipline."[28] For such democracy, elections are simply the punctuation of longstanding deliberation and concern for the public weal; elections are not substitutes for shared language but instead a provisional settlement of ongoing discussions. Elections are decidedly not decisions in which a citizenry shows a preference for a leader who will secure us greater individual liberty; rather, democracy is the ongoing effort to exercise self-governance over ourselves. At best, it understands that we, the electorate, are the government and that there is an intimate link between our personal behavior and our public commitments. For such democracy, the individual strives to understand his or her place in the fabric of the whole, seeing his or her good in the ongoing health of the community and the surrounding natural environment, which includes our decisions as individual consumers. A proper form of self-governance leads to a high degree of personal, familial, regional, and national self-sufficiency and a corresponding liberty from a slavish reliance upon foreign sources of satisfactions that outstrip local resources and thereby local limits. History has shown that slavish addiction to extraneous sources of desire fulfillment inevitably leads to greater concentration of power ever more distant from local sources, and thus in a corresponding decline of political self-governance. That is, the absence of personal governance of desire leads to the decline and ultimately the loss of political liberty.[29]

Above all, this means that democracy—as the classical theorists such as Aristotle, the philosopher Montesquieu, and the Anti-Federalists understood—requires an extraordinary degree of virtue that must needs be widespread throughout the citizenry.[30] Writing about the prospects for democracy in modern times, one of America's philosophers—George Santayana—wrote that the extraordinary must become ordinary, and the ordinary, extraordinary:

> If a noble and civilized democracy is to subsist, the common citizen must be something of a saint and something of a hero. We see, therefore, how justly flattering and profound, and at the same time how ominous, was Montequieu's saying that the principle of democracy is virtue.[31]

Saints and heroes are notable for their rarity and exceptionalness; their virtues, deemed praiseworthy in part due to their very infrequency, must pervade the citizenry, making them at once unexceptional for their very commonness and yet still extraordinary for their exceeding difficulty. Saints and heroes alike are most noteworthy for their willingness to sacrifice on behalf of the common weal, to exercise the denial of self for the sake of something greater than themselves. For this reason, Santayana saw democracy as the most "flattering" of political regimes because it pictures humanity at its noblest, while it is also the most "ominous" for the same reason—particularly given that Santayana was not optimistic about the likelihood of the achievement of such widespread self-sacrifice. Still, Santayana wrote: "For such excellence to grow general mankind must be notably transformed." While he was not sanguine at such prospects, he nevertheless pointed to the same necessary conditions of locality and scale that have been stressed by democratic thinkers ranging from Aristotle to Berry:

> What might happen if the human race were immensely improved and exalted there is as yet no saying; but experience has given no example of efficacious devotion to communal ideals except in small cities, held together by close military and religious bonds and having no important relations to anything external.[32]

Those virtues that must be long habituated and cultivated do not as a rule spring up ex nihilo but instead are the product of the explicit teachings of parents and teachers and the implicit teachings of culture. As such, for sustenance they require particular settings attuned to the possibilities and limits of place, history, and experience.

The paramount virtue of democracy is and remains self-governance, whether called moderation, temperance, or prudence. Self-governance means, above all, the learned and habituated capacity to deny oneself those wants that prove to be limitless and to which we thereby can too easily become enslaved. For democratic citizens of modern times—taught by liberalism that human happiness is commensurate with the satisfaction of wants—we must begin the hard lesson of learning to distinguish between wants and needs. Being able to draw distinctions between desires that are rightfully sated and those that demand inevitable diminutions of liberty is only the result of a difficult apprenticeship in the disciplines of citizenship.[33] This aspiration of liberty, and the democracy that is its result, receives no better expression than by Wendell Berry, today's leading articulator of democracy rightly understood:

> Free men are not set free by their government; they have to set their government free of themselves. . . . It is a matter of discipline. A person can free himself of a bondage that has been imposed upon him only by accepting another bondage that he has chosen. A man who would not be the slave of other men must be master of himself—that is the real meaning of self-government. . . .
>
> A person dependent upon somebody else for everything from potatoes to opinions may declare that he is a free man, and his government may issue him a certificate granting him his freedom, but he will not be free. . . . Men are free precisely to the extent to which they are equal to their own needs.[34]

Freedom is not in the conquest of the world but rather in the conquest of our insatiability. Only in waging that never-ending battle can a true path to democracy be struck.

8

# First They Came for the Horses: Wendell Berry and a Technology of Wholeness

## *Caleb Stegall*

To be sane in a mad time
is bad for the brain, worse
for the heart.
—"The Mad Farmer Manifesto: The First Amendment"[1]

There is a scene in Wendell Berry's novel *Remembering* in which the protagonist, Andy Catlett, coming to terms with having lost his hand in a farming accident, considers its technological replacement. Teaching himself not to be repulsed by the prosthetic, Andy tells himself, "*It is only a tool.* It is not a hand. . . . It is a tool, only a tool. His hand is gone."[2]

This captures at the most basic level Berry's posture toward technology. Our late-modern society is reflexive in its praise and genuflection before the spectacle of technological progress and advance. We are bedazzled. We are impressed. We marvel: "How do they do that?" "What will they think of next?" Berry, on the other hand, is wary. He knows that many tools represent not an addition but instead a profound subtraction. *It is not a hand. It is a tool. His hand is gone.*

In *Remembering*, Andy Catlett considers his life in light of his literal dismemberment. Catlett, of Berry's fictional Port William membership, grew up, got educated, and moved to the city to become a journalist for

89

agribusiness interests. At one point, he was sent by his magazine to interview the man named that publication's "Premier Farmer of the Year," Bill Meikelberger, "one of the leaders of the shock troops of the scientific revolution in agriculture."[3]

Andy discovers that Meikelberger farms two thousand acres, having patiently bought out all his neighbors. He "owned a herd of machines" and "had an office like a bank president's." "On all the two thousand acres there was not a fence, not an animal, not a woodlot, not a tree, not a garden."[4] But there was corn from wall to gullet. Andy arrives to find Meikelberger alone in his vast home, his wife at work in town and his children having flown the coop.

Andy is surprised during the interview to learn that the Premier Farmer is in debt and is told that "debt is a permanent part of an operation like this. Getting out of debt is just another old idea you have to junk. I'll never be out of debt. I never intend to be."[5] Meikelberger pops some pills for his stomach ulcer and declaims,

> You can't let your damned stomach get in your way. If you're going to get ahead, you've got to pay the price. You're going to need a few pills occasionally, like for your stomach, and sometimes to go to sleep. You're going to need a drugstore just like you're going to need a bank.[6]

Technologically advanced pharmaceuticals and the wizardry of capitalist financing are just tools in the Premier Farmer's toolbox. But to Berry, they are prosthetics, stand-ins for a healthy body and a self-sufficient and free family economy. They represent not an advance but a profound loss. "Meikelberger's ambition had made common cause with a technical power that proposed no limit to itself, that was, in fact, destroying Meikelberger, as it had already destroyed nearly all that was natural or human around him."[7] *His hand is gone.*

Upon leaving the dead zone of Meikelberger's premier farm, Andy comes across an Amishman working his fields with a team of horses. He is drawn to them; they remind him of his childhood working horses. After a short conversation, the Amishman offers Andy the reins.

As he drove the long curve of the plowland, watching the dark furrow open and turn, shining and fresh-smelling, beneath him, Andy could feel the good tilth of the ground all through his body. The gait of the team was steady and powerful, the three mares walked well together, and he could feel in his hands their readiness in their work. Except for the horses' muffled footfalls and the stutter of the plowshare in the roots of the sod, it was quiet. Andy heard the birds singing in the woods and along the creek.[8]

After a meal with the Amish family, Andy learns that they farm the same eighty acres that have been farmed by the family since their arrival a generation before. They have money in the bank and a thriving family economy. The farm is full of life—livestock, crops, garden, orchard, bees, and children. Andy wonders if the Amishman has ever considered buying more land and is told, "If I did I'd have to go in debt to buy it, and to farm it. It would take more time and help than I've got. And I'd lose my neighbor." Asked if he would consider mechanizing the farm, he replies, "What for? So my children can work in a factory?"[9]

By the end of the day, Andy realizes that while the Amishman is prosperous, content, and free, the man lauded as Premier Farmer of the Year is "on two thousand acres . . . liv[ing] virtually alone with his ulcer" and has become "the best friend that the bank and the farm machinery business and the fertilizer business and the oil companies and the chemical companies ever had."[10]

The catalyst of all of Andy's remembering is a conference he attends of assembled experts and corporate reps in San Francisco to address the topic "The Future of the American Food System." At the conference, one speaker after another forcefully asserts the argument of inevitability, culminating in the address of a man described only as a "high agricultural official." The High Official begins by saying that he "grew up a farm boy" but continues: "Let's face it. Those days are gone, and their passing is not to be regretted. . . . I want to live in a changing, growing, dynamic society. I want to go forward with progress into a better future."[11] After this litany of techno-bureaucratese, the High Official piously intones that "this is economics we're talking about. And the basic law of economics is: Adapt or die. Get big or get out." Those who have gotten big are "as savvy financially as bankers. And they are enjoying the amenities of life—color TV, automobiles, indoor toilets, vacations in Florida or Arizona."[12]

During this diatribe of inevitability, Andy recalls his own grandfather saying, "If you're going to talk to me, fellow, you'll have to walk."[13] This is Berry's invitation and quiet, almost unheard rebuke to the pontificators and bloviators of The Way Things Are.

*If you're going to talk to me, you'll have to walk.*

Walking has a way of gently imposing limits while opening a surprising expanse of the possibilities of being human. Here is Berry at his disarming finest. You want to talk technology to me, fellow, you'll have to walk. Berry knows that talk is cheap, but the walk is free, and that's the catch. Who has the courage for such freedom in the face of ubiquitous cheapness?

What Are People For?

> From the heron flying home at dusk,
> from the misty hollows at sunrise,
> from the stories told at the row's end,
> they are calling the mind into exile
> in the dry circuits of machines.
> —*A Timbered Choir*[14]

The work of Wendell Berry resists any system that might be imposed upon it. An honest encounter with Berry cannot help but leave one with the sense that here is something sui generis—the way the words fructify in the life, and the life in the words, and both in their fraternity with the reader. The work of the essayist, then, who steps by necessity outside this fraternity, is something of a betrayal. Attempts to analyze what Berry may be saying about any discreet subject amounts to an essential diminishing.

While Berry's juxtaposition of these two farmers in *Remembering* will admit to a certain amount of stereotyping and perhaps exaggeration to demonstrate a truth, it is a perfect illustration of Berry's method of answering the most vexing questions of late modernity. Berry recognizes that abstract arguments about any issue—the impact of modern toolmaking and using in this case—serve as an essential distraction that always ends up tilting the argument in favor of the inevitability of the status quo. Throughout his entire corpus, Berry resists, ferociously at times, being drawn into this dead end. He knows that man has always made tools—it is essential to who we are, and to civilization itself. He asks only whether any particular toolmaking and using represents a dismemberment or, as Andy discovered on the Amish plow, a profound amplification of what it means to be human.

What *can* be said is that Berry loves himself and his life. Or he loves the fact that he is a human being, a person who is alive and has been given a human body with hands and feet and eyes and ears and a human heart enmeshed with other people and the places their bodies occupy.

Berry is one of that rare and disappearing breed—an authentic humanist. He resists, sometimes violently, any classification, recruitment into any movement, and any reading that would place him on one side or the other of any "issue." Berry is no one's tool. He speaks only for himself and his own striving for that essential wholeness that is his one answer to the one question he deems worthy of asking: "What are people for?"

This realization, by itself, tells us quite a bit about what Wendell Berry thinks of technology (and everything else), if we will let it. Berry once wrote of Edward Abbey that his virtue was that "because he speaks as himself, he does not represent any group, but he *stands* for all of us."[15] So, too, Berry.

People are for *wholeness* says both Berry's talk and his walk. Teasing out the complexities, elegance, contradictions, beauty, tragedy, and deep mysteries of this basic principle has been the intense focus of Berry's life and work. He is a sane man in a mad time whose great, tenacious effort has been to "conserve *himself* as a human being in the best and fullest sense."[16] "He is fighting for the survival not only of nature but also of *human* nature, of culture, as only our heritage of works and hopes can define it."[17]

Berry, the poet, essayist, novelist, eulogist for rural America, and farmer, doesn't just walk the walk; he talks while he walks. In his poem "Horses," Berry laments:

The tractors came. The horses
Stood in the fields, keepsakes,
grew old, and died. Or were sold
as dogmeat. Our minds received
the revolution of engines, our will

stretched toward the numb endurance
of metal. And that old speech
by which we magnified
our flesh in other flesh
fell dead in our mouths.[18]

Against this "revolution of engines," Berry posits at least three things that people are for—utility, freedom, and membership—that can either be diminished or enhanced by our tools. Though Berry would never be caught stepping through a field of cow pies imposing such an analytical framework on the proper use of tools, it will be helpful to see more clearly his specific treatment of the question in light of each of these human purposes, that we might move once again toward magnifying ourselves in our tools.

## Utility

This modern mind sees only half of the horse—that half which may become a dynamo, or an automobile, or any other horse-powered machine. If this mind had much respect for the full-dimensioned, grass-eating horse, it would never have invented the engine which represents only half of him.
—Alan Tate, "Remarks on the Southern Religion"[19]

Berry's most direct treatment of technology is his essay "Why I Am Not Going to Buy a Computer," originally published in *Harper's*, in which he declares simply: "As a farmer, I do almost all of my work with horses. As a writer, I work with a pencil or a pen and a piece of paper." He elaborates briefly that his wife prepares his manuscripts on a reliable 1956 Royal standard typewriter. Berry resists the computer because, as he puts it, "I disbelieve, and therefore strongly resent, the assertion that I or anybody else could write better or more easily with a computer than with a pencil." He concludes the short essay by giving nine standards by which he judges technological innovation:

1.  The new tool should be cheaper than the one it replaces.
2.  It should be at least as small in scale as the one it replaces.

3. It should do work that is clearly and demonstrably better than the one it replaces.
4. It should use less energy than the one it replaces.
5. If possible, it should use some form of solar energy, such as that of the body.
6. It should be repairable by a person of ordinary intelligence, provided that he or she has the necessary tools.
7. It should be purchasable and repairable as near to home as possible.
8. It should come from a small, privately owned shop or store that will take it back for maintenance and repair.
9. It should not replace or disrupt anything good that already exists, and this includes family and community relationships.[20]

This is a fairly short, easy to grasp standard of utility, and anyone abiding by it won't be steered far wrong. Here Berry expresses his first measure of a tool—that it is for doing something well.

*Harper's* readers, however, raised a great hue and cry from quarters technophile and feminist, objecting to Berry's neglect of The Future and to his wife's enslavement to "drudgery." In response, Berry wrote a lengthy rebuttal called "Feminism, the Body, and the Machine." In it, he expands on his understanding of utility. "After several generations of 'technological progress,' in fact, we have become a people who *cannot* think about anything important."[21] Human thought is at the heart of all utility. Tools that eliminate thought eliminate usefulness as far as Berry is concerned, and those that amplify and magnify thought enhance a person's ability to do a task well.

Applied to the question of the pencil versus the computer, Berry argues that "the computer apologists . . . have greatly underrated the value of the handwritten manuscript as an artifact."[22] Handwritten pages look "hospitable to improvement," and as such, according to Berry, "the longer I keep a piece of work in longhand, the better it will be."[23] Here is a powerful argument, if true, in favor of the pencil over the computer strictly on the grounds of utility. Berry has the audacity to suggest that a pencil is actually a better tool for the task of writing. Here is something unexpected by the legions of techno-hawkers—an argument that challenges technological enhancement on its presumed home turf of superior utility.

But it is a fair question and deserves a fair hearing, as heretical as it may seem. Is a pencil the better tool? Berry offers a compelling case for the affirmative that, if nothing else, clarifies his essential posture towards any tool. "Much is made of the ease of correction in computer work, owing to the insubstantiality of the light-image on the screen; one presses a button and the old version disappears, to be replaced by the new."[24] On the other hand, "because of the substantiality of paper . . . one does not handwrite or typewrite a new page every time a correction is made."[25] What difference should this make? A tremendous difference, as it turns out.

Berry explains that a "handwritten or typewritten page therefore is usually to some degree a palimpsest; it contains parts and relics of its own history—erasures, passages crossed out, interlineations—suggesting that there is something to go back to as well as something to go forward to." Pixelized text can never achieve such historical solidity. It is part of what Berry terms the "industrial present, a present absolute." "A computer destroys the sense of historical succession, just as do other forms of mechanization. The well-crafted table . . . embodies the member of . . . the tree it was made of and the forest in which the tree stood. . . . All good human work remembers its history." Good writing, then, "is full of intimations that it is the present version of earlier versions of itself, and that its maker inherited the work and the ways of earlier makers."[26]

Utility requires thought; thought requires a past; a past requires a community of fellow laborers. Berry's insights in defense of the humble pencil are helpfully clarified by the thought and categories introduced by an earlier critic of technological progress, Ivan Illich. In *Tools for Conviviality*, Illich writes:

> I choose the term "conviviality" to designate the opposite of industrial productivity. I intend it to mean autonomous and creative intercourse among persons, and the intercourse of persons with their environment; and this in contrast with the conditioned response of persons to the demands made upon them by others, and by a man-made environment. I consider conviviality to be individual freedom realized in personal interdependence and, as such, an intrinsic ethical value. I believe that, in any society, as conviviality is reduced below a certain level, no amount of industrial productivity can effectively satisfy the needs it creates among society's members.[27]

Illich goes on to describe how convivial tools facilitate free and creative interplay between people, places, institutions, generations, and the memory that binds them all together as an indivisible "community." Industrial tools, on the other hand, come "pre-packaged." Their meaning is self-contained and imposed on the user who must acquiesce to the demands of the tool. The difference can be seen, for example, between a textbook and a work of literature. The former imposes its meaning on a user; the latter invites the reader to participate in a historical community composed of an unbroken chain of authors, texts, and readers.

Illich's categories elucidate Berry's argument that industrial tools simply are not as well equipped to perform their function. They diminish rather than enhance us; they are the prosthetic hook as opposed to the convivial hand. This understanding requires that we accept Berry's broad and deep definition of usefulness. To be useful, a person must be not only skilled but also joyful, creative, well rested, and in constant communication with others, past and present. Industrial tools cut off and reduce the possibility for all of these things.

A final aspect of utility for Berry is beauty. A useful tool is a thing of beauty. People know this instinctively, even if they resist the knowledge. Conversely, where there is no beauty, it is at least reasonable to question a tool's utility. Berry tells the humorous story of how he learned to dispose of his Weedwacker (a "power scythe" before the ad geniuses had a chance to do their work) in favor of a sleek, elegant hand scythe. The grass scythe is, Berry says, "the most satisfying hand tool that I have ever used."[28] It is light, easy to handle, adaptable, safe, quiet, never fails to start, and "runs on what you ate for breakfast." The hand scythe is a thing of beauty for two specific reasons—joy and rest—both of which turn out to be essential to a tool's usefulness.

"I never took the least pleasure in using the power scythe, whereas in using the [hand] scythe, whatever the weather and however difficult the cutting, I always work with the pleasure that one invariably gets from using a good tool," Berry writes in *The Gift of Good Land*. Furthermore, because it is quiet and safe, the hand scythe "allows the pleasure of awareness of what is going on around you as you work."[29] In addition to the pleasure of its use, the hand scythe is naturally limited by the "simple bodily weariness" of the cutter, which is always a prerequisite to his good and well-earned rest. "The power scythe, on the other hand, adds to the weariness of exertion the unpleasant and destructive weariness of strain." This is because the power tool "imposes patterns of endurance that are alien to the body" such that "as long as the motor is running there is a pressure to keep going."[30]

But without a doubt, the central symbol of conviviality in American life for Berry is the farm horse. Berry returns to the horse again and again in his essays, poetry, and novels as both the symbol and actual representation of technological perfection—and its perfection is most perfect in its beauty as a conduit for magnifying what is human. Human agricultural proficiency reached its technological apex in the era of horse-drawn implements. "The coming of the tractor made it possible for a farmer to do more work, but not better. And there comes a point, as we know, when *more* begins to imply *worse*. The mechanization of farming passed that point long ago . . . when it passed from horse power to tractor power."[31]

With the disappearance of the horse as the ubiquitous tool of the American farmer, in Berry's diagnosis, came a host of ills, all of them ugly. The "efficiencies" of the tractor displaced millions. Mass migration to cities has created a host of problems loosely grouped under names like "urban decay" or the "crisis of the American city"—"and the land is suffering for want of the care of those absent families."[32]

Thus, "the coming of a tool" such as the tractor "can be a cultural event of great influence and power."[33] Those who would dismiss Berry as "antitechnology" are guilty of a grievous misrepresentation. He is more in favor of tools of conviviality than anything else, but to the extent he recognizes the coming of industrial tools as a profound event of cultural loss, he resists. He declares, simply, "Do I wish to keep up with the times? No."[34] More often, however, Berry's work expresses the usefulness and beauty of convivial tools. Here he is hymning the wonder of the technology of the horse:

> . . . And so
> I came to a team, a pair
> of mares—sorrels, with white
> tails and manes, beautiful!—
> to keep my sloping fields.
> Going behind them, the reins
> tight over their backs as they stepped

their long strides, revived
again on my tongue the cries
of dead men in the living
fields. Now every move
answers what is still.
This work of love rhymes
living and dead. A dance
is what this plodding is.
A song, whatever is said.[35]

Could such lyrical praise ever be concocted for the computer hard drive, the electric can opener, or the Weedwacker?

Freedom

> A major characteristic of the agrarian mind is a longing for independence—that is, for an appropriate degree of personal and local self-sufficiency. Agrarians wish to earn and deserve what they have. They do not wish to live by piracy, beggary, charity, or luck.
> —*Citizenship Papers*[36]

After utility, people are for freedom. That is, without the ability to provide for our own needs and the needs of those closest to us, we are less than fully human. Berry clearly recognizes that certain tools magnify human freedom, while others diminish it. It is interesting, again, to note Illich's essential characterization of industrialization as a form of imprisonment:

> People need not only to obtain things, they need above all the freedom to make things among which they can live, to give shape to them according to their own tastes, and to put them to use in caring for and about others. Prisoners in rich countries often have access to more things and services than members of their families, but they have no say in how things are to be made and cannot decide what to do with them. Their punishment consists in being deprived of what I shall call "conviviality." They are degraded to the status of mere consumers.[37]

Berry advances this argument. Consumers are no better than well-treated prisoners, and the American economy of industrial tools is designed entirely around the project of reducing autonomous tool users into pathetic, imprisoned consumers. The essential characteristic of their imprisonment is a loss of what we have been calling, according to Illich's categories, conviviality.

The industrial age has given us many tools, says Berry, "but little satisfaction, little sense of the sufficiency of anything."[38] This is because the primary product of industrial tools is dissatisfaction and discontent. Perversely, this is by design, for only in dissatisfaction can the user be imprisoned in the status of consumer, always ready to snap up the next thing, helpless to do for himself.

Berry, like any humanist worth the title, resists vehemently the commodification of all things by an industrial economy and through industrial tools. But importantly, his resistance is founded primarily on a defense of human freedom.

[D]espite their he-man pretensions and their captivations by masculine heroes of sports, war, and the Old West, most men are now entirely accustomed to obeying and currying the favor of their bosses. Because of this, of course, they hate their jobs—they mutter, 'Thank God it's Friday' and 'Pretty good for Monday'—but they do as they are told. They are more compliant than most housewives have been. Their characters combine feudal submissiveness with modern helplessness. They have accepted almost without protest, and often with relief, their dispossession of any usable property and, with that, their loss of economic independence and their consequent subordination to bosses. They have submitted to the destruction of the household economy and thus of the household, to the loss of home employment and self-employment, to the disintegration of their families and communities, to the desecration and pillage of their country, and they have continued abjectly to believe, obey, and vote for the people who have most eagerly abetted this ruin and who have most profited from it. These men, moreover, are helpless to do anything for themselves or anyone else without money, and so for money they do whatever they are told.[39]

What an indictment! What a picture of servitude and, in fact, slavery to the industrial model by and through the use of industrial tools that dispossess and render helpless! Far from being an effete discussion of aesthetics (which is what the bosses and other boosters of industrial serfdom would have all the macho-pretenders believe—the better to keep them doing as they are told), Berry knows that a society's use of tools is foundational to its freedom or lack thereof.

Berry writes that these prisoners of industrial tools know "that their ability to be useful is precisely defined by their willingness to be somebody else's tool." This sentence is the guts of Berry's criticism of industrial technology. The desire to be useful—Berry's first answer to the central question of what people are for—is turned from a human virtue to a weapon. A weapon that feeds off of helplessness to strip- mine the most valuable human resource—human liberty. Best, it is not taken by force of whip and chain but surrendered under a perverse form of voluntary extraction.

Notice especially the particular form that this voluntary surrender takes—a "willingness to be somebody else's tool." The true end of industrial tools—the *telos* of an industrial tool—is not usefulness, it is not getting the job done, it is not even ease and speed and the "freeing" of leisure time in order that people may "escape" the drudgery of handiwork or "save" their "labor." Instead, in a reversal of language and meaning worthy of Orwell, these tools have as their primary function the essential reduction of human beings to tools themselves for the magnification of the bosses. Such perversity and insult! Should the masses ever grasp this fact, there will be violence in the streets.

It is a fair characterization of Berry to say that he is of the view that no sooner did man step out of the saddle and trade his horse for a tractor than he himself was saddled and put to the spur. First they come for the horses, and the next thing you know, the bit is in your mouth. It is an apt and chilling metaphor.

On the other hand, the tools that amplify man's essential freedom are those that make him sufficient to his work, able to enjoy the produce of that work, and dependent on no one farther away than the local repairman in a pinch. The "central figure" of an economy based on convivial tools "has invariably been the small owner or small-holder who maintains a significant measure of economic self-determination."[40] "A mind so placed meets again and again the necessity for work to be good." This convivial impulse "is less interested in abstract quantities than in particular qualities. It feels threatened and sickened when it hears people and creatures and places spoken of as labor, management, capital, and raw material. It is not at all impressed by the industrial legendry of gross national products."[41]

Instead, says Berry, the convivial mind is "forever fascinated . . . by questions leading toward the accomplishment of good work." Berry folds his categories into one another in layer after layer, utility fructifies in beauty, beauty in usefulness, both in freedom and self-sufficiency, and all in resistance to subservience; to becoming a tool in service to the machine. A technology of wholeness is the only answer to the technologies of dispossession and dismemberment. Tools can magnify people in their essential humanness or people can be tools. The choice is as stark and naked as the cold steel of Andy's prosthetic hand.

## Membership

> But our memory of ourselves, hard earned,
> is one of the land's seeds, as a seed
> is the memory of the life of its kind in its place,
> to pass on into life the knowledge
> of what has died. What we owe the future
> is not a new start, for we can only begin
> with what has happened. We owe the future
> the past, the long knowledge
> that is the potency of time to come.
> That makes of a man's grave a rich furrow.
> —"At a Country Funeral"[42]

[I] would insist only that any manufacturing enterprise should be formed and scaled to fit the local landscape, the local ecosystem, and the local community, and that it should be locally owned and employ local people. [I] would insist, in other words, that the shop or factory owner should not be an outsider, but rather a sharer in the fate of the place and its community. The deciders should have to live with the results of their decisions.
—*Citizenship Papers*[43]

Utility and self-sufficiency both naturally create and are naturally buttressed by the third condition that people are for, and that is *membership*, the final condition and resting place of wholeness. Industrial tools set apart, while convivial ones bind together. Nowhere can this be more clearly understood than in the field most often lauded by Futurists—medical technology.

Berry's short story "Fidelity" tells the simple story of Burley Coulter, eighty-two years old and a lifetime citizen of the Port William membership, and his son Danny Branch, of the same membership. Burley is dying, and his family and friends, in the struggle of their love and grief, submit his care to the "medical community." "Loving him, wanting to help him, they had given him over to 'the best of modern medical care'—which meant, as they now saw, that they had abandoned him."[44]

Now Burley lies comatose yet "treated," "lying slack and still in the mechanical room, in the merciless light, with a tube in his nose and a tube needled into his arm and a tube draining his bladder into a plastic bag that hung beneath the bed . . . he breathed with the help of a machine."[45] Realizing their mistake, Danny kidnaps Burley one night while the rest of the membership cover his tracks in the face of the investigation that ensues.

Danny tenderly cares for his dying father as he takes him out of that place of tubes and machines to Burley's favorite haunts among the fields and trees. "Listen," says Danny to Burley, "I'm going to take you home."[46] Meanwhile, Wheeler and Henry Catlett, counselors at law of the Port William membership, stall the police. "I'm just doing my duty," says the Officer. Henry replies, "And you're here now to tell us that a person who is sick and unconscious, or even a person who is conscious and well, is ultimately the property of the medical industry and the government. Aren't you? . . . Some of us think people belong to each other and to God."[47]

Danny gives him a few last sips of water as Burley briefly regains consciousness before finally slipping away. Danny digs a grave and, in the morning, after the passing, gently lays one of the membership down in the furrow he has made. Danny "let the quiet reassemble itself around him, the quiet of the place now one with that of the old body sleeping in its grave. Into that great quiet he said aloud, 'Be with him, as he has been with us.' And then he began to fill the grave."[48] *Be with him as he has been with us.* Membership means *being with.*

The Lawman has moved on to confront Wheeler now. "All I know is that the law has been broken, and I'm here to serve the law," he says.

"But my dear boy, you don't eat or drink the law, or sit in the shade of it or warm yourself by it, or wear it, or have your being in it. The law exists only to serve." "Serve what?" asks the Officer. Wheeler says, and we know he speaks for Berry, "Why, all the many things that are above it. Love."[49]

Is this some strange apologetic for assisted suicide? The question itself is rotten, of course, and Berry won't even admit it to be asked. To ask is to function from the perspective of the Lawman and the Medical Care Providers and the industrial mind, who have forged a culture of dismemberment from the fires of mechanism and instrumentalism. This mind starts with the notion that every person is their own possession: "It's my life, my body, my self." Berry says, no person is his own—that is not what people are for—people are for membership, and every decision and every tool must account for that belonging.

Again, Illich is helpful in clarifying Berry's central argument. In his essay "Brave New Biocracy," Illich writes:

> In societies confused by the technological prowess that enables us to transgress all traditional boundaries of coming to life and dying, the new discipline of big-ethics has emerged to mediate between pop-science and law. It has sought to create the semblance of a moral discourse that roots personhood in the "scientific ability" of bioethicists to determine who is a person and who is not through qualitative evaluation of the fetish, "a life." What I fear is that the abstract, secular notion of "a life" will be sacralized, thereby making it possible that this spectral entity will progressively replace the notion of a "person" in which the humanism of Western individualism is anchored. "A life" is amenable to management, to improvement and to evaluation in a way which is unthinkable when we speak of "a person." The transmogrification of a person into "a life" is a lethal operation, as dangerous as reaching out for the tree of life in the time of Adam and Eve.[50]

The medical, legal, political, scientific, and in fact the entire industrial apparatus are invasive in ways that buttress the total power of the machine based on a grossly dismembered conception of what constitutes the good life, or *a* good life, as the case may be. Berry's loyalties and loves are clear—to the membership rather than to the machine. Just so.

If You're Going to Talk to Me,
You'll Have to Walk with Me

> Better than any argument is to rise at dawn
> and pick dew-wet red berries in a cup.
> —"A Standing Ground"[51]

To every argument about the modern world, its goods and bads, its twists and travails, its surprises and degradations, Wendell Berry patiently answers—*walk with me; walk with each other and with God.* Tools can help. Man was made for tools. Man was made to magnify himself and his maker in his maker's gift that is this world. But man was not made to be a tool; neither to make of himself a tool for his own greed and plea- sure nor for him to be made a tool by others for their greed and pleasure. Berry says, walk with me, and I'll teach you the difference. The difference between a Weedwacker and a scythe; between a pixel of light and a stick of lead; between horsepower and a horse; between a hook and a hand; between a living death and the death that is life.

Walking while talking is the state of wholeness.

# 9

# Living Peace in the Shadow of War:
# Wendell Berry's Dogged Pacifism

*Michael R. Stevens*

### Vietnam as the Shaper of Berry's Peacemaking

In one of those strange confluences of the imaginative life, I wrote much of this essay on Wendell Berry's pacifism while watching the HBO television production *Band of Brothers,* which follows Easy Company, 101st Airborne, from their training in Georgia, through D-Day, Bastogne, and finally the occupation of Germany. Many parts of the film show with unflinching candor the horror and hellishness of war. But one voice-over by the protagonist, then-Lt. Dick Winters, at the end of the D-Day episode titled "Day of Days," is particularly apt for this extended reflection on Berry. As he watches the incessant shelling during a lull for Easy Company after a full day's fighting amid confusion and cruelty, Winters reflects that he prayed a prayer of thanks to God for his survival, and then, "if somehow I managed to get home again, I promised God and myself that I would find a quiet piece of land someplace and spend the rest of my life in peace."[1] Obviously, Lt. Winters doesn't become a pacifist on D-Day (though several of his men think he might be a Quaker); his is a narrative of duty executed with near-ideal acumen in the face of danger. But the hint of war driving one to long for peace is just the sort of hint to open up a discussion of Wendell Berry's vision for peaceable living in the face of incessant violence, from wars and rumors of wars to economic and

106

agricultural decisions that bring death in the guise of profit and pleasure. Berry's call to peace is a call to leave war behind and to seek an embodied, active, and actualized life, in a real place among real people, where the good of Creation can be affirmed and husbanded rather than exploited and annihilated. In the valley of the shadow of war, Berry refuses the motives of fear and retribution, and, like his Good Shepherd, he tends to his sheep as a way to give life fullness. The fact that pacifism is cognate to "passive" is rendered moot by Berry's fully lived and practiced peace.

I don't mean to mislead; Berry is definitely angry at war. He is fed up with the suggestion that violence can somehow function as the curb to violence. The shadow of war hovers over Berry's career and his work in ways heavy and surprising to those who want to read Berry as a nostalgist and idealist. His earliest memories are bound up in the changes wrought by World War II, in the lives of soldiers and sufferers on the homefront, and in the world of agriculture decisively mechanized in the postwar boom. A generation later, in the flush of his early career as a teacher and writer, Berry's response to the Vietnam War served as a hinge for his deliberate move back to the land, and back (or forward, perhaps) into a concern for the "first things" of human life. Finally, late in his career, Berry has emerged as an outspoken opponent of the war making tied to America's response to the 9/11 bombings and the ongoing war on terror. All of Berry's laments of the violence done upon land and people by corporate greed and industrialized versions of agriculture have been written beneath this pervasive shadow of war. His knowledge that no part of the Creation is safe from man's fallen desires, that the destruction of everything and anything can be masked as having a good end, that a perpetual state of war *is* the reality that we must perpetually resist—these ominous tenets motivate Berry to point always toward peace. For him, the redemptive work to which man is called must be to guard the creational good from the absolutizing violence toward which our fallen condition tends. His only option for redemptive living is the way of peace.

How has Berry's articulation of his pacifism developed over the course of a long career? We begin with Wendell Berry in 1968, that grim and tumultuous year. There is nothing unique in the fact that Berry's pacifism becomes clearly articulated in such a year—for many thoughtful young people of his generation, in Paris and in Prague as well as in the riotous cities of the United States, this was just such a year. What is unique in

Berry's vision is that he has found a way to embody peace through apt relationship to his land, his people, and his place. His farm, as a link to the rich and varied creational web that is human community and human care, is his attempt at making peace, at showing rightly ordered connections across difficult boundaries.

On February 10, 1968, Berry delivered "A Statement Against the War in Vietnam" at the Kentucky Conference on War and the Draft. The setting was his workplace at the time, the University of Kentucky, but Berry had other work afoot, as just a few years before, he and his family had moved to Port Royal to rehabilitate a small farm. And it is in the context of that farm, in the background of his peacemaking with that land and its people—his people—that Berry spoke against the violence half a world away. Just about a week before this speech, Berry had enacted, and then composed, a poem that would come out a few years later in the volume *Farming: A Hand Book*. The poem, "February 2, 1968," offers a succinct and resonant context out of which his pacifism grows: "In the dark of the moon, in flying snow, in the dead of winter, / war spreading, families dying, the world in danger, / I walk the rocky hillside, sowing clover."[2] This wild act of hope, of sowing the potential for life and harvest in the midst of winter's death grip, is the analogy of all Berry's peacemaking. Here, now, in the world as it is, we pursue life rather than accept death as the permanent, irrevocable way. So, when Berry stepped to the lectern on February 10, he spoke from somewhere, for something profound, not just against something heinous. The turning away, for Berry, always involves a turning toward. Hence, in a dark hour, Berry told his audience: "I will be steadfastly hopeful, for as a member of the human race I am also in the company of men, though comparatively few, who through all the sad destructive centuries of our history have kept alive the vision of peace and kindness and generosity and humility and freedom. . . . I wish to be a spokesman of the belief that the human intelligence that could invent the apocalyptic weapons of modern war could invent as well the means of peace."[3]

Berry's "turning toward" is dogged and central—there can be no peace in the abstract, merely in the enmity toward war. "Do we think peace is possible? If we do, then we must envision the particularities of that possibility. We must enact, and so substantiate, that possibility in our lives."[4] The sort of enacting called for here requires work and imagination, and the default to violence as the base solution to problems is fundamentally a failure of the imagination. We must be able to construct a vision for peace and continuity with the created order, and that is much harder than destroying what we do not want to live alongside. If those aspects of our national tradition that tend toward peaceful civic life, aspects that Berry embraces as "the best hope for the chance of every person to live fully and to be free,"[5] are meant to be the source of imagination, then the failure of imagination is a national tragedy. What we have leaned upon, instead, is the most unimaginative impulse—brute force: "We have come to depend obsessively on an enormous capability of violence—for security, for national self-esteem, even for economic stability. As a consequence we have become blind to the alternatives to violence."[6] War, for Berry, can never be a path to peace, can never be a "turning toward" the good:

> We assume, dangerously, that minds invested in war, and trained to be warlike, can, at the signing of a treaty, be simply withdrawn from warfare and made peaceable. But the training needed for peace cannot be the same as that which is necessary for war. Men cannot be taught and encouraged to kill by fostering those impulses of compassion and justice and reasonableness that make it possible to hope for peace.[7]

But Berry does not rest upon this lament. His call to the protest movement, of which his audience is a tiny fragment, is a call to construction and embodiment:

> The main objective of any expression or demonstration by peace groups should be to articulate as fully as possible the desirability and the possibility of peace. I believe that a great danger to the cause of peace is the possibility that the peace movement might become merely negative, an instrument of protest rather than hope.[8]

Hopeful protest cannot afford to be mere rhetoric, mere opposition; it must flower into a new, renewing vision for life.

This sober presentation at the University of Kentucky laid out Berry's essential notion of pacifism—we must press for wholeness, which is unavailable in war and not guaranteed even in times of suspended hostility. The watchword is vigilance. Even in the face of hope and promise, the press toward violence, the weight of its shadow, never goes away. No wonder the heavy tone of the poem "March 22, 1968": "The jonquils, half open, bend down with its weight. / The plow freezes in the furrow. / In the night I lay awake, thinking / of the river rising, the spring heavy / with official meaningless deaths."[9] Such a tone is not surprising, given the poetry Berry had been writing in the years prior to his protest speech, poems gathered in the 1968 volume *Openings*. Many of them point away from war toward some elusive, constructive good. In these early poems, Berry hammers out his "pacifism of embodiment" on a troubled and troubling anvil of social upheaval. "To My Children, Fearing for Them" borders on that ultimate lament, of bringing kids into the world at all, as Berry wonders " . . . What have I done? I / need better answers than there are / to the pain of coming to see what was done in blindness, / loving what I cannot save. . . ." But the bringing to life of the next generation is substance, is essence, of what we must do and be, so that Berry protests the fear that war and discord brings with a reversal: ". . . Nor, / your eyes turning toward me, / can I wish your lives unmade / though the pain of them is on me."[10]

"Against the War in Vietnam" is even shakier, though shy of abandonment to fear; there is a vision, a constructive ideal to draw upon, albeit one sublimated and ignored. Berry casts the hopeful sense in a rhetorical question, one thus far horribly answered by war: "Where are the plenteous dwellings / we were coming to, the neighborly holdings? / We see the American freedom defended / with blood, the vision of Jefferson / served by the agony of children, / women cowering in holes."[11] "Dark with Power" sets up a similar judgment, one where our ideal is turned on its head by the reality of our dependence on war. Here, as elsewhere, Berry indicts our war on our own land as an extension, or maybe a root, of our foreign violence, so that "Dark with power, we remain/the invaders of our land. . . ."[12] So sharp is the loss of our sense of order and justice, Berry suggests that we have lost all moral high-ground, and he offers this dying glimpse at our aspirations: "We are carried in the belly / of what we have become / toward the shambles of our triumph, far from the quiet houses."[13] The quietude of household, place, community—whether in Kentucky or California or Vietnam itself—is the hope latent in Berry's diagnosis, though he recognizes the magnetic appeal that "triumph" offers, no matter the human and moral cost.

This gentle but deliberately assertive peacemaking is a stronger theme in a few of the other poems from *Openings*. So, in "The Want of Peace," when Berry confesses that "I lack the peace of simple things. / I am never wholly in place. / I find no peace or grace. / We sell the world to buy fire, / our way lighted by burning men . . . ," that sharp disconcert rooted in war is set against the conditions laid out in the previous stanza: ". . . the contentments made / by men who have had little: / the fisherman's silence/receiving the river's grace, / the gardener's musing on rows."[14] That bright contrast is heightened in what must be reckoned one of his signature poems, "The Peace of Wild Things," a poem that starts out in literal and figurative darkness—"When despair for the world grows in me / and I wake in the night at the least sound / in fear of what my life and my children's lives may be"—as the shadow of war, and of total and final and absolute war, looms. Only by reference to that angst does the constructive alternative resonate most fully, as the turn to the given goodness of the created order shows peacemaking by peacefinding: "I come into the peace of wild things / who do not tax their lives with forethought / of grief. I come into the presence of still water."[15] The echo of Psalm 23 in that last line suggests the spiritual component that must inform the pursuit of lasting peace in such a troubled time.

Alongside this givenness of "the peace of wild things" is the peace of human kinship, the fundamental bond by which we are to function in the world. Berry sharpens this point, revealing the necessity to actively pursue kinship in the face of invented barriers and hatreds, in a poem with deep Cold War roots, "To a Siberian Woodsman (after looking at some pictures in a magazine)." "Who has invented our enmity?" asks Berry, in section 4 of the poem, and he responds with an assertion of each man's placed-ness, each man's at-home-ness in his sliver of the creation, providing the bond of peace that makes life possible: "Who has imagined that I would destroy myself in order to destroy you, / or that I could improve myself by destroying you? Who has imagined / that your death could be negligible to me now that I have seen these pictures of your face?"[16] In this "turning toward" the supposed enemy become friend, Berry shows one of the contours of peacemaking. It is decisive in the humanizing of the other and in the refusal to let one's own mind be made up by any preconceptions or groupthink. It is peace by means of resistance to the magnetic pull of war.

Returning to that tragic spring of 1968, we find the essay "Some Thoughts on Citizenship and Conscience in Honor of Don Pratt," written

> a little more than a week after the death of Martin Luther King, who lived as only the great live, in humble obedience to the highest ideals, in proud defiance of men and laws that would have required him to abide by a narrower vision and to dream a narrower dream. He stood for the American hope in its full amplitude and generosity. His martyrdom is the apparition of the death of that hope in racism and violence.[17]

In the wake of such disappointment, Berry celebrates the courage of his student Don Pratt, who has been imprisoned for refusing to serve in the military. Berry identifies the gestures of Pratt and other young men like him as the appropriate embodiment of peace: "Because they have not only believed in our highest ideals, but have also acted as they believed, the world is whole before them, and they are whole before the world."[18] What these men have avoided, according to Berry, is the abstraction of peace; the threat of such abstraction is not always clear when one serves the cause, but it is highly destructive, as Berry writes in *The Long-Legged House*:

> My impression is that the great causes of peace and brotherhood are being served these days with increasing fanaticism, obsessiveness, self-righteousness, and anger. . . . And pacifists and peace-workers especially should be aware of its enormous potential of violence. The problems of violence cannot be solved on public platforms, but only in people's lives.[19]

The difference between solving violence on a personal level rather than on public platforms is a crucial distinction for Berry, one that leads him powerfully in the direction of the necessary embodiment of peace, for if a man "is for peace he must have a life in which peace is possible. He must be peace-able. To be a peaceable man is to be the hope of the world . . . How can a man hope to promote peace in the world if he has not made it possible in his own life and his own household?"[20]

Here then is Berry's stake in the pacifist "movement": the enacting of a whole relationship to a finite people and place, "putting things right" in his tiny sphere, "the possibility of a protest that is more complex than permanent, public in effect but private in its motive and implementation. Hence, Berry asserts that "[one] can *live* in protest. I have in mind a sort of personal secession from the encroaching institutional machinery of destruction and waste and violence."[21] Berry's own choice to return to subsistence farming and rural hardships (and joys) is one such possibility, though he admits not the only one. But with enough people living in protest, an embodied opposition to the shadow of violence

> might invent a way of life that would be modest in its material means and necessities and yet rich in pleasures and meanings, kind to the land, intricately joined both to the human community and to the natural world—a life directly opposite to that which our institutions and corporations envision for us, but one which is more essential to the hope of peace than any international treaty.[22]

Though political protests may further the cause of peacemaking, Berry is skeptical of their costs and their abstractions. "Peaceableness and lovingness and all the other good hopes are exactly as difficult and complicated as living one's life, and can be most fully served in life's fullness."[23] Berry's pacifism is thus as little, or as much, as living life fully here and now, in a created order that gives and takes and honors loyalty. Peace is the fully located life. Berry's discovery about himself in the mid-1960s when he moved his family to the farm and Port Royal is thus a discovery about what a world wracked by war (in manifestations both obvious and subtle) desperately needs: lived peace.

## A Hazardous Thirty Year Interlude

Berry's testament, captured in his fiction, poetry, and essays throughout his career and backed up by his daily labors on Lane's Landing Farm, has been essentially "lived peace." Certainly his tone moved in the many pitches of traditional protest to the subsidiary violences of industrial agriculture, corporate rapaciousness, and self-destructive hedonism within

American culture. Such volumes of essays as *The Unsettling of America* and *A Continuous Harmony* from the 1970s, *Home Economics* in the 1980s, and *What Are People For?* and *Sex, Economy, Freedom, and Community* in the 1990s bear a varied but persistent witness against these subwars often raging in our own communities and civil structures. But at every turn, Berry offers the hope wrought by embodied wholeness.

Maybe the best place to look, through these decades of Berry's work, is again at the poetry, which reveals the tension and the tendencies of Berry's vision. Hence, in "The Mad Farmer's Love Song" from the 1973 collection *The Country of Marriage*, where Berry offers a poetic wink and nudge: "O when the world's at peace / and every man is free / then will I go down unto my love. / O and I may go down / several times before that."[24] A more pungent poem, both of dissent and assent, is "Manifesto: The Mad Farmer Liberation Front," with its peacemaking illogic at work: "Invest in the millennium. Plant sequoias. / . . . Put your faith in the two inches of humus / that will build under the trees / every thousand years."[25] To end such a poem, Berry summons perhaps his finest poetic phrase, an apt blending of the need to live here and now and the deep spiritual impulses that undergird that need. It is a phrase to place at the heart of the peacemaking endeavor: "Practice resurrection."[26] In the 1980 volume *A Part*, Berry reveals the way in which lived peace can dwell alongside violence when that violence is within appropriate order, couched in appropriate dignity. In the poem "For the Hog Killing," what appears as an ominous, warlike set of exhortations—"Let them stand still for the bullet, and stare the shooter in the eye, / let them die while the sound of the shot is in the air, let them die as they fall, / let the jugular blood spring hot to the knife, let its freshet be full"—becomes a celebration of an apt exchange between man and beast, a killing that is not war nor murder: "let this day begin again the change of hogs into people, not the other way around, / for today we celebrate again our lives' wedding with the world, / for by our hunger, by this provisioning, we renew the bond."[27] Such a poem pushes back against the oppressive shadow of war and multifarious destruction, showing that even death can have its place within the peaceable structure of things. In this right ordering of the farm, the properly tended and husbanded livestock fulfills a role within the bond that is the home economy. There is an aptness to the rendering of hog into bacon and ham that has, in Berry's heightened language, the covenantal resonance of a marriage. One need only turn to the monstrous example of the contemporary industrial hog farm, with hundreds of thousands of animals stuffed into a facility (the furthest thing from a farm) and subjected to the science of slaughtering, to see why Berry wants to show the crucial nature of process rather than just production. Done rightly, the hog-killing time is a redemptive ritual, a kinship within the creational order of things. So it is not killing itself that is a prohibited act; it is killing that disorders the given web of relationships, within which a man killing another man can never be an affirmation of the bond. Berry doesn't define closely the parameters within which killing can be a part of "lived peace." If he is beyond many vegan and vegetarian sensibilities already with this poem, he is still shy of those who want to define the possibilities of human killing human—in self-defense, perhaps, or just war or capital punishment—as part of an order of necessity. He is a farmer, and the farm is his judge.

The volume *A Timbered Choir: The Sabbath Poems 1979–1997* is also rife with examples of peace enacted and understood. Indeed, the very notion of the Sabbath poems, Berry's musings while walking his land on Sunday mornings throughout these years, resting in the particularity of his place and of God's placing, shows how deeply the active resistance of this one farmer has connected with peace. A few examples will have to stand for the rich body of verse, one of them a rare sonnet of Berry's, "Sabbath IV, 1983," which plays upon the delicate balance between Creator and stewards: ". . . The field is made by hand and eye, / By daily work, by hope outreaching wrong, / And yet the Sabbath, parted, still must stay / In the dark mazings of the soil. . . ."[28] This is work within acceptance of a certain powerlessness; this is doing alongside waiting; this is "lived peace." The curious dynamic is well captured in the final couplet: "Bewildered in our timely dwelling place, / Where we arrive by work, we stay by grace."[29] And so Berry has stayed by grace thirty-plus years on his farm, working with plow and with pen, cultivating and articulating the vision of a life that trumps war. But within the past decade, the wound that had scarred over, never fully mending, broke open again.


The Return of War and the Loss of Home


The events surrounding the aftermath of the September 11, 2001, terrorist bombings at the World Trade Center and the Pentagon have shaped the past decade of Wendell Berry's work, as they did the lives of many others. Berry's pacifism was both strengthened by this furor and threatened by it. It became more obvious than ever that war is a persistent parasite, morphing in form and focus, but never ceasing to feed on humanity's aspirations for "peace in our time," especially for aspirations fueled by warlike economic and diplomatic policies. Yet the ground upon which Berry has stood has been shaken by the loss of those freedoms that made good and true resistance possible. Berry is deliberate in pointing the finger inward at the beginning of his set of twenty-seven observations in "Thoughts in the Presence of Fear." When he asserts that "[w]e citizens of the industrial countries must continue the labor of self-criticism and self-correction,"[30] he echoes his claim from the Vietnam era, that peacemaking must begin with a rigorous self-appraisal. The problem with Berry's rhetoric here is that the context of 2001 was one of patriotic outrage without the widespread sense of chagrin that surrounded the distant and mediated Vietnam conflict. The proximity of the violence in 2001 made Berry's declarations seem ill-directed as a critique of domestic policy. Why didn't he upbraid the terrorists as his first act of censure? He seems perhaps to gloss over their outrageous violence when he declares that

> [o]ne of the gravest dangers to us now, second only to further terrorist attacks against our people, is that we will attempt to go on as before with the corporate program of global "free trade," whatever the cost in freedom and civil rights, without self-questioning or self-criticism or public debate.[31]

But Berry sees that the sharpest danger is a disintegration of citizenry, of the ability to think about our own obligations when we have some "others" to vilify. Hence, he offers this immediate follow-up point: "This is why the substitution of rhetoric for thought, always a temptation in a national crisis, must be resisted by officials and citizens alike."[32] And his warning is once again for the peace movement as much as the war movement, since peace protests that aren't embodied in lived practice become merely rhetorical gestures, taking on the contours of the very movements they mean to oppose.

But Berry does turn the corner back toward his embodied peacemaking in the final few points; hence, he offers his basic pacifist thesis when he asserts that "[w]hat leads to peace is not violence but peaceableness, which is not passivity, but an alert, informed, practiced, and active state of being."³³ Further echoes of Berry's "embodied peace" emerge in his examples: "Starting with the economies of food and farming, we should promote at home and encourage abroad the ideal of local self-sufficiency. . . . [P]roper education enables young people to put their lives in order, which means knowing what things are more important than other things; it means putting first things first."³⁴ He sees the economic root cause of war as the place to begin (and continue) making the embodied protest, and so his gesture of peace is a resistance to consumption that breeds destruction. His final phrase points ahead, by pointing toward what he has always practiced: "We do need a 'new economy,' but one that is founded on thrift and care, on saving and conserving, not on excess and waste. An economy based on waste is inherently and hopelessly violent, and war is its inevitable by-product. We need a peaceable economy."³⁵

The question of a "peaceable economy" is central for Berry in one of the pre-9/11 essays in *Citizenship Papers*, bluntly titled "The Failure of War" (1999): "But let us have the candor to acknowledge that what we call 'the economy' or 'the free market' is less and less distinguishable from warfare."³⁶ This is the sort of clarification that Berry has made from his earliest comments about war: the intertwined nature of it, the economic causes and catastrophic economic effects, the numbness toward our own maladies in the wake of accusing others. Berry unequivocally includes our own domestic preemptive strikes in this broader infamy of war when he declares that "[a]bortion-as-birth-control is justified as a 'right,' which can establish itself only by denying all the rights of another person, which is the most primitive intent of warfare."³⁷ Here Berry connects the perverse strands of logic that justify killing children in the name of securing our own well-being: "How many deaths of other people's children by bombing or starvation are we willing to accept in order that we may be free, affluent, and (supposedly) at peace?"³⁸

Indeed, it is the coming home of war, the coming of war into the inner workings of our social and psychological fabric, that motivated Berry to write "A Citizen's Response to 'The National Security Strategy of the United States of America.'" Berry's critique is rooted in his idea that peacemaking must be done by placed people in actual communities. Patriotism cannot be an abstraction (read: the Patriot Act), and citizenship must have a *civitas*, a city of origin: "Increasingly, Americans—including, notoriously, their politicians—are not *from* anywhere. And so they have in this 'homeland,' which their government now seeks to make secure on their behalf, no home *place* that they are strongly moved to know or love or use well or protect."[39] This has become a longer stretch, this placing of the self to make peace, but Berry is insistent that it is still possible, along the very lines of human effort that he articulated in the Vietnam era as essential: "A nation's charity must come from the heart and the imagination of its people. It requires us ultimately to see the world as a community of all the creatures, a community which, to be possessed by any, must be shared by all."[40] Constructive. Embodied. Enacted. Hopeful. A leap of the imagination in a world racked by violence toward the air we breathe, the water we drink, the ground itself and the food we grow from it, and certainly the human community in which we all dwell. This is Wendell Berry's pacifism. It must be active; it must be activated by superhuman diligence (since the human condition will not naturally tend there). As Berry exhorts at the end of "The Citizen's Response," "We can no longer afford to confuse peaceability with passivity. Authentic peace is no more passive than war. . . . If we are serious about peace, then we must work for it as ardently, seriously, continuously, carefully, and bravely as we have ever prepared for war."[41] One imagines the "Uncle Wendell Wants You!" poster, with the old farmer pointing not out of the poster but out toward his fields: "Go and make peace!"

And in this post-9/11 iteration, Berry's vision of peace is increasingly tied to the Gospels, to his perception of Christian teaching, as Berry proclaims rather unexpectedly in the midst of "The Citizen's Response": "The Christian gospel is a summons to peace, calling for justice beyond anger, mercy beyond justice, forgiveness beyond mercy, love beyond forgiveness."[42] This thread represents the decisive root of Berry's pacifism: it is the way of Christ. Hence, for a man at odds with the church for most of his adult life and troubled by the exclusionary hegemony with which official Christianity has treated the rural parish, Berry's publication of "The Burden of the Gospels" represents a surprising act of piety. First published in *The Christian Century*, and later collected in Berry's most recent volume, *The Way of Ignorance*, this essay plays a third role in a small volume brought out by Shoemaker & Hoard in 2005, thoroughly titled as *Blessed Are the Peacemakers: Christ's Teachings about Love, Compassion and For-*

*giveness.* This slender volume can be seen as something of a culmination of Berry's pacifism, with an introduction that throws a massive pipe wrench into the just- war tradition: "One cannot be aware both of the history of Christian war and of the contents of the Gospels without feeling that something is amiss."[43] The dozens of verses that Berry then puts on display from Matthew, Mark, Luke, and John serve to underscore this amissness, since Christ's counterintuitive teaching of loving enemies, withholding the death blow, and letting humility trump pride seems absurd in the aggregate. Indeed, by ending this little volume with "The Burden of the Gospels," Berry brings the reader to the very point that Berry has come to after seventy years in the presence of these teachings. Beneath the wonderment and edification, he points out that exposure to the Gospels "has caused me to understand them as a burden, sometimes raising the hardest of personal questions, sometimes bewildering, sometimes contradictory, sometimes apparently outrageous in their demands."[44] Chief among the outrages is the vision of the peaceable kingdom, to be lived not only then but also now. Here the Gospels, and their winsome vision for life amid death, push down with a heavy burden, one that, for Berry, must be distributed over a life of intentionality, of lived community, of place and people: "We don't need much imagination," Berry argues, "to imagine that to be free of hatred, of enmity, of the endless and hopeless effort to oppose violence with violence, would be to have life more abundantly."[45]

Having begun this developmental account of Berry's pacifism with a poem (in fact, with a number of poems), I want to return to the Sabbath poems once more, particularly to a few written after the 9/11 attacks and the resumption of warfare as status quo for our nation. There is a dark edge to these more recent Sabbath poems, a disappointment that appears often in the poems included within the larger volume *Given: New Poems*, from 2005. The first is a winter poem, "2002, I," a poem that in many ways parallels the dynamic of "February 2, 1968," with an act of agricultural husbandry functioning as protest to the reality of war. But whereas within the earlier poem, the movement is from grievous events to the small, significant act, here in the newer poem the act is somewhat swallowed up in the shadow of war: ". . . Weary, / an old man feeds hay / to the stock at the end / of a winter's day / in a time reduced / to work, hunger, worry, / grief, and as always / war, the killed peace / of the original world."[46] If hope is not extinguished here, it is at least exhausted, with no springtime in sight. But another of these late Sabbath poems is posited right in that cusp between winter and spring, in the time of lambing that Berry, the sheep farmer, knows so well. Sabbath poem "2004, III" is set immediately against the blackened backdrop but with a glint of hope: "They are fighting again the war to end war, / And the ewe flock, bred in October, brings forth / in March. This so far remains, this pain / and renewal, whatever war is being fought."[47] Amid all the fray of birth and blood, the engagement with reality is complete, and Berry asserts that "[t]here is no happiness like this . . . / This then may be the prayer without ceasing, / this beauty and gratitude, this moment."[48] This moment, and all such moments, of standing against the culture of death with life, even a tenuous and troubled life, accrue as the transforming vision of peace and life. With risks aplenty, and with hope as a pinprick of light under the shadowy gloom of brute death and the death-in-life of our consumptive, entertainment-throttled lives—even with the absurd companionship of topsoil and quietude and the generations of a single place to see us along the journey—we stumble forward into the Peaceable Kingdom, already promised, already (though not yet) come. And a tall old farmer poet comes striding alongside as well, good company on the long, hard road.


Epilogue on Narratives of War

I began with a quote from a WWII soldier, and with at least a passing claim that WWII was a significant early turning point for the world into which Wendell Berry grew from boyhood to manhood. But a return to the context of that war raises many hard questions regarding Berry's pacifism. When we left Lt. Winters in *Band of Brothers*, he was unsettled by his first combat experience on D-Day, thinking only of survival and a return to peace. But the narrative goes on, and in episode 9, "Why We Fight," Easy Company comes upon a concentration camp in the primeval woods of Austria. As the men, hardened by the rigors of combat, try to come to grips with the horrors of the Final Solution, the question of evil arises and lingers like the barbaric smoke of the ovens. In a fallen world, is there any bottom to the depths of depravity, any way, aside from the protracted violence of war, to end genocide and atrocity and the horror of such camps? What answer can Berry's pacifism offer to that shadow of war that would smother and block out all light? I want to end with a brief reflection on a few passages from Berry's fiction, where the theme of war (particularly WWII combat) is dominant and where we can glimpse, by the *via nega-tiva*, why peacemaking is so central to his life and work. Both excerpts set up the difficulty of the transition from warmaking to peacemaking, and though neither is definitive, each points toward hope. The concentration camps of Poland and of Southeast Asia are not part of Berry's narrative; he gives voice to the lament of war without answering all the questions of either war or peace. His voice is passionate; though, like all human voices, it is provisional.

The first passage is from the story "Making It Home," collected in the 1992 volume *Fidelity: Five Stories*. In the story, Art Rowanberry is return-ing home from the war, walking the last bunch of miles from the bus stop in town back to his family's farm outside Port William. It is a walk of recovery, or at least reflection, since Art bears both the physical damage of a wound and also the psycho-spiritual damage of bearing witness:

> The fighting went on, the great tearing apart. People and every-thing else were torn to pieces. . . . You got to where you could not look at a man without knowing how little it would take to kill him. . . . There was nothing you could look at that was whole— man or beast or house or tree—that had the right to stay whole very long.[49]

What Art Rowanberry discovers is the vicious absolutism of war, the incredible fragility of creational good in the presence of the fallen motives and modes of mankind. Everything he knows is made expendable, includ-ing his own being. How can a man so contorted ever be whole again? As it turns out, his healing gesture is along the classic Berryian contours—to return to his people and his place—and to respond to his brother Mart's invitation back across the boundary from war to peace. Amid his father's stunned and moving greeting of the returned soldier, the brothers reunite: "Mart came around onto the headland then and stopped his team. He and Art shook hands, grinning at each other. 'You reckon your foot'll still fit in a furrow?' Art nodded. 'I reckon it still will.'"[50] This ending is perhaps a bit pat; peace is achieved with stunning quickness, under the biblical gloss of Early Rowanberry's offering almost verbatim the words of the prodigal's father from Luke 15: "Tell your granny to set on another plate. For we have our son that was gone and has come again."[51] But the offer and acceptance of a return to the lived peace of farm, family, and welcome finitude is a sharply drawn portrait of Berry's vision.

Things aren't so clean nor so clear at the end of Berry's 2004 novel, *Hannah Coulter*. Here the peacemaking left in the wake of WWII's ravages is incomplete, awkwardly wrought, a set of scars that never quite fade. The title character, Hannah, has had to survive the loss of one husband, Virgil Feltner, as an MIA in Italy—this loss is at the center of Berry's early novel *A Place on Earth*—but her pain is assuaged by courtship and marriage to Nathan Coulter, himself returned from the savage fighting at the end of the Pacific campaign. Throughout their lives together, Hannah bears witness to Nathan's quiet, steadfast work on their hillside farm, his desire to be deeply identified with the people and place of Port William. There is much failure, most notably the defection of all three of their children to the cities and suburbs and careers that offer them ample promise and little lasting pleasure. Of his time in the war, and the battle of Okinawa, which culminated his combat experience, Nathan never offers more than a few mumbled words, and the tossing body of one with haunted dreams.

Yet after Nathan's death, Hannah decides to study the history and circumstances of that battle, to try and know that unknowable silence in her husband. And what she learns is both horrific and fulfilling—horrific because the battle tore at the very fabric of humanness for those flung into it. But fulfilling also, because Hannah realizes that Nathan's whole effort of a lifetime on the farm was a persistent attempt at peacemaking, a protest rooted in life's affirmation: "It is hard to live in Port William and yet have in mind the blasted and burnt, bloodied and muddy and stinking battlegrounds of Okinawa, hard to live in one place and imagine another. But imagination is what is needed. Want of imagination makes things unreal enough to be destroyed."[52] So Nathan had tried to imagine his way back to peace, by imagining and then embodying the ridge-top farm, by imagining a long, rich life with Hannah, and somehow getting the better part of such dreams. But such lived peace is never complete—that is why it must always be active, the vigilance of love in a hateful world. Hannah reflects amid her discoveries about the war that "eventually, in loving, you see that you have given yourself over to the knowledge of suffering in a state of war that is always going on. And you wake in the night to the thought of the hurt and the helpless, the scorned and the cheated, the burnt, the bombed, the shot, the imprisoned, the beaten, the tortured, the maimed, the spit upon, the shit upon."[53] To constantly make a space for the "others," those for whom your peacemaking means everything, one must suffer alongside—but this suffering has the grains of redemption in it. It is Christlike.

Such peace is never outside the shadow of war, but peaceableness is the constant and cognizant effort both to remember the horror and to eschew its inevitability by living for tangible good in the world of here and now. At times, the imagination must stretch to the furthest possibility, but one of the gifts given to humans is just such imaginative scope. When Hannah as an old woman comes to imagine Nathan the young man on a slope at Okinawa looking across the thousands of miles back toward Port William, she imagines him imagining home as he'd known it and, by some miraculous grace, might know it again. Hannah realizes that her husband's life was a peace protest: "And so I came to know, as I had not known before, what this place of ours had been and meant to him. I knew, as I had not known before, what I had meant to him. Our life in our place had been a benediction to him, but he had seen it always within a circle of fire that might have closed upon it."[54]

A lived benediction within a circle of damnable fire—there is perhaps the most allusive of Berry's articulations of his pacifism. And clearly it's more than half impossible. Too many forces of malice are at work in the world, with each and any of us in their crosshairs; a stance of self-defense seems the very least that we're forced to, and more likely a life of preemptive strikes to keep violence off our own backs. This is as true for business and education and neighborhood relationships as for national security. So it would seem. So logic and history and literature and television and our own guts seem to declare. But Wendell Berry points us elsewhere, toward the goodness of the created order, along a beam of redemptive living light that pierces the dark fallen fabric hanging over everything—but not forever.

# 10

# Wendell Berry's Unlikely Case for Conservative Christianity

## D. G. Hart

Everyone wants a piece of Wendell Berry's blessing, including many contemporary Christians. The evangelical Protestant magazine of record, *Christianity Today*, ran a story on Berry in 2006 with a subtitle proclaiming that the Kentucky farmer and writer "is inspiring a new generation of Christians to care for the land." The journalist who interviewed Berry for the article opined that "he is attractive to Christians because he offers a vision of care for Creation that is tied up with the sacredness of life."[1] Alan Jacobs, a professor at Wheaton College and another occasional writer for *Christianity Today*, also appealed to Berry in a piece that called evangelicals to a way of life that was at odds with the consumerism of modern culture. He cited Berry's remarks regarding a John Deere advertisement for a tractor that completely insulated the farmer from the weather, dust, smells, and sounds of farming. "The only real way," Berry concluded, "to get this sort of freedom and safety" to escape the hassles of earthly life "is to die." Jacobs feared that many evangelicals viewed the church in a similar way, as an "earth space capsule" that would provide a way to escape the "uncertainties and setbacks" of real earthly existence.[2]

Such appeals to Berry seem to be responsible, but claiming him as an inspiration for the institutional church, as the popular evangelical pastor Eugene Peterson has, may border on abusive. As many readers know, Berry has no shortage of critical comments about formal Christianity or the churches that keep it going. And yet, Peterson has written, quite plausibly I should add, that he has learned much about the nature of the Christian ministry from the anticlerical-sounding Kentucky poet. In Berry, "the importance of place is a recurrent theme—place embraced and loved, understood and honored," Peterson explains. "Whenever Berry writes the word 'farm,' I substitute 'parish,'" Peterson adds. "The sentence works for me every time."[3] To see how plausible this thought experiment is, consider the following passage from Berry with the substitution Peterson suggests. It is a passage from *A Continuous Harmony* in which Berry likens the work of a farmer to that of a teacher. But his comments could apply just as well to a preacher:

> An urban discipline that in good health is closely analogous to healthy agriculture is teaching [preaching.] Like a good farmer, a good teacher [preacher] is the trustee of a vital and delicate organism: the life of the mind [soul] in his community. The ultimate and defining standard of his discipline is his community's [congregation's] health and intelligence and coherence and endurance. This is a high calling, deserving of a life's work. We have allowed it to degenerate into careerism and specialization. In education [religious life] as in agriculture we have discarded the large and enlarging disciplines of community and place, and taken up in their stead the narrow and shallow discipline of economics. Good teaching [preaching] is an investment in the minds [souls] of the young, as obscure in result, as remote from immediate proof as planting a chestnut seedling. But we have come to prefer ends that are entirely foreseeable, even though that requires us to foreshorten our vision. Education [religious life] is coming to be, not a long-term investment in young minds [souls] and in the life of the community [congregation], but a short-term investment in the economy. We want to be able to tell how many dollars a community [congregation] is worth and how soon it will begin to pay.[4]

Peterson's experiment notwithstanding, as much as the advocates of the traditional church might learn from Berry about care and nurture, they have a hard time appropriating his remarks about the institutional church. In *The Unsettling of America*, for example, Berry argues that

Christianity has been responsible for cultivating the industrial tendency of specialization. "At some point," he writes, "we began to assume that the life of the body would be the business of grocers and medical doctors, who need take no interest in the spirit, whereas the life of the spirit would be the business of churches, which would have at best only a negative interest in the body." This division of labor established a spiritual economy based on stark competition. "If the soul is to live in this world only by denying the body, then its relation to worldly life becomes extremely simple and superficial." The result is that religion has no "worldly purpose or force." "To fail to employ the body in this world," Berry warns, "at once for its own good and the good of the soul is to issue an invitation to disorder of the most serious kind."[5] The lesson seems to be that whatever churches may learn from farming, the work of farmers bears no resemblance to that of contemporary pastors.

Can traditional Christians, then, legitimately appeal to Berry for support? The short answer is yes. The longer answer, the one that follows, is that to take Berry on his own terms about the health of persons and the need to overcome the modern dualism that separates body and soul, husband and wife, individuals and community, is not only to conceive of the church in rural or pastoral ways that run counter to the most popular forms of Christianity in the United States, such as evangelical Protestantism, but also will involve overcoming a dualism in Berry's own understanding of Christianity. As much as he rejects the division of the physical and the spiritual, Berry's own account of Christianity relies upon a division that pits the spirit of Christianity against its form (or body). Overcoming that dualism will necessarily involve other tensions and paradoxes. But the case that Berry makes unintentionally for a traditional and agrarian, as opposed to a modern and industrial, form of Christianity points the way toward recovering a churchly form of religion that shares Berry's concern for health and wholeness. That form of Christianity may even be one of his best allies in resisting the acids of industrialism.

The Greater Divorce

Arguably, Berry's most extensive reflection on religion comes in a section of *The Unsettling of America* where the author himself acknowledges that the stakes of healthy agriculture for bodies, the earth, and souls are high. To alert readers to the magnitude of those stakes, Berry raises the subject of suicide on the way to making a poignant observation about health. A book about agriculture should include the subject of suicide, he argues, because the isolation of the body from the earth that prevails in unsettled America inevitably produces the sort of loneliness and despair that exacerbate those spiritual wounds that aggravate an imperfect human existence.

In contrast to the modern idea of health as the absence of pain and disease, Berry contends for one grounded in wholeness. "To be healthy is to be whole." This wholeness is not merely physical but also spiritual and ecological. Berry quotes Blake, "Man has no Body distinct from the Soul," thus affirming the intimate tie between health and holiness. Yet, man's dependence on Creation also reveals that the wholeness of the individual body is bound up with the health of other bodies. "Our bodies are . . . not distinct," he writes, "from the bodies of other people, on which they depend in a complexity of ways from biological to spiritual."[6] To approach health simply as the domain of the medical profession is "absurd." In fact, to heal the body alone is to "collaborate in the destruction of the body" and to perpetuate wounds that cannot be healed, such as those that sometimes lead to suicide.

From this starting point, Berry shows how the isolation of the body winds up destroying the body. An important factor is a division between body and spirit that results in a competition between body and soul, a zero-sum game where the body thrives at the expense of the spirit and vice versa. The spirituality produced by this competition is an otherworldly faith in which the soul prospers by denying the body. The soul's relation to the world is too "simple and superficial" for faith to have "any worldly purpose or force." In turn, the body proceeds to devalue and exploit the spirit by comforting and indulging the body. Such disrespect for the body gives a bizarre twist to the so-called culture wars. Berry writes, "The 'dialogue of body and soul' in our time is being carried on between those who despise the body for the sake of its resurrection and those, diseased by bodily extravagance and lack of exercise, who nevertheless desire longevity above all things." These groups think they oppose each other, but in truth "they could not exist apart."[7]

The condition of the body in unsettled America, thanks to this existential duel, is not pretty. Berry asserts that "we are wasting our bodies exactly as we are wasting our land." "Our bodies are fat, weak, joyless, sickly, ugly, the virtual prey of the manufacturers of medicine and cosmetics." "After the games and idle flourishes of modern youth," we use our bodies "only as shipping cartons to transport our brains and our few employable muscles back and forth to work." The health of our souls, despite all signs from the leading spiritual indicators of gross national spirit, is no better. One source of spiritual comfort for many modern people is the thrill of buying goods. Another is the news. "No longer in need of the exalted drama of grief and joy," Berry laments, our souls "feed now on little shocks of greed, scandal, and violence."[8]

The question of spiritual health eventually leads Berry to criticize the church. By isolating the body and narrowing our idea of wholeness, "the life of the spirit for many Christians is reduced to a dull preoccupation with getting to heaven." The body has practically no responsibility to God's work of Creation. It may destroy the earth, or it may exploit other bodies, and yet the soul remains pristine and uncontaminated. Again, the body functions as a mere container, this time for the soul, a "mere 'package,' that will nevertheless light up in eternity, forever cool and shiny as a neon cross." For Berry, such spiritual Christianity is a blight upon the church. "This separation of the soul from the body and from the world is no disease of the fringe . . . but a fracture that runs through the mentality of institutional religion like a geological fault."[9]

Health for Berry, then, is a condition of wholeness. And the way to heal the divisions of unsettled society is to restore the connections between body and earth, persons and communities, husbands and wives, body and soul. These frayed relationships form a complex web that refuses any form of isolated or specialized treatment. "The body is damaged," Berry writes, "by the bewilderment of the spirit, and it conducts the influence of the bewilderment into the earth, the earth conducts it into the community, and so on." In contrast, healing restores "connections of the various parts—in this way restoring the ultimate simplicity of their union."[10] The question that Berry's understanding of health invites is whether modern Christianity is capable of assisting in the restoration of these connections.

Berry versus the Bible

Berry's reflections on the body and soul obviously reveal a man who is friendly to a theistic point of view even if he is not the best friend of organized Christianity. His beef with Christianity falls into two categories. The first is the more plausible critique and concerns the institutional church's uncritical embrace of the industrial economy. The second involves the church's misreading of the Bible itself, a claim that ironically commits Berry to furthering the divisions that exist between body and soul, this time between Christianity as a body and Christianity as a spirit.

Berry's criticism of organized religion runs from practical to theoretical considerations. One example of his practical concern comes from his objection to the way denominations treat rural congregations. The specific problem is that of using "the rural ministry as a training ground for young ministers, and as a means of subsidizing their education." The disrespect for rural people is twofold. First, it assumes that persons not yet eligible for ministry are qualified to minister to rural people. Second, it "encourages young ministers to leave rural parishes as soon as possible and to find a 'normal' congregation." Berry writes, "The denominational hierarchies . . . evidently regard country places in exactly the same way as 'the economy' does: as sources of economic power to be exploited for the advantage of 'better' places." The rural churches invariably receive the impression that "as country people, they do not matter much." In the words of one of Berry's Christian friends, "The soul of the plowboy ain't worth as much as the soul of the delivery boy."[11] Berry's plausible deduction is that if the church is "mostly indifferent to the work and the people by which the link between economy and ecosystem must be enacted, it is no wonder that [the church is] mostly indifferent to the fate of the ecosystems themselves."[12]

Along similar lines, Berry sees in the modern church no interest in any "feature of culture by which humankind connects itself to nature: economy or work, science or art." Sermons reflect almost no awareness of preaching as an art. Christian songs assume that "religion is no more than vaguely pious (and vaguely romantic) emotion." And "most modern churches look like they were built by robots without reference to the heritage of church architecture or respect for the site; they embody no awareness that work can be worship."[13]

Berry also detects that in its evangelistic endeavors, the church has embraced the models of the industrial economy. Modern Christianity has become "wholly concentrated upon the industrial shibboleths of 'growth,' counting its success in numbers, and upon the very strange enterprise of 'saving' the individual, isolated, and disembodied soul."[14] The modern church even presumes to try to save people in other countries who are often better stewards of the earth than are Christians. These realities lead Berry to conclude that modern Christianity has become "willy-nilly the religion of the state and the economic status quo." By concentrating its energy and resources on the spiritual, the church has generally stood "silently by, while a predatory economy has ravaged the world, destroyed its natural beauty and health, divided and plundered its human communities and households."[15] The indictment could not be more devastating for those of us who are members of the industrial church. The church, according to Berry,

> has flown the flag and chanted the slogans of empire. It has assumed with the economists that "economic forces" automatically work for good and has assumed with the industrialists and militarists that technology determines history. It has assumed with almost everybody that "progress" is good, that it is good to be modern and up with the times. It has admired Caesar and comforted him in his depredations and defaults.[16]

The defects of the modern church, Berry argues, flow directly from the theoretical flaw already mentioned, namely the divorce of body and soul. From childhood, most Christians are encouraged "to think of the church building as 'God's house,' while attaching a similar conception to their shops or farms or factories could only happen with great effort and embarrassment." The condition of the nonholy places is even worse than the artless church buildings that house holy activity. These places of employment are ones of "desecration, deeply involved in the ruin of Creation."[17] Because the church has nurtured the view that the "body is a kind of scrip issued by the Great Company Store in the Sky, which can be cashed in to redeem the soul," most modern Christians can appreciate only the spiritual or mental aspects of Creation. The flipside of this spiritualized view is a "semi-conscious hatred of the 'physical' or 'natural' part," and a willingness to destroy the physical for "'salvation,' for profit, for 'victory,' or for fun. This madness constitutes the normality of modern humanity and of modern Christianity."[18] This dualism, furthermore, is hardly religious or Christian. Berry reasons that when we divide the world into two parts and regard only the spiritual as "good or desirable," then the Christian's relation to Creation becomes "arbitrary." Creation's only value is quantitative. In turn, we set ourselves up as the judges and so inevitably "the destroyers of a world we did not make, and that we are bidden to understand as a divine gift."[19] So much for reverence and awe before the handiwork of God the Creator of all things visible and invisible.

Owing to his distrust of organized Christianity, Berry proposes a different version of salvation than the one chiefly promulgated by the institutional church. Instead of regarding belonging to the body of Christ as at least one important manifestation of spiritual wholeness, Berry conceives of salvation as the quest of the solitary individual who leaves home to discover the truth of reality. In some ways, the model for this quest is the Earl of Gloucester from *King Lear*, who, led by his son, Edgar, ascends what seems to be a cliff and throws himself off it only to regain his senses and so is "saved by a renewal of his sense of the world and his proper place in it."[20] Berry acknowledges that this is not uniquely a Christian idea but actually permeates the imagination and literature of the West. He describes it the following way:

> Seeking enlightenment or the Promised Land or the way home, a man would go or be forced to go into the wilderness, measure himself against the Creation, recognize finally his true place within it, and thus be saved both from pride and from despair. Seeing himself as a tiny member of a world he cannot comprehend or master or in any final sense possess, he cannot possibly think of himself as a god. . . . Returning from the wilderness, he becomes a restorer of order, a preserver. He sees the truth, recognizes his true heir, honors his forebears and his heritage, and gives his blessing to his successors.[21]

This perspective on the Creation and man's place in it is clearly a vision that organized churches lack. How could they possibly regard the relation between people and Creation this way when they have contributed to the isolation of body and soul?

At other times, Berry indicates that the sort of restorative vision that Gloucester obtained in *Lear* is also fundamental to the teaching of the Bible. He concedes that scripture sometimes gives "exhausting" detail to the forms and orders of religion, such as the Old Testament's instruction on the Temple, its rites, and the priests' duties and clothing. But he also contends that the "most significant religious events" in the Bible are "unorganized" and sometimes "profoundly disruptive of organization." "From Abraham to Jesus," Berry writes, "the most important people are not priests but shepherds, soldiers, men of property, craftsmen, housewives, queens and kings, manservants and maidservants, fishermen, prisoners, whores, even bureaucrats." As such, the "great visionary encounters" did not take place within the confines of organized religion but "in sheep pastures, in the desert, in the wilderness, on mountains, by rivers and on beaches, in the middle of the sea; when there was no choice, they happened in prisons." The liturgical lesson is that no matter how much God prescribed rites and religious ceremonies, he "just as strenuously repudiated them when they were taken to be religion."[22] This lesson even allows Berry to render the Amish as primarily a community and a culture without any significant reference to its religious order or organization. For instance, while Berry acknowledges that the Amish are bound together by "spiritual authority," he also fails to mention the church when listing Amish institutions. The Amish have "only two" institutions, the family and the community, both of which take care of all their needs as a people.[23]

The anti-institutional strain that Berry sees in the Bible prompts him to read the pages of Holy Writ in ways that are generally marginal to the main contours of historic Christian theology. For instance, Berry speculates that the Bible has been underappreciated as an outdoor book. "It is a 'hypaethral book,' such as Theoreau talked about—a book open to the sky." This means that it is best "read and understood outdoors, and the farther outdoors the better." "Passages that within walls seem improbable or incredible," he explains, "outdoors seem natural." The reason is that outside "we are confronted everywhere with wonders; we see the miraculous is not extraordinary, but the common mode of existence." Anyone who has truly considered the lilies of the field or the birds of the air, and pondered their improbability "in this warm world within the cold and empty stellar distances, will hardly balk at the turning of water into wine."[24] But to read the Bible in "a closed, air-conditioned building" is to miss entirely the extraordinary ordinariness of the book's message.

Buoyed by the Bible's affirmation of Creation and untethered from the constraints of organized religion, Berry has rendered some interpretations of different passages that would be hard to square with those of the doctors of the church. For instance, Christ's teaching in Matthew 6, "Therefore take no thought, saying What shall we eat? or, What shall we drink? or, Wherewithall shall we be clothed? . . . But seek ye first the kingdom of God, and his righteousness; and all these things shall be added unto you," becomes for Berry a pivotal piece of instruction about the "Great Economy," that is, "the ultimate condition of our experience and of the practical questions rising from our experience . . ."[25] As much as this text might have suggested originally an otherworldly orientation for Christ's disciples, Berry argues that such an interpretation "makes the text useless and meaningless to humans who must live in this world." For that reason, he takes these verses "as a statement of considerable practical import about the real nature of worldly economy." To read it in a dualistic way would "have the odd result of making good people not only feckless but also dependent upon bad people busy with quite other seekings." Consequently, the right understanding of the text points to giving an "obviously necessary priority to the Great Economy over any little economy made within it."[26]

Berry's reading is not without difficulty, since Christ at other places says that his kingdom is not of this world and also seems to indicate that his followers are a narrower portion of humanity than the universalistic implication of the Great Economy or the created order's claims upon all people who draw their sustenance from the earth. It is to be sure a valiant effort to reconcile the apparently otherworldy aspects of Christ's teaching with Berry's this-worldly concern for this world. But by venturing out into the wilderness with the Bible and returning to the community with his own interpretation, Berry has more or less repudiated Christian interpreters of scripture who even before the rise of industrialism recognized a religious holiness that pointed beyond this world to a new heavens and a new earth. To his credit, Berry has acknowledged that his estrangement from organized religion could lead to a form of religious individualism. "I am far from thinking that one can somehow become righteous by carrying protestantism to the logical conclusion of a one-person church."[27] Even so, his caution against going it alone is in tension with his own understanding of salvation as an individual quest for wholeness.

Which brings us back to folks like Eugene Peterson who have seen in Berry a confirmation of what the Bible teaches about the organized or institutional church. According to this perspective, Scripture's own conception of the church is pastoral or agrarian, and the formal qualities of salvation are analogous if not parallel to the ways that living things grow. This does not mean that Berry's critique of the contemporary church is without merit. The point is only that by reading the Bible and conceiving of salvation in a way that stresses the ecological and physical over a spiritual understanding that gives priority if not equal weight to the soul and the afterlife, Berry may actually have cut off a potential ally in his call for healing the dualism that afflicts our unsettled state of affairs. In other words, Berry may have failed to see how the ways of the institutional church, no matter how flawed in practice, actually resonate with his call for sensitivity to the interrelatedness of body and soul, the created order and the world of the spirit.

The places in scripture where Christian devotion and organized religion become comprehensible through natural or agrarian imagery are too numerous to mention. Jesus himself refers to his relationship with his followers as that between a shepherd and his flock. In John 10, Jesus identifies himself as the good shepherd who even dies for his sheep, in contrast to the hired servant who, when seeing a wolf about to attack the flock, flees because he does not care for the sheep. Later in John's Gospel (chap. 21), Jesus also uses the metaphor of a shepherd when restoring Peter to fellowship and commissioning him to feed Christ's sheep. Also in the Gospel of John is Jesus' instruction (chap. 15) in which the relationship between Christ and his followers is likened to the organic tie between a vine and branches. "Abide in me, and I in you. As the branch cannot bear fruit of itself, except it abide in the vine; no more can ye, except ye abide in me. I am the vine, ye are the branches: He that abideth in me, and I in him, the same bringeth forth much fruit: for without me ye can do nothing."

Jesus also tried to explain the preaching of the word in the parable of the sower, an illustration that could not help but give the organized church some awareness of farmers and the care of the land. Matthew 13:36–38 reads:

Behold, a sower went forth to sow; And when he sowed, some seeds fell by the way side, and the fowls came and devoured them up: Some fell upon stony places, where they had not much earth: and forthwith they sprung up, because they had no deepness of earth: And when the sun was up, they were scorched; and because they had no root, they withered away. And some fell among thorns; and the thorns sprung up, and choked them: But other fell into good ground, and brought forth fruit, some an hundredfold, some sixtyfold, some thirtyfold.

This is one of those rare parables where Jesus did not leave his disciples in the dark but explained the meaning to them. Part of his explanation involved this comparison between the planting of seeds and the preaching of the word: "But he that received seed into the good ground is he that heareth the word, and understandeth it; which also beareth fruit, and bringeth forth, some an hundredfold, some sixty, some thirty."

Another agrarian-friendly reading of organized Christianity comes from the apostle Paul in his first letter to the Corinthians where, to explain his relationship to other pastors, Paul compares himself to a farmer. He wrote: "Who then is Paul, and who is Apollos, but ministers by whom ye believed, even as the Lord gave to every man? I have planted, Apollos watered; but God gave the increase. So then neither is he that planteth any thing, neither he that watereth; but God that giveth the increase." One last example of the Bible's use of natural images to explain spiritual realities comes later in that same letter to the Corinthians when Paul, trying to explain the mystery of the resurrection of the body, resorts to the natural world. Paul writes:

All flesh is not the same flesh: but there is one kind of flesh of men, another flesh of beasts, another of fishes, and another of birds. There are also celestial bodies, and bodies terrestrial: but the glory of the celestial is one, and the glory of the terrestrial is another. There is one glory of the sun, and another glory of the moon, and another glory of the stars: for one star differeth from another star in glory. So also is the resurrection of the dead. It is sown in corruption; it is raised in incorruption: It is sown in dishonour; it is raised in glory: it is sown in weakness; it is raised in power: It is sown a natural body; it is raised a spiritual body. There is a natural body, and there is a spiritual body.

Whatever these stupendous analogies may mean, they do demonstrate how the spiritual and otherworldly aspects of Christianity, which are ministered by the institutional church, are deeply embedded in the ordinary world of bodies, plants, earth, and the physical universe.

These pastoral and organic conceptions of institutional Christianity find expression in various places within Western Christianity's formal teaching. A couple of examples will have to suffice for the purposes of this essay.[28]

The first example is part of the Belgic Confession's (1561) instruction on the Lord's Supper, a creed written for Protestant churches in the Low Lands and subsequently used by the Reformed churches in the Netherlands. It starts with an assertion of dualism that is by no means promising in the light of Berry's critique above.

Now those who are regenerated have in them a twofold life: the one corporal and temporal, which they have from the first birth and is common to all men; the other spiritual and heavenly, which is given them in their second birth, which is effected by the word of the gospel in the communion of the body of Christ: and this life is not common, but is peculiar to God's elect.[29]

More needs to be said about the exclusive or nonpublic dimension of organized Christianity, but for now what is worth observing in this article of faith is the analogy between physical and spiritual life. The Belgic Confession recognizes that they are both distinct and interrelated. Spiritual life cannot exist apart from the created world. The Confession goes on to observe the parallels between the means for sustaining body and soul:

In like manner God has given us, for the support of the bodily and earthly life, earthly and common bread which is subservient thereto and is common to all men, even as life itself. But for the support of the spiritual and heavenly life which believers have, he has sent a living bread which descended from heaven, namely, Jesus Christ, who nourishes and strengthens the spiritual life of believers when they eat Him, that is to say, when they apply and receive him by faith and in the Spirit.[30]

One of the important implications of this sacramental teaching is that spiritual life is not mechanical or instantaneous but actually is dependent on means of sustenance in the same way that bodies are dependent on the fruit of the earth. It renders the work of the institutional church as a relationship between pastors and people where ministers supply members with necessary nourishment in ways comparable to the farmer's provision for his crop or the shepherd's for his flock.

This conception of the Christian ministry and church membership produced counsel such as the following from the German Reformed Church as late as 1902. It was part of the denomination's instructions to catechumens who are about to participate in their first Communion. Not only does this counsel draw a parallel between bodily and spiritual development and health; it also contrasts its own character with a version of spiritual life that is instantaneous and almost industrial. In contrast to merely flicking a switch, this organic piety is gradual, taking root and bearing fruit over time. This fitness for confirmation "may be called a 'change of heart,' though this is only another name for conversion." The statement begins as follows:

> This change is not sudden, but runs through years. You have not had any wonderful religious experiences, such as you hear about in others; but the Holy Ghost has done much in you in a very quiet way. Nor need you doubt your conversion, your change of heart, because you cannot tell the day when it took place, as many profess to do. It did not take place in a day, or you might tell it. It is the growth of years (Mark 4:26–28), and therefore all the more reliable. You cannot tell when you learned to walk, talk, think and work. You do not know when you learned to love your earthly father, much less the heavenly. This is the Reformed doctrine of "getting religion." We get religion, not in bulk but little by little. Just as we get natural life and strength, so spiritual life and strength, day by day.[31]

What is notable is the way this understanding of religious devotion draws upon the realities of bodily existence. The soul is bound up with the body, to be sure. But even more than this obvious point, it affirms that the soul is dependent on the means of grace administered by spiritual overseers in ways similar to the sort of interdependence that exists between eaters and farmers, and bodies and the land. This is not simply a different understanding of salvation and spiritual health from the lone prophet who ventures into the wilderness. It is also a different notion about the life of the spirit that, while relying on an important distinction between body and soul, nevertheless recognizes the interdependence of bodies, souls, and Creation. The human spirit envisioned is not an autonomous entity that receives edification only from direct infusions of the divine Spirit, as if independent of the body. The older understanding of the soul reflected in Christianity's sacramental teaching and liturgical practices recognizes the soul's relationship to the body and the means by which the elements of bread, wine, water, and words read by the eyes and heard by the ears sustain spiritual life. This soul is not only dependent on the body for receiving the sacraments and religious guidance, but that same body is dependent on the created order that produces bread and wine for the Lord's Supper, unpolluted water for baptism, trees for the publication of Holy Writ, and healthy physicians of the soul who care for the flock.

This is by no means an airtight case for an agrarian-friendly conception of institutional Christianity. But the points mentioned thus far may be sufficient to indicate the ways in which a Christianity that tries to do justice to the otherworldly character of the faith—that is, to the real and substantial claims made for the priority of the soul over the body—is also a form of devotion that depends fundamentally and ordinarily on Creation, the body, and the bodies and communities that care for the land. Instead of leading to neglect and waste, this older form of Christianity and its high regard for the church's spiritual ministry through physical means, even its otherworldliness, cannot help but make its adherents aware of their dependence on Creation as well as the rhythms of the natural world that not only teach about but also embody the ways of faith. If this is so, then a better and older form of Christianity may actually provide the healing and wholeness that Berry advocates, this time by reconnecting body and soul, church and spirit, liturgical rites and spiritual vitality.

## Complications to Restoring Wholeness

If the reading of Berry and organized Christianity offered thus far has any plausibility, then reconciling the former's call for wholeness with the latter's version of healing may appear to be possible if not likely. At the same time, as much as the church would do well to appropriate Berry, tensions between his and the church's account of healing need to be acknowledged. Before concluding on what I hope is a chord in a major key, I need to give some attention to disagreements or complications that will sound less harmonious.

In his reflection on health, Berry rightly faults moderns for being excessively narrow, for thinking of human flourishing primarily as the absence of disease or being physically fit. But he may be guilty of a kind of narrowness by not paying sufficient attention to the soul in his own conception of wholeness. Granted, his concern in the particular passage from the *Unsettling of America* that I have in mind is the body and its dependence on the well-being of the earth, other persons, and their communities. Still, if it is wrong to discount the body when considering spiritual wholeness, why not give more attention to the soul, not as an aspect of the human person that is isolated from the body, but rather as one that has its own needs for spiritual nutrients? The impression yielded at points in Berry's writings is that a soul can be healthy through a body that is properly connected to the rest of Creation. For instance, he asks, how can the body be whole "and yet be dependent, as it obviously is, upon other bodies and upon the earth, upon all the rest of Creation, in fact?" Our bodies, he continues "are not distinct from the cycles of feeding and in the intricate companionships of ecological systems and of the spirit."[32] But aside from the sort of vision that comes to Gloucester at the end of *King Lear*, Berry does not attend to the equally complex systems of spiritual feeding and intricate religious relationships that affect a healthy embodied soul.

To be sure, Berry's understanding of Creation and explicit recognition of its Creator is a step toward a healthy spirit. Proverbs says that the fear of the Lord is the beginning of wisdom, and fear usually involves awe. Berry's recognition of a Creator-haunted universe is a crucial part of restoring the connections between creatures and their maker. But is it enough? Christianity's answer has generally been "no." The heavens declare the glory of God, but as the apostle Paul wrote in Romans, that knowledge is only sufficient to condemn fallen men and women.[33] Christianity has generally taught more than God as Creator. It moves on, perhaps too quickly, but still goes on to confess God as Redeemer.

The mention of redemption is another feature in Berry's account of wholeness that creates difficulties for harmonizing his arguments with traditional Christianity. Seldom mentioned in his accounts of alienation and division that proliferate in our earthly existence is the alienation between creatures made in God's image and their Creator. He asks, "[w]hat is the burden of the Bible if not a sense of the mutuality of influence, rising out of an essential unity, among soul and body and community and world?" Berry insists that the aim of the Bible, at least as he reads it, is as a "handbook" on the interaction of the spirit and the world. "The world," he explains, "is certainly thought of as a place of spiritual trial, but it is also the confluence of soul and body, word and flesh, where thoughts must become deeds, where goodness is to be enacted."[34] To call this rendering of the Bible this-worldly would not be inaccurate, and Berry would likely regard such a judgment as praiseworthy.

But Christianity has also interpreted the Bible as more than this-worldly. Scripture also has important if not necessarily otherworldly aspects that have directly to do with the division between God and man that resulted from the Fall. Berry is indeed correct to read the Bible as a rejection of Creation as evil and something from which to liberate the spirit. Still, an affirmation of Creation's goodness does not deal sufficiently with the Bible's record of man's fallenness. From the perspective of Genesis 3, one could plausibly argue that the aim of the Bible is to try to restore fellowship between God and Adam. That restoration is not independent of Adam's original call to work in the garden. But the work of gardening will not make up for Adam's disobedience—hence the need for redemption by the last Adam. That Berry does not address this part of the Christian message is not a reason for rejecting his laudable arguments for this world. But neither does his account of wholeness do justice to spiritual health as understood by historic Christianity.

To mention spiritual health as typically understood by the church is to raise the topic of a Christian spirituality that, as Berry has rightly noted, has forsaken the body and Creation. Consequently, if Berry has not given adequate attention to a healthy soul, the church has not done justice to healthy bodies. He has rendered a fairly good account of the church's fail-ure, but it is possible to extend his argument from a general objection about a dualism that the church has cultivated between body and spirit to a more specific critique of a certain sector of American Protestantism. Because Berry's own Christian practice has been conducted in the context of the Southern Baptist Convention, the failings that he notes may have even more to do with the spirituality latent in evangelical Protestantism than with the historic tensions in Western Christianity between form and spirit.

Indications that Berry intuits particular strains within evangelical Protestantism come from the repeated way that he invokes disparagingly the word *evangelist* to refer to the proponents of agribusiness, economic growth, industrialism, or even progress. For instance, in his discussion of contraception in *The Unsettling of America*, Berry writes that the "public-ity on this subject is typically evangelical in tone and simplistically moral; the operations are recommended like commercial products by advertis-ings complete with exuberant testimonials of satisfied customers and appeals to the prospective customer's maturity, sexual pride, and desire for freedom."[35] Later in the book when discussing agricultural practices and policies, he remarks about a "widespread orthodoxy of agriculture" that is comparable to orthodoxies in religion—"an agriculture, that is to say, which is nearly uniform in technology and in its general assumptions and ambitions over a whole continent, and which, like many religions, aspires to become 'universal' by means of a sort of evangelism proclaiming that 'Other countries would do well to copy it.'"[36] For whatever reason, Berry senses something intrinsic to the evangelist as someone who is always on the go, advancing a cause, never settled, never tied, never content.

This is an astute reading of evangelical Protestantism. This form of Christianity arose in the early eighteenth century as the driving impulse of the so-called First Great Awakening. Until that time, the model of the Protestant ministry, with the exception of the missionary who would not emerge as a permanent religious figure until almost a century later, was the local pastor or settled minister. He was typically rooted in a particular town or place, caring for the people in that community, and passing on the teachings and leading the practices of his particular branch of the Reformation. This Protestantism was primarily local and communal. It took international or cosmopolitan expression only in the form of church councils. With the revivals of the First Great Awakening, however, itinerant evangelists became legendary, and their quest for new converts (often reenergizing people already under the care of local pastors) took them wherever horses or ships could go. The new form of Protestantism elevated the spirit over the form of religion in a way unprecedented in the history of the church. Evangelists like George Whitefield sought in his listeners a new birth or conversion and did not care particularly about denominational affiliation, whether his own or that of his hearers who were often members of other churches. The devotion that he promoted was indiscriminate. No matter what a person's church membership or place of residence, he or she could belong to this grander movement of the Spirit by being born again. As such, the convert's identity as an evangelical was primarily interior or subjective and spiritual. Outward forms did not matter because they were not reliable indicators of genuine faith. By stressing experience as the sign of authentic faith, evangelicalism divorced the spirit of Christianity from its forms and bodies (both individual and communal). This was otherworldliness with a vengeance, which ironically unleashed a crusading spirit to bring heaven down to earth.[37]

This new form of Protestantism has been an enabler for industrialism, approaching Christianity and church work with most of the gusto of modernity's evangelists. Three examples of Berry's critique of industrialism apply with equal force to the mechanical practices and mind-set of evangelical Protestantism. The first concerns the notion of our era's spiritual crisis. Evangelicals often respond to the problems of immorality or secularism in the same way that the proponents of agribusiness react to the food crisis; they don't try to "do" church better but instead produce more forms of deformed piety. Berry's critique of agribusiness executives who use the reality of hunger to advocate poor farming practices is one that evangelical parachurch and megachurch leaders would well heed:

> Millions are threatened with starvation—so the argument runs— therefore we must continue to farm in larger monocultures on larger holdings with fewer farmers, larger and more expensive machines, more chemicals. . . . How the future might be served by careless and destructive practices in the present is a question that is simply overridden by the brazen glibness of official optimism. If there is a food crisis, then, according to specialist logic, we must produce more food more carelessly than ever before.[38]

The very premise for relying on the mass and crass forms of Christianity that flourish in the United States runs on the fuel that the spiritual crisis of our age is so great that it demands genetically engineered spiritual nourishment.

A second example concerns a similar tendency among evangelicals to behave in ways that Berry refers to as exploitation. That is a rough word, to be sure, but it does justice to the lack of care for nurture that many proponents of progress and vital religion display. Berry writes in *The Unsettling of America*:

> I conceive the strip-miner to be a model exploiter, and as a model nurturer I take the old-fashioned idea or ideal of a farmer. The exploiter is a specialist, an expert; the nurturer is not. The standard of the exploiter is efficiency; the standard of the nurturer is care. . . . The exploiter wishes to earn as much as possible by as little work as possible; the nurturer expects, certainly, to have a decent living from his work, but his characteristic wish is to work *as well* as possible. The competence of the exploiter is in organization, that of the nurturer is in order—a human order, that is, that accommodates itself both to other order and to mystery. The exploiter typically serves an institution or organization; the nurturer serves land, household, community, place. The exploiter thinks in terms of numbers, quantities, "hard facts"; the nurturer in terms of character, condition, quality, kind.[39]

Of course, many evangelicals would not recognize themselves or their labors in a quotation like that (if only because of sincere commitment to doing good). They don't believe they are destroying the religious environment. But they rarely consider the perspective of the settled pastors who have to clean up or work around the religious debris left by the itinerant evangelist or the numerous religious entrepreneurs who compete for adherents and financial support. Evangelicals often think that their work is done once they have secured a person's conversion. An ordinary pastor, though, is in for the long haul and feels compelled to shepherd those converts well beyond the first flush of faith.

The last example of parallels between evangelicalism and industrialism is a disposition toward globalism. Evangelicals rarely exhibit loyalty to denominations or theological traditions; their faith transcends such locales or particularities. This is why John Wesley could say with a straight face that the *world* was his parish. But Berry has a very different view of globalism and its inherent danger to the local:

> ... one cannot live in the world; that is, one cannot become, in the easy, generalizing sense with which the phrase is commonly used, a "world citizen." There can be no such thing as a "global village." No matter how much one may love the world as a whole, one can live fully in it only by living responsibly in some small part of it. Where we live and who we live there with define the terms of our relationship to the world and to humanity. We thus come again to the paradox that one can become whole only by the responsible acceptance of one's partiality.[40]

The same could well be said for Christianity's religious environment. A believer cannot be part of a global Christianity without accepting first one's own place in a local congregation and the tradition to which such a church belongs.

These examples indicate that the dualism Berry sees in modern Christianity is deeply ingrained in American Protestantism in ways that he could only intuit. Consequently, for the contemporary church to listen to Berry, it will need not simply a greater awareness of its place in Creation but actually another kind of Christianity, one that values rootedness, particularity, and the ordinary.

The Enduring Paradox

Yet even if these obstacles to reconciling Berry and traditional Christianity could be removed, a deeper tension may exist, one that separates the audiences for Berry's agrarianism from Christianity's organicism. In the end, one need not be a Christian to feel the force of Berry's arguments. In fact, one can be a good farmer without being baptized. The reverse relationship is not as obviously correct because those who have been baptized, as Berry well shows, have an obligation to be good stewards of the good gifts of their Creator and Redeemer. Indeed, one of the ironies of the church's grappling with Berry is that his arguments actually have more force with Christians specifically, and theists more generally, than with the average agnostic who is on the fence about whether Creation is actually created. As otherworldly as Christianity may be in its promise of a new heaven and new earth, its official versions have always rejected as heresies—such as Gnosticism, Manicheanism, and Docetism—any version of the faith that depicted Creation or embodiment as less than good or that suggested the body and the created order were unworthy of care and cultivation. The gospel may tempt Christians to flee the world, but the narrative of Genesis will not allow them to get very far. Even the promise of a new creation includes resurrected bodies, lions that don't eat lambs, and wedding feasts of some duration. Nevertheless, Berry's account of Creation does not require belief in the resurrection or a new creation. Consequently, his outlook has the potential of convincing people who are unconvinced of Christianity's truth, a possibility that reveals the paradoxical relationship between organic Christianity and Berry's agrarianism. To put this relationship as pithily as possible, Berry's arguments are cogent for everyone who eats, but Christian teaching is not necessary in this life for human bodies that depend on food.

Despite this admission of Christianity's exclusivity, the question remains whether Berry still needs Christianity, not in the sense that baptism will lead Christian farmers to use draft horses, but from the perspective of Christian communions that have sufficient resilience, wisdom, and vitality to resist the gospel of industrial progress. At the end of his essay "The Whole Horse," Berry responds to the repeated charge that his arguments lead to hopelessness because his critique of modernity leaves apparently the only alternative of "turning back the clock." "My own aim," he writes, "is not hopelessness. I am not looking for reasons to give up. I am looking for reasons to keep on. . . . to show how the effort of conservation could be enlarged and strengthened."[41] This effort of enlarging the conservationist impulse extends to all people working to save something of value—"not just wilderness places, wild rivers, wildlife habitat, species diversity, water quality, and air quality, but also agricultural land, family farms and ranches, communities, children and childhood, local schools, local economies, local food markets, livestock breeds and domestic plant varieties, fine old buildings, scenic roads, and so on."[42] Berry does not include small and local congregations on that list of things that people are trying to conserve, but I would venture the claim that he should if only because the behemoth that is the United States is populated by many people who go to church but have no understanding of the value of what is old, small, and given. If American Christians could be persuaded from pursuing a Home Depot form of ministry, whether advocated by the likes of a Rick Warren or a Joel Osteen, and realize the benefits that come from locally produced religion, overseen by spiritual shepherds who care for the health and quality of their flocks, they might actually be enlisted in what Berry calls the "sometimes lonely battles to preserve things of value that they cannot bear to lose."[43]

But for these believers to be enlisted in the "shared stewardship of all the diversity of good things that are needed for the health and abundance of the world," they will need to be able to see the difference between exploiters and nurturers, between efficiency and order, between account-ability and belonging—which is to say, they will need to reckon with Wendell Berry. His outlook is congenial to an older form of Christian-ity, whether Eastern, Roman Catholic, or Protestant, that highly regards the rites, ceremonies, holy days, and patterns of inheritance upon which Christians for most of two millennia relied. But these forms of Christian devotion and ministry have generally been the healthiest in out-of-the-way places on the margins of industrial society. Just as the health of a good farm depends on its ability to "produce independently of the ups and downs of the Dow Jones industrial averages or the vagaries of politics,"[44] so the health of a church depends on its ability to produce strong faith irrespective of the latest Gallup Poll or the fortunes of the Religious Right or the National Council of Churches. In other words, the church needs to understand that small and local are not only beautiful but also true and good. To do this, it needs to take Berry to heart—and also to body, soul, strength, and mind.

# II

# The Rediscovery of *Oikonomia*

## *Mark Shiffman*

Modern economics has an embarrassing old uncle it hid in the attic so long ago that it has pretty well managed to forget his existence. It is ashamed of this uncle and has repressed his memory for two reasons. First, it is named after this crazy old coot, who is called in distressingly archaic fashion "Oikonomia." Second, if it were to be mindful of its namesake, it would have to face up to its illegitimacy. For modern economics is draped in the mantle of a distinguished lineage: it is the child of modern science and modern political philosophy, which are recognized heirs of Lady Philosophy but with a rather shady title to the inheritance. *Oikonomia*, on the other hand, is a product of her union with Aristotle, a very respectable figure in his day.

But if Aristotle is less respectable today than when he begat *oikonomia*, the latter is far less respectable still. Perhaps this is a third reason for blotting out his memory: he is embarrassingly behind the times. He is in fact a mad farmer. Fortunately, he is not entirely confined in his prison. His voice and spirit have been channeled by another mad farmer, Wendell Berry. This channeling, if we attend to it carefully, can provide us the opportunity to judge for ourselves whether the old codger's madness is really derangement or whether it is, on the contrary, the divine madness that characterizes the true heirs of Philosophy.

Recovering the Œconomic Vision

The Greek word *oikonomia* appears first in Plato and Xenophon and is given a precise meaning by Aristotle. It is composed of the words *oikos* and *nomos*. The *oikos* is the household. We must resist our impulse to think of it as the "private sphere," as if it were part of a system of artificial demarcations, boundaries drawn according to human choice between public and private domains. That way of thinking is an effect of the historical and conceptual transformation we are trying to get back behind. *Oikos* has the more concrete meaning of dwelling place, estate, household goods—that which makes up the site and the concrete form of the life of a family.

*Nomos* in this classical period means primarily law or custom, or more generally the governing ordering of a place. "Place" deserves particular emphasis here, because if we dig back behind this its classical meaning, we find that the ancient meaning of *nomos* is "a place of pasturage," which then gives rise to meanings like "habitation" and "province" or "sphere of command." Thus the writers who gave us the term *oikonomia* would have heard in it a double emphasis on place, with the implication that the ordering arises in the place and is appropriate to the place, rather than being willfully imposed upon it (at least until the word is extended metaphorically to the context of imperialist domination). In Aristotle's terms, there are ordering principles natural to the household, because the household itself has a nature that implicitly tends or yearns in the direction of the order that befits it. This is so because it is the concrete form of community of a family, and the family has its own nature as a distinct form of community shared by persons who are ordered toward a good life.

For Aristotle, then, *oikonomia* can only be understood as one distinct part of practical philosophy. Practical philosophy has three parts: ethics, concerned with the right formation of character and the capacity to choose and act; Œconomy, concerned with the right formation and conduct of the household as a place in accord with its nature; and politics, concerned with the right formation and conduct of the city or community united by laws.[1] These three parts of practical philosophy are distinct, but not separable, since they all take their bearings from the human good and in turn shed slightly different lights on it. For the most part, Aristotle sees each higher level as opening possibilities for fulfillment that are not available to the lower level when left to its own confines. To give one example, he argues that the proper relationship between husband and wife is best understood as republican in character—an image of the relationship of fellow citizens—rather than in terms of the monarchical king-subject model or the despotic master-slave model, and that one of the distinctive features of the Greek polis-civilization is that it makes it possible to understand the relationship in these terms.[2]

On the other hand, the three parts of practical philosophy can also be in a certain tension with one another. Even though the political order is the fulfillment of a natural progression, in which the family-household finds its good more fully realizable through the village-neighborhood, and the latter finds its greater self-sufficiency in the polis, it may well be the case that once the polis exists it will attempt to redefine the good of the household and its members wholly in terms of civic priorities. Aristotle signals this phenomenon by the different beginnings of book 1 and book 3 of his *Politics*. In book 1, discussing the natural genesis of the polis, Aristotle looks upon the polis or city as composed of families and as fulfilling their potentialities. In book 3, however, which initiates the study of forms of government, Aristotle identifies the citizens as the parts of which the city is composed.[3] Through the political lens, those who exist as parts of a family are reinterpreted as parts of the city instead. It is important to note that in neither case is the human being imagined as an unencumbered, free-standing individual as in modern liberalism. One is always understood as a part, either of the family or of the city.

When he attempts to clarify the proper conduct of *oikonomia* in *Politics* I.8–11, Aristotle is at pains to distinguish the art of household management from the art of acquisition. The former looks to obtaining, preserving, and using "those goods a store of which is both necessary for life and useful for partnership in a city or a household."[4] The acquisitive art, on the other hand, seeks to discern "what and how to exchange in order to make the greatest profit."[5] Accordingly, *oikonomia* recognizes limits to acquisition, since it takes its measure by the standard of self-sufficiency with a view to a good life, which means a life embodying virtue and friendship. Those intent on profit, on the other hand, encounter no natural limit to their pursuit, since "they are serious about living, but not about living well; and since that desire of theirs is without limit, they also desire what is productive of unlimited things."[6]

When we turn to Wendell Berry, we find a strikingly similar account. For example, in recounting a deathbed visit to an aged and childless family friend named Lily, Berry is dumbfounded by the "stupidity and cowardice" of the doctor who at Lily's lowest ebb speaks of "getting her back on her feet": "The medical industry now instructs us all that longevity is a good in itself. . . . My purpose here is only to notice that the ideal of a whole or complete life . . . now appears to have been replaced by the ideal merely of a *long* life. And I do not believe that these two ideals can be reconciled."[7]

Lily, however, accepts her mortality with grace:

> Speaking of the sale of her possessions, she said, "I'm all finished now. Everything is done." She said this so cheerfully that I asked her, "Lily, is it a load off your mind?" She said, "Well, Wendell, it hurt me. I laid here the night when I knew it was all gone, and I could *see* it all, all the things I'd cared for so long. But yes, it is a load off my mind." I was so moved and impressed by what she said that I wrote it down. She had lived her life and met her hardships bravely and cheerfully, and now she faced her death fully aware and responsible and with what seemed to me a completed grace.[8]

According to Berry, this contrast between Lily and the doctor is parallel and bound up with the contrast between old and new modes of agricultural production: the medical-technological ideal of indefinitely increasing life expectancy finds its complement in the agricultural-technological ideal of indefinitely increasing farm productivity. This aim undermines the good life made possible by and embodied in a farm:

> The art of farming is also the art of living on a farm. The form of a farm is partly . . . in the arrangement of fields and buildings in relation to the life of the farm's human family whose focus is the household. There is thus a convergence or even a coincidence between the form of a farm and the form of a farming life. . . . The exclusive standard of productivity destroys the formal integrity of a farm just as the exclusive standard of longevity destroys the formal integrity of a life. . . . Driven by fashion, debt, and

bad science, the desire for more overrides completely the idea of a home or a home place or a home economy or a home community. . . . By indulging a limitless desire for a supposedly limitless quantity, one gives up all the things that are most desirable. One abandons any hope of the formal completeness, grace and beauty that come only by subordinating one's life to the whole of which it is a part, and thus one is condemned to the life of a fragment, forever unfinished and incomplete, forever greedy.[9]

This focus on the form of farm life as normative for the integrity of the household can easily seem idiosyncratic in the age of suburbia and the information economy; but for Berry, as for Aristotle, it provides the critical natural measure for diagnosing our ills. Aristotle maintains that the agrarian life is natural, both from the point of view of providing necessities and of focusing the effort of accumulation on natural goods.[10] Berry likewise, in his first extended discussion of the integrity of the household in *The Unsettling of America*, attempts "to define a pattern of disintegration that is at once cultural and agricultural," that is to say, a pattern necessarily understood against the backdrop of the widespread destruction of the farming form of life.[11] "In the urban-industrial situation . . . the man's duty to the household came to be simply to provide money."[12] The transformation of men into wage earners and women into consumer-homemakers; the separation of home and work and the denigration of household production; suburbanization, i.e., the abandonment of neighborhood communities in favor of storage spaces for commuters and their nuclear families—all this transforms what had been a complementary difference between men's and women's work into an unsatisfying division, as Berry writes:

A woman's work became less accomplished and less satisfying. It became easier for her to believe that what she did was not important. And this heightened her anxiety and made her even more avid and even less discriminating as a consumer. . . . The man's mind was not simplified by a degenerative process, but by a kind of coup: as soon as he separated working and living and began to work away from home, the practical considerations of the household were excerpted from his mind all at once. . . . And in this division the household was destroyed as a practical bond between husband and wife. It was no longer a condition, but only . . . the site of mutual estrangement. . . . And it is important to recognize that this division—this destroyed household that now stands between the sexes—is a wound that is suffered inescapably by both men and women. Sometimes it is assumed that the estrangement of women in their circumscribed "women's world" can only be for the benefit of men. But that interpretation seems to be based on the law of competition that is modeled in the exploitive industrial economy.[13]

Thus we find in Berry, as in Aristotle, a vision of the profound intertwining of the first two parts of practical philosophy, ethics and economics, such that both become deranged by an unbridled profit motive rooted in a failure to reckon wisely with mortality. Unlike Aristotle's vision, however, Berry's does not extend to and embrace the third part, politics, except to the extent that it identifies the causal role of public policies in the destruction of the productive household. We may better understand the reasons for this difference if we examine both the eclipse of *oikonomia* in modern political philosophy and the way Berry goes about recovering its power to illuminate our condition.

## The New "Economy"

The first occurrence in English of the word *economy* in reference to the regulation of the larger system of wealth of a nation is found in that classic of modern political philosophy, Thomas Hobbes's *Leviathan* (where we also find the classic and unforgettable description of the law of competition).[14] In *Leviathan* chapter 23, on public ministers, Hobbes notes that some offices are concerned with the "economy of a commonwealth," such as those that administer the public revenues. A word formerly used to denote the judicious management of the goods proper to a household here gets metaphorically extended to the management of the more abstract goods, namely monies, upon which the more abstract political association of the state nourishes itself; and this metaphorical use eventually usurps the place of the proper sense of the term, so that today economics concerns the market and is emptied of the normative character that it can only derive from being concerned with what is good for a household. In essence, Berry argues that this liberation of economics from the norms of the healthy household results in an economic theory and practice that accomplishes the destruction of the well-ordered household as well as of the good places or communities in which they need to be embedded.[15] Thus, what we call the economy can only be seen, from the point of view of the word's original meaning, as a *dys-oikonomia*.

Let's consider for a moment the significance of the fact that this alteration of meaning occurs in Hobbes. The first obvious observation to make is that the household has no important role to play in Hobbes's political philosophy. For Aristotle and the Scholastic tradition the household plays an important role because it is the site of the practical life of the family, which is considered a social entity in its own right, with its own integrity and proper goods. Two fundamental points in Hobbes's account of human nature prevent him from viewing the family and household in this way. The first point is that Hobbes conceives of the human being as a metaphysical individual, not fundamentally as a participant in any natural larger entities that have metaphysical weight of their own. This conception he inherits from medieval nominalism. The second point is that this individual, with his particular passions and temperament, is the one who determines what is called good and bad, because these terms are only expressions of his appetites and aversions.[16] There are no intrinsic goods and no natural system or hierarchy of goods. What exists by nature is the world of individual tangible beings and the laws of motion; everything else exists as a result of human willing and acting, and so is what it is because of that willing and acting.

Human life, lacking any natural hierarchy of goods to give it form, becomes what Aristotle said it would, a limitless desire for the means of survival, or as Hobbes puts it, "the restless desire of power after power, that ceaseth only in death."[17] Since the constant change of man's physiological constitution means that his appetites and aversions change, and thus also his opinions of what is desirable and good, power is only intelligible as "present means to attain some future apparent good," and thus money is power in its purest and most adaptable form.[18] By this account, the family, and hence also the household, is an artificial construct amid the natural war of all against all, designed to secure a kind of peace for the more effectively ordered pursuit of power (especially money). Thus the household differs only in scale and in the terms of its constituting covenant from the commonwealth, and the economy of the home does not essentially differ from the "economy" of the state.

Here we must remind ourselves of two points noted earlier. The political order tends to reinterpret the family member strictly as a member of itself, as a citizen tout court. To the extent that it achieves this reinterpretation, it thereby "liberates" individual citizens from their family-member identities, but in classical thought there is no point in this process in which the individual is considered as something other than part of a greater whole. Hobbes, on the other hand, appears to liberate the individual in imagination before swallowing it up again in the Leviathan. But there is some sleight of hand at work here. Hobbes is the first theorist of the nation-state, and it is arguable that the philosophical conception of the human being as atomic individual is the reinterpretation that best serves the purposes of the nation-state.

It is worth noting in this connection that the "economy" of the commonwealth does not yet refer in Hobbes to production and exchange in what we would call "civil society" but specifically to the accumulation of money by the state itself. It is tempting to say that the deformation of the domestic economy results from a kind of trickle-down *dys-oikonomia*. The modern nation-state faces a new imperative arising from a new dynamics of history identified by Adam Smith: after the invention of firearms and artillery, the generation of wealth now leads to strength rather than to weakness in relation to less luxurious nations.[19] Smith thus provides the strongest case for John Locke's argument that the "Prince who shall be so wise and godlike as by established laws of liberty to secure protection and incouragement to the honest industry of Mankind against the oppression of power and the narrownesse of Party will quickly be too hard for his neighbours." This Lockean program already understands agricultural productivity in purely numerical (indeed exponential) terms, looking upon nature as providing "almost worthless materials" for human labor to push to its productive limits.[20] It leads directly to the animating spirit of the agricultural policies Berry identifies as responsible for the decline of the farming life and the consequent proliferation of the disordered "home": the public policy conception that "food is a weapon" in our international struggles.[21]

Under ancient conditions of warfare, the city demanded certain virtues of the citizen, especially courage and patriotism. It thus implicitly upheld a distinct vision of the human good, a vision in some continuity and potential dialogue with the natural ends of the household. Under modern conditions, the acquisitive individual has proved to be a convenient and efficient motor of public industry and revenue, and thereby of national security. Could it be the case that the metaphysical individual of Hobbesian theory is at bottom the modern version of the reinterpretation of the family member in political terms—that, in fact, the freely contracting individual of libertarian theory is really the creature and tool of the national state? Could it be that the economics of rational choice, in linguistically displacing traditional *oikonomia* and casting it into obscurity (and even going so far as to shed its more revealing older title of "political œconomy"), serves to beguile us of our real nature as beings ordered toward achieving the good through the integrity of the household, neighborhood, and city? Economics claims to be a neutral player in human moral life and in our human self-understanding, but perhaps this very semblance of methodological neutrality harbors its complicity: it swears off any judgments about relative goodness and so by default has to measure and compare in terms of value, which ultimately means by the medium of money. It thus recasts our imagination of the life of production and consumption in the image of the unlimited acquisition of money rather than in the image of choices about goods that contribute to a good life, thereby neutralizing the distinctive claims that the life of the household makes on the moral shape of our lives.[22]

Let us examine Hobbes's articulation of individualism and how it underwrites his linguistic appropriation (or misappropriation). His nominalism and rejection of intrinsic goods, we have seen, reduces life to a perpetual competitive pursuit of power among atomistic individuals who have no natural belonging to any larger order. Since any larger institution is an artificial construct of the human will, the family and state are merely contractual structures of power-consolidation operating on different scales. The rejection of intrinsic goods is central to Hobbes's interpretation of human action. Hobbes presents his argument for the rejection of intrinsic goods as if it follows from his metaphysical individualism. In truth, the logic of the case is just the opposite. A brief foray into metaphysics is necessary to clarify this point, which we must do if we want to see more clearly the defect of modern political theory that Berry has his finger on, as well as the case to be made for his attempts to correct it.

## The Mysterious Goodness of What Is

Platonic metaphysics is explicit about a point that is a bit more implicit in Aristotle: the fundamental principle of all being and intelligibility is the Good.[23] For Aristotle, being is always some definite kind of being; for a thing to be is for it to be *what* it is. But being what it is means doing what it characteristically does. Being is an activity, an *energeia*, or being-at-work. But if each thing has its characteristic work and continues to be what it is by virtue of doing this work, this means that a thing is most fully what it is when it does its characteristic work well. A dull ax isn't much of an ax, and a one-winged bird isn't much of a bird, and before long will prove it by ceasing to be a bird altogether. In short, in order for something to be what it is, it has to do well what such a thing does. But this means that the well-doing, or the being-fully-what-it-is (what Aristotle calls *entelecheia*), is the real source of a thing's being. This is what Aristotle calls its form, the constellation of activities that make it what it is. The material is that in which the form occurs and is that which individualizes it.

So then to claim as Hobbes does that what is real is the individual is to elevate matter to the source of a thing's being, which is to reject form as the source; and this means to reject the standard inherent in each way of being according to which a thing does what it does well. In other words, the rejection of the Good as the fundamental metaphysical determination of each thing is already implied in an individualist metaphysics. So the rejection of inherent goods is not really a result of Hobbes's metaphysical individualism but rather its presupposition. Behind Hobbes's innovation in the use of the word *economy*, then, is the metaphysical revolution that rejects inherent goods, understood as the properly constituted forms of activity that make things what they are.

The notion of a household as a natural entity with standards of perfection clearly rests on a conception of the household as a form of activity ordered toward the embodiment of certain goods. In our post-Hobbesian liberal regime, there is a tendency supported both by ideology and by the pressure of our jurisprudence to consider the family and household as a contractual relationship, differing not in kind but rather in degree and scope from the political association. If, as the Aristotelian economics maintains, polis and *oikos* are intrinsically different kinds of things, then we have generated confusion by reducing both to voluntaristic constructs.

The crucial question, of course, is whether it is true that the family and household are historical constructs of the will, or whether they are instead entities governed and shaped by their own inherent goods. Here it might seem that we are confronted with two dialectical alternatives, and that if we want to assess Berry's anti-Hobbesian position, we ought to identify his position within the dialectical array of options, articulating his communitarian, localist, subsidiarist principles, and then assess the philosophical merits of each position. But to approach the question this way is to miss Berry's distinctive contribution to the question, in particular the decisive contribution made by his fiction.

The problem with pursuing this question dialectically (as valuable as that endeavor may be) is that the two positions do not differ merely in their presuppositions or fundamental tenets but also articulate different fundamental attitudes toward the world. Following the rhetorical theorist I. A. Richards, let us call these positions nominalist and metaphysical. Richards formulates the distinction as follows. Nominalists do all they can to avoid "the kind of exploration that knows in advance that depth after depth will endlessly open to it. The virtue which nominalism has really aspired to is tidiness, everything in its place."[24] Nominalists, as Richards puts it, don't want to be "taken in" and so profess that they can't make heads or tails of the poet's evocation of the ineffable penumbra of ordinary things. The realist and metaphysician, on the other hand, does not want to be "left out," does not want to fail to do justice to all that appears to us in any given thing, or to all hidden within it that may appear to us only with patient attention. "Inevitably," says Richards, "this makes him early acquainted with, indeed overfamiliar with, unintelligibility. He learns to tolerate it more easily than others. He grows accustomed to high pressures from incomprehensibles."[25] This acceptance of the high pressure exerted by incomprehensibles implies a recognition that these apprehensible but not fully comprehensible presences are real in the sense that they exercise influence on the phenomena that are more evident to us.

It is the articulation of this sense of the world and its consequences for our lives that provides the central program of Berry's essays in the collection *Home Economics*. As he puts it, the subject of the essays is "the fact, and ultimately the faith, that things connect—that we are wholly dependent on a pattern, an all-inclusive form, that we partly understand."[26] He elaborates his guiding idea more fully in the first essay. In response to a scientific explanation by one Dr. Jenny, that rainwater passes through an ecosystem in a regular pattern while it enters and leaves it "in random fashion," Berry observes that

> pattern is verifiable by limited information, whereas the information required to verify randomness is unlimited. . . . What is perceived as random within a given limit may be seen as part of a pattern within a wider limit. If this is so, then Dr. Jenny, for accuracy's sake, should have said that rainwater moves from mystery through pattern back into mystery. If "mystery" is a necessary (that is, honest) term in such a description, then the modern scientific program has not altered the ancient perception of the human condition a jot. . . . To call the unknown "random" is to plant the flag by which to colonize and exploit the known. . . . To call the unknown by its right name, "mystery," is to suggest that we had better respect the possibility of a larger, unseen pattern that can be damaged or destroyed and, with it, the smaller patterns. . . . But if we are up against mystery, then knowledge is relatively small, and the ancient program is the right one: Act on the basis of ignorance.[27]

Here Berry contrasts the tendencies of modern science to "colonization" with the ancient humility of knowledge of ignorance. This modern hubris can be more directly connected historically to the nominalist attitude if we recall that modern science prides itself on directing itself by rigorous method, and that the first articulation of this "conscience of method" (as Nietzsche calls it) is "Ockham's razor," which dictates that we "posit no unnecessary beings."[28] This principle is noteworthy for two points: first, it takes as its ultimate metaphysical principle beings rather than the good, admitting those beings into an account only to the extent that they are necessary for rendering that account intelligible; second, making the intelligibility of the account the measure of what is necessary means making the human mind the measure of what is admissible as a legitimate being and puts that mind into a posture of suspicion toward any purported being that doesn't fit that measure. It is not hard to see that this attitude of mind sets the agenda for enlightenment rationalism and modern science and is the background for what Heidegger characterizes as the "enframing" attitude toward being that is the relationship toward the world to which modern technology habituates us.[29]

Recapturing the more ancient attitude requires clarifying another word of Greek inheritance and its fate in modern thought, namely *theoria*. Today our sense of the meaning of *theoretical* is given primarily by the practices of modern scientific research. The theoretical is what is proposed as an explanatory hypothesis, and theoretical science is distinguished from applied science by being more concerned with the fundamental explanatory system. This sense of the word is clearly governed by the methodological ethic. The earlier meaning of *theoria* as developed by Plato and Aristotle is best captured by Simone Weil's elaboration of the concept "attention." Weil observes in *Waiting for God*: "Attention is an effort, the greatest of all efforts perhaps, but it is a negative effort."[30] Attention is laying ourselves open to receive into our awareness what is waiting to reveal itself to us. It is the opposite of self-exertion, of being trapped within our own thoughts and constructions, and attention in Weil's sense might best be thought of as the alternative to construction. It involves the negative effort of quieting our constant activity of building up a world of meanings and interpretations that revolve around our own preoccupations and wishes. Thus the ethic of attentiveness is the opposite of the methodological ethic inasmuch as the latter is governed by a project of understanding, which ultimately means that it is governed by a determination of the will in a particular direction toward a particular aim, so that the will determines the criteria of what is admissible.

This, then, is why a mere intellectual or dialectical encounter of the metaphysical and nominalist interpretations of reality is ultimately inadequate: they are fundamentally different attitudes toward the world that reveal the world differently. The case for the metaphysical interpretive stance can be made only by recovering the attitude of attentiveness that is its substance. Put another way, it is false but attractive to maintain that genuine skepticism ought to lead us to nominalism, because only by cultivating the capacity for the attentiveness to the world and its mysterious presences that is at the heart of the metaphysical attitude do we gain the capacity to judge the relative merits of the two positions. This is a hard lesson for those of us trained in the disciplines of academic discourse; typically the dissertations that earn us admission to the guild begin with a chapter on methodology, and methodological explicitness becomes part of our intellectual conscience.


Berry's Fiction: Restoring Our Vision

Berry's third novel, *Remembering*, dramatizes the kind of epiphany required for crossing over the divide between these two fundamental attitudes. The protagonist, Andy Catlett, an academically trained agricultural journalist writing for a magazine called *Scientific Farmer*, is assigned to write a story on the exemplary modern farm of a Mr. Meikelberger, who "was the fulfillment of the dreams of his more progressive professors."

> On all the two thousand acres there was not a fence, not an animal, not a woodlot, not a tree, not a garden. The whole place was planted in corn, right up to the walls of the two or three unused barns that were still standing. Meikelberger owned a herd of machines. His grain bins covered acres. He had an office like a bank president's. The office was a carpeted room at the back of the house, expensively and tastefully furnished, as was the rest of the house, as far as Andy saw it. It was a brick ranch house with ten rooms and a garage, each room a page from *House Beautiful*, and it was deserted.[31]

As it turns out, the three Meikelberger children have been carried off in various directions by the currents of professional success, and his wife works in town to help pay the extensive debt that Meikelberger never expects to be out of. The ulcer caused by anxieties about the debt and the running of the business keeps Meikelberger constantly popping antacids. Meikelberger observes, however: "You can't let your damned stomach get in the way. If you're going to get ahead you've got to pay the price." The encounter has an unsettling effect on Andy Catlett.

Andy did not learn anything from Meikelberger that surprised him, but he had not expected Meikelberger's frankness. He drove away with . . . some things in his mind that he would have trouble writing down in the language of *Scientific Farming*. The obstacle that now lay in his way was his realization, which Meikelberger himself had left him no room to avoid, that there was nothing, simply nothing at all, that Meikelberger allowed to stand in his way: not a neighbor or a tree or even his own body. Meikelberger's ambition had made common cause with a technical power that proposed no limit to itself, that was, in fact, destroying Meikelberger, as it had already destroyed nearly all that was natural or human around him.[32]

This leads Andy to reassess all the assumptions and especially the methodological simplifications behind the practice of farming that takes its direction from modern science, modern economics, and the agricultural policies that treat food as a weapon.

In this story, however, although Berry has identified the point of engagement at which his literary art must confront our imaginative sensibilities, he has not yet attained the perfection of his art, because the message resides too much on the surface; it is something of a tract in fictional form, which is plausible because of Andy Catlett's involvement in journalistic and academic discourse. Berry is talking about and advocating the life he recognizes as good but not bringing us into its atmosphere and living tissue.

The requirements of an art that cultivates the kind of attention to the concrete goods that constitute a fulfilled life in a healthy community are spelled out in Berry's essay "Style and Grace." Here Berry compellingly elucidates the stylistic analogue of the philosophical divergence between the nominalist and metaphysical attitudes. He examines two fishing stories by Ernest Hemingway and Norman Maclean. Hemingway's "Big Two-hearted River" exhibits a style "severely reductive of both humanity and nature," which, like "the similarly reductive technical and professional specializations of our time, . . . minimizes to avoid mystery" and triumphs in its "ability to isolate those parts of experience of which one can confidently take charge."[33] In "A River Runs Through It," by contrast, Maclean's is "a style vulnerable to bewilderment, mystery and tragedy—

and a style, therefore, that is open to grace."[34] Its aim is not to "impose its terms on its subject." As Berry points out,

> The story admits grace because it admits mystery. It admits mystery by admitting the artistically unaccountable. It could not have been written if it had demanded to consist only of what was understood or understandable, or what was entirely comprehensible in its terms. "Something within fishermen," the writer admits, "tries to make fishing into a world perfect and apart." But this story refuses that sort of perfection. It never forgets that it is a fragment of a larger pattern that it does not contain. It never forgets that it occurs in the world and in love.[35]

It is clear that Berry considers Maclean's style better suited to reality and to cultivating the attitude that recognizes the presence of the palpable but imperfectly comprehensible mysterious, the larger pattern that we must seek to situate ourselves within precisely by recognizing the contours of our ignorance.

Perhaps the novel in which Berry best accomplishes this stylistic cultivation of attentiveness is *Hannah Coulter*. It is told as a memoir in the voice of Hannah, a character who appears in other novels as one of the lynchpins of the Port William community. But although Hannah is telling her own story, it can never simply be her story, in part because no story in Port William, at least before it starts to become a bedroom community, can be isolated from the other stories. In fact, Hannah discovers in her own terms over the course of her life the truth of Aristotle's œconomic and metaphysical vision: the intrinsic goods that shape the household, the embeddedness in a neighborhood that is a condition of its fulfillment, and the essence of human life as participation in the goodness that structures all being.

Those who choose to give themselves to the shared life of Port William farming belong to the Port William membership, which Hannah contrasts in the following terms with the world of "employment":

> One of the attractions of moving away into the life of employment, I think, is being disconnected and free, unbothered by membership. It is a life of beginnings without memories, but it is

a life too that ends without being remembered. The life of membership with all its cumbers is traded away for the life of employment that makes itself free by forgetting you clean as a whistle when you are not of any more use. . . . "But the membership," Andy said, "keeps the memories even of horses and mules and milk cows and dogs."[36]

Accepting membership is accepting being part of a multifaceted story that makes claims on one's remembrance, a story that deepens and ramifies one's relationships with others. This is why all Berry's fiction is devoted to telling us more of the story of Port William, drawing the reader more deeply into that story and into a deeper attentiveness to the characters who belong to it.

But in another way, Hannah's story is not simply her own. She has become a member of Port William by becoming a member of one of its central families, and then of another after her first husband dies, and these are both farming families. As she puts it: "Our story is the story of our place."[37] The life she shares with her second husband is the life of caring for a place and sharing that activity with children, relatives, and neighbors. Even the life she had looked forward to with her first husband, who died within a year of their marriage, was presented to her in these terms. Of their courtship, she notes:

> He was trying to show me the shape of his life, and what might become the shape of it. He was seeing the time to come as a possibility, as a life that he loved. And though maybe neither of us fully understood what he was doing, he made me love it. It wasn't as though I was being swept away by some irresistible emotion. . . . When I imagined him entering the life he saw, I imagined myself entering it too. It was becoming a possibility that belonged to us both.[38]

As their courtship progresses and she gets to know the family, her awareness of what this marriage demands of her deepens:

> Like maybe any young woman of that time, I had thought of marriage as promises to be kept until death, as having a house,

living together, working together, sleeping together, raising a family. But Virgil's and my marriage was going to have to be more than that. It was going to have to be part of a place already decided for it, and part of a story begun long ago and going on. . . . It was something I needed to get into my mind. The love he bore me was his own, but also it was a love that had been borne to him, by people he knew, people I now knew, people he loved.[39]

After their marriage, when Virgil is off at war and pronounced missing and she, pregnant with his child, continues living with his parents, she remarks:

By kindness I was coming to understand what it meant to be in love with Virgil. He and I had been, we were, we are—for there is no escape—in love together. I went into love with Virgil, and of course we were not the only ones there. To be in love with Virgil was to be there, in love, with his parents, his family, his place, his baby.[40]

This experience leads her to introduce one of the central images of the book, her sense that "love is like a great room with a lot of doors." This simple but powerful image captures her growing awareness of the inadequacy of the terms deriving from an individualist metaphysics (or what we have called a nominalist antimetaphysics), which would see love precisely as an emotional state within an individual psyche negotiating its terms with another psyche, rather than as a reality into which one enters and that makes its own demands on one's integrity if one is to preserve its integrity. She goes so far as to embody this metaphysical sensibility in a very physical image of nursing her infant daughter:

As she nursed and the milk came, she began a little low contented sort of singing. I would feel milk and love flowing from me to her as once it had flowed to me. It emptied me. As the baby fed, I seemed slowly to grow empty of myself, as if in the presence of that long flow of love even grief could not stand.[41]

As she begins to recover from her grief and to love again, she reconceives her relationship to the world:

I began to trust the world again, not to give me what I wanted, for I saw that it could not be trusted to do that, but to give unforeseen goods and pleasures that I had not thought to want. . . . It was the light that shines in darkness drawing me back into time.[42]

This reference to the Prologue of the Gospel of John is by no means fortuitous. Looking back on her second love, for Nathan Coulter, she begins to see in metaphysical terms what she did not fully see at that time:

Now I know what we were trying to stand for: the possibility that among the world's wars and sufferings two people could love each other for a long time, until death and beyond, and could make a place for each other that would be a part of their love, as their love for each other would be a way of loving their place. This love would be one of the acts of the greater love that holds and cherishes all the world.[43]

As the narrative proceeds, her conception of this metaphysical reality of love becomes more explicitly theological:

The room of love is the love that holds us all, and it is not ours. It goes back before we were born. It goes all the way back. It is Heaven's. Or it is Heaven, and we are in it only by willingness. By whose love, Andy Catlett, do we love this world and ourselves and one another? Do you think we invented it ourselves? I ask with confidence, for I know you know we didn't.[44]

These reflections, embedded within a rich narrative of the ways in which marital, familial, and neighborly life have given substance to such insights, communicate effectively a growing sense of this larger reality of which we are part if we allow ourselves to see it as such. They also dramatize Hannah's implicit recognition that acknowledgment of this larger reality requires overcoming a nominalist attitude encouraged by modern liberalism in which we see ourselves as individuals contracting relationships at will. The vision communicated here might well be characterized as a Platonic-Christian vision of participation in the ultimate reality, which is divine love. But it is Aristotelian as well, because that participation is actualized in concrete social institutions with their own formal, enacted integrity. As Karl Polanyi observed, Aristotelian economics in the social sense sees the criterion for the regulation of prices not in the impersonal laws of supply and demand but rather in the need to maintain the community in both self-sufficiency and friendship.[45] Berry's vision is substantially the same. The family and the community give actual existence to the fundamental realities of love and friendship, and an economy directed to the human good seeks to maintain these active realities in their integrity in the course of its productive activities, as opposed to the liberal market economy, which seeks "maximum profit or power with minimum responsibility."[46]

Berry's fiction, then, communicates and nurtures in the most effective way possible the vision that restores us to what Aristotle understands as the natural starting points of political philosophy in the other two parts of practical philosophy. Recognizing this allows us to understand the peculiar fact that many political theorists find Berry so appealing, compelling, and enriching, even though his horizon stops almost entirely short of politics. What Berry seems to have done is to recover a genuinely œconomic reflection on the human good and to extend it as far as the fructifying village or neighborhood. Because our politics and economics are so deeply anti-œconomic in their animating principles, this reflection finds no natural passage to the political level, the level of the natural, circumscribed, self-sufficient polis, but rather encounters the antithetical state as adversary. Or perhaps it is more accurate to say that in Berry's case it finds this passage only very late in the day. For in a recent interview, when asked how an urban community can have a healthier connection to the land, Berry observes: "A better model, if we want to look for a historical one, would be the Greek cities."[47]

# 12

# Wendell Berry's Defense of a Truly Free Market

## Mark T. Mitchell

Berry is often perceived as an opponent of the free market. However, his work actually champions a truly free market against the depredations of a corporate capitalism that is anything but. He has long argued that the modern industrial economy is anti-human, anticommunity, and unsustainable. To grasp Berry's positive economic vision—what he calls the Great Economy—it is helpful to examine first his scathing description of the reductionist, imperialist program he calls the Total Economy. According to Berry, "a total economy is one in which everything . . . is 'private property' and has a price and is for sale."[1] The total economy is one where everything, including people and communities, has a price, and the market superintends over all.

Such a reduction can only be imagined, much less attempted, when moral virtue has been severely attenuated. In Berry's view, modern industrial economies discourage or even undermine the development and practice of virtue. He argues that a view of the world rooted in agrarian sensibilities will facilitate the cultivation of virtue and, thereby, complement a free market economy, preventing it from deteriorating into a total economy.

The Total Economy

The willingness, even enthusiasm, of some to reduce the world into quantifiable elements necessarily distorts qualities and requires a voluntary ignorance of those parts of reality that simply cannot be quantified. Both a willing distortion of reality and voluntary ignorance represent moral failures, for virtue, or excellence of character, is characterized by individuals who seek to grasp reality as it is.

The virtuous person does not willingly distort reality, for he possesses the humility to admit of essential human limits. According to Berry, the breakdown of communities, the pathologies of the untethered individual, and our various environmental crises are the result, at least in part, of an economic crisis, and our economic crisis is, ultimately, a crisis of character in which we refuse to see the world as it is. But what would induce such an ill-fated war on reality? The answer is as old as the human story: pride. The old lie, "ye shall be as gods," persists and, amplified by the power of the machine, the consequences of believing that lie are perhaps more acute than ever before. The longing for control is, of course, only a dream, yet we have pursued it with abandon. The desire to dominate reality necessarily leads to a willful simplification whereby the complexities of creation are shorn away and a new, though false, world is embraced as authentic.

The habit of voluntary ignorance easily and naturally extends to our everyday economic encounters. This takes the form of "proxies" by which we delegate responsibility to organizations about which we know very little.

> Most people in the "developed" world have given proxies to the corporations to produce and provide *all* of their food, clothing, and shelter. Moreover, they are rapidly increasing their proxies to corporations or governments to provide entertainment, education, child care, care of the sick and the elderly, and many other kinds of "service" that once were carried on informally and inexpensively by individuals or households or communities. Our major economic practice, in short, is to delegate the practice to others.[2]

When we delegate our responsibility—to care for our needs, for our children, for our aging parents—to corporations, Berry is convinced that sloppiness, indifference, and waste will be the likely by-products. Obviously, though, it is possible to learn something of the various corporations with which we do business. We can choose between those we perceive to be responsible and those that are not. But how often does this actually happen? What is it about a corporate economy that makes diligent oversight by individual consumers so difficult?

That we can, in fact, delegate much of our economic practices to organizations with no vested interest or long-term presence in our community indicates the way that sheer size can hamper economic responsibility. While it is, indeed, the case that economies of scale are capable of producing a quantity of goods and services that is dizzying to contemplate, Berry encourages his readers not to ignore the less obvious consequences. The giantism, which characterizes so much of our world, facilitates anonymity, and anonymity makes irresponsibility far more likely than what will occur in a local economy populated by locally owned businesses. Take, for instance, the small truck farmer versus the "agri-businessman." The truck farmer sells his produce at the local farmer's market. He meets his customers, many of whom are his neighbors. He can receive immediate feedback on his produce. Customers can request changes or additions. He can respond. Because he must live with his customers, his participation in their lives extends beyond the simple market exchange. He wants them to be happy not simply so they will continue to purchase his goods but also because he cares for many of them and is interested in their long-term good. His life and the lives of his family are entangled with the lives of his customers. Their economic relationship is merely a part of a larger relationship that extends beyond economics. It is easy to see how the giant corporate concern differs. A customer can, of course, request that the supermarket carry a new item. And one can influence, in a very small way, the products that are carried by virtue of the price mechanism, for when I choose to buy one item over another, I am sending a message that, when combined and amplified by all the other customer choices, can affect product selection and quality. But the personal connection is gone. Our relationship is stripped down merely to market forces.

According to Karl Polanyi, "The outstanding discovery of recent historical and anthropological research is that man's economy, as a rule, is submerged in his social relationships." But recent history has witnessed a profound change. "Instead of economy being embedded in social relations, social relations are embedded in the economic system."[3] Berry's condemnation of corporate capitalism and his championing of local economies gets at the same notion. An economy, when it is not firmly grounded in ideals and principles that go beyond supply and demand, is corrosive of communities and of neighborly virtues that help communities thrive.

The notion of the corporation itself comes under heavy fire from Berry. Our economy is, according to Berry, rooted in the idea "that what is good for the corporations will sooner or later—though not of course immediately—be good for everybody." But the modern corporation is an odd entity, the structure of which we must not ignore, as Berry writes in *Citizenship Papers*:

> The folly at the root of this foolish economy began with the idea that a corporation should be regarded, legally, as "a person." But the limitless destructiveness of this economy comes precisely because a corporation is *not* a person. A corporation, essentially, is a pile of money to which a number of persons have sold their moral allegiance. Unlike a person, a corporation does not age. It does not arrive, as most persons finally do, at a realization of the shortness and smallness of human lives; it does not come to see the future as the lifetime of the children and grandchildren of anybody in particular. It can experience no personal hope or remorse, no change of heart. It cannot humble itself. It goes about its business as if it were immortal, with the single purpose of becoming a bigger pile of money.[4]

The very structure of the corporation, while paving the way for economies of scale with all the obvious benefits therein, can reduce the opportunity, as well as the inclination, for the exercise of virtue. Consider the issue from the investment side. A person might, having prudently diversified his portfolio, hold a small amount of shares in a wide variety of corporations. This investor, like all investors, is interested in realizing a profit through share appreciation and/or regular dividends. He is, though, removed from the daily operations of the corporation. He may in some cases receive an annual report and have the opportunity to vote in the election of executives, but the bottom line in the report is his main focus, and his information is generally inadequate to vote wisely. The very scale and remoteness of the enterprise makes careful monitoring difficult. Of course, someone might argue that if this person were really concerned about virtue, he could investigate the behavior of the corporation as well as the background of each of its officers. True. But doing this for a portfolio of investments would be laborious, and few are willing to make such an effort. And even if such an endeavor is conceivable, the point is that the structure of the corporation makes it far easier for all involved to focus on profits rather than virtue. The same dynamic is even more pronounced when corporate shares are owned as part of a mutual fund. The investor is one more step removed from the corporation, and the quantifiable bottom line of the mutual fund itself—this time abstracted from the individual stocks—is the natural focus. The moral asymmetries are obvious.

Because of the scale and remoteness associated with the modern corporation, virtue is disadvantaged (which is not to say it is impossible or absent). Because of abuse, the natural response of the public, and therefore their elected representatives, is to attempt to regulate corporations. Because of the asymmetry between profits and virtue, a regulatory bureaucracy is erected to make up the difference. Regulations become a substitute for virtue. Of course, as regulations increasingly pressure corporate executives, they will naturally find themselves focusing on the bureaucratic minutiae of the regulations rather than on the self-imposed moral probity that virtue requires. Regulations, then, can have the unintended effect of distracting from the cultivation and practice of virtue.

Corporations, of course, can and do hire lawyers to lobby the federal and state governments. The voices of those businesses that can afford to retain full-time lobbyists will obviously be heard above the voices of the small farmer in Pennsylvania or the owner of the independent bank in Kansas. The result, not surprisingly, is that the bulk of regulations favor the large concern over the small. Even those regulations that appear benign can produce onerous barriers to the small business. If, for instance, in the interest of clean meat, federal and state regulations require butchering facilities, the description of which is well suited to the corporate meat producer but impossibly expensive for the small rancher, then the small rancher is disadvantaged. Of course, one could say that such regulations are all in the name of public safety. But if a small rancher wants to butcher a handful of steers on his property, and if his neighbors who trust him (know he is a man of virtue) want to buy the meat from him, why should the USDA get in the way? In one instance we have regulations attempting to substitute for virtue (and disadvantaging some), while in the other we have legitimate virtue operating between neighbors. Which option serves to create a healthier society?

In his neglected classic *The Servile State*, Hilaire Belloc argues that industrial capitalism is fundamentally unstable and is therefore a transitory condition. It is important, though, to pay careful attention to his definition of capitalism. "A society in which the ownership of the means of production is confined to a body of free citizens not large enough to make up properly a general character of that society, while the rest are dispossessed of the means of production and therefore proletarian, we call capitalist."[5] In Belloc's mind, there are only two resolutions to the instability of capitalism. The first is socialism, and the second is what he calls "the distributist state," or "the proprietary state," in which private property, specifically the means of production, is broadly distributed throughout the populace.

Why is capitalism unstable? Capitalism, as defined by Belloc, tends toward the centralization of economic power, but when economic power is centralized, it requires a strong political structure to manage it. Herein we see the connection between economics and politics: centralized economic power goes hand in hand with centralized political power. Belloc's friend and fellow distributist G. K. Chesterton argued that capitalism had come to an end and the evidence was that the capitalists appealed "for the intervention of Government like Socialists."[6] In light of the government response to the financial collapse of 2008–9, it is difficult not to see Chesterton's point.

F. A. Hayek argued that consolidation of economic power would invariably lead toward socialism. "A state which allows such enormous aggregations of power to grow up cannot afford to let this power rest entirely in private control." The blame, according to Hayek, does not fall exclusively upon the capitalist class. Instead, "the fatal development was that they have succeeded in enlisting the support of an ever increasing number of other groups and, with their help, in obtaining the support of the state."[7]

Polanyi argues that "laissez-faire itself was enforced by the state."[8] The formation of a market system required a significant government involvement. "The road to the free market was opened and kept open by an enormous increase in continuous, centrally organized and controlled interventionism." This, of course, seems counterintuitive, but Polanyi's point is that the market system that grew up in the nineteenth century was not a spontaneous product. It was planned. "Thus even those who wished most ardently to free the state from all unnecessary duties, and those whose philosophy demanded the restriction of state activities, could not but entrust the self-same state with the new powers, organs, and instruments required for the establishment of laissez-faire."[9] Of course, strictly speaking, interventionism is the opposite of laissez-faire, and if the ideal of laissez-faire could ever be established, interventionism would not be necessary. But, according to Polanyi, that ideal is a utopian dream the pursuit of which justifies temporary intervention. "For as long as that system is not established, economic liberals must and will unhesitatingly call for the intervention of the state order to establish it, and once established, in order to maintain it."[10] In short, corporate capitalism seems to require a powerful, centralized state. Berry makes the same sort of argument:

> The World Trade Organization gives the lie to the industrialist conservatives' professed abhorrence of big government. The cause of big government, after all, is big business. The power to do large-scale damage, which is gladly assumed by every large-scale industrial enterprise, call naturally and logically for government regulation, which of course the corporations object to. But we have a good deal of evidence also that the leaders of big business actively desire and promote big government. They and their political allies, while ostensibly working to "downsize" government, continue to promote government helps and "incentives" to large corporations; and, however absurdly, they adhere to their notion that a small government, taxing only the working people, can maintain a big highway system, a big military establishment, a big space program, and big government contracts.[11]

It is clear then that economic centralization and political centralization feed off one another. Far from being antagonistic, they are natural allies. The massive regulatory state emerged with the explosive growth of market capitalism, and according to Belloc as well as Berry, modern industrial capitalism is destructive of local communities, for it encourages absenteeism and anonymity; it is destructive of local ecologies, for it tends to treat the natural world merely as a resource to be exploited for a profit; and it is destructive of individual character, for it undermines the context within which the virtues are developed and practiced.

The problems of centralization and scale, then, are tied to the problem of virtue. Wilhelm Röpke clearly sees this relationship. In his classic *A Humane Economy*, he writes: "Market economy, price mechanism, and competition are fine, but they are not enough. They may be associated with a sound or an unsound structure of society." If we reduce our concerns only to those things visible to the lover of quantifiable reality, we will be unable properly to evaluate the health or ill health of the economy, much less that of the society as a whole. Röpke continues:

> Market economy is one thing in a society where atomization, mass, proletarianization, and concentration are the rule; it is quite another in a society approaching anything like the "natural order." ... In such a society, wealth would be widely dispersed; people's lives would have solid foundations; genuine communities, from the family upward, would form a background of moral support for the individual; there would be counterweights to competition and the mechanical operation of prices; people would have roots and would not be adrift in life without anchor; there would be a broad belt of an independent middle class, a healthy balance between town and country, industry and agriculture.[12]

A healthy market economy depends on cultural goods that are above and beyond the influence of supply and demand. Centralization, both economic and political, undermines these very goods by reducing the space necessary for them to flourish. Commercialism destroys these good things by subordinating them to the laws of supply and demand. The loss of virtue makes it impossible to distinguish the healthy from the sick.

It might seem a truism to insist that a healthy market economy requires virtue. After all, don't all human interactions require certain virtues if they are to be successful over the long term? The freedom that a market economy affords depends on a certain kind of citizenry. If a critical mass of participants in a market economy possesses the virtues of self-control, personal responsibility, the willingness to sacrifice for others, courage, etc., then that economy can be the means for increased freedom within the context of higher goods that are invisible to the market. If, on the other hand, a critical mass of participants shun responsibility, pursue immediate gratification, and refuse to sacrifice for others, then the market system will be a means by which the participants can debase themselves, others, and society at large.

Not all agree, though, that the health of a market economy depends on moral virtue. Bernard Mandeville, born in 1670, gained fame—and notoriety—with the publication of an allegory titled *The Fable of the Bees; Or, Private Vices, Publick Benefits*. As the title indicates, Mandeville argues that if everyone pursues private vice, the public will benefit.

> Vast Numbers throng'd the fruitful Hive;
> Yet those vast Numbers made 'em thrive;
> Millions endeavoring to supply
> Each other's Lust and Vanity. . . .
> Thus every part was full of Vice,
> Yet the whole Mass a Paradise.[13]

Those things that have been traditionally associated with vice are the very forces, according to Mandeville, that are most useful to society. If Mandeville is correct, it is not hard to imagine what an infusion of traditional virtues would do to profits.

Some have suggested that Mandeville was writing satire. Perhaps. What is certain is that John Maynard Keynes, the giant of twentieth-century economics, was no satirist. He strikes a note startlingly in concert with Mandeville in a 1930 essay titled "Economic Possibilities for Our Grandchildren." Writing in the darkest days of the Great Depression, Keynes expressed his undying faith in progress. He chided the economic pessimists for focusing on short-term misery at the expense of the long-term prospects on the horizon. Given the tremendous surge in prosperity witnessed in the nineteenth century, Keynes argued there was every reason to think that, over the long term, growth would continue. Keynes imagined a time in the not-too-distant future where the problem of scarcity would be solved. All people would have enough to meet their needs for life and well-being. Keynes, though, worries about a new challenge that will beset humanity once the problem of scarcity is resolved: boredom. But creating a satisfying life in a world of plenty is, according to Keynes, the glorious challenge proper to human beings. "Thus for the first time since his creation man will be faced with his real, his permanent problem—how to use his freedom from pressing economic cares, how to occupy the leisure, which science and compound interest will have won for him, to live wisely and agreeably and well."[14] In this future time of peace and plenty,

> we shall be able to rid ourselves of many of the pseudo-moral principles which have hag-ridden us for two hundred years, by which we have exalted some of the most distasteful of human qualities into the position of the highest virtues. We shall be able to afford to dare to assess the money-motive at its true value. The love of money as a possession—as distinguished from the love of money as a means to the enjoyments and realities of life—will be recognized for what it is, a somewhat disgusting morbidity, one of those semi-criminal, semi-pathological propensities which one hands over with a shudder to the specialists in mental disease.[15]

The implication here is striking. At present, we do not have the luxury of ridding ourselves of the "disgusting morbidity" and "semi-pathological" aspects of our collective character that, in a time of reflection, would constitute mental illness. Keynes looks forward to the day when humans are free "to return to some of the most sure and certain principles of religion and traditional virtue," but until the problem of scarcity is overcome, we must tarry a while in the land of putative insanity. "For at least another hundred years we must pretend to ourselves and to everyone that fair is foul and foul is fair; for foul is useful and fair is not. Avarice and usury and precaution *must be our gods* for a little longer still. For only they can lead us out of the tunnel of economic necessity into daylight."[16] With Mandeville, Keynes asserts that economic prosperity depends on greed, on the love of money, on the passion to acquire. On the backs of these vices, a world of prosperity can emerge; but if we prematurely turn from these vices, scarcity will reassert itself. Instead of acting in accord with traditional notions of virtue and sacrificing our material good for our posterity, according to Keynes, we must sacrifice our souls in the dim hope that our grandchildren will have the luxury of being virtuous.

According to Berry, it is precisely this optimistic view of the future that marks the modern mind. But because of his singular concern for the future, such a person is alienated from the present as well as the past. The past was, after all, a backward place inhabited by benighted, miserable wretches. What could they have to teach us? What have we to learn from *them*? As Berry puts it, "The modern mind longs for the future as the medieval mind longed for Heaven."[17]

But this longing for a perfect future is really only a thinly disguised attempt to dominate reality by controlling the future. This alienation from the past, however, leads to alienation from the present and, ultimately, to the destruction of communities, for the alienated individual is ill-equipped to withstand the pressures and enticements to leave home in search of those abstractions called "the future" and "a better place." As Berry puts it in *The Unsettling of America*, "The history of our time has been to a considerable extent the movement of the center of consciousness away from home."[18] Yet this perfect place in the future is never found, and the individual contents himself with a life of abstract possibility, never settling, so never disappointed. He becomes, in short, the cosmopolitan who fancies himself at home anywhere. But such a notion is only rendered plausible by an emaciated concept of home. According to Berry,

> one cannot live in the world; that is, one cannot become, in the easy, generalizing sense with which the phrase is commonly used, a "world citizen." There can be no such thing as a "global village." No matter how much one may love the world as a whole, one can live fully in it only by living responsibly in some small part of it. Where we live and who we live there with define the terms of our relationships to the world and to humanity.[19]

The unattached nomad plays a key role in the idealized world of efficiency-driven economic theory. Consider, for example, the concept of a free market in labor described by the economist Frank Knight:

> Every member of the society is to act as an individual only, in entire independence of all other persons. To complete his independence he must be free from social wants, prejudices, preferences, or repulsions, or any values which are not completely manifested

in market dealing. Exchange of finished goods is the only form of relation between individuals, or at least there is no other form which influences economic conduct. And in exchanges between individuals, no interest of persons not parties to the exchange are to be concerned, either for good or ill.[20]

While Knight's description is admittedly idealized, Ludwig von Mises makes the same point, which, he argues, holds true in "the real world." If workers "did not act as trade unionists, but reduced their demands and changed their locations and occupations according to the requirements of the labour market, they could eventually find work."[21] Indeed, that might be true, but it is the economist's constricted view of reality that makes it impossible for him to acknowledge that something good might be lost in this world of nomadic wage seekers.

Berry defines community by emphasizing continuity of place through time: "By community, I mean the commonwealth and common interests, commonly understood, of people living together in a place and wishing to continue to do so. To put it another way, community is a locally understood interdependence of local people, local culture, local economy, and local nature."[22] If, as Berry suggests, a healthy community consists of placed people who depend on each other and expect to share a future together, then it is precisely community that falls victim to the economist's reductionism. And without healthy communities, the cultivation of virtue becomes a much more tenuous enterprise.


The Great Economy

So much for the total economy. Berry's criticisms of this inhuman economic system stands in stark contrast with his description of a healthy economy rooted in a local community. Berry argues that the problem with "the industrial economy is exactly that it is not comprehensive enough; that, moreover, it tends to destroy what it does not comprehend; and that it is *dependent* upon much that it does not comprehend."[23]

The economy that encompasses all of reality is the Great Economy.

The Great Economy, like the Tao or the Kingdom of God, is both known and unknown, visible and invisible, comprehensible and mysterious. It is, thus, the ultimate condition of our experience and of the practical questions rising from our experience, and it imposes on our consideration of those questions an extremity of seriousness and an extremity of humility.[24]

Humans exist within the Great Economy, for it "includes principles and patterns by which values or powers or necessities are parceled out and exchanged," but there is still, with all that, a need for a "little economy— a narrow circle within which things are manageable by the use of our wits."[25] A little economy, though, can be healthy or sick. As we have seen, Berry diagnoses the modern industrial economy as unhealthy, destructive, and unsustainable. Furthermore,

the industrial economy does not see itself as a little economy; it sees itself as the only economy. It makes itself thus exclusive by the simple expedient of valuing only what it can use. . . . Once we acknowledge the existence of the Great Economy, however, we are astonished and frightened to see how much modern enterprise is the work of hubris, occurring outside the human boundary established by ancient tradition. The industrial economy is based on the invasion and pillage of the Great Economy"[26]

According to Berry, it is precisely the denial of the existence of the Great Economy that makes the industrial economy a Total Economy.

The alternative to industrialism—an alternative that submits to the strictures of the Great Economy rather than denying them—is the disposition Berry calls agrarianism. These are, to Berry's mind, the only real options, and the differences are profound. "I believe that this contest between industrialism and agrarianism now defines the most fundamental human difference, for it divides not just two nearly opposite concepts of agriculture and land use, but also two nearly opposite ways of understanding ourselves, our fellow creatures, and our world."[27] Where the model for industrialism is the machine and technological invention, Berry notes that agrarianism begins with givens: land, plants, animals, weather, hunger, and the birthright knowledge of agriculture. Industrialists are always ready to ignore, sell, or destroy the past in order to gain the entirely unprecedented wealth, comfort, and happiness supposedly to be found in the future. Agrarian farmers know that their very identity depends on their willingness to receive gratefully, use responsibly, and hand down intact an inheritance, both natural and cultural, from the past. Agrarians understand themselves as the users and caretakers of some things they did not make, and of some things that they cannot make.[28]

The agrarian is guided by gratitude. He recognizes the giftedness of creation and accepts the great and awful responsibility to steward it well. Such a recognition "calls for prudence, humility, good work, propriety of scale."[29] In the use of the land, soil, water, and nonhuman creatures, the final arbiter, according to Berry, is not human will but nature itself.[30] But this is not to suggest that Berry is some sort of pantheist. Instead, "the agrarian mind is, at bottom, a religious mind." The agrarian recognizes that the natural world is a gift, and gifts imply a giver. "The agrarian mind begins with the love of fields and ramifies in good farming, good cooking, good eating, and gratitude to God." By contrast, the "industrial mind "begins with ingratitude, and ramifies in the destruction of farms and forests."[31] The implication here is striking. The agrarian begins with gratitude for the gifts of the natural world, and this leads him ultimately to gratitude to God. The industrialist, on the other hand, begins with ingratitude, which precludes this upward movement. Where the agrarian mind is essentially religious, the industrial mind is essentially irreligious or even antireligious. It is characterized by the will to dominate the natural world. This mind fails to recognize that humans are an intrinsic part of the natural world, and to be destructive of the natural world is to jeopardize human existence itself. Such a way of thinking seems patently foolish, but one must never forget the technological optimism lying at the heart of the industrial mind. If the agrarian mind is essentially religious, the industrial mind is animated by faith in technological innovation, which will solve the very problems brought on by the hubris of an ungrateful mind.

The agrarian model is, moreover, characterized by a particular view of private property. Echoing the views of distributists like Belloc, Berry argues that the central figure of agrarian thought has invariably been the small owner or small holder who maintains a significant measure of economic self-determination on a small acreage. The scale and independence of such holding imply two things that agrarians see as desirable: intimate care in the use of land, and political democracy resting upon the indispensible foundation of economic democracy.[32]

That we have become, by and large, a nation of wage earners and the owners of mutual funds rather than landowners signifies an important cultural shift. At the same time, Berry is not arguing that a healthy economy is only possible when everyone owns land. "I don't think that being landed necessarily means owning land. It does mean being connected to a home landscape from which one may live by the interactions of a local economy and without the routine intervention of governments, corporations, or charities."[33] But while being landed does not necessarily mean that everyone possesses land, it does require that a critical mass of citizens own land and thereby shape the economic and cultural climate whereby every citizen, owner or not, can enjoy the benefits of property.

It is important, in this context, to distinguish property from wealth. Belloc insists that the craftsman, who owns his tools, is very different from the man who owns shares in a corporation. And although there are many who would argue that wealth in the form of corporate shares is a means to achieving economic freedom, Belloc disagrees. "As a craftsman at his work he is in full control, personal and alive; as a shareholder his control is distant, indirect and largely impersonal."[34] For Belloc, economic freedom is possible only when an individual owns some means of production and is trained in its use. Such a person is self-sufficient in a way the shareholder never is, for in difficult economic times, the craftsman or farmer can provide for themselves, at least partially, whereas the shareholder is completely unequipped to do so.

Joseph Schumpeter makes much the same point but on a larger scale. There are, he argues, political and social consequences associated with the loss of the idea of real property as opposed to the wealth of the shareholder. "The capitalist process, by substituting a mere parcel of shares for the walls of and the machines in a factory, takes the life out of the idea of property." Schumpeter goes on to describe, in his book *Capitalism, Socialism and Democracy*, how this life is drained away.

It loosens the grip that was once so strong—the grip in the sense of the legal right and the actual ability to do as one pleases with one's own; the grip also in the sense that the holder of the title loses the will to fight, economically, physically, politically, for "his" factory and his control over it, to die if necessary on its steps. And this evaporation of what we may term the material substance of property—its visible and touchable reality—affects not only the attitude of holders but also that of the workmen and of the public in general. Dematerialized, defunctionalized and absentee ownership does not impress and call forth moral allegiance as the vital form of property did. Eventually there will be *nobody* left who really cares to stand for it—nobody within and nobody without the precincts of the big concerns.[35]

Schumpeter believed that this was the direction that capitalism would eventually take. The institution of property would be altered, people would be content with wealth in the form of corporate shares and wages, and real property would become increasingly centralized. In short, the successes of capitalism would undermine itself and give birth to socialism.

Thomas Jefferson, for his part, famously championed the small, independent landholder as the kind of citizen best suited to political liberty. "Cultivators of the earth are the most valuable citizens. They are the most vigorous, the most independent, the most virtuous, and they are tied to their country, and wedded to its liberty and interests by the most lasting bonds."[36] In Jefferson's words, we see a striking connection between economic liberty and political liberty. Jefferson believed that owning and working one's own land served to cultivate the very kinds of virtues necessary to sustain free citizens. Today we live in a different world; however, if there is a connection between the ownership of property and political liberty, we do well to consider how the institution of private property can be protected and reinvigorated.

Private Property and the Cultivation of Virtue

Exactly what are those virtues? Röpke argues that the market economy cannot sustain itself if it is stripped from its bourgeois foundation. The term *bourgeois* has been used in a pejorative sense by Marx and his follow-ers, but Röpke means only that the market system is necessarily rooted in the culture and virtues of the property-holding middle class. "Indepen-dence, ownership, individual reserves, saving, the sense of responsibility, rational planning of one's own life—all that is alien, if not repulsive, to proletarianized mass society."[37] For Röpke, the proletarian society is one characterized by bored wage earners who care little about private property or saving for the future but seek to alleviate their boredom through con-sumption of disposable goods and popular entertainment.

In considering the virtues encouraged by private property, we can begin with a general statement: the virtues necessary to manage one's pri-vate property are different from the virtues necessary to manage one's portfolio. Or, at the very least, real property cultivates virtues more thor-oughly and completely than does the abstract wealth of a stock portfo-lio. Schumpeter argued that private property cultivates a willingness to hold fast to one's own. It creates a kind of affection and attachment that abstract wealth can never generate. A piece of land or a small business is rooted in a particular place, has particular features, and is susceptible to the creative hand of the owner. It is incarnate, for this kind of property is embodied in space and time. It is real and not abstract. If the land is not cultivated, it will stop producing; if the business is ignored, it will not sur-vive. The skillful time and attention of the owner who pours himself into the property improves it not only for himself but for his children and their children. This kind of owner is motivated by affection. And affection can-not exceed a particular scale without thinning out into an abstraction that is ultimately harmful. Berry writes:

> The right scale in work gives power to affection. When one works beyond the reach of one's love for the place one is working in, and for the things and creatures one is working with and among, then destruction inevitably results. An adequate local culture, among other things, keeps work within the reach of love.[38]

Owners of property tend to cultivate the ideal of saving as well as maintain a margin against unseen needs. If a person's property is his main source of sustenance, then he will seek to build up a barrier against lean times. He will be loath to live on the edge, for the edge represents suffering and loss not only for oneself but for all who depend on that piece of property for life. Today a significant percentage of wage earners live from paycheck to paycheck. Of course, many will reply that this is so because basic needs are expensive and, therefore, there is no opportunity to save. But this, in part, seems disingenuous if we consider that our standard of living is higher than ever. It appears that as soon as we earn more, we incorporate that additional money into increasing our consumption. Could it be that so many are living paycheck to paycheck because we have failed to acknowledge the idea of limits? Could it be that we have truly come to believe that we can have it all and that we can have it now? Or at least that we deserve to have as much as possible as soon as possible? Surely the amount of consumer debt Americans carry is indicative of an ethic of immediacy and a devil-may-care attitude about the morrow. Our private debt simply mirrors, on a smaller scale, our public debt and the lack of virtue that characterizes our common lives.

The ideal of saving is tied closely to the idea of responsibility, and responsibility requires the virtue of self-control. Property owners seek to protect their property by living within their means, and by so doing they create a margin between themselves and disaster. This is responsible to the present, but it is also responsible to the future, for property is something that can be passed to future generations, and we can work now to make our grandchildren's lives better. Obviously, debt, too, can be passed to the future, and it is an indication of our ill-formed virtue that we have accumulated a public debt beyond all imagination, and it is our shame that this is our legacy to future generations. What else is this than a lack of the virtue of self-control that manifests itself both privately and publicly?

Thrift is an old-fashioned virtue that Berry encourages us to dust off. Many of us have parents or grandparents who lived through the Great Depression (and a few among us remember it). Many raised large families during those lean years, and the frugal habits they acquired by necessity stayed with them the rest of their lives. They saved and mended and lived lives characterized by thrift. They were grateful to have a margin between their income and their expenses and thought it was wise to live modestly. What would our grandmothers say to us now as we struggle to maintain our "American way of life"? Furthermore, it is not clear that our economy could sustain itself if the idea of thrift caught on. After all, growth is the criterion by which we measure the health of our economy.

What if people began to live lives characterized by thrift? What if people began mending their clothes, growing some of their own food, sharing tools with neighbors, and attempting to purchase as little as possible? The growth economy would suffer a serious shock. But doesn't this lead us to a troubling conclusion? The virtue of thrift (that is, attempting to favor saving and preserving over wasting) is contrary to an economy whose primary measure of health is growth. If our present economy depends on the absence of virtue, just as Keynes suggested, then perhaps we need to take a serious look at the assumptions underlying our economic system. This is precisely what Berry asks us to do.

The self-sufficient, small-scale property owner extolled by Jefferson naturally acquires a profound appreciation of limits, and an appreciation of limits is not far from humility. The farmer realizes that he can sow and cultivate, and do these things well, but the harvest is ultimately beyond his ability to guarantee. He recognizes his dependence on gifts he can anticipate but not command. He may even become attuned to the work of grace in the world as the Divine Giver sends the gentle rains and the fair harvest moon.

In a proletarianized world, populated by pleasure-seeking wage earners, the touch of divine grace may be less easily felt. When government largesse is the primary means of addressing economic crises, it may even be that humility disappears. After all, the abstract wealth wielded by the government creates the impression of infinitude, and citizens will demand their right to a fair share of the limitless pie. Demanding one's share as a right is a far cry from gratefully accepting a gift. The perception of infinitude—rooted in fiat money and therefore fiat thinking—created by government largesse of breathtaking scale cultivates precisely the opposite of humility.

The virtues that private property serves to cultivate are necessary for the long-term health of a market economy and the long-term health of a free society. Private property is good because it is one of the best means of developing the virtues necessary for freedom. This is precisely the reason that the centralization of property is undesirable: it collects property into a few hands and reduces the rest to property-less wage earners. In this light it is possible to see the harm done when a big-box store is built on the edge of town and the small, family-owned concerns downtown are forced to shut their doors. The big-box store means fewer people will be

property owners and more will be mere wage earners. The obvious coun-
terargument is that the prices are lower at the big concern and times are
tight, so a person will take his money where it will go the furthest. This
is compelling and price is certainly not to be ignored. Economies of scale
can, in many instances, deliver more goods for lower prices. The question,
though, is whether there should be other considerations in addition to
price. Is there a price to focusing only upon price?

## The Ideal of Competition

The problem, according to Berry, is the universalization of the ideal of
competition, "which is destructive of both nature and of human nature
because it is untrue of both."[39] For Berry, competition destroys communities, for it divides rather than unites.

> The ideal of competition always implies, and in fact requires, that
> any community must be divided into a class of winners and a
> class of losers. This division is radically different from the other
> social division: that of the more able and the less able, or that
> of the richer and the poorer, or even that of the rulers and the
> ruled. These latter divisions have existed throughout history and
> at times, at least, have been ameliorated by social and religious
> ideals that instructed the strong to help the weak. As a purely
> economic ideal, competition does not contain or imply any such
> instruction.[40]

It is important to note that Berry is speaking of an idealized or absolute
form of competition. When competition is the ideal, problems inevitably
result. First, "the danger of the ideal of competition is that it neither proposes nor implies any limits."[41] This limitlessness is precisely the trouble,
for without limits, competition intrudes into aspects of life that simply
cannot flourish in the context of competition. This leads, then, to destruction of lives, or at least livelihoods, for when all is engulfed under the rule
of competition, there will be losers, and the best that can be said to them
is "find another line of work." To the extent that this creates nomadic wage
seekers, it destroys community. Finally, the ideal of unlimited competi-

tion "proposes an unlimited concentration of economic power."[42] Why is this the case? "Economic anarchy, like any other free-for-all, tends inevitably toward dominance by the strongest." This concentration of economic power takes practical form in the concentration of property where "the usable property of our country, once divided somewhat democratically, is owned by fewer and fewer people every year."[43] The obvious conclusion is that industrial capitalism, with its ideal of limitless competition, leads to plutocracy. Belloc saw this decades ago and predicted the rise of what he called the servile state.

This is not to say, of course, that competition has no place in a market economy. As Berry puts it,

> there is no denying that competitiveness is a part of the life both of an individual and of a community, or that, within limits, it is a useful and necessary part. But it is equally obvious that no individual can lead a good or a satisfying life under the rule of competition, and that no community can succeed except by limiting somehow the competitiveness of its members.[44]

Röpke expresses the same sort of concerns. "Historical liberalism never understood that competition is a dispensation, by no means harmless from a moral and sociological point of view; it has to be kept within bounds and watched if it is not to poison the body politic."[45] Thus, Röpke argues, while competition is one of the indispensable pillars upon which a just economic order rests, it must be kept within strict limits. Competition, he writes,

> is a means of establishing order and exercising control in the narrow sphere of a market economy based on the division of labor, but not a principle on which a whole society can be built. From the sociological and moral point of view it is even dangerous because it tends more to dissolve than to unite. If competition is not to degenerate, its premise will be a correspondingly sound political and moral framework.[46]

We see here a recurring principle voiced by Berry but also by Polanyi and Röpke: a market economy is one thing when it exists within a broader framework of social, moral, and religious commitments where the virtues are inculcated and practiced. These structures clearly define and limit the extent to which market forces impinge upon noneconomic aspects of life. A market economy is something entirely different when it becomes a Total Economy. Competition in the former is useful and limited in its scope. Competition in the latter is limitless and, as a result, destructive.

The price of the centralization of property is, ultimately, freedom. This is not difficult to understand. Citizens without property, that is, citizens who work for a wage, are often one pink slip from disaster, especially in times of economic downturn. Such people will have security always near the forefront of their minds, and for good reason. But in a democracy, where the people possess the franchise, this property-less class will express its deepest concerns at the ballot box. That is to say, citizens who do not possess property are not economically free in the way described by Jefferson, Belloc, Röpke, and Berry. At the same time, they are politically free insofar as they have the vote. Because they realize their own insecurity, they will, not surprisingly, vote for the candidate who promises the greatest security. The desire for security is understandable. The willingness to exchange freedom for security is made possible, and more likely, by the fact that these citizens have not had the opportunity to develop the virtues necessary for maintaining freedom. These are the virtues that private property helps to cultivate.

Berry's economic vision is a radical one. At the structural level, he asks us to reconsider the very idea of the corporation, especially corporate personhood. He asks us to consider the effects of an economic and political alliance oriented toward the centralization of power, both economic and political. He asks us to pause in our headlong rush to embrace global markets. He puts to question the fundamental axiom of modern economics that perpetual growth is both desirable and possible. While change at the structural level seems a distant prospect, Berry holds out hope, for humans are free and therefore human institutions can be reassessed and reformed. At the same time, individuals can seek to build and participate in healthy little economies forged by the simple acts made on a daily basis.

A healthy little economy is one that is firmly rooted in verities that extend beyond the economy. It is one characterized by informed choices rather than ignorance, by diversity rather than centralization, by love of things that cannot be bought or sold rather than the frenzied consumerism where everything has its price. A healthy economy is rooted in the ideal of property broadly distributed and stewarded with care. Berry calls us to live lives of gratitude, humility, and love where our lives consist of good work, neighborly acts, and care of the natural world. Berry calls us to think in terms of modest scale, of quality and not merely quantity. When shopping, we should learn to see beyond mere price. We should attempt to spend our money in ways that strengthen the local community and encourage ownership. Supporting local food producers is a modest but important step. Patronizing locally owned businesses is a way of using personal spending choices to encourage ownership. Ultimately, we must learn to see ourselves as participants in the Great Economy, a reality we can touch only tangentially but one through which we can feel the hum of mystery, beauty, and truth.

# 13

## The Restoration of Propriety:
## Wendell Berry and the
## British Distributists

*William Edmund Fahey*

There recently occurred in my town of Hollis, New Hampshire, the annual apple festival—the Hollis Apple Festival. Hollis is in the Merrimack River Valley, about two hundred miles south of Quebec and fifty miles north and west of Boston. The wide hills of the township are between four hundred and eight hundred feet above sea level; the soil is a rich, pebbly loam. Proximity to the Atlantic along with the broadening nature of the watershed means that temperatures are less dramatic in the fall and winter, frost less erratic. It is just the place for European plums, hardy peaches, pears, and apples, but especially apples. Hollis, for some time, has been filled with orchards, small and great. The town even boasts—or once boasted—of its own apple, developed by Deacon Stephen Jewett in the 1770s: the Nod Head, or Jewett's Fine Red as it is sometimes called. In 1874, a New Hampshire gazette blustered that "Hollis is one of the wealthiest towns in the county, and that everything pertaining to the farms and farmhouses betokens an air of wealth and thrift." To which that Thucydides of Hollis history, Samuel T. Worcester, replied, "A compliment well deserved as to many of them, but subject to exceptions."[1] The exceptions have grown over the decades; and even if the air smells of wealth, thrift has puffed out, and full-time farmers are rare.

Now, throughout the early autumn, anyone passing through Hollis would be enchanted by the fragrance of apples, the aroma teaching the history lesson that until very recently the majority of the town was involved in the cultivation, harvesting, packaging, and marketing of apples. Two family-run farms and orchards have popular stores near the town center, stocked with local produce. I have eaten more varieties of heirloom tomatoes than I can reasonably list; I have the ability to purchase a half-dozen different varieties of local honey, maple syrup, baked goods, vegetables, dairy products, and—of course—locally grown apples. There are familial apples: Haralson, Gravenstein, Macoun, and Jonathan; there are political apples: Liberty Apples, Empire Apples, Freedom, Spartans, and Regents; there are recently-arrived apples from the Orient: Fuji and Mutsu; and there are time-honored old apples of the West: Braeburn, Coxes, and Rome; there are sensuous apples: Honeygold, Honeysweet, Winesap, and Blushing. And finally, there are hoary, New England apples: Northern Spy, Roxbury Russett, and Gilliflowers. Hollis may be one of the few places where MacIntosh and Granny Smith are exotic.

And so you see, I found it strange that at the Hollis Apple Festival there were no apples from Hollis, or from farther parts of New Hampshire, or even from nearby Massachusetts. The Hollis Apple Festival is an annual gathering on the village commons to celebrate Hollis and its heritage and to raise money for the town band, which was there: members in splendid red jackets, beneath shuttering maple trees, brattling and booming away a mix of familiar tunes while ladies of the Hollis Women's Club nimbly sliced pies and generously ladled out crumble for the residents and Sunday visitors of our town. The autumnal light slanted across Monument Square against the stark face of the clapboard congregational church; and even longer and more solemn shadows stretched forth from the old tombstones of the village graveyard. It was a quintessential New England scene. Yet the apples were from New York. Every last one was shipped from the Empire State.

When I asked a very prim member of the Hollis Women's Club why I could not find a single Hollis apple in my Hollis Apple Festival crumble, the furnace of feminine ire opened upon me: "Perhaps Hollis farmers should offer apples at more competitive prices; then we could raise more money." I retreated, but continued pestering and prying and reading the local papers in search of an answer. Is it not one's right, after all, as a citizen of New England to be a crank?

It turns out that the local apple pie company moved away from Hollis to Merrimack (some ten miles away). This company previously would peel and core Hollis apples for the festival. The old company has now been transformed or absorbed into something bigger, which calls itself New England Country Pies of Merrimack. They provided the ladies with nine, forty-pound boxes of apples, grown, peeled, and cored in New York State. One of the local farmers considered purchasing the equipment for coring and peeling but determined that the equipment, which would cost some $16,000, was not worth it: "[I]t wouldn't have been cost effective," the local paper reported.[2]

Now then, if you feel that the Hollis Apple Festival was still—despite the interlopers of New York—a celebration of Hollis heritage and Hollis apples, and that there is nothing tragic about this tale, you will not appreciate the remainder of my essay. Yet if you sense that something is not quite right, then wait, just a bit, and read on. The issue I will examine over these pages is what lies near the very center of the humane vision championed by Wendell Berry. I shall attempt to address this by comparing his articulation of this vision with that of the British distributists. As I have a historical sensibility, permit me to begin with the distributists and move to Berry. I promise not to remain hidebound by chronology.

Up from Materialism:
The Essence and Origins of Distributism

Distributism is a convenient, if ugly, term used to describe a specific social, political, and economic orientation that emerged in the first half of the twentieth century in the British Isles.[3] There were many associated with the generation of principles that describes distributism and many more who tried, in Britain and elsewhere, to conduct their lives under the light of these principles. The chief architects of distributism were three friends: Hilaire Belloc, Gilbert Keith Chesterton, and Fr. Vincent McNabb. These men flourished from 1868 to 1953 (from the birth of McNabb to the death of Belloc). All three wrote with great fondness about—and from—the places where they lived: Fr. McNabb from Hawkesyard Priory in the English countryside and then for twenty-three years at the Dominican house and parish of St. Dominic in London; G. K. Chesterton from the grubby pubs of Fleet Street to his suburban cottage at Beaconsfield; and Belloc—well, Belloc wrote from Europe, inasmuch as he was the very embodiment of Old Europe. Yet from his boyhood on, his home and heart were always in a corner of Sussex. Eventually, he established himself at King's Land, a dilapidated brick house dating from the fourteenth century and set on five acres, a place evoked constantly in his writing.

Distributism may be described as a social disposition held by those who emphasize life as lived out in a local community. Distributists see this emphasis as the best response to the modern tendency of man to be attenuated by participation in larger, abstract associations. Distributists hold that there is an organic link between the person, the family, the homestead, the city, and the state. Yet distributists view concentrated political and economic power with suspicion and seek to influence private and public initiatives in such a way as to encourage a decentralized polity and the widespread distribution of property. Distributism encourages the orderly desire for ownership (in particular, the ownership of the means of production) among individuals, free families, and independent worker cooperatives.

The three men most closely identified with distributism were all leading participants in a cultural revival associated with the rebirth of Catholicism and a certain kind of Tory conservatism within the British Isles. The century from the battle of Culloden to the Oxford movement is, of course, marked by the Industrial Revolution, the rise of theories of progress, cultural materialism, economic liberalism, and the philosophical ascendancy of Enlightenment skepticism and empiricism. Science is increasingly triumphant, religion and tradition increasingly discredited. Kant replaces Aristotle and the tradition of the Schoolmen within ethics. The rise in urban centers, urban population, urban arts, and urban unrest during this period was unprecedented.

The distributist movement came as a response to the perceived twin evils of communism and the unrestricted capitalism generated by classical liberal ideology. Both of these systems emphasize the materialist dimension of man and are marked by a false faith in the continual unfolding of Progress. Vincent McNabb and Hilaire Belloc vociferously pointed to the unity between Marxism and most contemporary versions of capitalism in their materialistic leveling of man. The point has been reemphasized recently by Pope John Paul II's *Centesimus Annus*, his reflection on *Rerum Novarum*, where he notes that contemporary capitalism "agrees with Marxism, in the sense that it totally reduces man to the sphere of economics and the satisfaction of material needs."[4] From the beginning, the distributists opposed this Janus-faced materialism with two complementary traditions of European thought: Thomism, restored to prominence under Pope Leo XIII, and the anti-Whig medievalism of late-eighteenth- and nineteenth-century British cultural conservatives such as Cobbett, Coleridge, Ruskin, Newman, and Manning. On a deeper level—that of habit and custom—the distributists opposed the abstractions of industrial existence with the concrete lived reality of the European peasant, small craftsman, and town burgher.

Distributist ideas would enter into North America chiefly through the works of the English distributists and the growing influence of Roman Catholic social teaching in political and economic thought. The writings of Chesterton, Belloc, and McNabb had a deep and lasting influence on Catholics in America through numerous books published by the Newman, Bruce, and Sheed & Ward presses. Print works fostered personal contacts. The American Herbert Agar, as London correspondent for the Louisville *Courier-Journal* and a regular columnist for the *American Review*, became a close literary friend of Chesterton's and gave public prominence to distributism. Distributist ideas enjoyed broadening circulation in the 1930s and early '40s, especially in Catholic communities along the eastern seaboard and in the farming towns of the Midwest. This is little surprise given that the most successful American distributists in the early twentieth century were Catholics such as Peter Maurin, Dorothy Day, and members of the original Catholic Worker movement; Graham Walker and the New England Distributist League; and Virgil Michel, as well as those associated with the National Catholic Rural Life Conference.[5] Almost every economic handbook or text on Catholic social teachings published from the early 1920s until the beginning of the Cold War revealed the positive influence of the distributists.[6]

The distributists were among some of the first individuals to identify the destruction of the countryside and the erosion of the agrarian life as a wider social problem to be confronted through a posture of localist self-reliance. In the cities, American distributists were prominent in the fight to prevent unions from embracing communism, while simultaneously safeguarding workers from the predatory conditions of industrial and urban existence. In the face of the socialist tendencies of unions and the collusion of government and big business, the urban distributists championed smaller entrepreneurial enterprises and creation of worker sharehold-ing associations.

The closest allies of the distributists were the agrarians in the South and their northern associates, such as Agar and Ralph Borsodi, as well as the founder of the Catholic Worker movement, Peter Maurin. Like McNabb, Maurin was deeply influenced by the writings of Pope Leo XIII, was experienced as a farmer, and was something of a preacher himself. Maurin's original vision for the Catholic Worker movement had three essential parts: (1) roundtable discussions where laborers and intellectu-als studied Catholic social teaching together; (2) houses of hospitality— a restoration of the medieval hospice for the poor; and (3) agrarian col-leges for the education of the urban refugee to the land. Like McNabb and Ralph Borsodi, Maurin was distrustful of the alliance between government and business. In Maurin's case, the connection with McNabb is direct. McNabb's writings were part of the body of literature from which Maurin heavily drew.[7] Borsodi, on the other hand, is an American secular parallel to McNabb. Borsodi shared with McNabb a desire to convince people to return to self-sufficient homesteading.[8] Unlike McNabb, Borsodi viewed small-scale technology as a force that could assist this process.

McNabb has been described as the most practically influential of the British distributists and certainly the "most unabashedly radical."[9] He held that machinery simply tightened one's reliance on the structure of cities and industrialization and that any "back to the land" movement that relied on machines was ultimately inconsistent with the object of self-sufficiency. In this belief McNabb stands close to Andrew Lytle's position in "The Hind Tit":

How is the man who is living on the land . . . going to defend himself against this industrial imperialism and its destructive technology? One common answer is heard: industrialize the farm; be progressive; drop old-fashioned ways and adopt scientific methods. These slogans are powerfully persuasive and should be, but are not, regarded with the most deliberate circumspection, for under the guise of strengthening the farmer in his way of life they are advising him to abandon it and become absorbed. Such admonition coming from the quarters of the enemy is encourag-ing to the land-owner in one sense only: it assures him that he has something left to steal. Through its philosophy of Progress it is committing a mortal sin to persuade farmers that they can grow wealthy by adopting its methods. A farm is not a place to grow wealthy; it is a place to grow corn.[10]

Yet whereas Lytle was attempting a last-ditch defense of the men *on* the land, McNabb—holding to the same truths—was attempting to lead men *back to* it. Both men saw the industrial technology of their day as a menace to traditional rural life.

Together, the distributists and the agrarians stood for local traditions, self-sufficiency, an economic life centered on the household, the steward-ship of the land, and localist political activism. They stood against the mechanization of society, laissez-faire capitalism, consumerism, cultural homogenization, the destruction of rural and small town life, and the veiled socialism of the Roosevelt administration. Together the distributists and agrarians attempted to preserve what was described as a Jeffersonian position in American political life.[11] The journal *Free America* became the flagship publication for the distributist-agrarian alliance in America; within Catholic circles, the *Social Justice Review*, *Orate—Fratres*, and *The Catholic Worker* regularly printed the essays of distributists. In the British Isles, *Eye Witness*, *The New Age*, *The New Witness*, and *G.K.'s Weekly* were the principal venues, with the *Tablet*, the *Dublin Review*, and T. S. Eliot's *Criterion* occasionally weighing-in. Whereas the distributists anchored their thought in what they saw as a wider natural tendency for man to flourish in a local community, the Southern Agrarians worked out of a specifically regional milieu. The Southern Agrarians' quintessential, but exclusive (southern) regionalism made a lasting and effective union impos-sible, and the two remained allied forces achieving little public effect after the appearance of *Who Owns America?* in 1936, although *Free American* remained in circulation until the mid-1940s. In recent years, the chief heir to this tradition in North America has been Wendell Berry of Kentucky.[12]

After the Second World War, enthusiasm for the distributist and agrar-ian position ebbed, as most conservatives formed a common front in the struggle against Communism. American exceptions to this were Richard Weaver and Russell Kirk, both of whom were well-read in the distributist and agrarian literature. In Europe we find E. F. Schumacher and, to a great extent, Wilhelm Röpke espousing distributist ideas.[13] With a growing concern for environmental issues, the decline of the Soviet Union, and greater alarm for the destructive tendencies of a resurgent laissez-faire Capitalism, interest in Distributism began to wax anew in the last decade of the twentieth century. Indeed, within the ambit of conservatism, there are growing numbers who, to varying degrees, have broken with the classical liberal tradition on social, economic, and environmental issues.[14]

The thought of distributist thinkers can be set out according to the following canons: (1) Subsidiarity, or the understanding that the members of a primary association (e.g., the family) must structure their lives and direct their actions responsibly, and that higher associations should not—without grave cause—usurp a smaller organization's ability to accomplish its task, but rather at all times support its endeavors;[15] (2) Proprietary interest, or the commitment to the widespread ownership of property and the means of livelihood; (3) Defense of the local, or a suspicion of private or public entities that threaten subsidiarity or proprietary interest, and a willingness to support public policy that encourages small, locally controlled economies over the domination of large retail chains and global corporations; (4) Craftsmanship, or the confidence that local, community-based economies tend toward greater beauty, quality, and trust between the makers and the users of goods; and (5) Agrarianism, or the belief that a rural society is the best environment for safeguarding tradition, typically understood as a family-centered life, self-sufficiency, anti-majoritarianism, the dignity of labor and craftsmanship, good health, small communities, and religious vitality.

## Seeing with Wonder and Knowing Your Place: Wendell Berry's Social Vision

Obtaining a clear view of Berry's social vision has been a slow and pleasurable process for readers who have been following his writing over the past thirty years. In recent works, Berry has become increasingly precise in reassuring his audience that the vision is not his by creation but by inheritance and cultivation, and he has associated himself more and more explicitly with the agrarian tradition of Europe and America. He speaks of his "life as an agrarian writer" and states that this is to belong to a group "involved in a hard, long, momentous contest, in which we are so far, and by a considerable margin, the losers. What we have undertaken to defend," he writes in *Citizenship Papers*,

> is the complex accomplishment of knowledge, cultural memory, skill, self-mastery, good sense, and fundamental decency—the high and indispensible art—for which we probably can find no better name than "good farming." I mean farming as defined by agrarianism as opposed to farming as defined by industrialism: farming as the proper use and care of an immeasurable gift.[16]

Berry goes on to point out here (as elsewhere) that farming or agrarianism is a way of understanding oneself and one's place in nature and community. It is a vision that guides a man not to "think global and act local" but to think locally and act appropriately.

This is not to say Berry advocates an abandonment of the public sphere that extends beyond one's local community. Quite the contrary. If we turn back to one of his earliest works, *The Unsettling of America*, we can find a bold illustration of this agrarian vision forming or informing public policy. Here Berry is speaking of social and economic disintegration in his corner of Kentucky, but by extension and with adaptation it could be elsewhere.

> The first necessary public change is simply a withdrawl of confidence from the league of specialists, officials, and corporation executives who for at least a generation have had almost exclusive charge of the problem and who have enormously enriched and empowered themselves by making it worse.

Berry then turns to the early American republic and states,

> we must see again, as I think the founders of our government saw, that the most appropriate governmental powers are negative—those, that is, that protect the small and weak from the great and powerful, not those by which the government becomes the profligate, ineffectual parent of the small and weak after it has permitted the great and powerful to make them helpless.

He then turns to the issue of taxation as an instrument for encouraging the distribution of ownership. Like Belloc he does not focus on re-distribution or confiscation but rather on remembering and reimagining the whole social-economic order of things. Berry explicitly cites Jefferson writing to James Madison in 1785: "'Another means of silently lessening the inequality of property is to exempt all from taxation below a certain point, and to tax the higher portions of property in geometric progressions as they rise.'"[17] Elsewhere Berry suggests policies in agriculture that do not permit a price deflation that only benefits the large industrial business; subsidized loans for family farms rather than corporate farms; encouragement of localized markets rather than global trade; limitations on the application of technology within the farming sector; tariffs; and many other suggestions that could make a white-hot American conservative quail. One can debate about the particular merits of the policy suggestions. I only note two things: first, all these policies have been implemented or upheld in the past by conservatives and Republicans, as the work of Alan Carlson has shown.[18] Second, in print Berry has moved away from policy suggestions, which tend to be national, to testing principles based on his local knowledge and reflections. That Berry rarely allows himself to dwell on specific policies is in accord with his principle that policies must be adapted over time and for different regions. Global thinking—even national thinking—can only be abstract and ideological, and "Abstraction," notes Berry,

> is the enemy wherever it is found. The abstraction of sustainability can ruin the world just as surely as the abstractions of industrial economics. Local life may be as much endangered by those who would "save the planet" as those who would "conquer the world." For "saving the planet" calls for abstract purposes and central powers that cannot know—and thus will destroy—the integrity of local nature and local community.[19]

## With Minds and Bodies Changed by Place and Time: Some Distinctions and the Essential Unity of the Distributists and Berry

We should note that there are certain distinctions or contrasts between the distributists and Berry. First, while ownership of land and agrarian sensibilities are part of the distributist program, they are only a part. Second, within distributist writings there is diversity of thought on the best political regime, while Berry is consistently Jeffersonian and democratic. Belloc and Chesterton—and most distributists—briefly admired Mussolini, supported Franco, and were busily engaged in reviving notions of monarchy (or monarchical power) within a constitutional framework. Still, both groups are unanimous in defending common men, especially the marginal, the urban poor, the peasant, and country people. Third, while members of the Distributist League were all varieties of religious and nonreligious stripes, the vast majority were Roman Catholic or high-church Anglican. Berry—"by principle and often spontaneously, as if by nature, a man of faith"—is also, by his own admission, an "uneasy reader" of scripture, especially the Gospels. His Baptist affiliation is, at least on the surface, quite different from the apparent boisterousness of the Catholic distributists. Nevertheless, there is at the heart of both Berry and the distributists a central idea, and that idea I shall call, with Berry, "propriety."

Propriety: what is it? First, a little more of Berry's background is necessary. In an earlier autobiographical reminiscence, "A Native Hill," Berry described coming to an awareness of modern man's disconnection with his world and then the source of his own rare connection. Berry had begun his mature writing career as a university professor and writer in New York City. There he was held by the provincial intellectuals of that city as a young man of talent and promise. For all the encouragement that he received there, Berry felt cut off from reality, from the wellspring of his literary imagination. He also realized that his own understanding of what was "real" did not correspond to that of the city's literati. New cosmopolitian experiences, or at least "the modern experience," was not something Berry found sustaining. "What I had in my mind that made the greatest difference was the knowledge of the few square miles in Kentucky that were mine by inheritance and by birth and by the intimacy the mind makes with the place it awakens in."[20] Berry, then, returned to Kentucky to teach, and to write, and to farm.

Reflecting seriously on the history of the region, the customs of his people, and the natural life of his own farm, Berry came to see his life and work as rooted and nourished, like that of any living thing, in a specific locale. After many years on his small native hill, Berry reflected in an essay titled "A Native Hill" that he had become "free of a suspicion that pursued me for most of my life, no matter where I was, that there was another place I should be."[21] Place stood against ideological abstraction: "My mind became the root of my life rather than its sublimation."[22] Localism, or regionalism, was an awareness of a larger order, an order that was given before the particular individual entered upon the scene, a world that is one's native place shaping and informing one's experience, talents, and desires. This knowing of a specific place makes possible the ordering of meaning, not as it exists in the abstract, but rather as it exists in a world that can be communicated and shared with others.[23]

What, then, is propriety? In an early intimation, Berry saw it in the bearing of four rough-winged swallows along the river near his land. "They were neat, beautiful, gentle birds. Sitting there preening in the sun after their cold bath, they communicated a sense of domestic integrity, *the serenity of living within order*."[24] The serenity of living within order. Elsewhere Berry speaks of harmony, and it would seem that these two terms—harmony and propriety—are nearly interchangeable. Propriety is thus the diverse, vital, and beautiful coordination of man and his world, natural and created. Berry's most sustained and deliberate description of propriety can be found in *Life Is a Miracle*:

> "Propriety" is an old term, even an old-fashioned one, and is not much in favor these days. Its value is in its reference to the fact that we are not alone. The idea of propriety makes an issue of the fittingness of our conduct to our place or circumstances, even to our hopes. It acknowledges the always-pressing realities of context and influence; we cannot speak or act or live out of context. Our life inescapably affects other lives, which inescapably affect our life. We are being measured, in other words, by a standard we did not make and cannot destroy.[25]

The opposite of propriety is the abstract way of thinking. This abstract way of thought typifies political tyrants, as well as technological and economic determinists; that is, anyone who firmly pursues the so-called dynamic vision of man re-creating endlessly the world of his own imagination, the well-lit world of his own thought. This urge for the new and for change inevitably leads to conflicts with other visions and an utter confusion as to the individual's rights, roles, and place in the world. Again, Berry:

> [Such confusion] comes from the specialization and abstraction of intellect, separating it from responsibility and humility, magnanimity and devotion, and thus giving it an importance that, in the order of things and its own nature, it does not and cannot have. The specialized intellectual assumes, in other words, that intelligence is all in the mind. For illustration, I turn again to *Paradise Lost*, where Satan, fallen, boasts in "heroic" defiance that he has
>
> > A mind not to be chang'd by Place or Time.
> > The mind is its own place, and in itself
> > Can make a Heav'n of Hell, a Hell of Heav'n,
> > What matter where, if I be still the same, . . .
>
> I do not know where one could find a better motto for the modernist or technological experiment, which assumes that we can fulfill a high destiny anywhere, any way, so long as we can keep up the momentum of innovation; that the mind is "its own place" even within ecological degradation, pollution, poverty, hatred, and violence.[26]

Berry and the distributists before him founded their social views on the old truth that man is not mere intelligence, or even incarnated intelligence, but a creature, spiritual and material, possessed of intellect and a body, born into communities—communities with memories, narratives, knowledge, codes, and customs that, far from being possessed by his mind, formed and informed his mind, his body, his whole soul and self. He is a placed creature, and without place he loses or deforms those memories, narratives, bodies of knowledge, codes, and customs. When he does not attend to place, he jeopardizes all those traditions that he may seek to call his own—now or at some future date.

Placed Creation: Participation in Creation
and Society and Its Theological Roots

While the traditional Christian anthropology found in distributist writings is clear, there are various critics who wish to understand Berry as fundamentally secular, and so my comment on man as a "placed creature" in Berry's thought may require expansion.[27] For the sake of brevity here, I suggest to readers that two passages from Berry may be compared. First, let us turn to the novel *Jayber Crow*, where the main character, the barber Jayber, remarks that

> the Spirit that had gone forth to shape the world and make it live was still alive in it. I just had no doubt. I could see that I lived in the created world, and it was still being created. I would be part of it forever. There was no escape. The Spirit that made it was *in* it, shaping it and reshaping it, sometimes lying at rest, sometimes standing up and shaking itself, like a muddy horse, and letting the pieces fly.[28]

Berry does not use the language of a traditional theologian, of course; that would be incongruous with the narrator. Nevertheless, the theological underpinning of Berry's thought is the anchor to his protagonist's views in the novel. All men—indeed, all created things—are *placed* in a world—a created order—that allows for participation with the Creator. To ignore the implications and obligations of such placement is dangerous. Berry makes this point quite explicitly in a lecture he gave at the Southern Baptist Theological Seminary in Louisville, Kentucky. In reading Sacred Scripture, Berry states:

> We will discover that the Creation is not in any sense independent of the Creator, the result of a primal creative act long over and done with, but is the continuous, constant participation of all creatures in the being of God.[29]

That we are placed in the created order and have an obligation to stewardship establishes, for Berry, a communion in which God reveals

Himself, is present to, and interacts with all creatures. To reject our place in Creation and our stewardship of a place is to "fling God's gifts into His face."

> The Bible leaves no doubt at all about the sanctity of the act of world-making, or of the world that was made, or of a creaturely or bodily life in this world. We are holy creatures living among other holy creatures in a world that is holy.[30]

This emphasis on the holiness or goodness of Creation *may* put Berry at odds with traditional Baptist theology and, indeed, much of mainstream Protestant thought. He is also more comfortable speaking of the role of Spirit and of the Creator than talking about Jesus, and when he does speak of Jesus or Christ it is usually in the context of a lifelong effort puzzling over the meaning and consequence of Christ's advent, life, and teaching.[31] And yet Berry has always described himself as in the Bible-reading Christian tradition, not a deist or an agnostic or merely a spiritual person.[32]

Berry's dilemma and difficulty with the theology of his youth is a permanent fixture of American Christianity. From the very beginning there has been a tension in America between two Christian approaches to nature and the newfound land. The Puritan William Bradford, in his *Of Plimouth Plantation*, looked upon the natural order through a sharp Calvinist's spectacles—it was but a "hideous and desolate wilderness" filled with the most fallen of men and a mirror of unredeemed man. Yet for his contemporary, the high-Anglican Thomas Morton, "the beauty of the place . . . in [his] eyes, t'was nature's Masterpiece."[33] Berry may be in conscious reaction to restrictive Baptist theology, or in tradition with the anti-Puritanism of transcendentalists such of Thoreau, or a living echo of the other side of the American tradition exemplified by Morton, or—most likely—all of these at once. In any case, the fundamental goodness of Creation and the belief that it is a gift from a Creator still active in Creation is foundational to Berry's thought and analogous to that of the distributists.

In itself, Berry's belief in this fundamental goodness of Creation does not pose difficulties for the Catholic theology behind Distributism. Such an understanding of man's relationship to Creation and the Creator is essential to Catholic teaching. One can find modern papal writings from those of Pope Pius XII onward treating the communion that the farmer has with his Creator through nature.[34] And it is a commonplace in the writings of St. Augustine, St. Thomas Aquinas, and St. Bonaventure that the created order is fundamentally good and given in order to allow communication and participation with and in God.[35] Modern industrial society seemed to put layers between man and the created order and, thus, between man and the Creator. A fundamental axiom of traditional Christian humanism is that without an understanding of the Creator, man cannot understand himself and his true purpose. Working within and close to the created order allows man to participate in Being itself and to ponder the order and causes hidden within all Creation. The great closing of the gap between man, the created order, and the Creator came with the Incarnation.

It was for these reasons that distributists turned to the farmer, the homesteader, or as they liked to call him, the peasant. Of course, owning and working the land was a fundamental part of the economic side of Distributism, but it was not the deepest part. Listen to Chesterton:

> Rustic populations, largely self-supporting, seem to have amused themselves with a great many mythologies and dances and decorative arts; and I am not convinced that the turnip-eater always had a head like a turnip or that the top hat always covers the brain of a philosopher. But if we look at the problem from the point of view of the community as a whole, we shall note other and not uninteresting things. . . . A system based entirely on the division of labour is in one sense literally half-witted. That is, each performer of half an operation does really only use half of his wits. . . . The peasant does live, not merely a simple life, but a complete life. It may be very simple in its completeness, but the community is not complete without that completeness. The community is at present very defective because there is not in the core of it any such simple consciousness; any one man who represents two parties to a contract. Unless there is, there is nowhere a full understanding of those terms: self-support, self-control, self-government.[36]

Chesterton here looks explicitly to Virgil, who said, speaking of the small farmer, "happy is he who could know the cause of things." And behind Virgil stands Aristotle, who tells us in the *Metaphysics* that "all men desire to know." All men delight in their senses and delight in all forms of learning. But, of wisdom and the happiness that comes with it, he is clear: this comes only to the one capable of understanding "causes and principles," and that knowledge can be glimpsed only by those who can and do observe the whole.[37] This, Aristotle holds, is true in politics, friendship, economics, and every art and science, in the whole of human affairs.

Yet the distributists were not merely, nor even chiefly, Aristotelians; they were Catholics. Their view on human society was shaped chiefly by their understanding of how profoundly the Incarnation changed human society. Belloc himself said little directly on the Incarnation in his social criticism but rather concentrated his attention on the impact of the church and the creation of Christian society, both of which came into being and took their shape because of the Incarnation. The chief areas transformed by Christianity were slavery and the family. Slavery was gradually replaced with serfdom and then a peasant independence centered in the economics of a household, dignified by, and socially enshrined in, the Christian monogamous marriage. These are the two pillars of Belloc's economic views: first, a free household of a free family; and second, freedom itself given new meaning by the new understanding of human dignity.[38] Thus, the advent of Christianity, from the Bellocian view, restored part of what was originally proper to man but lost in the wave of human sinfulness. It restored two missing parts of social propriety: the harmony of man and woman in marriage and the freedom of families to work on the land and enjoy the fruit of their labor.

For McNabb, the Holy Family became the "Nazareth Measure," an essential image of the natural social unit by which all political life was to be evaluated. He warned politicians: "Let no guile of social usefulness betray you into hurting the authority of the Father, the chastity of the Mother, the rights and therefore the property of the Child. Social and economic laws are more subtle but not less infallible than physical law. No programme of good intentions will undo the mischief caused by an interference with family life."[39] In and through the family, men and women would find their place and naturally settle and form community.

For Chesterton, the presence and influence of the Incarnation was increasingly evident in his writings. The shining example remains the *Everlasting Man*. Yet, like Belloc, he never forced the reality of the Incarnation to the front of his prose, or forced his readers to assent to his own Catholic principles. Even at the end of his *Outline of Sanity*, in his chapter "The Religion of Small Property," which argues for the Catholic faith as the foundation for a distributist society, Chesterton avoids both sectarianism and the technical language of Catholic theology. In speaking of the success of French Canadians at establishing a humane social order, he underlines their Catholicism as the chief reason for the distinctive social order of colonial Quebec. This religious backdrop explained their success in establishing, in the new world, a society that was both Old European and new; stable and attractive, just and prosperous:

> In a sense a new world can be baptized as a new baby is baptized, and become part of an ancient order not merely on the map but in the mind. Instead of crude people merely extending their crudity, and calling that colonization, it would be possible for people to cultivate the soil as they cultivate the soul. But for this it is necessary to have a respect for the soil as well as for the soul; even a reverence for it, as having some association with holy things. But for that purpose we need some sense of carrying holy things with us and taking them home with us; not merely the feeling that holiness may exist as hope. In the most exalted phrase, we need a real presence. In the most popular phrase, we need something that is always on the spot.[40]

Neither Chesterton nor Belloc, for all the subsequent lampooning of their Catholic faith, bludgeoned their audience with the necessity for conversion to Catholicism.[41] Indeed, both were so committed to the sacrality of the created order that even friendly critics sometimes remarked on their apparent pantheism.[42] The key to both Berry and the distributists is that propriety could be observed and experienced because it was of the nature of man to be in a place and there to be able to see the harmony of things. The emplacement in relationship to land and other humans was a gift, given by design and by a generous Spirit, for human flourishing. For a just society to emerge, a determining number of families needed to participate in the created order, freely, and in a specific place over long periods of time. The chief mark of distinction between Berry and the distributists lies in the distributists' willingness to assert that such a gift was possible to realize and build again chiefly thanks to the Incarnation and the organic social order that arose in its wake.

Thus, the vision of the distributists and of Berry is a revival of a commonsense Christian metaphysics over and against the Miltonic (or Satanic) individualism of modernity, which cannot escape its own mind as the solitary judge, if not creator, of its own so-called reality. Such an illusory individualism animates even some of the most apparently sober of modern thinkers.[43]

The vision of propriety—that harmony that comes from knowing one's place, knowing the limits of oneself and that place—ironically lights up the only path toward freedom for the human thirsts. Consider the words of Belloc's character Grizzlebeard, the old man who has been one of the three companions of the narrator ("myself") in Belloc's masterwork *The Four Men*. Myself and his companions—the sailor, the poet, and Grizzlebeard—have journeyed from October 30 to November 2 across Sussex. The real Sussex and the imagined geography come together so that Belloc's creative powers allow him to see his world more deeply, as that world refines Belloc's self-understanding. At the end of the journey, Myself begs his companions to push on with him farther, for there are other inns and villages and Roman ruins to see and contemplate. Grizzlebeard responds with "dreadful solemnity":

> "No; we are all three called to other things. But do you go back to your home, for the journey is done." Then he added (but in another voice); "There is nothing at all that remains: nor any house; nor any castle, however strong; nor any love, however tender and sound; nor any comradeship among men, however hardy. Nothing remains but the things of which I will not speak, because we have spoken enough of them already during these four days. But I who am old will give you advice, which is this—to consider chiefly from now onward those permanent things which are, as it were, the shores of this age and the harbours of our glittering and pleasant but dangerous and wholly changeful sea."[44]

We cannot avoid living in a world that requires political action, at least now and again. Indeed, a reflection on our nature reveals that we do not desire complete severance from such action. We cannot avoid living in a world filled with economic activity in which we too play a part, and the active life is not one to be shunned or avoided. The localism of the distributists and Wendell Berry is not separatism; it is rather a traditional framing of the social life of man. I would suggest that without a firm commitment to those little communities that have claims on us: families, churches, towns—they will differ here and there, but they are united by actually being *here* or *there*—without a commitment to them, we cannot conceivably exercise the prudence (and sense of propriety) so needed in social life, because we will forever be trapped in a solitary mind.

Let us conclude and return to apples. The scandal of the Hollis Apple Festival is to me yet another sign that the fabric of our civilization is rent something terrible. One must ask what is being celebrated in such a festival, nominally dedicated to a specific community and its traditional economy, when apples are chosen outside the region solely for their low price. My simple question as to why no local apples were included elicited a bristling response. Perhaps the question had been asked before. In any case, my Women's Club interlocutor had her response down pat, delivered it crisply, but clearly was not happy with it. How could she be? She was kind and of the best intentions, but her unconscious acceptance of a narrow economic way of thinking abstracted her mind from the wholeness still possible in one little corner of our commonwealth. Not to see how the farmer's cultivation of apples and her baking of apples and my eating of the same apples would give a rich and concrete meaning to the Hollis Apple Festival leaves frayed to a perilous degree the cords of unity with our town. It shifted the balance in favor of an abstraction, pleasant to some inner eye, of saving money and gaining money. But where is the communion in that?

# 14

# The Integral Imagination of Wendell Berry

*Nathan Schlueter*

Writing about works of the imagination sometimes feels a little like brushing my teeth right after a good meal. It may be necessary, but it is not necessarily pleasant. The analogy is admittedly vulgar, but then I don't profess to be a poet. I am, by habit and inclination, an intellectual with a guilty conscience, inveterately sifting every experience through a framework of ideas, trading the solid substance of things for airy simulacra. Worse, writing about the imagination inevitably risks mimicking the growing industry of audio lectures that, by lecturing people on great literature, relieves them of the burden of reading the books for themselves. So if you have not yet read Wendell Berry, stop here and go enjoy the real thing first.

Despite its dangers, reflection on the imagination is in some sense natural and even necessary, for the imagination plays an important role in the life of every human being, whether for good or ill, and whether we are aware of it or not. Such reflection seems especially important in our time, when we are more saturated with images than ever before, and yet strangely find ourselves more impoverished than ever before in our ignorance of what these images mean for living well or poorly. Indeed, reflective deliberation is a constituent part of human nature, pointing to man's uneasy relationship with the rest of nature. Human beings, although a part of nature, do not exist in simple harmony with it. Even as we recognize in our bodies the same metabolic processes and material conditions that exist in the rest of the natural world, we possess in our reason, will, and imagination a constant reminder of our differences from that world. This natural complexity of human beings makes certain questions inescapable. "How do we fit in?" Wendell Berry asks in *Standing by Words*. "What is the possibility of a human harmony *within* nature?"[1]

Such harmony within human beings, and between human beings and the rest of nature, can never be spontaneous or immediate. It always involves an achievement of mediation. Something of this necessity is indicated by the fact that human experience *is* mediated experience, moving through sense, imagination, memory, history, and culture to the center of the self. The quality of these mediations in large part determines the quality of our lives. The attempt to escape the necessity of mediation does not result in immediacy but in ignorance, enslaving us willy-nilly to those mediation makers who would profit from it by giving us only the illusion of immediacy. I speak here primarily of the entertainment industry, whose implicit goal is the "Feelies" of Huxley's *Brave New World*. We forget that this story ends in an orgy of obscene and brutal voyeurism, which bears a striking resemblance to the "reality" television of today.

It is therefore a necessary and high responsibility of culture and politics to reflect upon, preserve, and promote those mediations that contribute to the wholeness proper to human beings. Sadly, the culture of our time is characterized by the insane ambition to destroy mediation, principally through the specialized separation of science and art. Ours is a culture against culture, an anticulture, and the consequences have been a tragic disintegration and fragmentation of individuals and communities. There is no better time therefore to recover serious reflection about wholeness and the integral role mediation plays in such wholeness, and there is no better place to begin such reflection than in the works of Wendell Berry.

Berry is himself a model of integral wholeness. He is simultaneously citizen, farmer, writer, activist, husband, father, and human being, in a way that, at least to his admirers, appears seamless.[2] His writings span the genres of prose, poetry, and fiction, mapping a world of meaning that seems as large as the world itself. At the center of this world is a humane vision that seeks to achieve the wholeness proper to human beings, and at the center of this vision is a restoration of the imagination to its rightful place in the order of things. This imagination is best described as "integral," a word whose Latin root means "whole" but can also mean "healthy" and "sane." An integral whole consists of a unity of parts, but such a unity is not achieved by reducing or resolving the parts into a simple whole. Rather, an integral whole preserves and protects the parts precisely by integrating them into the larger whole to which they are naturally ordered. When these parts are divided and separated, not only is the whole destroyed, but the parts themselves suffer as well. It is to this division I now turn.

## The Great Divorce between Reason and Imagination

It is not sufficiently appreciated that our anticulture culture originated in an attack on the imagination. Here is a pivotal passage from the fifteenth chapter of Machiavelli's *The Prince*:

> But since it is my intention to write a useful thing for him who understands, it seemed to me more profitable to go behind to the *effectual truth* of the thing, than to the *imagination thereof*. And many have *imagined* republics and principates that have never been seen or known to be in truth; because there is such a distance between how one lives and how one should live that he who lets go that which is done for that which ought to be done learns his ruin rather than his preservation—for a man who wishes to profess the good in everything needs must fall among so many who are not good.[3]

Machiavelli presents here a series of contrasting dichotomies (how one lives, how one ought to live; ruin, preservation; good, not good, etc.), the most significant of which is effectual truth, and the imagination thereof. According to Machiavelli, it is the "imagined republic and principates" (read Plato's *Republic* and St. Augustine's *City of God*) that "have never been seen or known to be in truth" that are the cause of the world's ruin.

Machiavelli makes clear his intent in the following chapters of *The Prince*. The "effectual truth" is that nature (including human nature) has no intrinsic goodness or purpose; it is rather a "violent river," indifferent if not hostile to human flourishing, which must therefore be conquered and directed by "embankments" and "defenses" (i.e., technology). "La mar" (feminine) thus becomes "el mar" (masculine), as Hemingway puts it in *The Old Man and the Sea*. In such a world, there is no higher good than preservation (or what will become for Thomas Hobbes "comfortable self-preservation"), and there are therefore no limits to its pursuit. In attacking the imagination, Machiavelli was attacking the entire traditional moral and metaphysical order that placed limits on the human will for the sake of goods deemed higher than mere preservation.

By driving a wedge between "the effectual truth of the thing" and the "imagination thereof," Machiavelli paved the way for the two most powerful movements of our time, modern science and romanticism. These in turn played an important role in the technological, political, and often-times bloody revolutions that have plagued the modern world.[4] Whereas modern science embraced an empiricist and mathematical methodology that had for its purpose "to renew and enlarge the power and empire of mankind in general over the universe,"[5] romanticism embraced the imagination as a "baseless fabric"[6] and celebrated "the cult of creativity" and "art for art's sake."

Yet Machiavelli knew the utility and power of the imagination, which he used to great profit in *The Prince* and elsewhere.[7] By associating imagination with ineffectuality, Machiavelli hoped through his own poetic discourse to destroy the imagined republics of the past and to create a new "imagined republic" on supposedly more realistic or effectual grounds, one whose essential nature would be disguised even from its own practitioners under scientific-sounding names like positivism, empiricism, and behaviorism. Far from an accurate description of reality itself, all of these *isms* are instead abstractive fictions for understanding or expressing general laws of reality. As Leon Kass has written:

> The so-called "empirical" science of nature is, as actually experienced, a highly contrived encounter with apparatus, measuring devices, pointer-readings, and numbers; nature in its ordinary course and as humanly experienced is virtually never encountered directly. . . . Science becomes not the representation and demonstration of truth, but an art: the art of *finding* the truth—or, rather, that portion of the truth that lends itself to be artfully found.[8]

The paradox of Machiavelli's poetry is that the imagination plays a more powerful role in our lives than ever before, yet we are largely unaware of this fact. Modern science thus conceals its own poetic ground, and the romantic cult of creativity reacts strongly by severing itself from the real. The result is a culture deeply divided between science without poetry (i.e., scientism) on the one hand, and poetry without intellect (i.e., romanticism) on the other. This cultural division in turn reflects and encourages a deeper division within the human person, producing what T. S. Eliot referred to as "a dissociation of sensibility,"[9] what Walker Percy called the "angelism-bestialism" neurosis,[10] and what C. S. Lewis identified as "men without chests."[11]

By his use of this phrase, Lewis showed a precise understanding of the problem I have been discussing, for the chest is the traditional metaphorical seat both of the imagination and emotion, as well as the mediator between reason and appetite in human beings. In that part of Plato's *Republic* that is most neglected (because it is most scorned) by modern educators, Plato describes in careful detail the education in poetry and music that provides the necessary foundation for the later education in the liberal arts. This education of the imagination begins the liberation of the soul from raw appetite, making it responsive to truth, goodness, and beauty. As Lewis puts it in *The Abolition of Man*:

> Aristotle says that the aim of education is to make the pupil like and dislike what he ought. When the age for reflective thought comes, the pupil who has been thus trained in "ordinate affections" or "just sentiments" will easily find the first principle in the Ethics: but to the corrupt man they will never be visible at all and he can make no progress in that science. Plato before him had said the same. The little human animal will not at first have the right responses. It must be trained to feel pleasure, liking, disgust, and hatred at those things which really are pleasant, likeable, disgusting and hateful. In *The Republic*, the well-nurtured youth is one "who would see most clearly whatever was amiss in ill-made works of man or ill-grown works of nature, and with a just distaste would blame and hate the ugly even from his earliest years and would give delighted praise to beauty, receiving it into his soul and being nourished by it, so that he becomes a man

gentle of heart. All this before he is of an age to reason; so that when Reason at length comes to him, then, bred as he has been, he will hold out his hands in welcome and recognize her because of the affinity he bears to her."[12]

Without this education in poetry, a liberal arts education becomes not only futile but also dangerous. It destroys our prejudices without deepening that understanding of them, which is the precondition for their correction. A liberal arts education without poetry ends in nihilism, a fact illustrated by the current state of higher education today.

Wendell Berry's Restoration of Reason and Imagination

Like C. S. Lewis, Wendell Berry locates the illness of our time in a great divorce between reason and imagination. The separation came with the advent of modern science and romanticism, which "specialized reason and imagination and turned them against one another,"[13] resulting in the "most destructive disease of dualism that afflicts us . . . a cleavage, a radical discontinuity, between Creator and creature, spirit and matter, religion and nature, religion and economy, worship and work, and so on."[14] Implicit in the specialization of reason and imagination is the outright denial that there is a unified whole that harmonizes the diversity of things. It is a denial of order. Though Berry dedicates separate books to each term of this division—*Standing by Words* to romanticism, and *Life Is a Miracle* to modern science—he insightfully brings out in both books what these two attitudes share in common, despite their evident differences. The common sentiment is expressed most concisely in words of Satan in *Paradise Lost*:

A mind not to be chang'd by Place or Time.
The mind is its own place, and in itself
Can make a Heav'n of Hell, a Hell of Heav'n.
What matter where, if I be still the same. . . . (I, 253–56)

Several characteristics common to romanticism and modern science are implicit here. First, both regard the natural world as somehow separate from the self and subject to it: "The romantic mind is a mind apart," Berry writes in *Standing by Words*. "It conceives itself as divided from nature and superior to it, not as stranded with it on the same mountaintop." Similarly, "To the romantic scientist, nature is a stock of natural resources to be used however seems necessary to further the human ascent toward a god-like autonomy and control."[15] In their specialized isolation of mind, both romanticism and modern science share a preoccupation with the new, and hostility for the old and for tradition; "the modern cult of creativity" in poetry, which is eager to "replace the old with the new,"[16] is paralleled in modern science by "the cult of innovation"[17] and "the cult of progress,"[18] which pursue "indefinite human progress"[19] through the reconstruction of nature by technology. "Both, in their different ways, propose that a new Eden, an earthly paradise, can be made solely by 'the discerning intellect of man.'"[20] Finally, both modern science and romanticism reject all limits, whether human or divine, to man's power over nature or his efforts at self-creation.

Despite their superficial differences, therefore, it is not surprising that modern science and romanticism would eventually meet in the "romantic scientist." Consider this passage from *Challenging Nature*, by Lee Silver, a molecular biologist at Princeton University:

> If we follow the only sustainable path that is really left open, then surely, over the centuries or millennia, human nature will remake Mother Nature in the image of the idealized world that exists within our own minds, and humankind will be better for it. We will establish stable ecosystems with animals that are friendly and roam free, and perhaps one day, a real-life Jurassic Park will come into existence alongside a forest of mythological creatures. And the creatures will be no more or less soulful than animals currently residing in the San Diego zoo. Of course, human beings are an integral part of the world that will be remade. Will they alone remain unchanged, or will they reconceive and reconstruct the human race—consciously or unconsciously—like everything else in the "natural" world?[21]

Silver wrote another book with the telling title *Remaking Eden*. Not surprisingly, the language of the biblical myth of Creation and of the Fall play prominently in Berry's writings, and his readers would do well to pay close attention to them as they occur. For Berry, these stories express poetically the foundational truths of man's nature and his condition in the world. The myth of the Fall in particular powerfully expresses the two basic attitudes human beings can take toward themselves and the world: either human beings are the ultimate creators of good and evil, or they are creatures capable of recognizing and cooperating with a prior order of good and evil they did not make. The implications for one's choice on this issue are vast and ultimately turn on man's ambiguous place within the whole.

Berry agrees that the mind is what distinguishes human beings from the rest of the natural order. The mind is the origin of both science and art, which exist in an uneasy relationship to one another and to the world. Through the mind, human beings are liberated from the realm of natural necessity and become capable of understanding the truth of things. And through the mind they modify nature in order to live in it. These two aspects of the mind force human beings to ask and answer pressing questions: What can I know? What must I do? What if any are the limits of knowledge and of art?

These questions are complicated by the fact that the human mind exists in a body, which places human beings firmly within the natural world. One implication of this fact is that the body necessarily conditions and mediates the operations of the mind. The body proves the futility of the quest for immediate or unmediated knowledge. Berry contrasts the modern scientific formula "mind=brain=machine" with what he calls "the Adam and Eve theory of the mind": "mind=brain+body+world+local dwelling place+community+history. 'History' here would mean not just documented events but the whole heritage of culture, language, memory, tools, and skills."[22] Culture and all its mediations are necessary extensions of what it means to have a body. To level these mediations, Berry suggests, does not empower the mind; it renders it isolated, impotent, and inert.

The presence of the mind in the body raises a further question of human identity: Am I a mind who happens to be in a body, or am I the unity of my mind and body? Berry firmly insists on the latter. Every individual human being is a composite of mind and body, and one of the challenges of culture is to achieve a harmony of the parts. "If human nature is double, then its two halves must meet and inform each other.

This seems to be one of the oldest cultural themes."[23] Further, "Body and soul delight as well as suffer in each other and are in a sense each other's crisis," he writes, but "to attempt or pretend to divide them is foolhardy, dangerous and evil."

> The real task is to bring them into unity or harmony, and this is to be done by the cultivation of the virtues, both practical and spiritual, which are enjoined upon us by what are called divine commandments and moral laws, and which may be understood as a set of instructions for preserving our place and ourselves within them.[24]

To recognize oneself as the unity of mind and body is to recognize oneself as limited, that is, mortal, dependent, and to some degree ignorant. This last quality is most important and most fateful; important because it reflects not merely our limits but also our somewhat painful awareness of our limits; fateful because how we deal with that knowledge will have great consequences for ourselves and the world. "Ignorance . . . is part of our creaturely definition," Berry writes in *The Way of Ignorance*, whose Socratic-sounding title is borrowed from T. S. Eliot's poem *The Four Quartets*.[25] Further, "We *have* to act on the basis of what we know, and what we know is incomplete." One function of culture therefore is to provide "an effective way of telling us that our knowledge is incomplete, and also of telling us how to act in our state of ignorance."[26]

A culture based upon the way of ignorance gives rites or forms to the ignorance, which is a constituent part of man's creaturely existence, encouraging an attitude of humility, wonder, reverence, respect, and responsibility toward the inexhaustible and irreducible mystery of life and living creatures. Such a culture reminds human beings of their true place in the order of nature, reconciling them to their condition and reinforcing in them patterns of proper behavior within that order. It opposes, however, those forms of ignorance that are morally culpable, which result from prejudice, fear, laziness, or greed. One such prejudice is the belief that science can in principle conquer all limits.

Both modern science and romanticism reflect this prejudice. They can both be characterized by the revolt of the mind against the natural limits of the body and of man's history and experience of living in the body—his own and the "body" of the world or nature. Modern science in particular is a revolt against uncertainty, especially the uncertainty of death, through technology. In this respect, modern science does not seek the elimination of mediation as such but rather the substitution of mechanical mediation for the mediation of the body. Because the senses distort the real quality of things, because our passions often distort our judgments, and because the body will die, we must remove it as much as possible in our quest to know and to live. Machines are now used in place of the body, constructed according to mathematical principles, mathematics being the most exact science because it has no real body and because everything within it is determined and predictable. Reduced to the laws of mathematical physics, nature becomes certain, predictable, and, in principle, controllable.[27] Thus the scientific method becomes the necessary means to "objective knowledge," a term that implies that all knowledge outside its boundaries is merely "subjective" and therefore is no knowledge at all.

The scientific and romantic revolt encourages a culture that is best understood as an anticulture, a form against all form. Rites that once made the human condition bearable and even joyful are recklessly destroyed as oppressive obstacles in the path to eternal youth and immortality. The fantasy endures despite abundant evidence of its falsehood. Death still comes, only now we die in our prosperity like the corpse in the vision of Ebenezer Scrooge, "plundered and bereft, unwatched, unwept, uncared for." As the rites fall, so does our memory of them, making it much more difficult for individuals to resist the mighty economic juggernaut of the progressive dystopia.

It is important to note that Berry concedes that science "has benefited us in so many ways,"[28] and he acknowledges the legitimate use of the scientific method. "Reductionism, like materialism, has uses that are appropriate,"[29] he writes. "There obviously is a necessary usefulness in the processes of reduction. They are indispensable to scientists—and to the rest of us as well."[30] What he opposes is what others have called "scientism," and what Berry calls the "religification and evangelizing of science, in defiance of scientific principles."[31] This is the imperialistic and tyrannical tendency of science to claim for itself the whole of knowledge and to remake all other knowledge in its own image. The fatuousness of this endeavor is captured in the ordinary language scientists use in their nonscientific lives. "The giveaway is that even scientists do not speak of their loved ones in categorical terms as 'a woman,' 'a man,' 'a child,' or 'a case.'"[32] The language of science is abstraction. And though Berry has claimed that "the Devil's work is abstraction,"[33] he writes, "Without some use of abstraction, thought is incoherent or unintelligible, perhaps unthinkable." However, "abstraction alone is merely dead,"[34] for it misses the miraculous and irreducible particularity of individual things:

> There is, empirically speaking, no average and no type. Between the species and the specimen the creature itself, the individual creature, is lost. Having been classified, dissected, explained, the creature has disappeared into its class, anatomy and explanation. The tendency is to equate the creature (or its habitat) with one's formalized knowledge of it.[35]

For this reason, the "objective" language that has become so popular in ordinary speech is not only incapable of accounting for basic aspects of human experience such as goodness, beauty, and mystery; it serves even to undermine them. Berry calls instead for a "whole, vital, particularizing language"[36] upon which familiarity, reverence, and responsibility rest. Art and the imagination play a large part in this language, for "art insists upon the irreducibility of its subjects; and works of art, as objects, are by nature not reducible."[37] Further, "the power of art tends to be an individuating power, and that tendency is itself an affirmation of the value of individuals and of individuality."[38]

Similarly, Berry writes:

> If we are to protect the world's multitude of places and creatures, then we must know them, not just conceptually but imaginatively as well. They must be pictured in the mind and in memory; they must be known with affection, "by the heart," so that in seeing or remembering them the heart may be said to "sing," to make a music peculiar to its recognition of each particular place or creature that it knows well. . . . To know imaginatively is to know intimately, particularly, precisely, gratefully, reverently, and with affection.[39]

Although Berry asserts that the imagination is necessary for this kind of particular knowledge, we would be profoundly mistaken to take from this that Berry believes the imagination lends to reality what it does not intrinsically possess. On the contrary, the attraction and value in this individuating power of art and imagination is truth: "If we didn't, to start with, feel that a work of art was true, we wouldn't bother with it, or not for long."[40] The observation points to Berry's criticism of the romantic turn in poetry. Berry commends in romanticism its "tradition of objection" to "the enterprise of science-industry-and-technology," such as "Blake's revulsion at the 'dark Satanic Mills' and Wordsworth's perception that 'we murder to dissect.'" He also finds in it, however, a strong impulse of specialization parallel to that in science, in which words, or autonomous creation, become the fundamental subject and goal of poetry.[41] This specialization of poetry results in the breakdown of "the union of beauty with goodness and truth."[42] Further, "Once imagination is divided from reason and from the material world, it loses its power over them; it loses, or begins to lose, even its power to refer to them."[43] "The subject of poetry is not words," Berry writes. "It is the world, which poets have in common with other people."[44]

Art and the imagination therefore are necessarily mimetic. They are also practical, concerned not just with representation but also with living. "The order of nature proposes a human order in harmony with it. There are beautiful ideas, but their beauty cannot be separated from their practicality."[45] For this reason, Berry makes clear his preference for the older poetry, represented by the Bible, Homer, Milton, Dante, and Pope, which understood the unity between the imagination and the truth on the one hand, and art and life on the other.

> The first aim of the propriety of the old poets . . . was to make the language true to its subject—to see that it told the truth. That is why they invoked the Muse. The truth the poet chose as his subject was perceived as superior to his powers—and by clear implication, to his occasion and purpose.[46]

Because the imagination, like reason, is ordered to the truth about reality, it must be subject to correction. "The extremes of reality and imagination, within the limits of human experience, are never pure,"[47] he writes. It is necessary therefore that they constantly correct one another: "Both imagination and a competent sense of reality are necessary to our life, and they necessarily discipline one another."[48] The touchstone for this discipline of the imagination and reason, art and science, is reality itself. "Science and art are neither fundamental nor immutable. They are not life or the world. They are tools."[49] But they are necessary tools, for "We join ourselves to the living world by the artifacts of art and science—by made things."[50] The harmonious joining of art and science, and of ourselves to the world, is the work of culture: "The only reason, really, that we need this kit of tools is to build and maintain our dwelling here on earth. . . . Our dwelling here is the proper work of culture."[51]

The human necessity for culture points again to the uneasy relationship between human beings and nature. How can something that is artificial or man-made be considered natural, and what is the status of that nature that can and must be so transformed? The difficulty turns somewhat on an ambiguity in the meaning of the term *nature*. In contemporary usage, nature most often denotes the pristine, or that which has not been modified by human action. In its older usage, however, nature refers to the proper use, end, or perfection of a thing, which might involve the assistance of art, such as language. Only in this older teleological sense can nature provide a standard for culture, and this brings us again to the dilemma presented by the myth of the Fall: Is the natural human need to transform nature somehow limited by nature as well? Is there a law of nature that directs and prescribes limits to human action?

For Berry the answer is clear: human beings are creatures existing within a created order they did not make and have no right or even ability to destroy. Recourse to the Christian account of reality, and especially the Chain of Being, seems indispensable here for providing the fullest or richest account of this condition. The Chain of Being sets boundaries to human action by reminding human beings that they "are neither gods nor beasts,"[52] a notion, incidentally, that plays large in the writings of the American founding. "This idea of just compass can be derived only from such an idea as the Chain of Being, for without the idea of hierarchical order the just compass of any human must be defined solely by power—power, that is, *replaces* justice."[53] In Berry's understanding, the Chain of Being not only sets limits; it also establishes "the condition upon which we truly are set free, admitted to the Creation and the community of creatures."[54]

The hierarchy among creatures within the Chain of Being rests on natural differences in "ability, intelligence and power" among creatures, but these differences do not license indiscriminate power and control. They point rather to the need for virtue and law, including human law: "These discrepancies which exist by nature, define, among humans, the need for moral law and governmental justice. The idea has always been a *just* hierarchy, not *no* hierarchy."[55]

Based upon what has been said above, it is not surprising that Berry sees in the Chain of Being not merely a poetic invention but also a reflection of reality itself.

> It would be a mistake to assume, because the Chain of Being is so manifestly present in writings, that it is only a literary or philosophical artifact. Long before it became explicit in literature, the moral implications of the human place within it were well understood. It is easy to suppose that the roots of the idea go back to whatever events first differentiated humans from animals.[56]

Though they did not create the reality, traditional poets gave it form through which human beings might preserve this knowledge of themselves and the world, both in theory and in practice.

> One of the necessary services of the poets was to reunderstand and renew this idea, reimagine its human embodiments and catastrophes, and keep it alive. Poetry, then, was—and it may be—a part of the necessary cultural means by which we preserve our union, the possibility of harmony, with the natural world and "higher law."[57]

## Wendell Berry's Humane Vision

These last remarks shed important light upon Berry's poetic vision. *Vision* is a favorite word of Berry's. It means not only the natural power of the sense of sight but also the suprasensible if not supernatural power of poetry at its highest or most profound. This play on the word's intrinsic meaning is significant, for poetic visions have the capacity to correct or transform our natural sight, threatened as it always is by fear, pride, greed, lust, anger, and envy. "The walls of the rational, empirical world are famously porous," Berry has written. "What comes through are dreams, imaginings, inspirations, visions, revelations."[58] These imaginings and inspirations can powerfully reorient how human beings perceive and act in the world.

The point is illustrated in one of Berry's favorite literary episodes, Act IV of Shakespeare's *King Lear*, in which Edgar tricks his blind, despairing father into believing that his life has been miraculously saved from an attempted suicide. The drama reaches its climax in Edgar's exhortation to his father: "Thy life's a miracle. Speak yet again."[59] "This is the line," Berry writes, "that calls Gloucester back—out of hubris, and the damage and despair that inevitably follow—into the properly subordinated human life of grief and joy, where change and redemption are possible."[60] Henceforth Gloucester will no longer seek control over his life. "He has given up his life as an understood possession, and taken it back as miracle and mystery."[61] Gloucester "dies 'smilingly' in the truly human estate."[62] Gloucester's transformation is not the result of an argument but of an experience. Moreover, Edgar brings to this experience a form that provides it with meaning. For this reason, Berry calls it a "rite of death or rebirth."[63]

The objects around Gloucester have not changed. Nature remains as it is, and Gloucester still dies of a "flawed heart." What has changed is how Gloucester sees nature. The change is fundamental. If nature is viewed as indifferent or even hostile to human flourishing, one will approach it as an adversary to be overcome, and then one is well on the way to the Baconian enterprise of conquering nature for the relief of man's estate, and the consumerist economy will closely follow. If, on the other hand, human beings are part of a nature that has an intrinsic value, then human beings must learn to live humbly and even joyfully within these limits. Both ways of viewing nature cannot be true, and yet the truth will surely have consequences for human happiness. One's way of seeing nature will necessarily involve how one imagines the unknown, the unpredictable, the mysterious. Berry occasionally calls this part of nature "the Wilderness," that wild untamed portion of reality beyond the limits of human control, and he explains why true imaginative visions properly originate in the Wilderness and return to it.[64] In the Port William fiction, the unpredictable, unconventional, and always lovable Burley Coulter personifies this necessity to "preserve the necessary connections between the domestic and the wild,"[65] a point made clear in Berry's poignant short story "The Wild Birds."[66]

Though it rests at the heart of all his fiction, the clearest and most dramatic glimpse of Berry's transformative vision can be found in his lovely novel *Remembering,* in many ways the most singular of the Port William fiction with its mythic quality, use of fantasy, and principal setting outside of Port William. The title of the story captures its action. In the journey from despair through memory (remembering) to wholeness (re-membering), *Remembering* recapitulates the *Divine Comedy* in a modern idiom, reenacting while correcting the American myth of individualism and self-creation. It is in fact a bold poetic attempt to reestablish the American identity according to less celebrated yet more stable tradition.

At the beginning of the novel, Andy Catlett, like Dante, finds himself lost in the dark. "It is dark. He does not know where he is." Andy is far from home, having left the encumbrances of family, place, and history in search of something better. Like so many others before him, he has moved westward and finds himself at the very edge of the frontier and of civilization. He gazes out into the vast Pacific Ocean and rattles the Chain of Being as he entertains in his imagination the temptation of autonomous self-creation. "Where might he not go? Who knows where he is? He feels the simplicity and lightness of his solitude. Other lives, other possible lives swarm around him."[67]

But Berry ingeniously complicates the myth and thereby reveals its more fundamental mechanism: the desire to escape the human condition. Having lost his right hand to a mechanical corn picker in a farming accident, Andy cannot accept the humiliation of dependency and his loss of self-reliance. In that humiliation and pride, Andy is fleeing his home, his family, his community, and his history. In Andy's bodily wound, Berry figures the essential condition of all human beings: we enter the world in complete and utter dependency, and we experience in our bodies the constant reminder of necessity and mortality. This is evident in the most radical wound of all, sexuality, whose mark upon the body forever testifies to the futility of the human quest for complete autonomy.[68] In Berry's telling, the persistent, pervasive, and restless American desire to "move west" is best understood, at root, as the attempt to escape from the body and its limits. It therefore naturally finds its next frontier in the utopianism of biotechnology, which promises to conquer suffering and death.

To experience human dependence as a wound, however, already reveals a basic error. If in fact the erotic experience of incompleteness and of human dependency points to a larger wholeness, it is no longer a wound but a possibility and a promise. Everything turns once upon how one *sees* the same object, and the myth of *Remembering* is the reversal from the blindness of seeing human dependence as a wound to the clarifying vision of seeing it as a gift.

Just as he is fantasizing the possibilities of his new self, Andy is called back to himself in memory by the voice of his grandmother Dorie Wheeler. This memory takes him way back, even before his childhood, to a time outside his personal memory when first "the shuttle flung . . . though the web of his making."[69] There he sees distant relatives reenacting the rites that made him what he is, moving through to his personal memory in the home of his grandmother Wheeler, where, gathering eggs together in the evening, she looks down at him smilingly and says, "Oh, my boy, how far away will you be sometime, remembering this?"[70] This is the "thy life is a miracle" memory, bringing Andy to tears. The lines are worth quoting in full, for both their pathos and beauty:

> He is held, though he does not hold. He is caught up in the old pattern of entrances: of minds into minds, minds into place, places into minds. The pattern limits and complicates him, singling him out in his own flesh. Out of the multitude of possible lives that have surrounded and beckoned to him like a crowd around a star, he returns now to himself, a mere meteorite, scorched, small, and fallen. He has met again his one life and one death, and he takes them back. It is as though, leaving, he has met himself already returning, pushing in front of him a barn seventy-five feet by forty, and a hundred acres of land, and six generations of his own history, partly failed, and a few dead and living whose love has claimed him forever. He will be partial, and he will die; he will live out the truth of that. Though he does not hold, he is held. He is grieving, and he is full of joy. What is that Egypt but his Promised Land?[71]

Andy's Egypt, of course, is Port William. In Berry's fiction Port William is a place of both conviviality and roguishness, where fragile rites of courtship and marriage (*Hannah Coulter*), child-rearing and work (*Andy Catlett*), aging and death (*The Memory of Old Jack*) temporize with the Wilderness, protecting each person in his dependency, preserving him in his dignity, and bringing him at last to the final resting place. It is what Burley Coulter calls "the membership," a term pointing to another important play on the title of *Remembering*. The term *membership* as applied to human community originates in Christian ecclesiology and is based upon an analogy to the body: "For just as the body is one and has many members, and all the members of the body, though many, are one body, so it is with Christ" (1 Cor. 12:12).[72] It is to this membership that a broken, humbled, hopeful Andy returns at the end of *Remembering*.

In Andy's imagination, Egypt is transformed into the Promised Land. *Remembering* concludes with a magical vision, a rare device for Berry, who ordinarily writes in a more natural style. The vision occurs as Andy, sleeping in a valley outside Port William, is awakened from a dream by a man, "dark as a shadow," who guides him Virgil-like to the top of a hill overlooking the town. It is indeed Port William, but transformed, and within it "are people of such beauty that he weeps to see them. He sees that these are the membership of one another and of the place and of the song or light in which they live and move."[73] Among them Andy sees "men and women he remembers, and men and women remembered in memories he remembers, and they do not look as he ever saw or imagined them."[74] Andy desires to go to them, but his guide prevents it. "He is not to stay. Grieved as he may be to leave them, he must leave." The concluding lines, gently evocative of Psalm 137:5, are as joyful as the first are somber:

He has come into the presence of these living by a change of sight, by which he has parted from them as they were and from himself as he was and is.

Now he prepares to leave them. Their names singing in his mind, he lifts toward them the restored right hand of his joy.[75]

Through re-membering, Andy's wounded body and soul are both restored to wholeness. In this story, as in his other Port William fiction, Wendell Berry provides his readers a poetic vision that corrects and heals the escapist desires behind modern science and romanticism. It does so by revealing how human life, mediated by imagination and culture, can be lived beautifully and richly within the confines of grief and love, dependency and death. For some Americans of an older generation, something of this vision is present to actual memory, but for a younger generation, whose memories are marred by the abandonment of divorced parents, deracination by the global economy, fragmentation by consumerism, alienation from ties of history and tradition, Berry's fiction becomes memory itself. In a very real way, they do not merely read about Port William; they participate in it.

## Wendell Berry's Edenic Imagination

There is one aspect of Berry's integral imaginative vision that seems to contradict what has been said so far. It offers no positive vision of formal mediating institutions, especially those historical institutions that have been most foundational to the growth of Western civilization, religion, and politics. Port William possesses no government itself, and when government does make an appearance from outside, it is always to disrupt or destroy the common good of Port William, never to protect or preserve it. Wars are never just or noble or heroic, and there is little pride of country or patriotism, little identification with a just cause for war, in the men of Port William. Upon returning from war, Art Rowanberry, Ernest Finley, and Nathan Coulter all share a cynical sense of alienation and exploitation by a powerful "other" with interests separate from themselves and their own. Similarly, although Port William does have a church, its occasional, feckless minister, though not vicious, never manages to become an integral part of the membership. His efforts to minister to the suffering souls of Port William are received with suspicion, and sometimes even contempt.

In short, Berry's imagination seems to point to a vision of rational anarchy, in which culture and community are established and preserved purely on the basis of cooperation and consent, without support, encouragement, or protection from formal political or religious institutions. Berry's apparent anti-institutionalism seems to cut against his better knowledge of the important and necessary role mediating forms play in human flourishing.[76] Political and religious institutions, flawed as they inevitably are, are such necessary forms, providing communities a ruling instrument for securing and preserving their common good, hopefully by deliberation, though often by coercion. One aspect of that common good is defense against the organized aggression of other political communities, a fact that makes war a proper, and occasionally even a noble, pursuit. The form of politics, like the form of marriage, properly instituted, gives discipline, protection, and direction to natural human inclinations, ordering them into the more perfect whole where they might realize their full perfection. In this respect, politics, like marriage, is a natural extension of the body and its condition of living in the world, a fact indicated by its omnipresence across cultures and history. Berry's evident hostility to the mediation of formal institutional structures seems to reflect that romantic imagination he otherwise opposes in his writings. It suggests something of what Russell Kirk, following Irving Babbitt, called the idyllic imagination, which is characterized by the desire to be emancipated from duty and convention, and even from the body itself.[77]

I might suggest, however, that Port William reflects not a perverse idyllic imagination so much as a positive Edenic one. Whereas both of these imaginations represent a state of things that is in some sense impossible given what we know about human beings, their impossibilities rest upon vastly different grounds; indeed, on different accounts of what it means to be human. The idyllic imagination is based upon a false understanding of human nature itself: it is not only impossible; it is unimaginable. Idyllic man, separated from all mediation—others, the body, the world, suffering, death, and the consciousness of death—is not even recognizable as a human being. Edenic man, on the other hand, we somehow know, for he keeps before us the latent memory of our deeper, our truer selves. John Paul II, in *The Theology of the Body*, gives us some sense of the meaning of this mystery:

> The state of sin is part of "historical man." . . . That state, however—the "historical" state—plunges its roots, in every man without exception, in his own theological "prehistory," which is the state of original innocence. . . . It is impossible to understand the state of historical sinfulness without referring or appealing (and Christ appealed to it) to the state of original (in a certain sense, "prehistoric") and fundamental innocence. Therefore, right from the beginning, the arising of sinfulness as a state, a dimension of human existence, is in relation to this real innocence of man as

his original and fundamental state, as a dimension of his being created in the image of God. . . . Historical man is, so to speak, rooted in his revealed theological prehistory. So every point of his historical sinfulness is explained (both for the soul and the body) with reference to original innocence. It can be said that this reference is a "co-inheritance" of sin, and precisely of original sin. If this sin signifies, in every historical man, a state of lost grace, then it also contains a reference to that grace, which was precisely the grace of original innocence.[78]

Eden therefore provides the imaginative ground for making sense of man's fallen, historical state. More important, it keeps alive in the midst of history what is truest about human beings and their relationship to nature and to God. Without this informing vision of things, history only *is*, possessing no larger meaning or purpose that might inform and guide human action in the midst of suffering and evil. A world without Eden is the world of romanticism and modern science. In Eden, human beings discover their full freedom and happiness in a giving of self that is ordered to community, beginning with the family and extending to civic, religious, and political associations. Such an order is necessarily hierarchic without being despotic. In Eden, human beings are not the masters but rather the stewards of nature, recognizing its intrinsic value and cooperating with it to bring forth its inner perfection.

Through the Edenic imagination, we also see the true value and purpose of formal mediating institutions as a remediation of man's fallen condition. Though necessary, they are always and only a means to human flourishing, never an end in themselves. This idea is captured remarkably well by C. S. Lewis in an essay significantly entitled "Membership":

> The secular community, since it exists for our natural good and not for our supernatural, has no higher end than to facilitate and safeguard the family, friendship, and solitude. To be happy at home, said Johnson, is the end of all human endeavor. As long as we are thinking only of natural values we must say that the sun looks down on nothing half so good as a household laughing together over a meal, or two friends talking over a pint of beer, or a man alone reading a book that interests him; and that all

economies, politics, laws, armies, and institutions, save insofar as they prolong and multiply such scenes, are a mere ploughing the sand and sowing the ocean, a meaningless vanity and vexation of spirit.[79]

Although it has one foot in Eden, Port William has the other firmly planted east of Eden. We recognize in it the usual combinations of good and evil: marriage, family, and work in Port William are suffused with good cheer, generosity and affection, but women still suffer in childbirth, men still work by the sweat of their brow, and Cain still assaults Abel. The Edenic myth accounts for this double quality of human experience by the notion of original sin. Adam and Eve's disobedience is the pivotal event of the story. As a result, there occurs a rupture in man's original integral wholeness, both within and without; he is expelled from the garden, and he is launched onto the path of salvation history. Original sin therefore points to the limits of achievable wholeness east of Eden. It also explains and justifies the positive, temporizing function of formal, second-ary mediating institutions and their actions, including the organization of worship and of politics, which, properly ordered, serve to restore and preserve as much as possible what remains of that original wholeness.[80]

How does Berry account for this double experience? Given the evident influence of biblical Christianity on his imagination, it is surprising that he rarely if ever mentions original sin, upon which so much turns. The absence of the original sin narrative, with all that it implies, as opposed to the mere recognition of occasional human waywardness, suggests that Berry's imaginative vision is incomplete. This is perhaps the root of Berry's strong inclination toward pacifism, which seems to many of his admirers incongruent with his otherwise well-grounded good sense.

It also might explain his ambiguous treatment of formal worship, or liturgy. The liturgical orientation of biblical Christianity is prefigured in the Exodus story, about which two important things stand out: First, God calls and saves human beings not simply as individuals but also as an ordered community of persons, as an *ecclesia*. Second, the *ecclesia* finds its very identity and purpose in worship. The justification for the Exodus is not liberation but rather liturgy: "Let us go a three days' journey into the wilderness, that we may sacrifice to the Lord our God"(Exod. 3:18). The Exodus event finds its fulfillment in the Paschal mystery, which is the foundation of the Christian *ecclesia*. Liturgy, communal in its very nature, is the goal of Creation, the place where cosmos and history come together and find their meaning.[81] It is therefore the primary analogate from which all notions of membership take their meaning and without which all forms of membership must inevitably collapse.

Nevertheless, although the Port William fiction lacks a positive representation of formal mediating institutions, it does not point to an idyllic emancipation from mediation. It points rather to emancipation *through* mediation. The members of Port William discover themselves *through* its history, order, form, memory, hierarchy, authority, and responsibility. In the Port William "membership," every person is embedded within a social and economic order and given a particular role within it that provides the context for and measure of his or her identity and responsibility. Much of the dramatic power in Berry's fiction follows from the degree to which individuals embrace or refuse to embrace their places within the membership—places that are sometimes given unaccountably, and whose outcome is always unpredictable—and the subsequent joy and grief supervening upon these responses. The absence of formal mediating institutions in Port William therefore indirectly serves to illuminate those primary mediations that formal institutions are designed to serve. This is not the false and fantastical perfection of escapism from the body and its limits; it is the true sight of things as they are, in their proper wholeness. Andy Catlett's restorative vision at the end of *Remembering* does not occur as he gazes out at the Pacific Ocean, with its mythic hint of primordial formlessness and creative possibility; it occurs when he returns home, gazing down upon the concrete realities of his own land, history, and people.

In Andy's vision of wholeness we discover how the forms of perfection that operate through the imagination can help to humanize life, counteracting the inevitable brutality that follows when necessity becomes an end rather than a means. War with no vision of perfect peace, politics with no vision of perfect justice, marriage with no vision of perfect union, inevitably become instruments of cruelty and oppression rather than of liberation. An integral imagination requires and points to an Edenic imagination, which is to say that a humane life without places like Port William is inconceivable. By representing good human actions in a way that makes them appear both beautiful and attractive, without being sentimental, Berry achieves the rarest poetic achievement, almost singular in the history of the novel. In this, Berry's vision is truly humane, giving us a powerful glimpse of what it means to be fully human, and then helping us to live it.

# 15

# Earth and Flesh Sing Together: The Place of Wendell Berry's Poetry in His Vision of the Human

*Luke Schlueter*

When one thinks of the work of Wendell Berry, it is not typically his poetry that first comes to mind, in spite of the fact that Berry has published more than sixteen volumes of poetry dating back to the early 1960s. This may be due in part to the fact that Berry wears three different hats, two of which claim the attention of the typical reader—those of novelist and essayist. Were Berry to wear only the hat of poet, he would undoubtedly be better known as such, even if he would no doubt enjoy a fraction of the readership he enjoys today. As it stands, most readers of Berry's work will think he dons this last hat at odd times, perhaps when the stories have spun themselves out and the natural philosopher has tramped, for a time, his last bit of woods. Berry, in his resistance to commenting on his poetry over the years, has done little to persuade readers that these apparently "odd" times—times when Berry must feel that the peculiarities of a certain kind of thought and experience are best given expression in lyric form—are theirs too. There is a suggestion in what little Berry has said that makes it seem as if poetry is his indulgence in personal revelry. In a recent interview, for example, Berry stated, "I feel a kind of intimacy with my work as a poet that makes me not very eager to talk about."[1] One may surmise that while Berry may make himself vulnerable enough to publish his poetry, that is as far as he is willing to go.

It is perhaps not surprising, then, that the typical reader of Berry's work tends to view Berry's poetry as being the odd child in the family, a personal extravagance that won't provide the easy comfort and genial pleasures of the fiction and prose. It is also possible, of course, that the typical reader of Berry's work, not unlike the typical contemporary reader more generally, has lost both the capacity for and interest in engaging with verse. Such readers will be interested to discover that Berry's poetry provides a rich and distinctive pleasure, one that harks back to the idea of poetry as being a crucial vehicle for the representation of goodness, beauty, and truth. Readers of Berry's work may also be interested to discover that Berry's poetry constitutes a unique and powerful expression of his vision of human things, and for this reason has a critically important place in this vision. Readers who privilege the fiction and prose over the poetry risk losing something of the integrity and wholeness of Berry's humane vision. As Berry himself once noted in an interview when asked about his poetry, "My various kinds of writing are not involved in a race for first place, but in something more like a neighborhood; they have been necessary and helpful to each other."[2] An understanding and appreciation of Berry's work can accordingly be enhanced to the degree that we can discern the specific ways in which Berry's poetry has been "necessary and helpful" to his fiction and prose. But my concern here goes beyond the question of utility. I also want to make clear how Berry's poetry possesses an excellence in its own right; how it carries some essential and finally incommensurable expression of Berry's vision of human things. In order to do this, I first want to describe how Berry sees the place and function of poetry in human existence more generally. I then want to sketch an outline of Berry's poetic project. And finally I want to look at a small number of poems in order to illustrate how Berry uniquely realizes in his poetry his vision of human things.

While Berry has been a most reluctant interlocutor in addressing the nature of his own poetry, he has, happily, been less reticent in expounding upon the estate of poetry more generally. And while we are under no obligation to take Berry's remarks as descriptive of his own work, in their articulation of a basic stance toward poetry and the poetic function, they do serve to outline something of the spirit that animates Berry's poetry. What becomes clear is that Berry's vision of poetry, no less than his vision of all human activity, counters the modern conception of the poet as someone who is concerned chiefly with dramatizing the contents of his own private, deeply subjective experience and who, accordingly, traffics in a language that typically defeats the possibility of shared meanings. Berry's vision of poetry, rather, expresses something of the old ideal of the poet speaking to and on behalf of a community of persons who are bound together by a shared sensibility. Berry's poetry is finally persuasive because of how it engages with this ideal in a contemporary idiom—one not without precedent (how could it be in light of Berry's own commitments to traditional forms and modes of representation?) but that nonetheless becomes something uniquely identifiable as his own.

Readers of Berry's work may have been surprised at the stir created by Dana Gioia's pronouncement in 1991 that "American poetry now belongs to a subculture. No longer part of the mainstream of artistic and intellectual life, it has become the specialized occupation of a relatively small and isolated group."[3] Berry, after all, had said essentially the same thing more than fifteen years earlier in "The Specialization of Poetry," in which he lamented that the situation of poetry in the contemporary world corresponds to the drive toward specialization in all the arts and sciences. This drive, he claims, inheres in the desire for perfection—a perfection only imaginable within the narrow context of the specialist's particular sphere of action and that "depends upon the abandonment of all the old ideals of harmony, symmetry, balance, order, in favor of the singular totalitarian ideal of control."[4] The consequence for the poet is that he is left "isolated and specialized and that the old union of beauty, goodness, and truth is broken."[5] This remark lines up with Berry's more general philosophy of human nature in which all human activity, including the aesthetic, achieves its highest good when it is driven by man's fundamental desire for goodness, beauty, and truth. Berry's conception of poetry—his embrace of the "old ideals"—counters, again, the more reductive conceptions of the poetic function that have dominated poetry for the past fifty or so years and that are embedded within a set of practices that have become increasingly distanced from the lives and interests of the majority of readers. Berry's own particular poetic project, following upon his conception of the poetic function, significantly involves an attempt to dramatize through the lyric form something of his own felt sense of reality and human experience, which inevitably, and by virtue of Berry's own sense of our shared humanity, will work against the more narrowly defined (i.e. "specialized") projects of his contemporaries.

The outlines of a poetics, then, can be espied in Berry's rejection of a poetic sensibility that has its raison d'être in an atmosphere of specialization and exclusivity. This rejection clears a space for Berry to imagine what an "unspecialized" poetry might look like. It is perhaps inevitable that such a poetry will reclaim what Charles Altieri, in his study of American poets writing in the 1960s, calls an "immanentist" vision. Altieri sees this mode of poetry as having its origins in Wordsworthian romanticism, where the immanentist poet "stresses the way an imagination attentive to common and casual experience can transform the mind and provide satisfying resting places."[6] Altieri cites Heraclitus—"Man is estranged from the familiar"—in calling attention to the basic project of these poets to "restore the familiar in its many modes of merging."[7] Berry's particular investment in this tradition, as we will see, is to dramatize the exchanges that occur between human beings in the context of community and in their relationship to the natural world. Even the more private poems Berry writes—poems for his wife, for example—are shaped by this sensibility, where human love becomes an expression of an attunement to the encompassing realities that give it its purpose and meaning.

Berry also expresses in his poetry a sense of how these realities evade our attempts to understand them. (Berry's argument against the modern project of reason and control has implications here.) For example, Berry oftentimes will dramatize in his poems the limits of knowing, but rather than identifying these limits with the abyss of modern existence—a move made by many of his contemporaries—he sees them as being invitations to mystery. In the essay "Poetry and Marriage," for example, Berry, in working out an analogy between the "forms" of marriage and poetry, states:

> It may be, then, that form serves us best when it works as an obstruction to baffle us and deflect our intended course. It may be that when we no longer know what to do we have come to our real work and that when we no longer know which way to go we have begun our real journey. The mind that is not baffled is not employed. The impeded stream is the one that sings.[8]

It is through a pattern of living, a way of life, that the unknowns and uncertainties of human experience become not handicaps to living but rather serve to draw us more fully into what our lives would have us be.

And it is this same fundamental vision that Berry attempts to dramatize and express in his own poetry.

Berry's poetics are informed, likewise, by his vision of how lyric poetry constitutes a kind of interface between spirit and flesh, body and song:

> The rhythm of a song or a poem rises, no doubt, in reference to the pulse and breathe of the poet . . . It rises also in reference to daily and seasonal—and surely even longer—rhythms in the life of the poet and in the life that surrounds him. The rhythm of the poet resonates with these larger rhythms that surround it; it fills its environment with sympathetic vibrations. . . . Song, then, is a force opposed to specialty and to isolation. It is the testimony of the singer's inescapable relation to the world, to the human community, and also to tradition.[9]

Berry's project here is to identify the lyric poet as a singer who celebrates and enacts the rhythms and resonances that obtain between himself and the world. This self, however, and the rhythms and resonances that he enacts in his song, are embedded in a vision and practice of life that is fundamentally communal. To ears distressed by the accumulation of nearly a century of Anglo experimentation, this idea of poetry may sound quaint, just as traditionalism at any given historical moment must suffer the prejudices of progressivism. But it is finally not so much a return that Berry signals, as we shall see, as it is the development of a particular lyric sensibility that sees the place of lyric within a broader context of communal knowing and experiencing. The typical speaker of Berry's poetry celebrates the shared commitments and mutual investments of a community of persons living both within and across historical time. As he writes in the title essay of *Standing by Words*, "Two epidemics of our time—upon both of which virtual industries of cures have been founded—are the disintegrations of communities and persons."[10] And he likewise observes in "Notes: Unspecializing Poetry": "Nothing exists for its own sake, but for a harmony greater than itself, which excludes it. A work of art, which accepts this condition, and exists upon its terms, honors the Creation, and so becomes part of it."[11]

This isn't to suggest that Berry's vision of poetry is solely, or even fundamentally, idyllic. His vision, in fact, very much takes into account the reality of human suffering, including the reality of death and the transitory nature of human life. But we can call Berry's poetic vision redemptive because of how these realities are suffused with transindividual meanings. The private voice we hear in the Berry poem is, when all is said and done, profoundly public. It expresses a sense of purpose and value that clearly is linked to the individual's relationship to the informing realities of the world outside himself, whether these be those of the natural world, or of other human persons, or of some mixture of these. His poetic vision, finally, is a kind of embodied expression of his belief that "the source of our poetry is the idea that poetry must be used for something, must serve something, greater and higher than itself. It is a way to learn, know, and celebrate the truth—or, as Yeats said, to 'bring the soul of man to God'"[12]

While Berry's own poetic project necessarily follows from his understanding of the place and function of poetry in human existence more generally, it is at the same time true to say that his poetry constitutes a unique intervention in the poetic tradition. And while it should come as no surprise that Berry's poetic project follows from the unique and vital vision that informs his work as a whole, it is nonetheless interesting to note how Berry distinguishes the function of his poetry from that of his other work. For example, Berry has written, "I have always been attracted to the poetry of William Carlos Williams because of his use of the art of writing as an instrument by which a man may arrive in his place and maintain himself there."[13] Berry's understanding of Williams's project mirrors his own: poetry as a method of recollection, recovery, and renewal. Alternatively, we can think of Berry's project, read through Williams, as serving a purpose beyond itself; it constitutes both a method of knowing and a manner of remembering: "A poem—a good poem—exists at the center of a complex reminding, to which it relates as both cause and effect."[14]

The slow-brewing wisdom that informs much of Berry's work likewise reflects a sense in which poetry becomes a means of aesthetically engaging with the shapes, forms, and patterns of quotidian life. Gary Snyder, an accomplished poet who shares many of Berry's concerns, may come closest to identifying the true provenance of Berry's work when he writes of poets "who have composed themselves and turned part of themselves back to themselves to become richer and stronger, like Wendell Berry, whose poetry lacks glamour but is really full of nutrients."[15] A careful reading of Berry's poetry reveals that these nutrients constitute a pleasure that is both aesthetically rich and deeply humanizing to the extent that it reminds readers of their own relationship to the world around them— both natural and human.

Taken together, the ideas of poetry as "an instrument by which man may arrive in his place and maintain himself there," poetry as an act that centers a "complex reminding," and poetry as a kind of composting of the self suggest a basic outline for Berry's poetic project. It is an outline that has proved to be remarkably consistent throughout the entire body of poetry that Berry has published, beginning with *The Broken Ground* in 1964 and culminating in his 2011 volume, *Leavings*. It is a body of work that testifies in turn to the multitudinous forms of knowledge and experience that inform Berry's vision of human existence.

In turning to the poetry itself, I want to focus upon how it expresses some of the central themes in Berry's vision of human things. In light of Berry's dual vocation as farmer-poet, it should be unsurprising that work is one important form of knowledge and experience in this vision. Berry's interest in expressing an ethos of work in his poetry connects him with a line of poets (such as Virgil, Whitman, Frost, Williams, Sandburg, and Snyder) whose creative work is deeply informed by the work of their hands. In 1965, after a string of successes as a writer and teacher, Berry took the unconventional step of buying a farm near his native stomping grounds of northern Kentucky and has since then devoted the better part of his career to working and maintaining a small-scale farming operation. It should come as no surprise that a number of Berry's poems follow from his work and identity as a farmer, and dramatize more generally Berry's recognition that labor is a fundamentally humanizing force in the life of man and therefore eminently worthy of representation.

Berry sees an analogy between physical labor and the work of the poem insofar as both constitute important means by which the farmer-poet "maintains himself in place." His perception of the relationship between farming and poetry ("In both one must be concerned for the way things are joined together, in one's mind and art and in the world"[16]) furthers the case. Berry again looks to William Carlos Williams as an important influence in this regard: "[Williams] has always about him the awareness that poetry, as much as the axe or the plow, is a necessity of discovery and settlement, and of the husbanding and neighboring that must follow."[17] The most successful of Berry's work poems have it both ways: they dramatize the metaphoric "discovery and settlement" accomplished by the poem through a depiction of the "discovery and settlement" accomplished by physical labor. One such poem is "The Stones" (1970). In the opening lines to the poem, Berry imagines the worker as a crucial agent in the recycling of nature and history:

> I owned a slope full of stones.
> Like buried pianos they lay in the ground,
> shards of old sea ledges, stumbling blocks
> where the earth caught and kept them
> dark, an old music mute in them
> that my head keeps now I have dug them out.[18]

In this poem, Berry initially positions himself as something of a geologist describing the history of the stones and their presence on his land. But while the "shards of old sea ledges" suggests a time frame that supersedes the human, the association of the stones with pianos grants them a human dimension, a sense in which they reflect human purposes even in their hiddenness. Likewise, by granting the earth agency (it "caught and kept" the stones), Berry draws the human and the natural into creative tension with each other. This tension resolves itself in the question Berry asks himself upon liberating the stones from the earth: "What bond have I made with the earth, / having worn myself against it?"[19]

This question, which neatly summarizes the thematic of the poem, richly suggests Berry's sensitivity to the humanizing force of labor. Of course, there is nothing intrinsically humanizing about the kind of physical labor Berry describes here. A different person working under different conditions or under a different set of assumptions might find such work dehumanizing. What makes the difference here is the powerful act of imagination Berry brings to his work where the object of his labor—removing the stones from the ground—becomes an act of participation in reshaping the ground that he inhabits. Or, rather, the poem suggests that it is finally the subjectivity of the worker that is more nearly reshaped by his labor, just as the subjectivity of the musician is ultimately shaped by his music:

> The stones have given me music
> that figures for me their holes in the earth

and their long lying in them dark.
They have taught me the weariness that loves the ground,
and I must prepare a fitting silence.[20]

The "me" in each of its three instances constitutes Berry as receiver rather than taker, as acted upon rather than acting. There is a sense that labor, even while serving human purposes, is ideally receptive to the transformative power of its object. The laborer finally genuflects before the stones, his weariness compelling him to "prepare a fitting silence" for what has come of his day's work.

In "Enriching the Earth" (1970), Berry again imagines himself as an active participant in the work of earth's renewal and dramatizes once more the mysterious nature of this participation. In the first part of the poem, Berry, after describing his work of planting, sowing, and plowing, states that "all this serves the dark." Berry takes up the question of darkness, of a labor engaged with the mysterious energies of nature's own workings, in the second half of the poem which concludes with the following:

After death, willing or not, the body serves,
entering the earth. And so what was heaviest
and most mute is at last raised up in song.[21]

A strong association between death, body, and earth is forged in the first sentence, presenting a realistic appraisal of death's power. But a redeeming vision of death is presented in the final line as the laborer, heavy and mute in the earth, at last becomes part of the song of re-creation. Much like the stones that become pianos in the earlier poem, Berry's vision here is of selves that for a time may be buried beneath the weight of the earth but are at last transformed into song. "Enriching the Earth," like "The Stones," again dramatizes the act of imagination that attends the farmer's labor by envisioning labor as being a humanizing force in the laborer's life. This dramatization turns upon a perspective of the farmer's labor where the earth, the object of labor, sponsors both the farmer's death and his life. The true service of the body is in its final submission to the earth upon death, where it becomes the raw material feeding nature's and man's renewal.

Poems that express Berry's ideal of work are complemented by numerous other poems that dramatize the relationship between nature and man.

Nature is represented in many of Berry's poems as offering human beings a source of consolation and an opportunity for meaningful repose. In "The Peace of Wild Things" (1968), Berry counteracts the temptation to despair by lying down "where the wood drake / rests in his beauty on the water, and the great heron feeds."[22] Berry concludes the poem with the following:

> And I feel above me the day-blind stars
> waiting with their light. For a time
> I rest in the grace of the world, and am free.[23]

Berry's predominant use of monosyllabic words combined with unvarnished nouns tends to give extra emphasis to those moments when he does use modifiers, as in the "day-blind stars" that wait with their light. Nature constitutes either foreground or background depending upon the reader's perspective. There is at once the figure of the poet observing and embracing the natural world; but when viewed from another angle, there is the natural world that observes and embraces the human. Berry's resistance to privileging one over the other lends such poems an air of quietude, a sense in which the human and nature achieve a momentary stasis against the pressures of time and activity.

While Berry can view nature as a humanizing force insofar as it provides the opportunity for consolation and reflection, many of his poems also dramatize a deeply subjective identification with nature in which the human becomes entirely subsumed by the natural, as for example in the poem "Sleep" (1970):

> I love to lie down weary
> under the stalk of sleep
> growing slowly out of my head,
> the dark leaves meshing.[24]

The long vowels ("weary," "sleep," "growing slowly," "leaves meshing") carry the music of the poem, while the bracing metaphor (sleep as an unfolding stalk) rides the crest of the music into the reader's mind. The lovely music and the striking identification neatly dramatize how Berry sees the natural world as being a crucial ground of self-knowledge. The poem suggests an imagination that is not only shaped by the natural world but is at some level constituted by this identification. This play between the imagination and nature suggests, even further, something about the crucial place poetry has in the career of Berry. Berry's dramatization in his poetry of the interpenetration of nature and the imagination serves to reveal some deep and lasting truths about this relationship. As Jacques Maritain writes in *Creative Intuition in Art and Poetry*, "Man's art and vision . . . are one of the ways through which mankind invades Nature, so as to be reflected and meant by her. Without the mirrors worked out by generations of painters and poets, what would our aesthetic penetration of nature be?"[25] The power and grace of Berry's "aesthetic penetration of nature" in his poetry is redoubtable. His thought at this level sings where elsewhere it is content to merely speak.

While nature and work can be thought of as two thematic poles in Berry's poetry, one crucial grounding force in Berry's vision is the domicile. Marriage is a theme that serves both as a metaphor for what Berry wants to say about engaged, embodied human activity and that also concretely exemplifies what he wants to say about the nature and power of the particular bond that constitutes his marriage to Tanya, his wife of fifty years.

While the human tendency is to reject or shun the unknown, the great value of marriage for Berry lies precisely in its association with an experience of being that is marked more by interpersonal relationship than by categories of reason that confine the individual to an enclosed or shut-off experience of self. Berry is conscious of how his version of marriage differs from contemporary versions. In his essay "Feminism, the Body, and the Machine," he writes:

> Marriage, in what is evidently its most popular version, is now on the one hand an intimate "relationship" involving (ideally) two successful careerists in the same bed, and on the other hand a sort of private political system in which rights and interests must constantly be asserted and defended. Marriage, in other words, has now taken the form of divorce: a prolonged and impassioned negotiation as to how things shall be divided.[26]

Berry counters such a version of marriage through depicting in his poetry one constituted by intangibles such as care, consideration, and regard. These values are funded by an ideal of commitment. Where modern marriage lacks the sort of commitment, both emotional and psychological, that would bind the couple together in a shared engagement with the world, Berry's vision of marriage, through embodying the values of legacy, history, desire, memory, and dream, offers the possibility of a rich and lasting engagement with the world—one defined by the centering idea in his work of "fidelity."

What makes Berry's love poems so rich is how they oftentimes dramatize the inner life of an angst-ridden speaker who finally discovers, or rediscovers, his love to be a stabilizing force against the shifting ground of his emotional life. As Berry writes in "Notes: Unspecializing Poetry," "Love poems that are meant as such aspire to the real world, not a word world. They have tried autonomy and found it lonesome; they seek to 'form a more perfect union.'"[27] Marriage constitutes a fundamental ground of being that centers the speaker of the love poems and gives his life purpose, direction, depth, and meaning. Marriage in Berry's work can also be read in this way as a kind of metaphor for any intentional bond, as between farmer and earth, or individual and community.

"Envoy" (1968) presents a rich and complex picture of marital love through dramatizing marriage as a healing force over against an experience of fragmentation and disconnection. The poem is organized as a sonnet in which the first part poses a problem that is resolved in the second part. The problem here is Berry's sense of disease and disconnection: "Love, all day there has been at the edge of my mind / the wish that my life would hurry on."[28] Berry dramatizes the desire for self-oblivion (interestingly) through a work image:

> For I felt myself a man carrying a loose tottering bundle
> along a narrow scaffold: If I could carry it
> fast enough, I could hold it together to the end.[29]

The work image is a deceptively simple one. The sense of disproportion and mismanagement in the bundle being both "loose" and "tottering" expresses Berry's sense of carrying an emotional burden that he is only barely able to manage. The second part of the image, "If I could carry it fast enough . . . ," suggests the extent to which this experience of self is an agonizingly private one. And precisely by virtue of its private, subjective character we surmise that there is no accounting for this burden in this life; it is simply something to be born, even as it threatens the dissolution of self.

Were the poem to end at this point, we would be left with the despairing view that there is no end to the turmoil of fragmented selfhood, that the self is driven inescapably toward death and nullity. In the second part of the poem, however, Berry rediscovers in his love, imaged as a kind of domestic interior, a containing, healing space that offers the possibility of a transformed selfhood: "I come within the boundaries of your life, an interior / clear and calm." It is also a possibility that comes with a condition: "You could not admit me unburdened." The possibility of intimacy is premised upon Berry's willingness to be stripped of despair, the despair that had ruled him prior to coming into the beloved's presence. And so it is that by relinquishing his dis-ease and entering into the interior space of his beloved, the world-weary speaker is cleansed of his internal confusions.

This space, interestingly, which is at first imagined as a domestic one, is soon reconfigured as a maternal one, suggesting the lover's acknowledgement that romantic or erotic love is at some level funded by a desire for nurturance and healing. It is through the speaker's vulnerability at this level that the richest form of marital intimacy is achieved. That the beloved must learn to speak "the tongue of my joy that you do not know" suggests her own challenge and happiness. And so it is through this exchange that the lover and beloved come to know "the deep leisure of the filling moon." The transition in the poem is complete. The speaker recovers a sense of the fullness of life expressed in the concluding prayer, "May I live long."

Complementing those poems that dramatize the humanizing and healing force of marriage are poems that dramatize the nature of familial inheritance. The poem "The Gathering" (1973) is organized around the image of fathers holding sons, where Berry's experience of holding his own son results in an intense sense of companionship with Berry's grandfather, who is further imagined as one link in a chain of male holding going back to his own father. The first four lines depict Berry's memory of being cradled in his father's arm:

At my age my father
held me on his arm
like a hooded bird,
and his father held him so.[30]

The soft, short vowels ("father," "arm," "bird," "father") lend to the poem a conversational tone, while the pet image of the "hooded bird" recalls a class of other such affectionate terms, such as the idea of a child being a "pup." The image of the child as a hooded bird has the further advantage, however, of suggesting the father's knowledge that this bird will one day leave the brood, even as it will inevitably return, just as the hawk is trained to do. In the lines that follow, the physical intimacy between father and son takes on a rich psychological resonance. As Berry holds his son on his arm, he enters into a "brotherhood of thought" with his own father:

> Now he speaks in me
> as when I knew him first,
> as his father spoke
> in him when he had come
> to thirst for the life
> of a young son.[31]

The vowels open up ("speaks," "knew," "spoke," "life") as the tone of the poem shifts from the conversational to the gently visionary. Berry's "thirst" to know "the life" of his son, prompted by the physical intimacy of holding him, presents a rich perspective of fatherhood (and one that at the time the poem was published was quite countercultural). The sharing of thought between consecutive generations of fathers in the final lines of the poem, furthermore, richly dramatizes Berry's vision of the vital interconnectedness of generations:

> My son
> will know me in himself
> when his son sits hooded on
> his arm and I have grown
> to be brother to all
> my fathers, memory
> speaking to knowledge,
> finally, in my bones.[32]

This self-knowledge is driven by a sense of generational knowledge as each man recognizes his identity in the identity of his father. Fatherhood as marked by a receptivity to otherness defines Berry's experience of manhood, where the goal of growth is an increased understanding of the extent to which our emotional and psychological lives are dependent upon an experience of otherness. The domicile is the space that holds these relationships, allowing the self to integrate progressively the private world of emotional vulnerability with the public world of knowledge. The two are ultimately seen as two sides of the same coin. Knowledge is finally not a form of thought divorced from emotion but rather is enfleshed in emotion, an idea that Berry captures in the image of memory speaking to knowledge in his bones.

In the poem "Our Children, Coming of Age" (1982), Berry more directly addresses the transmission of domestic value from parents to children. The poem, framed by the image of the dance, acknowledges the necessary separation of children from parents while also recognizing that the children through this separation take up their places in the larger dance, what Berry calls "the great circle." The first several lines of the poem suggest that it is only through this separation that the children become aware of the music that has subtly drawn them into this circle:

> In the great circle, dancing in
> and out of time, you move now
> toward your partners, answering
> the music suddenly audible to you
> that only carried you before
> and will carry you again.[33]

The present progressive tense in the first several lines ("dancing," "answering") and the evocative metaphor of the dance might at first obscure the fact that Berry is in fact talking about the encompassing dance of life, one driven by a kind of cosmic music that beckons the lives of the young dancers into it. Berry presents a more complex picture of this dance in the next several lines as a note of realism enters the poem.

> When you meet the destined ones
> now dancing toward you,
> we will be in line behind you,
> out of your awareness for the time,

we whom you know, others we remember
whom you do not remember, others
forgotten by us all.[34]

The lovely interplay between the "you" of the young and the "we" of the elders evokes the "great circle" that is Berry's controlling metaphor in the poem. Even while romantic love will for a time captivate the attentions of the young as they go to meet "the destined ones," and even as they in the process lose sight of their elders, Berry understands that both generations are nonetheless participating in the great dance that involves them all.

The final lines of the poem evoke an equally rich sense of how the old finally provide a kind of informing and encompassing light for the young:

When you meet, and hold love
in your arms, regardless of all,
the unknown will dance away from you
toward the horizon of light.
Our names will flutter
on these hills like little fires.[35]

One imagines an outdoor dance lit by candlelight. In the "great circle" that is Berry's true subject, however, these candles become the names of the elders who light the way for the young, who make their movements visible and their love possible. The poem wonderfully dramatizes Berry's vision of intergenerational vitality through choreographing the dance of life where the young, even amid their temporary forgetfulness, are surrounded by those luminous figures that give their life and love purpose and meaning.

The importance of communal inheritance is perhaps most powerfully dramatized in those poems that memorialize the deceased. Berry was once asked in an interview about what happens to us if we forget the dead. His response neatly summarizes the value of this kind of knowing: "Well, if you didn't know the past, you literally wouldn't know anything. You'd have no language, no history, and so the first result would be a kind of personal incompleteness."[36] The elegy functions in this way as one crucial vehicle by which a community comes to know and understand itself.

Berry's poem "Elegy" (1982) dramatizes the passage of wisdom from the old to young through elegizing the memory of Owen Flood, a lifelong friend and mentor who significantly influenced many of Berry's agricultural ideals. Berry once shared with an interviewer a memory of Flood that suggests the nature of this relationship. After having spent a long night drinking and dancing, Berry showed up the next morning for work, cutting tobacco for Flood, in no very good shape:

> He went out ahead of me as usual and expected me to follow, and I made my way through that terrible day. It got up in the evening, with still a long way to go, and I became aware that he'd stopped to watch me fumbling along. After a while he said, "That social life don't get down the row, does it, boy?" . . . It was one of the best days of his life, I imagine. But you know it was profoundly instructive, the way he did it. It was an educational work of genius, really.[37]

In the poem, then, Berry dramatizes the dynamic presence of the memory of his friend and teacher in his own sense of self and community. Berry begins the poem by speaking to the function of memory in rooting selves to a given place. He does so by playing on the idea of the ground as literally holding the deceased and of the deceased as representing a body of memory that grounds the living:

> To be at home on its native ground
> the mind must go down below its horizon,
> descended below the lightfall
> on ridge and steep and valley floor
> to receive the lives of the dead. It must wake
> in their sleep, who wake in its dreams.[38]

In a lovely metaphor, Berry describes how the mind, like a seed, must be implanted in the earth in order to receive the nutrients of the dead who have fertilized the soil. The mind in this sense becomes one with the earth as it becomes one with the deceased. In another sense, however, the ground is imagined as a holding place for the deceased, which the living must, in a motif borrowed from Homer and Virgil, visit in order to understand life. Death, in its associations with sleep, is not represented as an interim period in which the deceased await the resurrection of the body at Christ's final coming, but rather it is imagined as a kind of interface where the living and the dead commingle and by doing so keep each other alive. Transmission is imagined as a vital interchange between the living and the dead, and therefore supports the continuity of life and the possibility of a community.

Berry proceeds to imagine himself as one who is beckoned to enter this ground. While walking "On the rock road between / creek and woods in the fall of the year," Berry is struck by a series of sounds. At first he hears, in conformity to the natural setting, "the cries / of little birds high in the wind." The natural, however, is quickly exchanged for the supernatural: "And then the beat of old footsteps / came around me, and my sight was changed." Immediately Berry must let go of the need to attend only to what is visible and must learn to "see" what lies behind appearances, in this case the summoning of the past. Caught up in this vision, and in a movement that again plays upon the visits Odysseus and Aeneas make to the underworld, Berry follows the summons and enters the earth:

> I passed though the lens of darkness
> as through a furrow, and the dead
> gathered to meet me. They knew me,
> but looked in wonder at the lines in my face,
> the white hairs sprinkled on my head.[39]

The metaphysical image where Berry passes through the "lens of darkness" is striking. The image is further modified by an agricultural metaphor ("as through a furrow"), bringing the sublime action into the very specific context of Berry's farming community. Among the dead who come to meet Berry are several who have managed their deaths well, who have learned to accept death as they accepted their lives. One man, however, attracts Berry's attention:

> I saw one standing aside, alone,
> weariness in his shoulders, his eyes
> bewildered yet with the newness
> of his death.[40]

Berry recognizes the man as Owen Flood. Sorrow is mixed with gladness at the sight of his friend, whose first words, punctuated with a grin, are "Wendell, this is not a place / for you and me." Berry is gratified that his friend has lost none of his dry wit and stubbornness: "It was his principle to doubt / all ease of satisfaction."

Death, in the following stanza, is at first imagined as a division, a sharp separation between the living and the dead, where any possible communion is offset by the impermanence of the one and the permanence of the other. Flood, however, rises momentarily above his melancholy state to resume his former relationship in life to Berry:

> It seemed to me then that he cast off
> his own confusion, and assumed
> for one last time, in one last kindness,
> the duty of the older man.[41]

The images are both simple and striking as Flood "casts off" his confusion and takes up one last time the mantle of wise elder. The wisdom that is communicated by Flood has fundamentally to do, then, with the importance of intergenerational relationships and in particular of the vital importance of companionship to the life of men:

> He spoke of our history passing through us,
> the way our families' generations
> overlap, the great teaching
> coming down by deed of companionship:
> characters of fields and times and men,
> qualities of devotion and of work—
> endless fascinations, passions,
> old as mind, new as light.[42]

One can imagine the scene: the two men for one last time bound together in a shared vision of life, the older man presenting the younger with "the great teaching" that is precisely the history of relationship and communion between the men and all the persons they have known and loved. The last two lines in particular express something of the force and vigor of this vision, a sense in which a life lived under such conditions achieves its deepest satisfaction. The poem becomes a cosmic vision that expresses the vital companionship between men whose lives are invigorated by mutual labor and shared history. Berry sums up this vision by using the metaphor of song, one which in this case expresses the force of life that draws human beings together, giving their lives purpose and meaning:

> There is a song in the Creation:
> it has always been the gift
> of every gifted voice, though none
> ever sang it. As he spoke
> I heard that song. In its changes and returns
> his life was passing into life.
> That moment, earth and song and mind,
> the living and the dead, were one.[43]

The rich weave of song and voice here dramatizes the possibility of intergenerational communion; it is a weave that binds the living to the living and the living to the dead. The motif of song is made all the more meaningful by the song of the poem that puts proof to the function of poetry in keeping alive the memory of the dead. The elegy finally acknowledges the role of the deceased in ensuring the vitality of the community where all that has been fragmented becomes, through participating in song, whole. It is Berry's willingness to listen to this song that has given Flood his life back to him, just as Berry, in the final lines of the poem, returns to life with a profound sense of what he has been given: "And I, inheritor of what I mourned, / went back toward the light of day."

Each of the poems treated in this essay represents the uniquely expressive power that Berry's poetry has in dramatizing his vision of human experience. They not only reflect Berry's sense of the poem as "an instrument by which a man may arrive in his place and maintain himself there" through illustrating the interdependencies that exist between human beings whose lives are ordered by their fidelity to each other and to the place in which they live, but also illustrate Berry's sense of how the poem "exists at the center of a complex reminding, to which it relates as both cause and effect." This reminding can involve the relationship of human beings to the earth; it can also involve the relationship of husbands to wives, parents to children, teachers to students, and friends to friends. In each case, Berry's poetry expresses a rich vision of selfhood, one that finds its deepest meaning not in the search for an elusive "I" but rather in the recognition that the "I" only has meaning within the context of external realities that both stabilize the "I" and give it breadth and depth.

From poems of praise and thanksgiving to poems of mourning; from simple poems of noticing and observance to longer poems of memorial and of communal remembering; from poems of love to poems of loss; from poems of acute self-doubt to poems of despair redeemed; from poems of political witness to poems of wisdom; from work poems to leisure poems; and from religious poems and to poems of secular joy; there is no poem Berry has written that doesn't dramatize something of Berry's belief in the essential provenance of poetry—its power to render something of the created world and the reality of embodied human experience in a language that sings softly and deeply, just as it exchanges "glamour" for some vital expression of lasting human things.

That Berry's fiction and prose have begun to move from the fringes of popular consciousness into the center is a testament to its vitality, richness, and relevance. It is not difficult to imagine a point in time when his poetry, likewise, will be recognized for the unique and significant achievement that it is. Readers who desire the fullest and richest experience of Berry's vision of human things would do well not to neglect this body of work.

# 16

# If Dante Were a Kentucky Barber

## *Anthony Esolen*

> Those meetings happened from time to time over a period of fourteen or fifteen years. I don't know how many there were—fewer than you would think, perhaps, seeing that they made up so important a part of my life. Since none was ever planned, each one was different, surprising in its way. And yet the terms never changed. Mattie always preserved a certain discretion, not in anything she said, but in the way she was, the way she carried herself and looked. She was with me, but not for me, if you can see what I mean. There was a veil between us. We both kept her vow, as I alone kept mine. I knew there was a smile of hers that I had never seen. And that was well. That was all right.
>
> —Jayber Crow[1]

I begin this essay with what seems an easy assumption. In his novel *Jayber Crow*, Wendell Berry, having structured his hero's early manhood after the pattern of Dante's wandering in the dark woods at the beginning of the *Inferno* and his struggle up the mountain of Purgatory, has cast his gentle heroine, Mattie Keith, later to be Mattie Chatham, in the role of Beatrice.

No doubt, if Mattie is meant to suggest Beatrice, it is as a lovely counterpoint. She is bound to her duties on this earth, among the people she loves. Mattie is here, not beyond. Dante's beloved reserves her smile, the "second beauty" more dazzling than her eyes, for the moment after the poet has been cleansed of the memory of his sins in the River Lethe, at the top of Purgatory mountain.[2] It is a smile that brings to a climax the prayers and the dance of those ladies called Faith, Hope, and Love. Dante will soon gaze into Beatrice's eyes and find himself as a man "soaring beyond man."[3] Mattie will never smile so upon Jayber; her beauty and goodness rather cause him, if not to soar, at least to struggle upward to manhood. It does not send him to heaven, but it does help him to see the shadows of heaven about him. It does not usher him among the communion of saints, but it does place him firmly within the communion of sinners, wondrous in its own right, in a place called Port William. The smile that Jayber Crow says he has never seen and will never see on earth is reserved to the private love between Mattie and her unappreciative husband, Troy. And that, says Jayber, was well.

Now we cannot see Mattie as playing the part of Beatrice without turning our minds to the nature of heaven and hell. Berry demands that we consider how this life on earth may be like a choral hymn preparatory to the songs above or like a long and wearying drill for the loneliness below. For when, with masterly patience, Berry finally reveals most clearly that "this is a book about Heaven,"[4] implying that Mattie has been its Beatrice, Jayber is near the end of his memoirs, and we have but a page or two to turn, with Mattie's death the only event to come. Then, with the slow surprise of an opening flower, our minds are led to reminisce and reconsider, as Jayber himself has done. We must ask, not while we are first reading but only afterward, just what this little place, the "Port William Membership," with its barber shop and bank, its school on the hillside, its clearing in the woods for all-night "worter dranking," even its cemetery, has to do with heaven. And that, if we have eyes to see and ears to hear, should rouse in us both wonder and contrition: wonder, that so splendid a world, and so real a communion, and so exalted a love, should be so near to us; contrition, that we should so often barter it for the drab, lonely, idle dreams of pride.

When Jayber first lays eyes on Mattie, she is a teenage girl coming home arm in arm between two other girls, and all he is, nothing more, nothing less, is a barber living in the garret above his shop, "a tall, lean, baldish man, almost twice their age, smiling down upon them from the threshold."[5] The incongruity makes their laughter all the merrier. Mattie certainly seems to be no walking embodiment of theological truth—or perhaps that sort of thing is not so obvious in the hills of Kentucky. Yet even in her youth, she possesses a presence, a womanliness, that penetrates to the heart: "It was her eyes that most impressed me. They were nearly black and had a liquid luster. The brief, laughing look that she had given me made me feel extraordinarily seen, as if after that I might be visible in the dark."[6]

That moment is reminiscent of the first two times Dante sees Beatrice, as he recounts them in his youthful *La vita nuova*. In the ninth year of his age, Dante says, he saw the young girl whom people called Beatrice, the lady who blesses, even when they did not know her name. It is a strange thing to say, a signal that the beautiful Beatrice touches the minds of those who see her, making them vaguely aware of a deeper world beyond and within the ordinary world of Florence. In other words, from the outset Beatrice is at once a young woman, even a nine-year-old girl, and a locus of allegorical symbolism. This appearance would come to govern Dante's life and art, though the boy of *La vita nuova* could not possibly have been aware of it at the time. Then he meets the same lady of his thoughts nine years later, walking between two other ladies, and she greets him. Dante will never be the same after that. He dreams that evening of a majestic and commanding figure, carrying in his arms the sleeping Beatrice, draped in scarlet. It is the God of Love, who looks to Dante and utters the words that will be the key to all of the man's poetry: *"Ego dominus tuus,"* he says; "I am your Lord."

Now that is a challenge to the world, especially our world, as we fancy ourselves our own masters. To hark back to Dante is not exactly to bring back the whole Ptolemaic universe that forms the staging for the *Divine Comedy*. But it is certainly to bring back the *meaning* of that universe; a world of beauty and life, not inert matter to be shaped and pounded to gratify our appetites; a providential world, and therefore a world whose script we do not ourselves write, we with our tedious plots and dull, trite habits. So Jayber, now an old man thinking about Uncle Othy and Aunt Cordie, who took him in when he was a little orphan boy, looks about the river and the valley and considers "the great unearned beauty of the place,"[7] always gloriously impractical and half wild. So too as Jayber recalls his life, its geography is not exactly that of the *Divine Comedy*, "starting, say, in the Dark Wood of Error, and proceeding by logical steps through Hell and Purgatory and into Heaven,"[8] but the terrain of Dante's life is there beneath the Appalachian underbrush. "My life has come to me," says Jayber, "or I have gone to it mainly by way of mistakes and surprises. . . . I have been unable to shake off the feeling that I have been led—make of that what you will."[9]

It is crucial to note, then, that Mattie, like Beatrice, is a character who *appears,* rather than one who takes active part in most of the everyday events of Jayber's life. One warm summer afternoon, Jayber is pottering about at his job as church groundskeeper, when Mattie brings a group of little children from Vacation Bible School outside to play, guiding their play yet playing with them as if she were a child herself; of such, says Jesus, is the Kingdom of Heaven. Then, says Jayber, "I was all of a sudden overcome with love for her. It was the strongest moment I had known, violent in its suddenness and completeness, and also the quietest. I had been utterly changed, and had not stirred."[10] The moment is an epiphany, a vision given as a grace, a mystery from without. It seems to cause Port William and all the world to fall away, and yet it transforms that world too; it is in the world, and works through the world, but it is not, finally, *of* the world.

Nor is the natural world itself *of the world.* "Thy life's a miracle," says Edgar to his despairing father in *King Lear,* a line that Berry uses as the touchstone for *Life Is a Miracle,* a collection of essays urging us to see the gifts we so ungratefully despise or forget entirely. Mattie is not the only bringer of grace in the novel, as Beatrice is not the only bringer of grace in Dante's *Comedy.* Think of the swirling flood of the Kentucky River that fairly arrests the young Jayber, aiming for Louisville in order to "make something of himself," as the deeply atheistic phrase puts it, and washes him back to his home village and to life. The river is a bringer of grace. So is the truck driver from Port William who gives Jayber a lift. For a short time, that fellow is like a Virgil in the midst of the Dark Woods, come to lead Dante eventually to the threshold of Heaven, there to see once more, after so many years of dryness and death, the blessed Beatrice.

For Berry, as for Dante (and, for that matter, all the medieval romancers), the things that most build the man are not those he chooses but rather those he allows to choose him, to shape him, and to inspire him, as Galahad and his companions in the Quest of the Holy Grail board the pilotless ship of faith and go they know not where. Mattie may or may not be a locus of allegory, but she certainly is a beautiful woman in love with Port William, its simple people, its well-tended farms, its homely work, and its mysterious woods, whose glory is not reducible to human utility. If the *Divine Comedy* is less an account of the love between a man and a woman than the story of that man's surrender to all that Beatrice is in the eyes and the providence of God, so *Jayber Crow* is less an account of the love between Jayber and Mattie than the story of his surrender to all that Mattie is in the eyes and the providence of God, yes, but made incarnate in the bustling life of Port William. We may say that Beatrice finally leads us to the mystery of Christ, the second person of the Trinity, God made man; and Mattie, without any conscious design, to the body of Christ manifest in a community on earth, bound together, despite our many sins, by the grace of God and by the slow leavening words of Jesus.

## Port William, the Body

Mattie, like Jayber, is a part of what Berry calls the "Port William Membership," and the allusion to Saint Paul is clear and, in our day, provocative. "For the body is not one member, but many."[11] It is important to understand what this does *not* mean in Port William. It does not imply any complicated system of government. Port William has no mayor, and no policemen; its informal officers of righteousness, the ill-behaved Regulators—a wicked spoof on government destroyers of innocent local pastimes and customs and businesses—are a gang of vandals who destroy moonshine stills so that they can corner the market for their own. Discipline is mainly maintained by the constant vigilance of the members, especially the old folks, who are everywhere and who get into some amiable mischief of their own. Business, too, is simple, straightforward, and personal. When Jayber comes back to town as a young man looking for work, he is able to view the vacant barber shop, meet the man who holds the mortgage, put a down payment on the loan, and sign the papers, in a single evening. That can only happen because of a complex fabric of long-standing relationships, memory, and trust. Says the owner to Jayber:

> "Mr. Crow, I'm Mat Feltner. I'm glad to know you. I knew your
> mother's people. I remember the Daggets very well."

There was nothing glancing or sidling about the way he
looked at you. He looked right through your eyes, right into you,
as a man looks at you who is willing for you to look right into
him.[12]

Jayber persuades him that he can cut hair and that he is willing to
make a go of it. When they agree on the rather strict terms, Jayber has
to give over the down payment—a wad of bills tied up with string and
stuffed into the lining of his jacket, and another wad stuffed into his shoe.
And Matt Feltner, the owner, having seen *the man* and not the poverty,
"sat there as if not a man in Port William had ever paid for anything without taking off his shoe."[13]

What in any other author might be an occasion for flippancy—with
an obligatory look askance at the backscratching ways of the hillbillies—
Berry sees rather as an expression of the potency of moral uprightness,
of plain virtues practiced in the sight of one's fellows. It is what allows
the loan to come off. Even in the dismal terms of economic materialism,
diligence, honesty, and plain dealing usually pay. It is vice, whether or
not it seems to pay off in quick cash (and it usually defaults on its promises; think of the entangling excesses of avarice, or the spiritual enervation
caused by lust), that is uneconomical, a drag on the health of the community. Of course, one cannot practice virtue for money; its very nature
places it within the economy of gift and gratitude. Compare, for example,
Jayber the Barber with Troy Chatham, the machine-obsessed lad, perpetually up-to-date and therefore perpetually adolescent, whom Mattie falls
in love with and marries. Jayber is not a success in the eyes of the World
(the Flesh has a little better success with him for a while, and the Devil a
very little, but the World, almost none at all). He never will make enough
money to support a wife and children, though that will not matter to him
much once it becomes clear to him that he must remain devoted to Mattie
and never marry. But he is a good barber, and Troy is a bad farmer. Why,
and what does it have to do with Mattie, whom the barber loves and the
farmer supposes he loves?

The answer is not skill, exactly, or not skill in the first instance. Jayber
in fact jests about the limits of his talent:

Burley came on in. "I need to get my hair cut bad," he said.

And I said, glad of a reason to grin, "Well, that's the way I cut it."[14]

Whether or not we take him at his word here, it is clear that for Jayber a barber is far more than a human machine who performs a certain sartorial function. As he shaves and cuts the hair of men who come to his shop, he comes to share their thoughts, their joys, and their sorrows. He becomes a part of their common story, mainly by listening to their stories. "My shop," he says, "was a democracy if ever anyplace was."[15]

In other words, it was a place of community, governed in part by Jayber's tact and in part by the tacitly acknowledged moral authority of old men. Most notable among those old men is Athey Keith, Mattie's father. One day a young and too-familiar upstart of a preacher attempts to patronize him with his breezy good cheer, asking him how he is and expecting the meaningless answer. Athey puts him in his place, with an irony that should remind him of the humility of the human condition:

> "Well, sir," Athey said, "where I used to be limber I'm stiff and where I used to be stiff I'm limber. Do you know what I'm talking about?"
> "Yessir," said Brother Wingfare.
> *"Nosir,"* said Athey.
> "Nosir," said Brother Wingfare.[16]

It is hard for us to remember now, but not so long ago men went to a barber shop—in my own small town they still did this when I was a boy—to engage in masculine banter about money, sports, the weather, aching bones, women, cars; to *be with* one another, even when they did not like one another.

It is from that care for each man, or that particular fellow who is a member of his community, that Jayber learns to be a good barber in all senses of the phrase. He cuts hair well because he wishes to do so for those he serves. It is the same for his care for the church and his tending of the cemetery. These things are matters not of industrial efficiency but rather of love.

In other words, Berry sees that the skill to become a really fine workman is founded in the community and aims for the good of the community. What happens when one cuts oneself off from that community is told in the pathetic tale of Troy Chatham. Enveloped in his good looks and above-average intelligence, Troy rejects the wisdom of his fellow farmers in his own day and that of his forebears who worked the land long ago. He is a modern man, severed from the past; a man who would not tend a cemetery but plow it up for the sake of a blacktopped plaza with a franchise doughnut shop. Troy must always go in for the biggest and most expensive machines. He buys a tractor for his fields because he has already accommodated both himself and nature to the exigencies of the machine:

> Troy went into debt and bought his new equipment because he didn't want to be held back by demanding circumstances. He was young and strong and ambitious. He wanted to be a star. The tractor greatly increased the power and speed of work. With it he could work more land. He could work longer. Because it had electric lights and did not get tired, he could work at night.[17]

He works, then, not *with* the natural rhythms of the day and the natural fertility of the land, but instead against them, or as indifferent to them. And as machines never call unto machines, so it is that such work, as Berry presents it, is essentially lonely, too. Athey Keith attempts to teach his son-in-law the methods of farming he learned from long experience, his own and that of his father and his father's father. "Such knowledge," says Jayber, "ought to have passed from Athey to Troy as a matter of course, in the process of daily work and talk."[18] It does not, because Troy, in his pride, alienates himself from the old farmers. They are but obstacles in the path of his machine:

> Troy had begun to see Athey and the others as "in the way." He would tell of working with them, for instance, on the same mowing land, and having to slow down until they could pull out at the turns to let him and his tractor go ahead. "By God," he would say, "I just wanted to drive right over the top of 'em!"[19]

We should not see in Berry's judgment a sentimental rejection of technology. Is it, after all, merely sentimental to demand that tools serve human purposes rather than that men subserve the tool? What's wrong with Troy is that he does not in fact really care for farming, as he does not care for his father-in-law, or for Port William. Because he does not love his land—and his village, with its fascinating little past and present—he will take no advice from his fellows. He will not stoop to learn. He does not use tools well, he does not honor the power and the beauty of the natural world, and he does not understand what it is to be a true member of a community. He must always outdo; and his pitching himself into debt is but the economic manifestation of a moral house in disarray. His consummate act of irresponsibility, at the end of the novel, is to destroy the Nest Egg, the woods that Mattie loved. While she lies dying in the hospital, helpless to dissuade him, he harvests the woods for timber, for money to pay off debts he never should have incurred. Amid the roar of bulldozers and the whine of the chainsaw, Jayber sees that Troy's ceaseless gamble of equity and relentless work against debt has finally come up snake eyes. The man is now so isolated, and so strangely unaware of his smallness, that "in his desperation to salvage something, even just a little dab of pride, he had had to look on Mattie's illness as providential."[20]

Mattie, it is true, fell in love with this impudent popinjay. Such things happen. But she does not complain of him. She gives him what love he can accept from her. And that is her way. For Mattie, without fanfare, and certainly without political bustle, loves her fellow villagers and the beauty of the land wherein the village is nestled. It is an important point to understand. Modern man may hang about roadhouses as Troy does, picking up wenches on the side, but he is lonely, as he defines himself as distinct from the democracy of the dead—what Chesterton called tradition—and from the claims of the annoying people among whom he happens to live. But Mattie is not lonely. Even when we find her alone, she is but dwelling in solitude, that tranquillity of heart that is at once most private and most receptive of the beauty and generosity of being. So Jayber finds her one day, after he awakes from a nap in the woods, "idly walking along, looking at everything as she went." When Beatrice first appears to Dante in earthly Paradise, she is preceded by a grand liturgical pageant, and by angels strewing her path and her chariot with "a mist of flowers / that leapt like spray."[21] That same admiring crowd is unseen but sensed as Mattie walks among the things she loves:

> She had picked a little bouquet of violets, both the blossoms and the pretty leaves, and was carrying it as she might have done when

she was a girl, pleased to have their beauty with her. She seemed surrounded by almost a singing of her sense of rest.[22]

What kind of woman can love a stand of trees and a hillside so simply and deeply? She is not an environmentalist, if by that we mean someone with a program for making herself feel righteous and her neighbors uncomfortable. She is emphatically unlike Cecelia Overhold, whose sense of her own virtue and intelligence causes her to despise everything about Port William, including such earthy things as "public loafing and spitting."[23] What Mattie enjoys is not some abstraction called "nature," surrounding her, but *this wood, this hill, these trees, those flowers.* Such a woman, even when no one is near, is a member of a community, and retreats from her fellows in the village not to be away from them but instead to be the more simply and intimately with other beautiful things that God has made. Such a woman is a good housewife, a good neighbor. "Mattie Chatham," says Jayber, "as time went on and the older women became less able, had a way of being involved and seeing to things. Her way was quiet and unobtrusive—and effective; she got things done."[24] Again, it is not a matter of a merely technical skill. It is a virtue, learned in and by love. In that love, work itself is folded into the joy of the Sabbath. So Berry writes, in a subtle poem connecting our need to work with our greater need to feast with one another:

The crop must drink, we move the pipe
To draw the water back in time
To fall again upon the field
So that the harvest may grow ripe,
The year complete its ancient rhyme
With other years, and a good yield
Complete our human hope. And this
Is Sunday work, necessity
Depriving us of needed rest.
Yet that necessity is less
Being met, not by one, but three.
Neighbors, we make this need our feast.[25]

I doubt very much that Berry *needed* to go to Dante for his insights into the relationship between community and virtue. Still, he did go to

Dante, and if we look at the *Divine Comedy* in light of Berry's apparent understanding of it, we may find passages that illuminate both works. For example, it is common knowledge that Dante was a political player in his day, exiled from his beloved Florence when the opposition party, abetted by Pope Boniface VIII, took control of the city. The history of medieval Florence certainly makes for fascinating reading, with its assassinations and party reversals and civil wars; but what critics of the *Divine Comedy* often overlook is that, for Dante, politics is never merely political but is also supposed to be ordained to assist man in his attaining of his final end, the beatific vision of God. And that is our true end, Dante maintains, because it is the fulfillment of our nature as social beings. Our oneness in community reflects the oneness of God:

> Mankind is in a good (indeed, ideal) state when, to the extent that its nature allows, it resembles God. But mankind most closely resembles God when it is most a unity, since the true measure of unity is in him alone; and for this reason it is written: "Hear, O Israel, the Lord thy God is one." But mankind is most a unity when it is drawn together to form a single entity.[26]

It is true that Dante favored a universal empire, though in the Middle Ages so strong was the sense of local allegiance and so rudimentary were the bureaucracies of emperor and king that nothing like the vast homogenizing modern state was even imaginable. The point is that man was created for community, both in the beginning—"It is not good that the man should be alone," says God[27]—and in the end, when God shall establish forever the community of the righteous:

> And I John saw the holy city, new Jerusalem, coming down from God out of heaven, prepared as a bride adorned for her husband.
>   And I heard a great voice out of heaven saying, Behold, the tabernacle of God is with men, and he will dwell with them, and they shall be his people, and God himself shall be with them, and be their God.[28]

Throughout his great poem, Dante aims at that consummate city and against it judges the earthly cities that ought to be foretastes of Paradise.

Hence the loneliness of Hell, its severe separation of classes of sinners fore-
shadowing the ultimate in separation, the traitors fixed in ice. Hence also
the genuine gregariousness of Purgatory, where the citizens-to-be form a
real brotherhood of suffering and mutual assistance in worship and prayer.
On that mountain, even when we seem to meet the recluse, we find we
are really in the company of a hearty patriot. Virgil is trying to determine
which way he and Dante should take to proceed on their ascent when they
catch sight of a soul "proud and full of dignity" watching them quietly
"as a lion / at rest will watch and never turn his head."[29] But when Virgil
approaches him,

> he made no response
> But to inquire about our native land
> and who we were in life; and the sweet guide
> began with "Mantua," when that desert shade
> Rose up from where he'd stood so firm in place–
> "We share one country, you of Mantua!
> I am Sordello!"—and the two embraced.[30]

The man hasn't even waited for Virgil to finish his sentence! No talk
of party or faction here! All that matters to the poet Sordello—who is in
for a wondrous surprise when he learns his fellow Mantuan's name—is
that he and Virgil come from the same *terra,* the same sweet land. It is not
only true that communities foster such love. Such love, devotion to the
small place of one's birth, is essential to community.

Apparently it is also blessed in the kingdom of God. So, for example,
from his great-great-grandfather Cacciaguida, the Athey Keith of *Parad-
iso,* Dante hears what it was like once to live in Florence, when Florence
was a true community, with true members, unlike the wealth-ridden city
of Dante's day:

> Bellincion Berti I have seen go, girt
> in leather and bone, his good wife coming from
> her mirror with no paint upon her face;
> I have seen Nerli and Vecchietto come
> content to carry wallets of mere skin,
> their wives contented with the wool and loom.

Fortunate women! sure of tombs within
their own town walls—and no one left to lie
alone by husbands moneying in France:
One at the cradle watches quietly
and in her parents' own sweet lisping talk
consoles her baby with a lullaby;
Another draws the wool skein off the shock
and with her household spins the ancient tales
of Trojans, of Fiesole, and Rome.[31]

The point is not that there is a special virtue in leather leggings but rather that a community whose highest aim is material wealth, as Thomas Merton notes in his introduction to Saint Augustine's *City of God,* will always be a "makeshift," at best a truce, as all its members submit, in Augustine's words, to being "ruled by the lust to rule."[32] Caught by such lust, Florentine husbands will leave their wives to sleep alone so that they may go courting money in France. Caught by such lust, a Troy Chatham will grow bored with Mattie, weary of the farm he cannot manage, so that he may buy a flashy piece of machinery he cannot use or bed down a roadhouse blonde he does not love.

How different is Mattie, whom we sometimes see in solitary contemplation but who even so is never alone, while her husband Troy is always about town, even patronizing Jayber's shop, without the slightest awareness of who the other men really are, including the barber who must restrain his hand as he slides the razor across his neck. Here she is, visiting the grave of her little daughter Liddie:

Walking in her grief, she had followed the old path that in her childhood she and the other children had followed, coming up out of the river bottom to school in the days before school buses, and then she had cut across through the Feltner place to the graveyard. She lay on the raw mound of the grave as if trying to shelter it with her body, ever so still and given up and small. . . . I knew that in all the world I was the only one who knew where she was.[33]

Note the path: it emerges from the past, from happy days with her friends; it crosses a neighbor's yard; it ends in that small community of the dead, beside the church, and, as it happens, beside the one man in the world who understands her and loves her, who is as it were married to her but not in the flesh, faithful to her, though she does not acknowledge his love and does not turn her heart from her husband.

It is true, as I have noted, that Mattie's is also an active love as she effortlessly matures into her duties as one of the women whose simple charity holds a community together. Yet that love is never divorced from simplicity: "Mattie loved wildflowers. She loved almost everything that grew out of the ground, but wildflowers especially. She loved just to look at them, and she loved to gather them (the ones that would last) in bouquets to take to church."[34] Berry has in mind perhaps the woman of whom Dante dreams, as a forerunner of Beatrice, when he reaches earthly Paradise, at the top of the mountain of Purgatory. She, too, artless and gentle, combines a love for the simple act with a gaze toward transcendent beauty:

> In that hour when Venus shines
> upon the mountainside her orient gleam,
> ever enkindled by the fire of love,
> A young and lovely lady in a dream
> appeared to me upon the meadowland,
> gathering flowers, and she said in song,
> "Let anyone who may demand my name
> know I am Leah, and I go to make
> myself a garland by my lovely hands.
> Here I adorn myself for the delight
> I will enjoy when looking in my glass.
> My sister Rachel never leaves that sight
> But gazes in her glass the whole day through.
> She for her lovely eyes, I for my hands—
> her yearning is to see, and mine to do."[35]

Mattie gathers flowers for her church. Leah, symbol of a life of active virtue, calls our attention to her contemplative sister, Rachel; their union is made manifest in the person of Beatrice, whom Dante is soon to meet again after many years, renewing his youthful love.

A Theology of Love

The only virtue that can bind together the oddments of humanity that populate Port William, transforming it from a vague geographical area to a "membership," is love. But we should not suppose that love is to be valued merely for that utility, no matter how important it is. Berry never claims to be a theologian; he is far more modest in his theological than in his economic forays. More modest, and more successful. For he is attempting, like Dante, to fashion a poetic vision that will flesh out the deepest significance of love. Says the theologian Jean Danielou, "Love is therefore as primary as existence," and Berry, in sympathy with that insight, will show us that if we do not know love, we miss not only the beauty of Mattie Chatham and the beauty of the woods above Port William. We also miss ourselves and all the created world. We miss what it means, finally, to be.

In this good and earthy Kentucky metaphysic, as in the narrowing funnel of Dante's *Inferno,* Hell is our entrapment in lusts, in the hatred that "always finds its justifications and fulfills itself perfectly in time by destruction of the things of time."[36] So we meet souls in the *Inferno* utterly unable to leap the bounds of time, as they were unable to love God and neighbor: a Farinata, a sort of failed Sordello, fixed forever in the political feuds of his native city, whose sole preoccupation is the fortune of his kin. "Who were your family?" he asks Dante. It seems a natural enough question. Anyone in Port William might ask it of a stranger. But in Farinata, it is the resumption of civil war. He does not wish to look back upon his kinsmen with wistful affection but rather to place the poet in an everlasting grid of Florentine strife.

But there is something about love that will not be so bound. The old question "Why is there something, and not nothing?" implies, in the heart of the lover, the richer question "Why should there be such beautiful things to love?" And just as the things themselves cannot answer why they should exist, so they cannot answer why they are to be loved; those answers arrive to us, in moments of intuition, from somewhere or Someone beyond the foundations of the world:

> But love, sooner or later, forces us out of time. It does not accept that limit. Of all that we feel and do, all the virtues and all the

sins, love alone crowds us at last over the edge of the world. For love is always more than a little strange here. It is not explainable or even justifiable. It is itself the justifier.[37]

That is an astonishing passage. Christian poets have long dwelt upon the strangeness of this life, for the wayfaring Christian is to learn from Abraham, who left his home in the Chaldees and became a stranger in a strange land, following the call of the Lord. Yet Berry's hero, in returning *home,* and in loving that home as deeply as any man can love a place and a time, finds by that very love that he has been crowded "over the edge of the world," set free from place and time. The Benedictine monks of old, wishing to be pilgrims and not vagabonds, took a vow of stability that rooted them in one place, to work there, to pray, and to assist one another in the Christian journey. Jayber essentially takes such a vow. It allows him to encounter wonder in his love for the familiar. In this he is unlike the restless and loveless Troy Chatham, who thinks he has everyone reckoned up and who therefore is reduced in the end to an old, self-pitying child in need of a single friend to whom he can complain.[38]

Says the Psalmist:

Make a joyful noise unto the LORD, all ye lands.
Serve the LORD with gladness: come before his presence with singing.
Know ye that the LORD he is God: it is he that hath made us, and not we ourselves.[39]

In that fine old Hebrew hymn, too, being and loving are at one. We are, and we burst into praise that we should be, for we did not make ourselves, nor have we made even the joy that sweeps us away. Berry understands. We do not judge a thing and then determine whether to love it. It is love that judges us:

We do not make it. If it did not happen to us, we could not imagine it. It includes the world and time as a pregnant woman includes her child whose wrongs she will suffer and forgive. It is in the world but is not altogether of it. It is of eternity. It takes us there when it most holds us here.[40]

Or it ravishes us when we freely give our freedom away. "It does not hold us," writes Berry, "except we keep returning / to its rich waters thirsty." Willing to give ourselves up to it, we enter "into the commonwealth of its joy."[41]

Berry does not care for precise Christological definitions—he is in that regard an old-fashioned Baptist. But even if he might be wobbly on the sovereign freedom and the omniscience of God, his sense that Love has come down from above and dwells among us would warm the heart of the great definer Athanasius. "Could I not see," says Jayber, "how even divine omnipotence might by the force of its own love be swayed down in to the world? Could I not see how it might, because it could know its creatures only by compassion, put on mortal flesh, become a man, and walk among us, assume our nature and our fate, suffer our faults and our death?"[42] Just as love sets our feet firmly on the little plot of earth to be loved, while ravishing our hearts into eternity, so Love, from eternity, has come down to us, as it is through Love that all things were made, and then "dwelt among us," that we might behold his glory.[43]

We see then that to love these things aright—these things that proclaim in gratitude, "It is he that hath made us, and not we ourselves"—we must ourselves be seized by that Being of love, who has loved them into existence. It is then true and not true that Port William leads Jayber Crow to the church, or that Mattie Chatham leads him to Christ. If what we mean by "lead" is that they serve as ladders, which when they are climbed may be dispensed with, we have mistaken Love entirely. They lead only because the One to whom they lead is already here. If we love them rightly, we love them for the sake of the Father, whose love sustains them in their very existence. We are in the position of Dante, who is transported from earth to Paradise by beholding the eyes of Beatrice, as she beholds the eternal beauties of Heaven:

Into the everlasting wheels of light
Beatrice gazed with silent constancy;
on her I gazed, far from that central sight.
Her countenance had the same effect in me
as did the plant that Glaucus tasted when
it made him share the godhood of the sea.
To signify man's soaring beyond man

words will not do: let my comparison
suffice for them to whom the grace of God
Reserves the experience.[44]

Mattie is the Beatrice for Jayber, in her being only and yet fully what
she is, an ordinary woman, with a profound capacity for love. She needs to
be no more than that, because that is itself a wonder, inexplicable in terms
of matter and place and time. It was after all a good thing, says Jayber,
that he never would be married to Mattie, since the normal life might have
obscured the wonder. "I saw," he says, "that Mattie was not merely desirable, but desirable beyond the power of time to show." That desirability,
Jayber observes, springs not from her amiability or her physical beauty, but
from her very being: "She was a living soul and could be loved forever." Her
being, so ordinary, among the ordinary flowers and shrubs and walkways
of time, yet spills over time. "That was why," says Jayber, "as she grew older,
I saw in her always the child she had been, and why, looking at her when
she was a child, I felt the influence of the woman she would be."[45]

For the child passes, and behold, she is still here, and the one we love
dies, and yet lives again. Dante will be granted a vision of the mystic rose,
all the blessed saints in Heaven. Jayber Crow sees something very like
that, transposed into the key of Kentucky. He wakes from a nap in the
church he tends, and suddenly in his twilight of half-sleep there appear
before him "all the people gathered there who had ever been there": his
Aunt Cordie and Uncle Othy, who had taken care of him as an orphan
child; the men, "quiet or reluctant or shy"; the sick and the lame; "the
young married couples full of visions; the old men with their dreams";
generations of people whose hearts themselves span the generations, men
creased with work; women cheerfully singing, and they say nothing to
him, because nothing needs to be said, beyond the inexpressible joy of
being. "I seemed to love them all," says Jayber, "with a love that was mine
merely because it included me."[46] Why should the saints in Heaven, Dante
the pilgrim asks, desire their bodies again in the resurrection, when they
are already perfectly blessed? Well, our souls are the sorts of creatures that
are meant to animate human bodies; that is the theological answer he
receives from Solomon. But the poet gives us a better and bolder answer
than does the theologian. For when Solomon ceases, the crowd of saints
about him cries out:

So prompt and ready was the loud "Amen!"
both choirs responded, it was clear to me
how much they yearned to see their flesh again,
Maybe less for themselves than for their mamas,
their fathers, and the others they held dear
before they had become eternal flames.[47]

In the love of God, says Edmund Spenser, "there is nothing lost, that may [not] be found, if sought."[48] He who loves Heaven, says C. S. Lewis in his introduction to *The Great Divorce*, will receive earth into the bargain. The resurrection of the body is for the communion of saints.

How wondrous and self-leaving a thing it is, finally, to praise. That bit of dust called man, says Saint Augustine, wishes to praise God: "You arouse him to take joy in praising you, for you have made us for yourself, and our heart is restless until it rests in you."[49] But what is praise, if it is alone? When Augustine learned to praise God aright, he learned also to love his friends and his saintly mother Monica aright, she who "took care as though she had been mother to us all,"[50] and who, standing beside her son in Ostia, shortly before she would be called from this world, was rapt with him into the "region of abundance that never fails," wherein God feeds "Israel forever upon the food of truth, and where life is that Wisdom by which these things are made, both which have been and which are to be."[51] And how should our bliss not be a love that embraces all things and all our brethren and all times? For God Himself, as Christians affirm, is a communion of love. "O Light that dwell within Thyself alone," cries Dante, beholding the Trinity in wonder, "who alone know Thyself, are known, and smile / with love upon the Knowing and the Known!"[52] It is love, not calculations of utility, but passionate love for Beatrice, that gives Dante the courage to pass through the wall of purgatorial fire. It is love that rouses in him the will to rise:

Will above will now surged in such delight
to climb the top, that with each step I took
I felt my feathers growing for the flight.[53]

"This is a book about Heaven," says Jayber,[54] and that is because it is a book about the love that made both heaven and earth and that can gather together even the broken hearts of men. To be gathered together in love, for love, by the Love that moves the sun and the other stars, is to be at last. So Berry suggests in a poem worthy of Dante's last vision. When we have been true to what we love here on earth, love in turn is true to us, and in death we rise:

> Past the strait of kept faith
> the flesh rises, is joined
> to light. Risen from distraction
> and weariness, we come
> into the turning and changing
> circle of all lovers. On this height
> our labor changes into flight.[55]

# 17

# Wendell Berry:
# A Latter-Day St. Benedict

*Rod Dreher*

Irecently read a passage from a Wendell Berry essay that struck me as an acutely perceptive diagnosis of the present political moment in America:

> It appears to me that the governing middle, or the government, which supposedly represents the middle, has allowed the extremes of left and right to force it into an extremism of its own. These three extremes of left, right, and middle, egged on by and helplessly subservient to each other's rhetoric, have now become so self-righteous and self-defensive as to have no social use. So large a ground of sanity and good sense and decency has been abandoned by these extremes that it becomes possible now to think of a New Middle made up of people conscious and knowledgeable enough to despise the blandishments and oversimplifications of the extremes—and roomy and diverse enough to permit a renewal of intelligent cultural dialogue. That is what I hope for: a chance to live and speak as a person, not as a function of some political bunch.[1]

Berry wrote that in 1970. Apparently, things haven't improved. Though I write as a conservative by conviction and a Republican by default, I too hope for a chance to live and speak as a person, not as a function of some political bunch. In fact, for the first time since my teen-age years, when the election of Ronald Reagan brought me to politically consciousness, I no longer feel that I am part of any political bunch.

My usual bunch, the Republicans, are a mess. They gave themselves over wholly to the support of a war that ought never to have been launched and to a stance toward the world that never seems to have met an occasion for foreign entanglement it didn't like. When given command of the nation's economic policy, they spent profligately, abandoning all pretense of prudence and treating their responsibility to regulate finance as if original sin ceased to exist for that industry's elites. They have shown themselves to be irresponsible on global warming and environmental stewardship, captives to an inflexible ideology of market individualism over the common good. On issues important to social conservatives, the Republicans talk a good game but rarely act with force and vigor. There is among Republicans little if any appreciation of how the party's enthusiasm for laissez-faire capitalism—and the idea that economic growth is the raison d'être of our common existence—undermines the communal and social bonds necessary to support the traditional family-centered morality Republicans claim to esteem.

One looks to the Democrats for relief and finds little or none. They have been ineffective in opposing the war in Iraq, and under the Obama administration developed a Strange New Respect for policies they (rightly) deplored under the Bush presidency. In some quarters, Democrats coast on a decades-old reputation as defenders of the common man's economic interests against Wall Street's predation, but even a cursory glance at the party's financial regulatory policies from Bill Clinton forward will find little daylight between the party of FDR and the GOP. They might conceivably be better on health care, the economy, and the environment, but for most disaffected social conservatives, the Democrats' hostility to traditional moral values obviates their appeal. It strains my conscience to imagine voting for a party that supports redefining marriage into a purely contractual phenomenon at a time when the traditional family is unraveling. Similarly, at a historical moment when genetic engineering and medical advances threaten to redefine what it means to be human, I cannot vote for a party for which the absolute right to abortion on demand is nonnegotiable and, in turn, whose worldview subordinates the sanctity of human life to an ethic of instrumentality.

As tempting as it is to blame the Republicans and the Democrats for being out of touch and unresponsive to the real concerns of the American people, the fact is they represent with a fair degree of accuracy the way Americans think philosophically. We are a people given over to autonomous individualism. Mainstream liberals are more sympathetic to sexual autonomy; mainstream conservatives to economic autonomy. The ferocious contempt partisans of both sides have for each other obscures their fundamental philosophical agreement. As the philosopher Alasdair MacIntyre has said, all modern political arguments come down to disputes "between conservative liberals, liberal liberals and radical liberals."[2] He meant that in our culture, nearly all political factions accept as given that the choosing individual is the base unit of our political order, and all claims must be made in terms of expanding freedom to choose.

And that, Wendell Berry knows, accounts for our common dilemma and the seemingly insurmountable difficulty of resolving it. "The conventional public opposition of 'liberal' and 'conservative' is . . . perfectly useless," Berry writes in one of his best diagnostic essays, "Sex, Economy, Freedom & Community." Conservatives, he writes, exalt the family as a sort of "public icon" but will not stand against economic practices that undermine the family's structure and purpose. Liberals exalt sexual emancipation and the abrogation of established traditions governing sexual relations but refuse to recognize how their libertine ethic undermines the community they claim to support.[3] Neither side can offer a credible solution to the current crisis because neither side has a credible answer to the question once posed by Berry: "What are people for?"

And if neither political party can answer that question credibly, neither can ordinary people answer it with much conviction, or at least persuasiveness. We have lost a common moral sense and with it the kind of moral vocabulary with which to articulate political principles. We are no longer citizens but consumers. A conservative policy analyst I ran into at a social event said she didn't understand why so many otherwise sensible people on the political right were against unlimited immigration. After all, she said, don't they know that this is why we have so much to choose from at such low prices? I thought she was putting me on, but she was dead serious. I realized, then, that this is what citizenship came down to for this bright and articulate young conservative. She thinks she lives in the United States of America, but deep down, she's taken her stand in what the bumper sticker advertises as Walmart Country.

In Walmart Country—in which, whether they know it or not, liberals live too—if you ask them what people are for, what do you think they would say? They would say that people are for the non-negotiable right to live as we like. As Alan Ehrenhalt said in his 1995 book, *The Lost City*, about the degradation of community in American life, most post-1960s Americans believe "in individual choice and [have] suspicion of any authority that might interfere with it."[4]

So while it is satisfying to bewail the failures of the Republicans and the Democrats, let's not deceive ourselves. Our problems come not so much because American political parties have lost their way but rather because we, the American people, have lost our way. There are no votes in telling people this, so politicians don't. Still, the wise among us will heed Wendell Berry's verdict: "Our country is not being destroyed by bad politics; it is being destroyed by a bad way of life."[5]

You can only judge a way of life "bad" if you have a standard for the good. Kimberly K. Smith identifies the essence of Berry's politics as working "to preserve the land and culture on which it depends."[6] Berry's politics are built on an ethic of stewardship and husbandry, for the sake of maintaining within the human community social bonds across the generations—including those yet to be born. Our way of life, and our way of practicing politics, guarantee fragmentation and disintegration—of nation, of community, of family, and ultimately of the self.

Indeed, the valorization of the autonomous self is precisely the problem. Edmund Burke counseled on the inescapability of our moral duties, in this passage from his "Appeal from the New to the Old Whigs":

> Dark and inscrutable are the ways by which we come into the world. The instincts which give rise to this mysterious process of nature are not of our making. But out of physical causes, unknown to us, perhaps unknowable, arise moral duties, which, as we are able perfectly to comprehend, we are bound indispensably to perform. Parents may not be consenting to their moral relation; but consenting or not, they are bound to a long train of burthensome duties towards those with whom they have never made a convention of any sort. Children are not consenting to their relation, but their relation, without their actual consent, binds them to its duties; or rather it implies their consent because the presumed

consent of every rational creature is in unison with the predisposed order of things. Men come in that manner into a community with the social state of their parents, endowed with all the benefits, loaded with all the duties of their situation. If the social ties and ligaments, spun out of those physical relations which are the elements of the commonwealth, in most cases begin, and always continue, independently of our will, so without any stipulation, on our part, are we bound by that relation called our country, which comprehends (as it has been well said) "all the charities of all." Nor are we left without powerful instincts to make this duty as dear and grateful to us, as it is awful and coercive.[7]

This principle—that our natural state imposes duties and limits upon us and our relations to others—is increasingly foreign to the American way of life, which rejects limits, natural or prescribed. As the military historian Andrew Bacevich has argued, with reference to Jimmy Carter's disastrous attempt to convince Americans to live within our means (the so-called malaise speech), we have become a people who will tolerate war in the Middle East as the price for maintaining the right to live without limits. It is, or has become, the American way.[8]

The crisis of indebtedness that threatens to sink our economy is, deep down, a moral crisis. We have, both individually and corporately, thrown aside the old habits of thrift and a sense of honor that comes with paying what one owes. A California homeowner told the *New York Times* that he felt bad that he had defaulted on his home mortgage—until he engaged the services of a company that helped him walk away from his debt. "They took the negativity out of my life," he chirruped.[9] But that man, as dishonorable as his ethic is, was formed by institutions—public and private—that encouraged such behavior. As a disgusted friend in the mortgage industry told me, plain old greed, aided and abetted by a sense that nobody was responsible for anything except his own personal profit, corrupted every level of his business—from Main Street to Wall Street.

An honest acceptance of duties and limits is at the heart of Wendell Berry's countercultural communitarianism. If his politics can be summed up in a word, it is "responsibility." Berry advocates the terribly unfashionable proposition that we should not live beyond our means. We should care both for the land we have been given and for its people. We should treat with pious respect the authoritative traditions we have been handed that make the cohesion and continuity of the community possible. Our liberty is only meaningful if it is ordered and disciplined. We should treat the world and the living things in it as mysteries to be loved, not as instruments to be manipulated, problems to be solved, or adversaries to be conquered, for we live "in a world rooted in mystery and in sanctity."[10] And finally: stay where you are and, to paraphrase Burke, learn to love the little platoon and the little place you have in society.

That last idea—that we should renounce our mobility—may be the most radical and antimodern of all Berry's principles. But it is also, I think, the key to his politics. He notes that "the history of our time has been to a considerable extent the movement of the center of consciousness away from home."[11] We are nomads, strangers to our land, our neighbors, our tradition, and, therefore, to ourselves.

In his 1988 essay "The Work of Local Culture," Berry explores the impoverishment of individual and communal life resulting from the command imposed by mass culture to leave home. It is literally a command to abandon the place where you were born and raised, a command that our economy makes hard to resist. But it goes deeper than that. Our literal and metaphorical homelessness, and all the wreckage our nomadism entails, comes out of a culture in which we know ourselves only by our lifestyle choices, the multiplicities of which are endless.

Moreover, technology has created a media culture that exacerbates this fragmentation and alienation. Sven Birkerts puts the problem in the form of a question:

> How do you believe yourself bound to a place and time when you live in the midst of a pure potentiality of space and time? How do you sustain a consistent presence, a clarity of thought and imagination, when you are bombarded at every instant by waves of distracting stimuli, with an endless menu of possible conceptual frameworks?[12]

What does any of this have to do with the politics of the present moment? This: we have to understand more clearly the nature of the illness before we can begin to think about a prescription for the cure.

Alasdair MacIntyre counseled rejecting both political parties in 2004 "not primarily because they give us the wrong answers, but because they answer the wrong questions."[13] Do you see either the Democrats or the Republicans asking the right questions? I don't. Still, the political failure of the GOP does not mean vindication for the Democrats' political vision, inasmuch as they don't have much of one. The next few election cycles will likely be a time of philosophical murkiness, as we await the emergence of the Next Big Idea, which will transform American politics as much as Reaganism did, and the New Deal before it.

Where does that leave us? Are we prepared to be satisfied with exquisite lamentation, or are there practical things we can do to redeem the time? I believe in angels but not in angelism, which is why I try to resist the temptation to turn my back entirely on party politics, especially at the local level. But I am convinced that conservatives have placed far too much stock in political action and far too little in the work of culture. "Society's long-term direction is not set mainly by politicians," the political theorist Claes Ryn recently wrote. "It is set by those who capture a people's mind and imagination."[14]

Conservatives who can read the signs of the times would do well to busy themselves with building the institutions, communities, and networks that can sustain and transmit the ideas, virtues, and traditions that make human flourishing possible, especially under adverse conditions of the sort that the end of cheap oil will likely bring upon America in the years and decades to come.

Let me sketch out briefly why I believe pursuing conventional politics is a weak bet for the kind of cultural reformation adequate to the crisis. I return to MacIntyre. In his 1998 essay titled "Politics, Philosophy and the Common Good," he praises farming as historically sustaining "virtues that are central to all human life."[15] He praises Wendell Berry for understanding this and asks why the prophetic antimodern writings of Berry and others have had so little impact on the national debate.

In reply, MacIntyre argues that these fundamental questions have simply been excluded from discussion. I can testify from my own experience discussing the neotraditionalist themes in my book *Crunchy Cons* that in the media, which set the terms of public debate, asking these basic questions about first principles either is actively and irrationally resented—Jonah Goldberg sets the gold standard here—or, as is more common, viewed as eccentric and irrelevant.

MacIntyre goes on to say—in an echo of the central thrust of his masterwork *After Virtue*—that we have lost the ability to think and deliberate in terms of the common good. We have lost a shared standard for evaluating the common good because we can't agree on what constitutes virtue. Absent a considerable degree of shared culture, and acceptance of custom and tradition, it will be difficult to reach a politically meaningful definition of the common good. We find it hard to deliberate together on how best to achieve the good society because we have such radically different ideas of what constitutes the good society. We settle on a definition that is individualist and minimalist—the good society as a rough conglomeration of private goods—but one that ends up creating a political society to whose survival a diminishing number of people feel loyalty.

For MacIntyre, the kind of polity worthy of free and rational men and women is one in which its citizens recognize their responsibility to live within the laws of nature and to balance their individual good with the common good. It has to be a place where citizens grasp the deeper meaning of following the law. It's not just about yielding to rules but also about creating a social environment in which people may best become what they were made to be. "Such societies," writes MacIntyre, "must be small scale and, so far as possible, as self-sufficient as they need to be to protect themselves from the destructive incursions of the state and the wider market economy."[16] And they need to be small-scale for the sake of mutual accountability. The ideal polity will favor small-scale economics—small farmers, small manufacturers, small merchants—because that is the kind of society in which people are most likely to develop in wisdom, virtue, and happiness.

MacIntyre acknowledges that such a society would not make the kind of material progress that our society has. But then again, to believe that wealth is the only significant measure of the worth of an individual, a family, or a community is to reject the teaching of nearly every religion and wisdom tradition that ever was.

It will be perfectly obvious to Wendell Berry's readers that the political ideal MacIntyre teaches is wholly consonant with the ideals Berry has been living out and advocating all his life. Both MacIntyre and Berry stand for a humane alternative to the dominant liberal tradition, one that conceives of liberty in terms of natural law, virtue, and commonality.[17] Given that this tradition has never been central to American life and shows no sign of mounting a threatening challenge to the liberalism inherent in both parties, where does that leave disconsolate traditionalists?

For one thing, it leaves us with what I call the Benedict Option. The phrase comes from the famous final paragraph of *After Virtue*:

> A crucial turning point in that earlier history occurred when men and women of good will turned aside from the task of shoring up the Roman imperium and ceased to identify the continutation of civility and moral community with the maintenance of that imperium. What they set themselves to achieve instead . . . was the construction of new forms of community within which the moral life could be sustained so that both morality and civility might survive the coming ages of barbarism and darkness. If my account of our moral condition is correct, we ought also to conclude that for some time now we too have reached that turning point. What matters at this stage is the construction of local forms of community within which civility and the intellectual and moral life can be sustained through the new dark ages which are already upon us. And if the tradition of the virtues was able to survive the horrors of the last dark ages, we are not entirely without grounds for hope. This time however the barbarians are not waiting beyond the frontiers; they have already been governing us for quite some time. . . . And it is our lack of consciousness of this that constitutes part of our predicament. We are waiting not for a Godot, but for another—doubtless quite different—St. Benedict.[18]

Well. Should we all head for the monasteries, then? Not necessarily, though I note with delight that some latter-day traditionalist Benedictines are now raising a monastery in rural eastern Oklahoma and that scores of Catholic families have purchased land near this monastery, with the intention of living a more Benedictine life. The monks are already engaged in organic farming and learning how to raise livestock and crops without machines or chemicals. One imagines that the community of laypeople forming around them will learn the same techniques, as well as participate in the ancient liturgical traditions of the Church.

Should we emulate them, lighting out for the countryside or for small towns? Perhaps. I occasionally encounter fellow urbanites who fantasize about escaping to a small town, where they imagine old-fashioned communal virtues still obtain. As someone born and raised in a small town, I have to warn them that television and popular culture are as effective in setting moral standards there as anywhere else, and the residual conformity present in small towns can make it harder for those who wish to raise their kids by traditional moral values to do so.

In any case, and contrary to some of his critics, Berry does not demand that we empty out the cities and send everyone to the countryside. As he has written,

> any thinkable human economy would have to grant to manufacturing an appropriate and honorable place. Agrarians would insist only that any manufacturing enterprise be formed and scaled to fit the local landscape, the local ecosystem, and the local community, and that it should be locally owned and employ local people. They would insist, in other words, that the shop or factory owner should not be an outsider, but rather a sharer in the fate of the place and its community.[19]

Keeping in mind Berry's critical insight that we have disordered politics because we have disordered souls—we should strive within the limits of our own particular situations to construct new forms of community to repair and redeem the moral imagination distorted by modern life. We should begin to think of our homes as domestic monasteries and to cultivate thoughtfulness and purposefulness in the way we go about our daily lives. Withdrawing consciously from practices that cloud our minds and alienate us from essential wisdom is the first step toward healing. In this sense, turning off the television is a giant step toward healthy political reform. Many families are turning to homeschooling to reclaim their children for the family from the state schools and the increasingly barbaric culture ruling their hallways. Farmer's markets are booming around the country, as urbanites and suburbanites support the work of local family farmers, thus building up local agriculture while learning to think more deeply about where food comes from. A new appreciation for craftsmanship is causing small producers of beer, wine, and cheese to arise. Evangelical Christians, the most dynamic religious community in America, are discovering a new sense of stewardship for the natural world. And however slowly, more and more people are coming to realize that our environmental policies are unsustainable and are working at the local level to make change happen.

And in some places around the country, traditionalists are already living in physical community, realizing that it really does take a village to raise a child and to form an authentically human soul. In Eagle River, Alaska, a small community of Orthodox Christians that formed around St. John's Cathedral have built a small school and live out their lives literally on the same streets surrounding their church. They are not cloistered and remain open to the world. They are already into the second generation in that community. In Augusta, Georgia, some like-minded Catholic laypeople pooled their money in the 1970s, bought houses together in a run-down part of town, and renovated them so their families could live in community. In my book, I recount the story of Rachel and Paul Balducci, who grew up in that community as children, returned to raise their own children there—even though Paul's salary as a lawyer could have bought them a McMansion in a gated development. Rachel told me that the chance to raise her kids in a neighborhood where people share the same moral vision is priceless.[20]

The point is, despite our generally woebegone situation, there are undeniable signs of a new springtime. More and more people are coming to understand that the model America has been following is destined to fail because it hides or denies the true cost of things. Though the seeds of renaissance are still at the margins of American life—and have shown few if any signs of politically meaningful organization—it is much closer to the mainstream than when Wendell Berry first began his prophetic writing. I am encouraged by Pope Benedict's idea of the role of "creative minorities" in the restoration of a healthy culture. He takes the term from the British historian Arnold Toynbee, who held that every culture depends on its creative minorities to keep it spiritually alive. In his recent book *Without Roots*, Benedict foresaw a rump of Catholic true believers, and fellow travelers, holding tightly but joyfully to the faith and being a light to the world. The pope writes:

> The [early] Christians were able to demonstrate persuasively how empty and base were the entertainments of paganism, and how sublime the gift of faith in the God who suffers with us and leads

us to the road of true greatness. Today it is a matter of the great-est urgency to show a Christian model of life that offers a livable alternative to the increasingly vacuous entertainments of leisure-time society, a society forced to make increasing recourse to drugs because it is sated by the usual shabby pleasures. Living on the great values of the Christian tradition is naturally much harder than a life rendered dull by the increasingly costly habits of our time. The Christian model of life must be manifested as a life in all its fullness and freedom, a life that does not experience the bonds of love as dependence and limitation but rather as an open-ing to the greatness of life. Here, too, I refer to the idea of the creative minorities that enrich this model of life, present it in a convincing way, and can thus instill the courage needed to live it.[21]

Thus, the Benedict Option—which, minus the overt sectarian appeal, could have been written by Wendell Berry. Christian or not, traditional-ists can best change the culture, and thus, over time, change our politics, through the Benedict Option. This means finding each other and work-ing together to build communities and institutions united by the kind of moral vision that has shown Wendell Berry the way through the present dark age. And because our work must be local, we have to work to accept the Benedictine proposition that runs most counter to the spirit of the age: the vow of stability.

The Benedictine order more or less saved European civilization in the Dark Ages, and the most important thing the Benedictine monks did to that end was live out their vow of stability. That meant that when a Bene-dictine monk took his vows, he promised to live in that same monastery until the end of his days. Peasants knew that the monks were not going to abandon their posts, or them, come what may. So they settled near the monasteries and learned from the monks. Over many generations, those settlements became towns and great cities. The point is, the monks stayed put and bore witness. In so doing, they showed a lost and scattered people how to be more fully human. In a time of great chaos, their decision to remain fixed points converted and saved an entire culture. Such is the power of a creative minority.

In a more secular spirit, if we live by the humane vision and resolute spirit of Wendell Berry, who can say what and who we might save in the end simply by doing the right thing? What I propose is that we not wait for politicians to save us but rather that we get busy now forming intentional communities and supporting localism, communal self-reliance, the common good, and a small-is-beautiful ethic. Let's not be daunted by the plain fact that ours is a minority pursuit at the present time. As Berry has written, "Thoreau gave the definitive reply to the folly of 'significant numbers' a long time ago: Why should anybody wait to do what is right until everybody does it? It is not 'significant' to love your own children or eat your own dinner, either. But normal humans will not wait to love or eat until it is mandated by an act of Congress."[22]

We do await a new, and doubtless very different, St. Benedict, to show us how to build a humane community in the evening shadows of the American empire. It is my conviction that his prophetic forerunner is among us now: our old, and unquestionably very different, Wendell Berry.

# Acknowledgments

One benefit that comes from reading the works of Wendell Berry is an enhanced sense of gratitude. Although we cannot acknowledge here the many gratuitous acts, both large and small, that made this book possible, a few should not be overlooked. First, to the sponsors of ISI's Lehrman Summer Institute in 2005: ISI, Lewis, Lehrman and Robert P. George. It was here that our idea for this book was born. Also to Jeremy Beer, who midwifed this project through its early stages with enthusiasm, encouragement and advice. Next to ISI, the Philadelphia Society, and Gary Gregg at the McConnell Center for sponsoring a conference in 2007 on "The Humane Vision of Wendell Berry," from which many of the chapters for this book were taken. To Jed Donahue and Christian Tappe at ISI Books for helping hone this book into its final form. To Joby Mitchell and Elizabeth Schlueter, and to our children, for helping us to bring the meaning of this book out of our heads and into our daily lives. Above all, we thank Wendell Berry for the gift of his life and his art. Throughout this process he has been sometimes curious, often humorous, and always gracious.

# Notes

Introduction

1. Anne Husted Burleigh, "Wendell Berry's Community," in *Conversations with Wendell Berry*, ed. Morris Allen Grubbs (Jackson, MS: University Press of Mississippi, 2007), 135.
2. Wendell Berry, "The Agrarian Standard," in *Citizenship Papers: Essays* (Washington, DC: Shoemaker & Hoard, 2003), 149.
3. Thomas Jefferson, "To James Madison," October 28, 1785, in *The Portable Thomas Jefferson*, ed. Merrill D. Peterson (New York: Penguin Books, 1977), 397. Quoted in Berry, "The Agrarian Standard," *Citizenship Papers*, 149.
4. Berry, "The Agrarian Standard," in *Citizenship Papers*, 144.
5. Wendell Berry, "Health Is Membership," in *Another Turn of the Crank* (New York: Counterpoint, 1995), 89.
6. Ibid., 153.
7. This is the title of a collection of essays by Berry, as well as one of the essays in that collection. See Wendell Berry, *The Way of Ignorance: And Other Essays* (Berkeley, CA: Shoemaker & Hoard, 2005). The phrase is from T. S. Eliot, "East Coker" in *Four Quartets*.

Chapter 2: Marriage in the Membership
Anne Husted Burleigh

1. Wendell Berry, "Pray Without Ceasing," in *Fidelity: Five Stories* (New York and San Francisco: Pantheon Books, 1992), 4.
2. Anne Husted Burleigh, "Wendell Berry's Community," *Crisis* 18:1 (January 2000): 28–33, reprinted in *Conversations with Wendell Berry*, ed. Morris Allen Grubbs (Jackson, MS: University Press of Mississippi, 2007), 138.

3. Wendell Berry, "Sabbaths 1998, I," in *Given: New Poems* (Washington, DC: Shoemaker & Hoard, 2005), 55.

4. Wendell Berry, *Jayber Crow: The Life Story of Jayber Crow, Barber, of the Port William Membership, as Written by Himself* (Washington, DC: Counterpoint, 2000), 254.

5. Burleigh, "Wendell Berry's Community," in *Conversations with Wendell Berry*, 145.

6. Wendell Berry, "Sex, Economy, Freedom, and Community," in *Sex, Economy, Freedom, and Community: Eight Essays* (New York: Pantheon Books, 1992), 161.

7. Berry, *Jayber Crow*, 248.

8. Ibid., 248.

9. Wendell Berry, *Hannah Coulter: A Novel* (Washington, DC: Shoemaker & Hoard, 2004), 140.

10. Ibid., 141.

11. Wendell Berry, "Standing by Words," in *Standing by Words: Essays* (San Francisco: North Point Press, 1983), 30.

12. Wendell Berry, "Sabbaths 1999, IX," in *Given*, 78.

13. Berry, "Sex, Economy, Freedom, and Community," in *Sex, Economy, Freedom, and Community*, 138.

14. Ibid., 139.

15. Wendell Berry, "How to Be a Poet (to Remind Myself)," in *Given*, 18.

16. Berry, *Hannah Coulter*, 57.

17. Wendell Berry, *Remembering: A Novel* (San Francisco: North Point Press, 1988), 95–96.

18. Wendell Berry, "It Wasn't Me," in *The Wild Birds: Six Stories of the Port William Membership* (San Francisco: North Point Press, 1986), 68.

19. Ibid., 67.

20. Berry, *Remembering*, 51–52.

21. Ibid., 62–63.

22. Ibid., 63.

23. Wendell Berry, "The Boundary," in *The Wild Birds*, 96.

Chapter 3: Not Safe, nor Private, nor Free: Wendell Berry on
Sexual Love and Procreation
Allan Carlson

1. Angus Fenwick, "Improve Your Sex Life Tonight—The Amish Way," *Weekly World News* (March 10, 2003): 1–2.

2. Wendell Berry, "Rugged Individualism," in *The Way of Ignorance: And Other Essays* (Berkeley, CA: Shoemaker & Hoard, 2005), 9–11.

3. Wendell Berry, "Letter to Daniel Kemmis," in *The Way of Ignorance*, 141–44.

4. Wendell Berry, "Sex, Economy, Freedom, and Community," in *Sex, Economy, Freedom, and Community: Eight Essays* (New York: Pantheon Books, 1992), 142.

5. Ibid., 120–21.

6. Wendell Berry, *The Unsettling of America: Culture and Agriculture* (San Francisco: Sierra Club Books, 1977), 117, 131.

7. Berry, "Sex, Economy, Freedom, and Community," in *Sex, Economy, Freedom, and Community*, 142.

8. Berry, *The Unsettling of America*, 133–34.

9. Wendell Berry, "The Conservation of Nature and the Preservation of Humanity," in *Another Turn of the Crank: Essays* (New York: Counterpoint, 1995), 82.

10. Berry, "Sex, Economy, Freedom, and Community," in *Sex, Economy, Freedom, and Community*, 138, 143.

11. Berry, "The Conservation of Nature and the Preservation of Humanity," in *Another Turn of the Crank*, 79. Emphasis added.

12. Ibid., 78–79.

13. Ibid., 80–81.

14. Ibid., 82.

15. Berry, "Sex, Economy, Freedom, and Community," in *Sex, Economy, Freedom, and Community*, 142.

16. Berry, *The Unsettling of America*, 117.

17. Wendell Berry, "The Whole Horse," in *The New Agrarianism: Land, Culture, and the Community of Life*, ed. Eric T. Freyfogle (Washington, DC: Island Press–Shearwater Books, 2001), 64.

18. Berry, *The Unsettling of America*, 132, 135.

19. Wendell Berry, "The Broken Ground," in *Collected Poems, 1957–1982* (San Francisco: North Point Press, 1987), 25.

20. Berry, *The Unsettling of America*, 117, 130, 132.

21. Ibid., 117, 130; Berry, "The Conservation of Nature and the Preservation of Humanity," in *Another Turn of the Crank*, 81–82.

22. Berry, *The Unsettling of America*, 115, 132–35.

23. Wendell Berry, "Preserving Wildness," in *Home Economics: Fourteen Essays* (San Francisco: North Point Press, 1987), 149–50.

24. Wendell Berry, "Renewing Husbandry," in *The Way of Ignorance*, 96–100.

25. Wendell Berry, *Hannah Coulter: A Novel* (Washington, DC: Shoemaker & Hoard, 2004), 67–68.

26. Wendell Berry, *The Memory of Old Jack* (Washington, DC: Counterpoint, 1999), 103.

27. Wendell Berry, *A World Lost: A Novel* (Berkeley, CA: Counterpoint, 2008), 55.

28. Wendell Berry, "A Jonquil for Mary Penn," in *Fidelity: Five Stories* (New York: Pantheon Books, 1992), 79.

29. Fenwick, "Improve Your Sex Life Tonight—The Amish Way," 1. In this article, the last two words of the sentence are "Amish style."

Chapter 4: An Education for Membership:
Wendell Berry on Schools and Communities
Richard Gamble

1. Wendell Berry, *Remembering: A Novel* (Berkeley, CA: Counterpoint, 2008), 36.

2. Ibid., 54.

3. Ibid., 55.

4. Ibid., 53.

5. Ibid., 57.

6. Ibid., 70.

7. Ibid., 59.

8. Wendell Berry, *Jayber Crow: The Life Story of Jayber Crow, Barber, of the Port William Membership, as Written by Himself* (Washington, DC: Counterpoint, 2000), 82.

9. Wendell Berry, *Hannah Coulter: A Novel* (Washington, DC: Shoemaker & Hoard, 2004), 67.

10. Ibid., 112.

11. Wendell Berry, "The Work of Local Culture," in *What Are People For?: Essays* (San Francisco: North Point Press, 1990), 160–61.

12. Ibid., 161–62.

13. Wendell Berry, *Life Is a Miracle: An Essay Against Modern Superstition* (Berkeley, CA: Counterpoint, 2001), 56–57.

14. Berry, "The Work of Local Culture," in *What Are People For?*, 162.

15. Wendell Berry, Commencement Address at Bellarmine University, May 2007, available at http://www.bellarmine.edu/studentaffairs/Graducation/berry_address. asp, accessed June 13, 2011.

16. Berry, "The Work of Local Culture," in *What Are People For?*, 163.

17. Berry, *Jayber Crow*, 8.

18. Ibid., 279.

19. Wendell Berry, *The Hidden Wound* (San Francisco: North Point Press, 1989), 134.

20. Berry, *Jayber Crow*, 70–71.

21. Ibid., 160.

22. Berry, *Life Is a Miracle*, 35.

23. Berry, *The Hidden Wound*, 72. Berry wrote this section in 1968–69.

24. Ibid., 112.

25. Ibid., 113.

26. Ibid., 184.

27. Wes Jackson, *Becoming Native to This Place* (Lexington, KY: The University Press of Kentucky, 1994), 3.

28. Berry, *Life Is a Miracle*, 136.

29. Ibid., 116.

30. Berry, *Remembering*, 65.

31. See the conversation between Jayber and his teacher Dr. Ardmire in *Jayber Crow*, 53–54.

32. Berry, "The Work of Local Culture," in *What Are People For?*, 169.

33. These words come from Berry's own writing teacher, Wallace Stegner, in the introduction to *Where the Bluebird Sings to the Lemonade Springs: Living and Writing in the West* (New York: Random House, 1992), xxii. "Boomers" are "those who pillage and run." "Stickers" are "those who settle, and love the life they have made and the place they have made it in."

Chapter 5: And for This Food, We Give Thanks
Matt Bonzo

1. Wendell Berry, "The Gift of Good Land," in *The Gift of Good Land: Further Essays Cultural and Agricultural* (New York: North Point Press, 1982), 270.

2. See our discussion of the idea of gift/call in the work of Wendell Berry in J. Mat-

thew Bonzo and Michael R. Stevens, *Wendell Berry and the Cultivation of Life: A Reader's Guide* (Grand Rapids, MI: Brazos Press, 2008), 74ff.

3. Berry, "The Gift of Good Land," in *The Gift of Good Land*, 270.

4. I am appealing to Berry's understanding of the sympathetic mind in Wendell Berry, "Two Minds," in *Citizenship Papers: Essays* (Washington, DC: Shoemaker & Hoard, 2003).

5. Wendell Berry, "The Whole Horse," in *Citizenship Papers*, 116–17.

6. See Wendell Berry, "Let the Farm Judge," in *Citizenship Papers*.

7. Wendell Berry, "The Satisfactions of the Mad Farmer," in *Farming: A Hand Book* (New York: Harcourt Brace, 1970), 60.

8. Wendell Berry, "Two Economies," in *Home Economics: Fourteen Essays* (New York: North Point Press, 1987), 54.

9. It is fascinating to note the number of times in the Bible there is an identification between God and food. To mention just a couple of obvious examples, Jesus' ministry is described as the bread of life, water, and wine.

10. Wendell Berry, "The Pleasures of Eating," in *What Are People For?* (New York: North Point Press, 1990), 145.

11. Berry, "Two Economies," in *Home Economics*, 61.

12. Ibid., 61.

13. Wendell Berry, *The Unsettling of America: Culture and Agriculture* (San Francisco: Sierra Club Books, 1997), 9–10.

14. Jared Diamond, *Guns, Germs, and Steel: The Fates of Human Societies* (New York: W. W. Norton and Co., 1999).

15. As the Israelites left Egypt and headed towards the Promise Land, they were fed with manna they were not allowed to store. This could be understood as God reminding them that he was their resource even in battle.

16. Berry, *The Unsettling of America*, 9.

17. The recent food crisis in Zimbabwe is an excellent example. Once the breadbasket of the region, Zimbabwe saw most of its farms devastated as the result of political interference. The result was an inability to provide food even for itself.

18. Berry, *The Unsettling of America*, 9.

19. Ibid., 9.

20. Ibid., 10.

21. Ibid., 10.

22. Wendell Berry, "The Purpose of a Coherent Community," in *The Way of Ignorance: And Other Essays* (Berkeley, CA: Shoemaker & Hoard, 2005), 79. Berry concludes the essay with "that is why a house for sale is not a home." See also Martin Heidegger, "Building Dwelling Thinking," in *Poetry, Language, Thought*, trans. Albert Hofstadter (New York: Colophon Books, 1971).

23. See Steven Bouma-Prediger and Brian J. Walsh, *Beyond Homelessness: Christian Faith in a Culture of Displacement* (Grand Rapids, MI: Eerdmans, 2008), for an excellent overview and analysis of contemporary North American society using a broad understanding of homelessness.

24. Wendell Berry, "The Agrarian Standard," in *Citizenship Papers*, 152.

25. Berry, "Two Minds," in *Citizenship Papers*, 88.

26. Wendell Berry, "Agriculture from the Roots Up," in *The Way of Ignorance*, 109.

27. Wendell Berry, "The Way of Ignorance," in *The Way of Ignorance*, 63.

28. Berry, "The Agrarian Standard," in *Citizenship Papers*, 146.

29. Ibid., 147.

30. Wendell Berry, "Prayer after Eating," in *The Selected Poems of Wendell Berry* (Washington, DC: Counterpoint, 1998), 83.

Chapter 6: The Third Landscape: Wendell Berry and
American Conservation
Jason Peters

1. Wendell Berry, *The Unsettling of America: Culture and Agriculture* (San Francisco: Sierra Club Books, 1977), 27.

2. Wendell Berry, "Word and Flesh," in *What Are People For?: Essays* (San Francisco: North Point Press, 1990), 197.

3. Wendell Berry, "In Distrust of Movements," in *Citizenship Papers: Essays* (Washington, DC: Shoemaker & Hoard, 2003), 44–45.

4. Wendell Berry, "Why I Am Not Going to Buy a Computer," in *What Are People For?*, 177.

5. "In saying this," he added, "I do not mean to belittle the importance of protest, litigation, lobbying, legislation, large-scale organization—all of which I believe in and support. I am saying simply that we must do more. We must confront, on the ground, and each of us at home, the economic assumptions in which the problems of conservation originate." See Wendell Berry, "The Whole Horse," in *Citizenship Papers*, 123. Elsewhere Berry has insisted on the "impossibility of separating economic significance from ecological significance" and enjoined biologists to teach their discipline in such a way as to "foster the hope that economic responsibility and ecological responsibility might become a single practice." See his foreword to *Kentucky's Natural Heritage: An Illustrated Guide to Biodiversity*, ed. Greg Abernathy, Deborah White, Ellis L. Laudermilk, and Marc Evans (Lexington, KY: The University Press of Kentucky, 2010), xvi and xiii.

6. Wendell Berry, "Conservationist and Agrarian," in *Citizenship Papers*, 166.

7. Ibid., 166.

8. Wendell Berry, "Below," in *Collected Poems, 1957–1982* (San Francisco: North Point Press, 1987), 207.

9. Wendell Berry, "Conservation Is Good Work," in *Sex, Economy, Freedom, and Community: Eight Essays* (New York: Pantheon Books, 1992). The first kind of conservation preserves grand scenery, the second hopes to conserve "natural resources," and the third "is what you might call industrial troubleshooting" (27). All are "urgently necessary and all of them [are] failing" (31).

10. For example, John Wesley Powell, George Perkins Marsh, Gifford Pinchot, Rachel Carson, Stewart Udall, and Roderick Nash.

11. But also such terms and phrases as "the American progressivist doctrine" and the hypermobility expressed as "deracination," among others. See Twelve Southerners, *I'll Take My Stand: The South and the Agrarian Tradition*, ed. Louis D. Rubin Jr. (Baton Rouge, LA: Louisiana State University, 1977), xxxvii–xlviii. Berry discusses his indebtedness to this book in "Still Standing," "The Whole Horse," and "The Agrarian Standard" in *Citizenship Papers* (Berkeley, CA: Counterpoint, 2010).

12. Wendell Berry, "The Whole Horse," in *Citizenship Papers*, 117–18.

13. So neither the Hobbesian nor Darwinian notions of man, for example, impress him. It is our privilege and responsibility to live not by desire or instinct or competition but instead by justice, mercy, and restraint—to live not merely as creatures in an ecosystem but also as men and women in neighborhoods and communities. The Great Chain of Being, on Berry's account, at least had the benefit of assigning to us a place in the world. See also Berry's "Faustian Economics" in *What Matters? Economics for a Renewed Commonwealth* (Berkeley, CA: Counterpoint, 2010): "Our cultural tradition is in large part the record of our continuing effort to understand ourselves as beings specifically human: to say that, as humans, we must do certain things and we must not do certain things" (47). And again: "To deal with the problems, which after all are inescapable, of living with limited intelligence in a limited world, I suggest that we may have to remove some of the emphasis we have lately placed on science and technology and have a new look at the arts. For an art does not propose to enlarge itself by limitless extension but rather to enrich itself within bounds that are accepted prior to the work" (51).

14. I should also say that I acknowledge but must leave aside such distinctions as exist, or are imagined to exist, among, say, "conservationists," "preservationists," and "environmentalists." The history of conservation broadly conceived is a somewhat thorny terrain I do not intend to enter here. I will use "conservationist," "preservationist," "environmentalist," as well as variations on them, and mean something like "people who are concerned about the natural world, or who wish to conserve it, or who want certain tracts of land left untouched." That is not "robust," as the definers like to say, but it isn't for that reason inaccurate or uncharitable either. For the present purpose, I will speak in general rather than specific terms about "American conservation." I assume that the words *conserve* and *preserve* are not difficult to understand, notwithstanding the abuses they and *environment* sometimes suffer.

15. Interview with Vince Pennington, *The Kentucky Review* 13:1–2 (Spring 1996), 57–70. Reprinted in *Conversations with Wendell Berry*, ed. Morris Allen Grubbs (Jackson: University Press of Mississippi, 2007), 41; see also "Conservation Is Good Work," in *Sex, Economy, Freedom, and Community*, 34–35.

16. Wendell Berry, "The Conservation of Nature and the Preservation of Humanity," in *Another Turn of the Crank: Essays* (Washington, DC: Counterpoint, 1995), 73.

17. Ibid., 74.

18. Much misdirected blame descends from Lynn White, Jr's., famous and somewhat confused essay "The Historical Roots of Our Ecological Crisis" in *Science* 155, no. 3767 (March 10, 1967): 1203–7.

19. Berry, "The Conservation of Nature and the Preservation of Humanity," in *Another Turn of the Crank*, 75.

20. Ibid., 74.

21. Interview with Carol Polsgrove and Scott Russell Sanders, *The Progressive* 54:5 (May 1990), 34–37; reprinted in Morris Allen Grubbs, ed., *Conversations With Wendell Berry*, 27.

22. Berry, "Word and Flesh," in *What Are People For?*, 201; "The Conservation of Nature and the Preservation of Humanity," in *Another Turn of the Crank*, 71.

23. cf. Berry, "Conservation Is Good Work," in *Sex, Economy, Freedom, and Community*: "Solving these problems is not work merely for so-called environmental organi-

zations and agencies but also for individuals, families, and local communities" (33). And also: "There is now no end to the meetings and publications in which the horrifying statistics are recited, usually with the conclusion that pressure should be put on the government to do something. Often this pressure has been applied, and the government has done something. But the government has not done enough and may never do enough. It is likely that the government *cannot* do enough" (38; emphasis Berry's).

24. Berry, "Word and Flesh," in *What Are People For?*, 200–201. The quotation from Orwell can be found in George Orwell, *A Collection of Essays* (1946; New York: Harcourt Brace Jovanovich, 1953), 120.

25. Berry, "Word and Flesh," in *What Are People For?*, 201.

26. Berry, "The Conservation of Nature and the Preservation of Humanity," in *Another Turn of the Crank*, 71. Aaron Sachs has said well that "[b]y celebrating only faraway 'wilderness' areas allegedly full of biodiversity, we tacitly endorse the industrial system that has fractured our society and devastated the environments where the majority of Americans live. We seem to have forgotten that all places are connected and, ultimately, equally valuable, that life depends on all the mutually dependent features of the cosmos." See Aaron Sachs, *The Humboldt Current: Nineteenth-Century Exploration and the Roots of American Environmentalism* (New York: Viking, 2006), 342–43.

27. Berry, "The Conservation of Nature and the Preservation of Humanity," in *Another Turn of the Crank*, 71.

28. Ibid., 71–2. On the "rules of land-use" see Wendell Berry, "Conservation and Local Economy," *Sex, Economy, Freedom, and Community*, 3–4; see also 11, 16.

29. This paradox is important and bears illustrating: "Perhaps our most serious cultural loss in recent centuries is the knowledge that some things, though limited, are inexhaustible. For example, an ecosystem, even that of a working forest or farm, so long as it remains ecologically intact, is inexhaustible. A small place, as I know from my own experience, can provide opportunities of work and learning, and a fund of beauty, solace, and pleasure—in addition to its difficulties—that cannot be exhausted in a lifetime or in generations" (Berry, "Faustian Economics" in *What Matters?*, 50).

30. "Solar energy—if you know how to capture and use it: in grass, say, and the bodies of animals—is cheaper than petroleum" (Berry, "Conservationist and Agrarian," in *Citizenship Papers*, 172).

31. The true costs of industrial farming are conveniently kept off the books. In "Still Standing," for example, Berry says that the "World Resources Institute estimates that the net operating income of a Pennsylvania corn and soybean farmer would be reduced by 55% if soil depreciation were to be considered a cost of production" (Wendell Berry, "Still Standing," in *Citizenship Papers*, 159). This leaves aside the costs in aquifer depletion, groundwater contamination, loss of farms, farming communities, farmers, and edible food.

32. Berry, "Conservationist and Agrarian," in *Citizenship Papers*, 165.

33. Ibid., 166.

34. Berry, "In Distrust of Movements," in *Citizenship Papers*, 48.

35. Cf. Berry, "The Conservation of Nature and the Preservation of Humanity," in *Another Turn of the Crank*, 71.

36. Wendell Berry, "Preserving Wildness," in *Home Economics: Fourteen Essays* (San Francisco: North Point, 1987), 146.

37. Berry, "Why I Am Not Going to Buy a Computer," in *What Are People For?*, 174

38. Wendell Berry, "Think Little," in *A Continuous Harmony: Essays Cultural and Agricultural* (1970; rpt. Washington, DC: Shoemaker & Hoard, 2004), 78.

39. Edward Abbey, *Desert Solitaire: A Season in the Wilderness* (New York: Simon and Schuster, 1968), 39.

40. Berry, "Conservationist and Agrarian," *Citizenship Papers*, 167.

41. Food production is but one instance of economic abstraction. It is one example of our massive withdrawal from economic responsibility. On its exemplary status, however, see, e.g., Berry, "Conservation Is Good Work," in *Sex, Economy, Freedom, and Community*: "The economic system that most affects the health of the world and that may be most subject to consumer influence is that of food" (41).

42. Berry, *The Unsettling of America*, 138.

43. Berry, "Think Little," in *A Continuous Harmony*, 79.

44. Ibid., 78–79.

45. Berry, *The Unsettling of America*, 138.

46. See, e.g., Berry, "In Distrust of Movements," in *Citizenship Papers*: "I am not suggesting, of course, that everybody ought to be a farmer or a forester. Heaven forbid! I *am* suggesting that most people now are living on the far side of a broken connection, and that this is potentially catastrophic. Most people are now fed, clothed, and sheltered from sources, in nature and in the work of other people, toward which they feel no gratitude and exercise no responsibility" (48)

47. Berry, "Conservationist and Agrarian," in *Citizenship Papers*, 167.

48. Ibid., 170. Berry acknowledges that many farmers obviously do increase this debt, mainly because there is little or no economic incentive not to, and he is "not asking conservationists to support destructive ways of farming" (ibid., 170). Meantime, farmers who do not increase the ecological deficit continue to be paid poorly for the good that they do and the goods they produce.

49. Ibid., 171.

50. Ibid., 173.

51. Ibid.

52. Ibid., 174; cf. Wendell Berry, "Nature as Measure," in *What Are People For?*: "If agriculture is to remain productive, it must preserve the land, and the fertility and ecological health of the land" (206). See also the foreword to *Kentucky's Natural Heritage: An Illustrated Guide to Biodiversity*: "The idea that farmers should be conservationists has been fairly common since at least the 1930s, and it is a fact, to some extent acknowledged, that the survival of agriculture depends upon the conservation of nature. But too few experts and officials have realized that conservation in agriculture requires an adequate number of farmers adequately paid. You can't expect a minimal farm population, minimally paid and struggling for survival, to be devoted conservationists" (xii).

53. Berry, "Think Little," in *A Continuous Harmony*, 72.

54. The conference, sponsored by Georgetown College (Lexington, Kentucky), was titled "The Future of Agrarianism: *The Unsettling of America* Twenty-Five Years Later." "The Agrarian Standard" would be published the following year not only in *Citizenship Papers* but also in *The Essential Agrarian Reader: The Future of Culture, Community, and the Land*, edited by the convener of the conference, Norman Wirzba (Lexington: The University Press of Kentucky, 2003). "Conservationist and Agrar-

ian," which originally appeared as "For Love of the Land" in *Sierra* (May-June 2002), is, like *The Unsettling*, an attempt to get conservationists to pay attention to the land economy and in particular to its iterations in agriculture. In both of the later essays, Berry mentions being on the "losing" side of things. In "The Agrarian Standard," he says that agrarians have been involved in a "hard, long, momentous contest" in which they are "so far, and by a considerable margin, the losers" (*Citizenship Papers*, 143); in "Conservationist and Agrarian," Berry says that his "sorrow in having been for so long on two losing sides"—the side of small farmers and conservationists—"has been compounded by knowing that those two sides have been in conflict, not only with their common enemy, the third side, but also, and by now, almost conventionally, with each other" (*Citizenship Papers*, 165–66).

55. "Over the last twenty-five or thirty years," Berry says, "I have been making and remaking different versions of the same argument" ("In Distrust of Movements," in *Citizenship Papers*, 43).

56. Berry frequently uses the term "kindly use" in *The Unsettling of America*; see, e.g., 30.

57. The essay recalls in many ways *The Unsettling*, at least two of which bear mentioning in this context. One is that in *The Unsettling*, Berry began by comparing foreign and domestic colonialism: "Now, as then, we see the abstract values of an industrial economy preying upon the native productivity of land and people. The fur trade was only the first establishment on this continent of a mentality whose triumph is its catastrophe" (*The Unsettling of America*, 6–7); in "The Agrarian Standard," Berry says, "The industrial economy . . . is inherently violent. It impoverishes one place in order to be extravagant in another, true to its colonialist ambition" (*Citizenship Papers*, 146). The other is that in the later essay, Berry, true to the project of *The Unsettling*, still proceeds from the premise—that "land is a gift of immeasurable value . . . to all the living in all time"—to the question "that begins the agrarian agenda and is the discipline of all agrarian practice: What is the best way to use land?" ("The Agrarian Standard," in *Citizenship Papers*, 152).

58. Berry, *The Unsettling of America*, 97.

59. Ibid., 22.

60. *Kentucky's Natural Heritage: An Illustrated Guide*, xvii.


Chapter 7: Wendell Berry and Democratic Self-Governance
Patrick J. Deneen

1. Thomas Hobbes, *Leviathan*, ed. Richard Tuck (New York: Cambridge University Press, Revised Student Edition, 1996), 88.

2. Ibid., 90.

3. John Locke, "A Letter Concerning Toleration," in *The Works of John Locke, in Nine Volumes*, 12th ed., vol. 5, (London: Rivington, 1824).Emphasis added.

4. Aristotle, *Politics*, 1277b 7–15.

5. Ibid., 1317a-b.

6. Wendell Berry, "Rugged Individualism," in *The Way of Ignorance: And Other Essays* (Washington, DC: Shoemaker & Hoard, 2005), 9–11.

7. Wendell Berry, "In Distrust of Movements," in *Citizenship Papers: Essays* (Washington, DC: Shoemaker & Hoard, 2003), 45.

8. Wendell Berry, *The Unsettling of America: Culture and Agriculture* (San Francisco: Sierra Club Books, 1997), 4.

9. See Louis Hartz, *The Liberal Tradition in America* (New York: Harcourt, 1991). See also Vernon L. Parrington, *The Main Currents in American Thought.* 3 vols. (New York: Kessington Publisher, 2005).

10. For "defenders" of this tradition, alternatively called by some the "republican" or "communitarian" or "civic democratic" traditions, see for examples Wilson Carey McWilliams, *The Idea of Fraternity in America* (Berkeley, CA: University of California Press, 1973); Christopher Lasch, *The True and Only Heaven: Progress and Its Critics* (New York: Norton, 1991); Robert Booth Fowler, *The Dance with Community: The Contemporary Debate in American Political Thought* (Lawrence, Kansas: University Press of Kansas, 1991); and Michael Sandel, *Democracy's Discontent: America in Search of a Public Philosophy* (Cambridge, MA: Belknap, 1998).

11. Wendell Berry, "Agriculture from the Roots Up," in *The Way of Ignorance*, 107–8.

12. Wendell Berry, "Two Economies," in *Home Economics: Fourteen Essays* (New York: North Point Press, 1987) 70–71.

13. Wendell Berry, "Preserving Wildness," in *Home Economics*, 138, 139.

14. Wendell Berry, "Feminism, the Body, and the Machine," in *What Are People For?: Essays* (San Francisco: North Point Press, 1990), 195. He goes on: "If we want to have a world fit and pleasant for little children, we are surely going to have to learn to draw the line where it is not so easily drawn" (196).

15. Wendell Berry, "Nature as Measure," in *What Are People For?*, 208.

16. Ibid., 209.

17. Wendell Berry, "Economy and Pleasure," in *What Are People For?*, 141–2. Cf. Aristotle, *Politics*, I.

18. Wendell Berry, "The Way of Ignorance," in *The Way of Ignorance*, 56–57.

19. Wendell Berry, "The Work of Local Culture," in *What Are People For?*, 154.

20. Wendell Berry, "Higher Education and Home Defense," in *Home Economics*, 51.

21. Ibid., 52.

22. See Berry, *The Unsettling of America*, 7–9.

23. Wendell Berry, "Sex, Economy, Freedom, and Community," in *Sex, Economy, Freedom, and Community* (New York: Pantheon Books, 1992), 120.

24. Ibid., 120–21.

25. Ibid., 157.

26. Lest anyone believe that this critique of liberal "standardization"—most often in the form of national, and increasingly international, legal imposition—implies that the Left or the Democratic Party is the understood target of the critique, see as a counter-example the recent article "Bullies Along the Potomac" by Nina Mendelson in the *New York Times* (July 5, 2006) at (http://query.nytimes.com/gst/fullpage.html?res=9C02E FDA1230F936A35754C0A9609C8B63, accessed June 15, 2011). Mendelson relates that the Republican-controlled Congress—far from insisting upon states' rights—has since 2001 enacted twenty-seven laws "that preempt state authority in areas from air pollution to consumer protection," including one law she discusses entitled "National Uniformity for Food Act." Or, in the domain of education, consider the standardizing effect of President Bush's landmark "No Child Left Behind" program, or the rumblings for the potential standardization in the area of higher education being threatened by the Secretary of Education's "Commission on the Future of Higher Education."

27. Edmund Burke, *Reflections on the French Revolution*, ed. J. G. A. Pocock (Indianapolis: Hackett, 1987), 85. Berry expresses his admiration for Burke in among other places, *Citizenship Papers*, 1, 7.

28. Wendell Berry, "Property, Patriotism, and National Defense," in *Home Economics*, 101.

29. "But there is a paradox in all this, and it is as cruel as it is obvious: as the emphasis on individual liberty has increased, the liberty and power of most individuals has declined." Berry, "Sex, Economy, Freedom, and Community," in *Sex, Economy, Freedom, and Community*, 151.

30. "Loyalty, devotion, faith, self-denial are not ethereal virtues, but the concrete terms upon which love is kept alive in this world. Morality is neither ethereal nor arbitrary: it is the definition of what is humanly possible, and is the definition of the penalties for violating human possibility. A person who violates human limits is punished or he prepares a punishment for his successors, not necessarily because of divine or human law, but because he has transgressed the order of things. . . . By clarifying the human limits, morality tells us what we risk when we forsake the human to behave like false gods or like animals." Wendell Berry, "Discipline and Hope," in *A Continuous Harmony: Essays Cultural and Agricultural* (Washington, DC: Shoemaker & Hoard, 1970) 158.

31. George Santayana, *The Life of Reason or The Phases of Human Progress*. One-volume edition (London: Constable & Co., Ltd, 1954), 148.

32. Ibid., 147.

33. "A better economy, to my way of thinking, would be one that would place its emphasis not upon the *quantity* of notions and luxuries but upon the *quality* of necessities." Berry, "Discipline and Hope," in *A Continuous Harmony*, 117.

34. Berry, "Discipline and Hope," in *A Continuous Harmony*, 124.

Chapter 8: First They Came for the Horses: Wendell Berry and
a Technology of Wholeness
Caleb Stegall

1. Wendell Berry, "The Mad Farmer Manifesto: The First Amendment," in *The Selected Poems of Wendell Berry* (Berkeley, CA: Counterpoint 1998), 89.

2. Wendell Berry, *Remembering: A Novel* (Berkeley, CA: Counterpoint, 2008), 58.

3. Ibid., 60–61.

4. Ibid., 61.

5. Ibid., 62.

6. Ibid., 63.

7. Ibid.

8. Ibid., 65.

9. Ibid., 69.

10. Ibid.

11. Ibid., 9.

12. Ibid., 10.

13. Ibid., 15.

14. Wendell Berry, "1990: II," in *A Timbered Choir: The Sabbath Poems 1979–1997* (Washington, DC: Counterpoint, 1998), 117.

15. Wendell Berry, "A Few Words in Favor of Edward Abbey," in *What Are People For?: Essays* (New York: North Point Press 1990), 44.

16. Ibid., 40.

17. Ibid.

18. Wendell Berry, "Horses," in *The Selected Poems of Wendell Berry*, 121.

19. Quoted in Wendell Berry, *Citizenship Papers: Essays* (Washington, DC: Shoemaker & Hoard, 2003), 113.

20. Berry, "Why I Am not Going to Buy a Computer," in *What Are People For?: Essays* (New York: North Point Press, 1990), 171–2.

21. Wendell Berry, "Feminism, the Body, and the Machine," in *What Are People For?*, 187.

22. Ibid., 192.

23. Ibid., 193.

24. Ibid.

25. Ibid.

26. Ibid.

27. Ivan Illich, *Tools for Conviviality* (New York: Harper & Row, 1973), 11.

28. Wendell Berry, "A Good Scythe," in *The Gift of Good Land: Further Essays Cultural and Agricultural* (New York: North Point Press, 1981), 173.

29. Ibid., 174.

30. Ibid.

31. Wendell Berry, "Horse-Drawn Tools and the Doctrine of Labor Saving," in *The Gift of Good Land*, 105.

32. Ibid.

33. Ibid.

34. Wendell Berry, "Feminism, the Body, and the Machine," in *What Are People For?*, 190.

35. Berry, "Horses," in *The Selected Poems of Wendell Berry*, 122–23.

36. Berry, "The Whole Horse," in *Citizenship Papers*, 117.

37. Illich, *Tools for Conviviality*, 11.

38. Wendell Berry, "The Prejudice Against Country People," in *Citizenship Papers*, 111.

39. Berry, "Feminism, the Body, and the Machine," in *What Are People For?*, 184–85.

40. Wendell Berry, "The Whole Horse," in *Citizenship Papers*, 117.

41. Ibid., 116.

42. Wendell Berry, "At a Country Funeral," in *The Selected Poems of Wendell Berry*, 92.

43. Berry, "The Whole Horse," in *Citizenship Papers*, 121.

44. Wendell Berry, "Fidelity," in *That Distant Land: Collected Stories* (Washington, DC: Shoemaker & Hoard, 2004), 376.

45. Ibid., 372.

46. Ibid., 383.

47. Ibid., 411–12.

48. Ibid., 414.

49. Ibid., 418.

50. Ivan Illich, "Brave New Biocracy," in *New Perspectives Quarterly* 11 (Winter 1994): 4.

51. Wendell Berry, "A Standing Ground," in *The Selected Poems of Wendell Berry*, 73.

Chapter 9: Living Peace in the Shadow of War:
Wendell Berry's Dogged Pacifism
Michael R. Stevens

1. "Day of Days," *Band of Brothers*, DVD, written by John Orloff, directed by Richard Loncraine (HBO Home Video, 2002).
2. Wendell Berry, "February 2, 1968," in *Collected Poems: 1957–1982* (New York: North Point Press, 1985), 108.
3. Wendell Berry, "A Statement against the War in Vietnam," in *The Long-Legged House* (Washington, DC: Shoemaker & Hoard, 2004), 66.
4. Ibid., 67.
5. Ibid., 67–68.
6. Ibid., 70.
7. Ibid.
8. Ibid., 73.
9. Wendell Berry, "March 22, 1968," in *Collected Poems*, 108.
10. Wendell Berry, "To My Children, Fearing for Them," in *Collected Poems*, 60.
11. Berry, "Against the War in Vietnam," in *Collected Poems*, 66.
12. Wendell Berry, "Dark with Power," in *Collected Poems*, 66.
13. Ibid.
14. Wendell Berry "The Want of Peace," in *Collected Poems*, 68.
15. Wendell Berry, "The Peace of Wild Things," in *Collected Poems*, 69.
16. Wendell Berry, "To a Siberian Woodsman," in *Collected Poems*, 96–97.
17. Wendell Berry, "Some Thoughts on Citizenship and Conscience in Honor of Don Pratt," in *The Long-Legged House*, 80.
18. Ibid., 81.
19. Ibid., 83–84.
20. Ibid., 85.
21. Ibid., 87.
22. Ibid., 89.
23. Ibid., 91.
24. Wendell Berry, "The Mad Farmer's Love Song," in *Collected Poems*, 162.
25. Wendell Berry, "Manifesto: The Mad Farmer Liberation Front," in *Collected Poems*, 151.
26. Ibid.
27. Wendell Berry, "For the Hog Killing," in *Collected Poems*, 200.
28. Wendell Berry, "Sabbath IV, 1983," in *A Timbered Choir: The Sabbath Poems 1979–1997* (New York: Counterpoint, 1998), 59.
29. Ibid., 59.
30. Wendell Berry, "Thoughts in the Presence of Fear," in *Citizenship Papers: Essays* (Washington, DC: Shoemaker & Hoard, 2003), 17.
31. Ibid., 19.
32. Ibid.
33. Ibid., 20.
34. Ibid., 21.
35. Ibid., 22.
36. Wendell Berry, "The Failure of War," in *Citizenship Papers*, 27.

37. Ibid., 24. In an intriguing "Postscript" added to the essay in 2003, Berry responds to apparent criticisms of his anti-abortion statements in "The Failure of War" in as succinct a fashion as I have ever witnessed: "It is killing, of course. To kill is the express purpose of the procedure." As for the question of what is killed, Berry goes to plain sense: "Generally, pregnant women have thought and spoken of the beings in their wombs as 'babies.' . . . No living creature is 'viable' independently of an enveloping life-support system" (30).

38. Ibid., 29.

39. Wendell Berry, "A Citizen's Response to 'The National Security Strategy of the United States of America," in *Citizenship Papers*, 6.

40. Ibid., 9.

41. Ibid., 16.

42. Ibid., 14.

43. Wendell Berry, "Blessed Are the Peacemakers," in *Blessed Are the Peacemakers: Christ's Teachings about Love, Passion, and Forgiveness.* (Washington, DC: Shoemaker & Hoard, 2005), 4.

44. Wendell Berry, "The Burden of the Gospels," in *Blessed Are the Peacemakers*, 50–51.

45. Ibid., 63.

46. Wendell Berry, "Sabbath I, 2002," in *Given: New Poems* (Washington, DC: Shoemaker & Hoard, 2005), 103.

47. Wendell Berry, "Sabbath III, 2004," in *Given*, 140.

48. Ibid.

49. Wendell Berry, "Making It Home," in *Fidelity: Five Stories* (New York: Pantheon Books, 1992), 88.

50. Ibid., 104.

51. Ibid., 105.

52. Wendell Berry, *Hannah Coulter: A Novel* (Washington, DC: Shoemaker & Hoard, 2004), 168.

53. Ibid., 171.

54. Ibid., 173.

Chapter 10: Wendell Berry's Unlikely Case for Conservative Christianity
D. G. Hart

1. Ragan Sutterfield, "Imagining a Different Way to Live," *Christianity Today* (November 2006): 62.

2. Alan Jacobs, "Choose Life," in *Books & Culture* (March 1, 2006), 8.

3. Eugene H. Peterson, *Take and Read: Spiritual Reading: An Annotated List* (Grand Rapids, MI: Eerdmans, 1996), 63.

4. Wendell Berry, "Discipline and Hope," in *A Continuous Harmony: Essays Cultural and Agricultural* (New York: Harcourt, Brace, Jovanovich, 1972), 136–37.

5. Wendell Berry, *The Unsettling of America: Culture and Agriculture* (San Francisco: Sierra Club Books, 1977), 104, 105.

6. Ibid., 103.

7. Ibid., 105, 106.

8. Ibid., 108.

9. Ibid.

10. Ibid., 110.

11. Wendell Berry, "God and Country," in *What Are People For?: Essays* (San Francisco: North Point Press, 1990), 97.

12. Ibid., 97–98.

13. Wendell Berry, "Christianity and the Survival of Creation," in *Sex, Freedom, Economy, and Community,* (New York: Pantheon Books, 1992), 113.

14. Ibid., 114.

15. Ibid., 114–15.

16. Ibid., 115.

17. Ibid., 100.

18. Ibid., 107.

19. Ibid., 109.

20. Berry, *The Unsettling of America*, 101.

21. Ibid., 99.

22. Berry, "Christianity and the Survival of Creation," in *Sex, Freedom, Economy, and Community,* 102.

23. Berry, *The Unsettling of America*, 212.

24. Berry, "Christianity and the Survival of Creation," in *Sex, Freedom, Economy, and Community,* 103.

25. Wendell Berry, "Two Economies," in *Home Economics: Fourteen Essays* (New York: North Point Press, 1987), 57.

26. Ibid., 58.

27. Berry, "God and Country," in *What Are People For?,* 101.

28. Both examples here come from the Reformed branch of Protestantism. The reason for their selection stems less from pride of place (for the sake of full disclosure, I am a Presbyterian) than from what I know relatively well.

29. Belgic Confession, Article 35.

30. Ibid.

31. Reformed Church in the United States, *Heidelberg Catechism, 20th Century Edition* (Philadelphia: Sunday School Board of the Reformed Church in the United States, 1902), 184–85.

32. Berry, *The Unsettling of America*, 103.

33. Rom. 1:18ff.

34. Berry, *The Unsettling of America*, 109.

35. Ibid., 134.

36. Ibid., 175.

37. For further elaboration of the differences between old and new Protestantism, see D. G. Hart, *The Lost Soul of American Protestantism* (Lanham, MD: Rowman & Littlefield, 2002); and D. G. Hart, *Recovering Mother Kirk: The Case for Liturgy in the Reformed Tradition* (Grand Rapids, MI: Baker Books, 2003).

38. Berry, *The Unsettling of America*, 59.

39. Ibid., 7–8.

40. Ibid., 123.

41. Wendell Berry, "The Whole Horse," in *Citizenship Papers* (Washington DC, Shoemaker & Hoard, 2003), 122.

42. Ibid., 124.

43. Ibid., 124.
44. Berry, *The Unsettling of America*, 184.


Chapter II: The Rediscovery of *Oikonomia*
Mark Shiffman

1. See Avicenna, *On the Divisions of the Rational Sciences*, in *Medieval Political Philosophy: A Sourcebook*, ed. Ralph Lerner and Muhsin Madhi (Ithaca, NY: Cornell University Press, 1963), 97; Thomas Aquinas, *Commentary on Aristotle's Nicomachean Ethics* (Dumb Ox Books, 1993), I.1.6, 3; and Bonaventure, *The Journey of the Mind to God* (Hackett, 1990), III.6, 22.
2. Aristotle, *The Politics*, trans. Carnes Lord (Chicago: University of Chicago Press, 1984), 1259b1.
3. See Aristotle's *The Politics*, book 1: 1252a21–3; book 3: 1274b39–1275a2. In between these two discussions, Aristotle examines those cities, both imagined (e.g. Plato's *Republic*) and actual (e.g. Sparta), considered to have the best regimes. In this context the problems resulting from the tendency to undermine the family in favor of civic identity come to the fore.
4. Aristotle, *The Politics*, 1256b28–9.
5. Aristotle, *The Politics*, 1257b4–5.
6. Aristotle, *The Politics*, 1256b31–2; 1257b41–1258a2.
7. Wendell Berry, "Quantity vs. Form," in *The Way of Ignorance: And Other Essays* (Washington, DC: Counterpoint, 2006), 81.
8. Berry, "Quantity vs. Form," in *The Way of Ignorance*, 82.
9. Berry, "Quantity vs. Form," in *The Way of Ignorance*, 87–89.
10. Aristotle, *The Politics*, 1258a37–8. He also argues that it is the best foundation for democracy (1319a4–6). Aristotle's agrarian vision entails two classes of farmers: patrician landholders who have the leisure (because of slave labor) to engage in politics, and a much larger body of yeoman farmers who have the solid virtues to recognize good character in others but neither the leisure nor the interest to get very involved in political rule. Berry's vision, of course, includes only the latter. On the question of the character of the citizens who provide the broad foundation of a decent republic, the two are in agreement with one another—as well as with James Madison. See "Republican Distribution of Citizens," in *Writings*, ed. Jack Rakove (New York: The Library of America, 1999), 511–13.
11. Wendell Berry, *The Unsettling of America: Culture and Agriculture* (San Francisco: Sierra Club Books, 1997), 123.
12. Ibid., 113.
13. Ibid., 115–16.
14. *Oxford English Dictionary*, 2nd ed. (Oxford, UK: Oxford University Press, 1989), 5:60; Thomas Hobbes, *Leviathan* (Indianapolis, IN: Hackett Publishing, 1994), 156.
15. See, for example, Wendell Berry, "The Purpose of a Coherent Community," in *The Way of Ignorance*, 78–79.
16. Hobbes, *Leviathan*, VI.6–7, 28–29.
17. Ibid., XI.1–2, 57–58.
18. Ibid., X.1, 50.

19. Adam Smith, *The Wealth of Nations*, bk. 4, chap. 1, pt. 1 (New York: Modern Library, 1965), 669.

20. John Locke, *Two Treatises of Government* (Cambridge, UK: Cambridge University Press, 1994), II.42.24–27 and 43.21–22, p.298.

21. Berry, *The Unsettling of America*, 8.

22. Viewed from this point of view, one of the most decisive moments of American history is Washington's acquiescence in the "economic" program of Adam Smith's most influential disciple, Hamilton, against the agrarian republicanism of his fellow Virginians Jefferson and Madison. According to Joseph Ellis, uppermost in Washington's mind was the need for a national system of revenue that could "provide resources in the reliable fashion of the British ministry" so as to enable a national military to stand up against the British forces. See Ellis, *His Excellency: George Washington* (New York: Vintage Books, 2004), 170, 218.

23. Plato, *Republic* (New York: Basic Books, 1968), 508e–509b; cf. Aristotle, *Nicomachean Ethics* (Newburyport, MA: Focus Publishing, 2002), 1094a1–3; *Physics* (Newburyport, MA: Focus Publishing, 1995), 195a24–26; 198b8–9.

24. I. A. Richards, "Realism, Nominalism, Conceptualism / Logic, Metaphysics, Psychology," in *Richards on Rhetoric: I. A. Richards, Selected Essays (1929–1974)* (Oxford, UK: Oxford University Press, 1991), 171.

25. Ibid., 172.

26. Wendell Berry, *Home Economics: Fourteen Essays* (San Francisco: North Point Press, 1987), Preface, ix.

27. Wendell Berry, "Letter to Wes Jackson," in *Home Economics*, 4.

28. This formulation, which acquired the name "Ockham's Razor," is not in fact Ockham's but nonetheless is "authentically Ockhamist Doctrine." See Paul Vincent Spade, "Ockham's Nominalist Metaphysics: Some Main Themes," in *The Cambridge Companion to Ockham* (Cambridge, UK: Cambridge University Press, 1999), 101. For Nietzsche, see *Beyond Good and Evil*, in *Basic Writings of Nietzsche* (New York: Modern Library, 1968), section 36.

29. Martin Heidegger, *The Question Concerning Technology* (New York: Harper & Row, 1977), 26–28.

30. Simone Weil, *Waiting for God* (New York: Harper & Row, 2000), 6.

31. Wendell Berry, *Remembering: A Novel* (Berkeley, CA: Counterpoint, 2008), 61.

32. Ibid., 63.

33. Wendell Berry, "Style and Grace," in *What Are People For?: Essays* (New York: North Point Press, 1990), 65–66.

34. Ibid., 66.

35. Ibid., 69.

36. Wendell Berry, *Hannah Coulter: A Novel* (Washington, DC: Shoemaker & Hoard, 2002), 133–34.

37. Ibid., 5.

38. Ibid., 28.

39. Ibid., 33.

40. Ibid., 50.

41. Ibid., 55.

42. Ibid., 57, 63.

43. Ibid., 68.

44. Ibid., 158–59.

45. Karl Polanyi, *Primitive, Archaic and Modern Economies: Essays of Karl Polanyi* (New York: Anchor Books, 1968), 107

46. Wendell Berry, "Two Economies," in *Home Economics*, 72.

47. Lauren Wilcox, "Wendell Berry: An Interview," in *World Ark* (January/February 2008): 17.

Chapter 12: Wendell Berry's Defense of a Truly Free Market
Mark T. Mitchell

1. Wendell Berry, "The Total Economy," in *Citizenship Papers: Essays* (Washington, DC: Shoemaker & Hoard, 2003), 72.

2. Ibid., 64.

3. Karl Polanyi, *The Great Transformation: The Political and Economic Origins of Our Time* (Boston: Beacon Press, 2001), 48, 60.

4. Berry, "The Total Economy," in *Citizenship Papers*, 69–70.

5. Hilaire Belloc, *The Servile State* (Indianapolis: The Liberty Fund, Inc.: 1977), 107.

6. G. K. Chesterton, *The Outline of Sanity* (Norfolk, VA: IHS Press, 2001), 42.

7. F. A. Hayek, *The Road to Serfdom* (Chicago: The University of Chicago Press, 1994), 214, 215.

8. Polanyi, *Great Transformation*, 145.

9. Ibid., 147.

10. Ibid., 155.

11. Wendell Berry, "The Whole Horse," in *Citizenship Papers*, 120.

12. Wilhelm Röpke, *A Humane Economy: The Social Framework of the Free Market* (Wilmington, DE: ISI Books, 1998), 35.

13. Bernard Mandeville, *The Fable of the Bees; Or, Private Vices, Publick Benefits*, vol. 1, ed. F. Kaye (Indianapolis: Liberty Classics, 1988), 18, 24.

14. Keynes, John Maynard, "Economic Possibilities for Our Grandchildren," in *Essays in Persuasion* (New York: Harcourt, Brace and Company, 1932), 367.

15. Ibid., 369.

16. Ibid., 372. Emphasis added.

17. Wendell Berry, *The Unsettling of America: Culture and Agriculture* (San Francisco: Sierra Club Books, 1997), 58, 56.

18. Ibid., 53.

19. Ibid., 123.

20. Frank H. Knight, *Risk, Uncertainty and Profit* (Chicago: University of Chicago Press, 1971), 77.

21. Ludwig von Mises, *Socialism: An Economic and Sociological Analysis*, trans. J. Kahane (New Haven: Yale University Press, 1951), 485.

22. Wendell Berry, "Sex, Economy, Freedom, and Community," in *Sex, Economy, Freedom, and Community* (New York: Pantheon Books, 1992), 119–20.

23. Wendell Berry, "Two Economies," in *Home Economics: Fourteen Essays* (New York: North Point Press, 1987), 54–55.

24. Ibid., 56–57.

25. Ibid., 57.

26. Ibid., 64–65.

27. Wendell Berry, "The Agrarian Standard," in *Citizenship Papers*, 144.

28. Ibid., 146.

29. Ibid., 147.

30. Berry, "The Whole Horse," in *Citizenship Papers*, 117.

31. Ibid., 118.

32. Ibid., 117.

33. Berry, "The Agrarian Standard," in *Citizenship Papers*, 150.

34. Hilaire Belloc, *An Essay on the Restoration of Property* (Norfolk, VA: IHS Press, 2002), 75.

35. Joseph Schumpeter, *Capitalism, Socialism and Democracy* (New York: Harper & Row, 1942), 142.

36. Thomas Jefferson, "To James Madison," October 28, 1785, in *The Portable Thomas Jefferson*, ed. Merrill D. Peterson (New York: Penguin Books, 1977), 397.

37. Röpke, *A Humane Economy*, 99.

38. Wendell Berry, "Out of Your Car, Off Your Horse," in *Sex, Economy, Freedom, and Community*, 24.

39. Wendell Berry, "Economy and Pleasure," in *What Are People For?: Essays* (New York: North Point Press, 1990), 130.

40. Ibid., 130–31.

41. Ibid., 131.

42. Ibid., 132.

43. Ibid.

44. Ibid., 134.

45. Wilhelm Röpke, *The Social Crisis of Our Time* (New Brunswick: Transaction Publishers, 1992), 52.

46. Ibid., 181.

Chapter 13: The Restoration of Propriety: Wendell Berry and
the British Distributists
William Edmund Fahey

1. The classic study of Hollis yet remains Samuel T. Worcester, *History of the Town of Hollis, New Hampshire, From Its First Settlement to the Year 1879, with Many Biographical Sketches of Its Early Settlers, Their Descendants, and Other Residents* (Nashua, NH: Press of O.C. Moore, 1879).

2. *Hollis Brookline Journal* (Friday, October 12, 2007), 1.

3. A sturdy and sympathetic introduction to distributist thought is still forthcoming, but a good starting point is Jay P. Corrin, *G. K. Chesterton & Hilaire Belloc: The Battle Against Modernity* (Athens, Ohio and London: Ohio University Press, 1981), which also provides a very fine bibliography to major distributist works.

4. John Paul II, *Centesimus annus. Encyclical letter on the hundreth anniversary of Rerum Novarum*, § May 1, 1991, 19.

5. See, in particular, the National Catholic Rural Life Conference's *Manifesto on the Rural Life* (Fargo: The Bruce Publishing Company, 1939).

6. See, for example, standard works such as John F. Cronin, *Catholic Social Principles:*

*The Social Teaching of the Catholic Church Applied to American Economic Life* (Milwaukee: Bruce Publishing Company, 1950), 633, 641, 652, and a full bibliography of Distributism at 767.

7. Maurin's writings are diffuse; for an overview, see Anthony Novitsky, "Peter Maurin's Green Revolution: The Radical Implications of Reactionary Social Catholicism," *The Review of Politics* 37.1 (1975), 83–103.

8. See, in particular, Ralph Borsodi, *Flight from the City* (New York: Harper and Row, 1933).

9. John F. Corrin, *Catholic Intellectuals and the Challenge of Democracy* (Notre Dame: University of Notre Dame, 2002), 158–59.

10. Twelve Southerners, *I'll Take My Stand: The South and the Agrarian Tradition* (1930; Baton Rouge and London: Lousiana State University Press, 1977), 204–5.

11. The principal texts for the thought of the Southern Agrarians remain *I'll Take My Stand: The South and the Agrarian Tradition* and *Who Owns America?: A New Declaration of Independence*, ed. Herbert Agar and Allen Tate (1936; Wilmington, DE: ISI Books, 1999).

12. Berry, it should be said, time and again has rejected leading or being embedded within any "movement." Nevertheless, I believe it is fair to situate him within the distributist-agrarian tradition. Berry's works are numerous, but a fine introduction to his social thought may be found in *The Art of the Commonplace: The Agrarian Essays of Wendell Berry*, ed. Norman Wirzba (Washington, DC: Counterpoint, 2002). For an anthology of agrarian revivalist writers, see *The New Agrarianism: Land, Culture, and the Community of Life*, ed. Eric T. Freyfogle (Washington, DC: Island Books, 2001).

13. See Joseph Pearce, *Small is Still Beautiful: Economics as if Families Mattered* (London: Harper Books, 2001), and John Zmirak, *Wilhelm Roepke: Swiss Localist, Global Economist* (Wilmington: ISI Books, 2001). In addition, see the enjoyable study of Allan C. Carlson, *Third Ways: How Bulgarian Greens, Swedish Housewives, and Beer-Swilling Englishmen Created Family-Centered Economies—and Why They Disappeared* (Wilmington: ISI Books, 2007).

14. For general discussion, see John R. E. Bliese, *The Greening of Conservative America* (Boulder and Oxford: Westview Press, 2001), and Allan C. Carlson, *The New Agrarian Mind: The Movement Toward Decentralist Thought in Twentieth-Century America* (New Brunswick and London: Transaction Books, 2000).

15. On which, see Joshua P. Hothschild, "The Principle of Subsidiarity and the Agrarian Ideal," *Faith & Reason* 27.2–4 (2002): 117–55.

16. Wendell Berry, "The Agrarian Standard," in *Citizenship Papers: Essays* (Washington, DC: Shoemaker & Hoard, 2003), 144–45.

17. Wendell Berry, *The Unsettling of America: Culture and Agriculture* (San Francisco: Sierra Club Books, 1977), 219–220.

18. In addition to Carlson's *The New Agrarian Mind*, cited above, see also his *The "American Way": Family and Community in the Shaping of the American Identity* (Wilmington, DE: ISI Books, 2003).

19. Wendell Berry, "Out of Your Car, Off Your Horse," in *Sex, Economy, Freedom, and Community: Eight Essays* (New York: Pantheon Books, 1992), 23.

20. Wendell Berry "A Native Hill," in *The Long-Legged House* (Washington, DC: Shoemaker & Hoard, 2004), 176.

21. Ibid., 198.

22. Ibid., 178.

23. See, for example, Wendell Berry, "The Regional Motive," in *A Continuous Harmony: Essays Cultural and Agricultural* (New York: Harcourt Brace Jovanovich, 1972), 67.

24. Berry, "A Native Hill," in *The Long-Legged House*, 211–12. Italics my own.

25. Wendell Berry, *Life Is a Miracle: An Essay Against Modern Superstition* (Washington, DC: Counterpoint Books, 2000), 13.

26. Wendell Berry, "Standing By Words," in *Standing by Words: Essays* (Washington, DC: Shoemaker & Hoard, 2005), 57. The quotation from *Paradise Lost* comes from book 1, 253–56.

27. The secularity of even Berry's spiritual sensibility is argued for by Kimberly K. Smith, *Wendell Berry and the Agrarian Tradition: A Common Grace* (Lawrence: University of Kansas, 2003), esp. 155–178. I am arguing that this nontranscendent interpretation of Berry is a result of configuring him only within a mainstream Protestant tradition. Comparing Berry's spiritual outlook with the longer Catholic tradition would lead to a nonsecular understanding of his religious thought.

28. Wendell Berry, *Jayber Crow: The Life Story of Jayber Crow, Barber, of the Port William Membership, as Written by Himself* (Counterpoint Books: New York, 2000), 83.

29. Wendell Berry, "Christianity and the Survival of Creation," in *Sex, Economy, Freedom, and Community*, 97.

30. Ibid., 98–99.

31. Most recently see Berry's "Burden of the Gospels," *The Way of Ignorance: And Other Essays* (Washington, DC: Shoemaker & Hoard, 2005), 127–37.

32. See for example, his comments in the preface and afterward of *Blessed Are the Peacemakers: Christ's Teachings about Love, Compassion and Forgiveness* (Washington, DC: Shoemaker & Hoard, 2005).

33. Cf., William Bradford, *Of Plymouth Plantation: Bradforth's History of the Plymouth Settlement 1608–1650* (London, 1647), chap. 9, and Thomas Morton, *New English Canaan* (Amsterdam, 1637), book 2, chap. 1. Bradford, disdainful of nature and the natural men he found therein, has passed down through history as a venerable Puritan founder. Morton, who loved the new wilderness, favored cooperative living with the Indians, transplanted festivities such as Maypole dancing, and saw goodness in the sale and consumption of alcohol, was scorned by the Puritans and is now virtually unknown. Morton's community, Merry Mount, prospered through the first quarter of the seventeenth century. Eventually under orders from Governor William Bradford, Myles Standish and Puritan militia raided Merry Mount, arrested Morton for his views, and marooned him off the coast of New Hampshire. John Endicott destroyed the community in the following year. The contrast between the two philosophies is captured in Nathaniel Hawthorne's short story "The May-Pole of Merry Mount."

34. See my introduction to Vincent McNabb, *The Church and the Land* (Norfolk, VA: IHS Press, 2003), 20–28.

35. Cf., St. Augustine, *De Civitate Dei*, books 11, 12, and 13—see esp. book 11, 21–22; St. Thomas, *Summa Theologiae*, book 1, 99.44–45; St. Bonaventure, *Itinerarium Mentis in Deum*, book 1.

36. G. K. Chesterton, "The Real Life on the Land," in *Outline of Sanity* (Norfolk, VA: IHS Press, 2001), 113–14.

37. Aristotle, *Metaphysics*, 980a25–982a1.

38. Cf., Hilaire Belloc, *The Servile State* (1913; Indianapolis: Liberty Fund, 1977), 68–83; *The Crisis of Civilization* (New York: Fordham University Press, 1937), 31–35. Belloc was perfectly capable of expressing himself in terms free of specific mention of the Catholic faith; see *The Restoration of Property* (1936; Norfolk, VA: IHS Press, 2002), 30. But even here, his use of the language of human dignity hints at his Christian humanism.

39. McNabb, *The Church and the Land*, 103.

40. G. K. Chesterton, "The Religion of Small Property," in *The Outline of Sanity*, 165–66.

41. Belloc was, in fact, aware of the caricature and made fun of it; see *An Essay on the Restoration of Property* (Norfolk, VA: IHS Press, 2002), 52–53.

42. See the comments of Lord Stanley of Alderly at xii-xiii in his introduction to Belloc, *The Cruise of the Nona* (London: Constable and Co., 1955); eg., "There is a Living Spirit who rules the sea and many attendant spirits about him."

43. Consider the comments of F. A. Hayek, *The Road to Serfdom* (Chicago: The University of Chicago Press, 1994), 66–67, where Hayek, on the one hand, marks the "limits of our powers of imagination" and so is wary of ideology; on the other hand, because he holds so firmly that "the scale of value can only exist in individual minds," cannot find a way to conclude anything but that the individual must be "the judge of his ends." It would be beneficial to establish the common ground as well as the distinctions between the metaphysics and epistemology of Hayek and Aristotle.

44. Hilaire Belloc, *The Four Men* (London: Thomas Nelson and Sons, 1912), 302–3.

Chapter 14: The Integral Imagination of Wendell Berry
Nathan Schlueter

1. Wendell Berry, "Poetry and Place," in *Standing by Words: Essays* (Berkeley, CA: Counterpoint Press, 1983), 157.

2. Berry does acknowledge the precariousness of this unity: "The conflicts of life and work, like those of rest and work, would ideally be resolved in balance: *enough* of each. In practice, however, they probably can be resolved (if that is the word) only in tension, in a principled unwillingness to let go of either, or to sacrifice either to the other. But it is a *necessary* tension, the grief in it both inescapable and necessary." Wendell Berry, "The Specialization of Poetry," in *Standing by Words*, 22.

3. Niccolo Machiavelli, *The Prince*, trans. Leo Paul S. de Alvarez (Prospect Heights, IL: Waveland Press, 1989), 93. Italics mine.

4. For more on Machiavelli as the founder of modern political science, see Leo Strauss, *Thoughts on Machiavelli* (Chicago: The University of Chicago Press, 1958). See also Strauss's essay "What Is Political Philosophy" in *What Is Political Philosophy? And Other Studies* (Chicago: The University of Chicago Press, 1958), 9–55.

5. Francis Bacon, *The New Organon*, book 1, chap. 129.

6. See Shakespeare, *The Tempest*, I.4.151.

7. Indeed, *The Prince* is itself a rhetorical masterpiece, drawing powerfully on images and the imagination. See especially chapter twenty-six, which is florid to the point of being a burlesque.

8. Leon Kass, "Science, Religion, and the Human Future," in *Commentary* (April 2007): 47.

9. T. S. Eliot, "The Metaphysical Poets," in *Selected Essays* (London: Faber & Faber, 1999), 281–91.

10. See Walker Percy, *Love in the Ruins* (New York: Picador, 1999); and *The Thanatos Syndrome* (New York: Picador, 1987).

11. C. S. Lewis, *The Abolition of Man* (New York: MacMillan Publishing Company, 1955), 34.

12. Ibid., 26–27, quoting Plato's *Republic*, 402a.

13. Berry, "Poetry and Place," in *Standing by Words*, 138.

14. Wendell Berry, "Christianity and the Survival of Creation," in *Sex, Economy, Freedom, and Community* (New York: Pantheon Books, 1992), 105.

15. Berry, "Poetry and Place," in *Standing by Words*, 184–85

16. Wendell Berry, "The Specializaton of Poetry," in *Standing by Words*, 13.

17. Wendell Berry, *Life Is a Miracle: An Essay Against Modern Superstition* (Berkeley, CA: Counterpoint, 2001), 65.

18. Ibid., 69.

19. Ibid., 67.

20. Berry, "Poetry and Place," in *Standing by Words*, 184–85, quoting Keats, *Tintern Abbey*.

21. Lee M. Silver, *Challenging Nature* (New York: HarperCollins Publishers, 2006), 313–14.

22. Berry, *Life Is a Miracle*, 48.

23. Berry, "Poetry and Place," in *Standing by Words*, 194.

24. Ibid., 191.

25. Wendell Berry, "Preface," in *The Way of Ignorance: And Other Essays* (Washington, DC: Shoemaker & Hoard, 2005), ix.

26. Berry, *Life Is a Miracle*, 10–11.

27. For a concise overview and assessment of the scientific method, see Kass, "Science, Religion, and the Human Future," *Commentary*.

28. Berry, *Life Is a Miracle*, 23.

29. Ibid., 38.

30. Ibid., 39.

31. Ibid., 19.

32. Ibid., 41.

33. Wendell Berry, "The Gift of Good Land," in *The Gift of Good Land: Further Essays Cultural and Agricultural* (New York: North Point Press, 1982), 279.

34. Berry, *Life Is a Miracle*, 136.

35. Ibid., 39.

36. Ibid., 137.

37. Ibid., 113.

38. Ibid., 114.

39. Ibid., 137–8.

40. Ibid., 117.

41. Ibid., 73–74. *Romanticism* is of course a word capable of many meanings, not all of them consistent with one another. For purposes of this paper, romanticism refers precisely to the celebration of the autonomous imagination that Berry traces both in Romantic poets like Shelley and Keats as well as in a good deal of contemporary poetry and contemporary art more generally.

42. Berry, "The Specialization of Poetry," in *Standing by Words*, 5, quoting John Crowe Ransom.

43. Berry, "Poetry and Place," in *Standing by Words*, 168.

44. Berry, "The Specialization of Poetry," in *Standing by Words*, 8.

45. Berry, "Poetry and Place," in *Standing by Words*, 158.

46. Berry, "Standing by Words," in *Standing by Words*, 29.

47. Berry, *Life Is a Miracle*, 85.

48. Ibid.

49. Ibid., 121.

50. Ibid., 83.

51. Ibid., 122.

52. Berry, "Poetry and Place," *Standing by Words*, 186.

53. Ibid., 153.

54. Ibid., 183.

55. Ibid., 148–49.

56. Ibid., 186.

57. Ibid.

58. Berry, *Life Is a Miracle*, 100.

59. *King Lear*, 4.6, 55, *The Pelican Shakespeare*.

60. Berry, *Life Is a Miracle*, 5.

61. Ibid., 10.

62. Wendell Berry, *The Unsettling of America* (San Francisco: Sierra Club Books, 1977), 99.

63. Ibid.

64. See for example *The Unsettling of America*, 130–31, and also *Standing by Words*, 191–207.

65. Berry, "Poetry and Place," *Standing by Words*, 192.

66. Wendell Berry, "The Wild Birds," in *That Distant Land* (Washington, DC: Shoemaker & Hoard, 2004), 337–64.

67. Wendell Berry, *Remembering* (Berkeley, CA: Counterpoint, 2008), 42

68. In Plato's *Symposium* (189e–194e), the poet Aristophanes describes the sexual division at the root of Eros as a wound inflicted on originally unified human beings by the Olympian gods as punishment for their pride. My own understanding of human sexuality is informed here by John Paul II, especially *Love & Responsibility*, trans. H. T. Willets (New York: Farrar, Straus, and Giroux, 1991) and *The Theology of the Body*, ed. John S. Grabowski (Boston: Pauline Books and Media, 1997).

69. Berry, *Remembering*, 42.

70. Ibid., 47.

71. Ibid., 48.

72. For an insightful discussion of this notion, see C. S. Lewis's essay "Membership," in *The Weight of Glory* (San Francisco: HarperCollins Publishers, 1980), 158–76.

73. Berry, *Remembering*, 102.

74. Ibid.

75. Ibid., 103.

76. Berry is doubtless aware of this tension. See for example Harold K. Bush Jr., "Hunting for Reasons to Hope: A Conversation with Wendell Berry," *Christianity and Literature*, vol. 56, no. 2 (Winter 2007): 219: "[Individualism] has a deep appeal for me, maybe too much appeal. You know, I worked at being a loner, and it's odd that somebody like me

would have become a defender of the idea of community, would have thought as hard as I have about what a community is and does and might do. Maybe, on the other hand, it's logical that people who try to be individuals find pretty soon how limited that is."
77. Russell Kirk, *The Essential Russell Kirk*, ed. George A. Panichas (Wilmington, DE: ISI Books, 2007), 208.
78. John Paul II, *The Theology of the Body*, ed. John S. Grabowski (Boston: Pauline Books and Media, 1997), 32–33.
79. Lewis, "Membership," *The Weight of Glory*, 161–62.
80. The most direct biblical evidence for the divine institution of government is Romans 13, though it is indirectly suggested throughout the New Testament.
81. For a wonderful treatment of this subject, see Joseph Cardinal Ratzinger, *The Spirit of the Liturgy* (San Francisco: Ignatius Press, 2000).


Chapter 15: Earth and Flesh Sing Together: The Place of Wendell Berry's Poetry in His Vision of the Human
Luke Schlueter

1. Harold K. Bush Jr., "Hunting for Reasons to Hope," in *Christianity and Literature* 56, no. 2 (2007), 222.
2. Gregory McNamee and James R. Hepworth, "The Art of Living Right: An Interview with Wendell Berry," in *Conversations with Wendell Berry*, ed. Morris Allen Grubbs (Jackson, MS: The University Press of Mississippi, 2007), 20.
3. Dana Gioia, "Can Poetry Matter," in *Can Poetry Matter* (Saint Paul, MN: Graywolf Press, 1992), 1.
4. Wendell Berry, "The Specialization of Poetry," in *Standing by Words: Essays* (Washington, DC: Shoemaker & Hoard, 2005), 5.
5. Ibid., 5
6. Charles Altieri, *Enlarging the Temple: New Directions in American Poetry During the 1960s* (Granbury, NJ: Associated University Presses, 1979), 17.
7. Ibid., 49.
8. Wendell Berry, "Poetry and Marriage," in *Standing by Words*, 97.
9. Berry, "The Specialization of Poetry," in *Standing by Words*, 17.
10. Wendell Berry, "Standing by Words," in *Standing by Words*, 25.
11. Wendell Berry, "Notes: Unspecializing Poetry," in *Standing by Words*, 85.
12. Wendell Berry, "Poetry and Place," in *Standing by Words*, 112.
13. Wendell Berry, "A Homage to Dr. Williams," in *A Continuous Harmony: Essays Cultural and Agricultural* (New York: Harcourt Brace Jovanovich, 1972), 56.
14. Wendell Berry, "The Responsibility of the Poet," in *What Are People For? Essays* (New York: North Point Press, 1997), 88.
15. Gary Snyder, "The East West Interview," in *The Real Work: Interviews and Talks 1964–1979* (New York: New Directions, 1980), 123.
16. Gregory McNamee and James R. Hepworth, "The Art of Living Right," in *Conversations with Wendell Berry*, 19.
17. Berry, "A Homage to Dr. Williams," *A Continuous Harmony*, 56.
18. Wendell Berry, "The Stones," in *Collected Poems 1957–1982* (New York: North Point Press, 1996), 103.

19. Ibid., 103.

20. Ibid., 103–4.

21. Wendell Berry, "Enriching the Earth," in *Collected Poems*, 110.

22. Wendell Berry, "The Peace of Wild Things," in *Collected Poems*, 69.

23. Ibid., 69.

24. Wendell Berry, "Sleep," in *Collected Poems*, 107.

25. Jacques Maritain, *Creative Intuition in Art and Poetry* (New York: Meridian Books, 1954), 8.

26. Wendell Berry, "Feminism, the Body, and the Machine," in *What Are People For?*, 180.

27. Berry, "Notes: Unspecializing Poetry," in *Standing By Words*, 82.

28. Wendell Berry, "Envoy," in *Collected Poems*, 99.

29. Ibid., 99.

30. Wendell Berry, "The Gathering," in *Collected Poems*, 161.

31. Ibid., 161.

32. Ibid., 161–62.

33. Wendell Berry, "Our Children, Coming of Age," in *Collected Poems*, 264.

34. Ibid.

35. Ibid.

36. Jordan Fisher Smith, "Field Observations: An Interview with Wendell Berry," in *Conversations with Wendell Berry*, 89.

37. Katherine Dalton, "Rendering Us Again in Affection: An Interview with Wendell Berry," in *Conversations with Wendell Berry*, 197.

38. Wendell Berry, "Elegy," in *Collected Poems*, 234.

39. Ibid.

40. Ibid., 235.

41. Ibid.

42. Ibid., 236.

43. Ibid., 240.

Chapter 16: If Dante Were a Kentucky Barber
Anthony Esolen

1. Wendell Berry, *Jayber Crow: The Life Story of Jayber Crow, Barber, of the Port William Membership, as Written by Himself* (Washington, DC: Counterpoint, 2000) 350–51

2. Dante Alighieri, *Purgatory*, trans. Anthony Esolen (New York: Random House, 2004), 31.138.

3. Dante Alighieri, *Paradise*, trans. Anthony Esolen (New York: Random House, 2007), 1.70.

4. Berry, *Jayber Crow*, 351.

5. Ibid., 9.

6. Ibid., 10.

7. Ibid., 25.

8. Ibid., 133.

9. Ibid.

10. Ibid., 191.

11. I Cor. 12:14.

12. Berry, *Jayber Crow*, 101.

13. Ibid., 102.

14. Ibid., 195.

15. Ibid., 213.

16. Ibid.

17. Ibid., 184.

18. Ibid.

19. Ibid., 187.

20. Ibid., 360.

21. Alighieri, *Purgatory*, 30.28–29.

22. Berry, *Jayber Crow*, 347.

23. Ibid., 151.

24. Ibid., 190.

25. Wendell Berry, *Sabbaths: Poems* (San Francisco: North Point Press, 1987) 1984; III.

26. Dante, *Monarchy*, ed. Prue Shaw (Cambridge: Cambridge University Press, 1996), 1.8.

27. Gen. 2:18.

28. Rev. 21:2–3.

29. Alighieri, *Purgatory* 6.62, 65–66.

30. Alighieri, *Purgatory*, 6.69–75.

31. Alighieri, *Paradise* 15.112–26.

32. Augustine, *The City of God,* trans. Marcus Dods; intro. Thomas Merton (New York: Random House, 1950), 1.1.

33. Berry, *Jayber Crow*, 206.

34. Ibid., 198.

35. Alighieri, *Purgatory*, 27.94–108.

36. Berry, *Jayber Crow*, 249.

37. Ibid.

38. Ibid., 361.

39. Psalm 100:1–3.

40. Berry, *Jayber Crow*, 249.

41. Wendell Berry, "The Country of Marriage," in *The Country of Marriage: Poems* (New York: Harcourt, Brace, Jovanovich, 1973), 66–68.

42. Berry, *Jayber Crow*, 251–52.

43. John 1:14.

44. Alighieri, *Paradise* 1.64–73.

45. Berry, *Jayber Crow*, 249.

46. Ibid., 164–5.

47. Alighieri, *Paradise* 14.61–66.

48. Edmund Spenser, *The Faerie Queene*, ed. Thomas P. Roche Jr. (London: Penguin, 1978), 5.2.39.9.

49. Augustine, *Confessions*, Tr. John K. Ryan (New York: Doubleday, 1960), 1.1.

50. Augustine, *Confessions*, 9.9.

51. Ibid., 9.10.

52. Alighieri, *Paradise*, 33.124–26.

53. Alighieri, *Purgatory*, 27.121–23.

54. Berry, *Jayber Crow*, 351.

55. Wendell Berry, "Passing the Strait," in *Collected Poems 1957–1982* (San Francisco: New Point Press, 1985), 263–64.


Chapter 17: Wendell Berry: A Latter-Day St. Benedict
Rod Dreher


1. Wendell Berry, "Discipline and Hope," in *A Continuous Harmony: Essays Cultural and Agricultural* (Washington, DC: Shoemaker & Hoard, 1970) 84.

2. Alasdair MacIntyre, *Whose Justice? Which Rationality?* (Notre Dame: University of Notre Dame Press, 1988), 392.

3. Wendell Berry, "Sex, Economy, Freedom, and Community," in *Sex, Economy, Freedom, and Community* (New York: Pantheon Books, 1992) 122.

4. Alan Ehrenhalt, *The Lost City: The Forgotten Virtues of Community in America* (New York: Basic Books, 1995). Republished as "The Lost City: The Case for Social Authority," in *The Essential Civil Society Reader: The Classic Essays*, ed. Don Eberly (Lanham, MD: Rowman & Littlefield, 2000), 253

5. Wendell Berry, "A Few Words in Favor of Edward Abbey," in *What Are People For?* (New York: North Point Press, 1990), 37.

6. Kimberly K. Smith, "Wendell Berry's Political Vision," in *Wendell Berry: Life and Work*, ed. Jason Peters (Louisville: The University Press of Kentucky, 2007), 50.

7. Edmund Burke, "Appeal from the New to the Old Whigs," in *Further Reflections on the Revolution in France* (Indianapolis: Liberty Fund, Inc., 1992), 161.

8. Andrew Bacevich, *The New American Militarism: How Americans Are Seduced by War* (New York: Oxford University Press, 2005).

9. Raymond Zulueta, quoted in "Facing Default, Some Walk Out on New Homes," in *New York Times*, Feb. 29, 2008 (http://www.nytimes.com/2008/02/29/us/29walks.html, accessed June 19, 2011).

10. Wendell Berry, "The Agrarian Standard," in *Citizenship Papers* (Washington, DC: Shoemaker & Hoard, 2003), 146.

11. Wendell Berry, *The Unsettling of America: Culture and Agriculture* (San Francisco: Sierra Club Books, 1997), 53.

12. Sven Birkerts, "Looking the Technological Gift Horse in the Mouth," in *Wendell Berry: Life and Work*, 236

13. Alasdair MacIntyre, "The Only Vote Worth Casting in November," published on the Notre Dame Center for Ethics and Culture website, undated. (http://www.brandon.multics.org/library/Alasdair_MacIntyre/macintyre2004vote.xhtml, accessed June 30, 2011).

14. Claes Ryn, "What Is Left? What Is Right?" *The American Conservative* (August 28, 2006), 26.

15. Alasdair MacIntyre, "Politics, Philosophy and the Common Good," in *The MacIntyre Reader*, ed. Kelvin Knight (Notre Dame: University of Notre Dame Press, 1998), 237.

16. Ibid., 248.

17. It's not for nothing that Patrick Deneen calls Berry a "Kentucky Aristotelian"; given the Christian sources of Berry's thought, he might have dubbed him a "hillbilly

Thomist" if Flannery O'Connor hadn't already claimed the term for herself. *Wendell Berry: Life and Work*, 304ff.

18. Alasdair MacIntyre, *After Virtue*, 2nd ed. (South Bend: University of Notre Dame Press, 1984), 263

19. Wendell Berry, "The Whole Horse," in *Citizenship Papers*, 121

20. Rod Dreher, *Crunchy Cons* (New York: Crown Forum, 2006), 111–14.

21. Pope Benedict XVI and Marcello Pera, *Without Roots*, trans. Michael F. Moore (New York: Basic Books, 2006), 125–26.

22. Wendell Berry, "Feminism, the Body, and the Machine," in *What Are People For?*, 195.

# The Works of Wendell Berry:
# A Selected Bibliography

Nonfiction

*Another Turn of the Crank: Essays.* Washington, DC: Counterpoint, 1996.

*The Art of the Commonplace: The Agrarian Essays of Wendell Berry.* Ed. Norman Wirzba. Washington, DC: Counterpoint, 2002.

*Blessed Are the Peacemakers: Christ's Teachings about Love, Compassion & Forgiveness.* Washington, DC: Shoemaker & Hoard, 2005.

*Citizenship Papers: Essays.* Washington, DC: Shoemaker & Hoard, 2003.

*A Continuous Harmony: Essays Cultural & Agricultural.* New York: Harcourt, Brace, Jovanovich, 1972 (Shoemaker & Hoard, 2004).

*Farming: A Hand Book.* New York: Harcourt, Brace, Jovanovich, 1970.

*The Gift of Good Land: Further Essays Cultural and Agricultural.* San Francisco: North Point Press, 1981.

*The Hidden Wound.* Boston: Houghton Mifflin, 1970.

*Home Economics: Fourteen Essays.* New York: North Point Press, 1987.

*In the Presence of Fear: Three Essays for a Changed World.* Barrington, MA: Orion, 2001.

*Life Is a Miracle: An Essay Against Modern Superstition.* Washington, DC: Counterpoint, 2000.

*The Long-Legged House.* New York: Harcourt, Brace, Jovanovich, 1969 (Shoemaker & Hoard, 2004).

*Sex, Economy, Freedom and Community: Eight Essays.* New York: Pantheon Books, 1992.

*Standing by Words.* San Francisco: North Point Press, 1983 (Shoemaker & Hoard, 2005).

*The Unsettling of America: Culture and Agriculture.* San Francisco: Sierra Club Books, 1977; Avon Books, 1978; Sierra Club Books, 1986.

*The Way of Ignorance: And Other Essays.* Washington, DC: Shoemaker & Hoard, 2005.

*What Are People For?* New York: North Point Press, 1990.


Fiction

*Andy Catlett: Early Travels.* Washington, DC: Shoemaker & Hoard, 2006.

*Fidelity: Five Stories.* New York: Pantheon Books, 1992.

*Hannah Coulter: A Novel.* Washington, DC: Shoemaker & Hoard. 2004.

*Jayber Crow: The Life Story of Jayber Crow, Barber, of the William Membership as Written by Himself.* Washington, DC: Counterpoint, 2000.

*The Memory of Old Jack.* New York: Harcourt, Brace, Jovanovich 1974. (revised Counterpoint 2001).

*Nathan Coulter: A Novel.* Boston: Houghton Mifflin, 1960 (revised North Point Press, 1985).

*A Place on Earth: A Novel.* Boston: Harcourt, Brace, 1967 (revised North Point Press, 1983; Counterpoint, 2001).

*Remembering: A Novel.* San Francisco: North Point Press, 1988.

*That Distant Land: The Collected Stories.* Washington, DC: Shoemaker & Hoard, 2004.

*Three Short Novels (Nathan Coulter, Remembering, A World Lost).* Washington, D.C.: Counterpoint, 2002.

*Two More Stories of the Port William Membership.* Frankfort, Kentucky: Gnomon, 1997.

*Watch with Me and Six Other Stories of the Yet-Remembered Ptolemy Proudfoot and His Wife, Miss Minnie, Née Quinch.* New York: Pantheon Books, 1994.

*Whitefoot: A Story from the Center of the World.* Berkeley, CA: Counterpoint, 2009.

*The Wild Birds: Six Stories of the Port William Membership.* San Francisco: North Point Press, 1986.

*A World Lost: A Novel.* Washington, DC: Counterpoint, 1996.


Poetry

*The Broken Ground.* New York: Harcourt, Brace & World. 1964.

*Clearing.* New York: Harcourt, Brace, 1977.

*The Collected Poems, 1957–1982.* San Francisco: North Point Press, 1985.

*The Country of Marriage: Poems.* New York: Harcourt, Brace, Jovanovich, 1973.

*Entries: Poems.* New York: Pantheon, 1994 (reprint Washington, DC: Counterpoint, 1997).

*Farming: A Hand Book.* New York: Harcourt, Brace, Jovanovich, 1970.

*Given: New Poems.* Washington DC: Shoemaker & Hoard, 2005.

*Openings: Poems.* New York: Harcourt, Brace, Jovanovich, 1968.

*A Part.* San Francisco: North Point Press, 1980.

*Sabbaths: Poems.* San Francisco: North Point Press, 1987.

*Sabbaths 2002.* Monterey, Kentucky: Larkspur, 2004.

*Sabbaths 2006*. Monterey, Kentucky: Larkspur, 2008.

*The Selected Poems of Wendell Berry*. Washington, DC: Counterpoint, 1998.

*A Timbered Choir: The Sabbath Poems 1979–1997*. Washington, DC: Counterpoint, 1998.

*The Wheel*. San Francisco, North Point Press, 1982.

*Window Poems*. Washington, DC: Shoemaker & Hoard, 2007.

# About the Authors

**MATT BONZO** has taught philosophy at Cornerstone University since 1998. He is also the proprietor of Small Wonders Farm, a community-supported agriculture experiment that he runs with his wife Dorothe and his son Matthias on his land in Newaygo County. He is the author of *Indwelling the Forsaken Other* (Pickwick Publications) and with Michael Stevens, *Wendell Berry and the Cultivation of Life* (Brazos Press) and *After Worldview* (Dordt College Press).

**ANNE HUSTED BURLEIGH** is a freelance writer, wife of 47 years, mother, and grandmother, who lives in Rabbit Hash, Kentucky. She has written many articles and columns for such publications as *Modern Age*; *Intercollegiate Review*; *Crisis Magazine*; *Magnificat*; *Catholic Dossier*; *Canticle*; *Homiletic & Pastoral Review*; *National Catholic Register*; *Sacred Architecture*; and *Communio*. She is the author of *Journey up the River, A Midwesterner's Spiritual Pilgrimage* (Ignatius Press) and *John Adams* (Transaction Publishers). She is also the editor of *Education in a Free Society* (Liberty Fund). Anne has published numerous pieces on Wendell Berry, including an interview with Berry that was republished in *Conversations with Wendell Berry* (University Press of Mississippi). In April, 2008, she presented the Founder's Day lecture, "Wendell Berry on Membership," for the 173rd anniversary of the Mercantile Library, Cincinnati, Ohio.

**ALLAN CARLSON** is President of the Howard Center for Family, Religion & Society and also Distinguished Visiting Professor of Political Science and History at Hillsdale College. He serves on the editorial boards of *Intercollegiate Review* and *Touchstone*. His books include *The New Agrarian Mind* (Transaction Publishers), *Third Ways* (ISI Books), *Conjugal America: On the Public Purposes of Marriage* (Transaction Publishers), and *American Way: Family and Community in the Shaping of the American Identity* (ISI Books).

**PATRICK DENEEN** is an associate professor of government at Georgetown University and is the Founding Director of the Tocqueville Forum on the Roots of American Democracy. He is the author of two books: *The Odyssey of Political Theory* (Rowman & Littlefield) and *Democratic Faith* (Princeton University Press) and co-editor of *Democracy's Literature* (Rowman & Littlefield). He is also the author of a number of articles and reviews on ancient and American political thought as well as areas of religion and politics and literature and politics.

**ROD DREHER** is a Philadelphia writer and author of *Crunchy Cons How Birkenstocked Burkeans, Gun-loving Organic Gardeners, Evangelical Free-Range Farmers, Hip Homeschooling Mamas, Right-Wing Nature Lovers, and their Diverse Tribe of Countercultural Conservatives Plan to Save America (or at least the Republican Party)*.

**ANTHONY ESOLEN** is a professor of English at Providence College. His books include *Ironies of Faith* (ISI Books), *The Politically Incorrect Guide to Western Civilization* (Regnery), *Ten Ways to Destroy the Imagination of your Child* (ISI Books), and the Modern Library translation of Dante's *Divine Comedy* (three volumes, Random House).

**WILLIAM FAHEY** is a Classicist and President of the Thomas More College of Liberal Arts. He is interested in all authors that inflame his love of learning and desire for God. He has co-edited (with Joseph Pearce) a volume of Hilaire Belloc's political thought, as well as an anthology on the principle of subsidiarity (with Thomas Stork). He hopes one day to return to his translating of forgotten spiritual and political works of the West. Until then, he is more than satisfied raising a family with his wife in southern New Hampshire. He has a small orchard.

**RICHARD M. GAMBLE** is Anna Margaret Ross Alexander Professor of History and Political Science at Hillsdale College in Hillsdale, Michigan. He is the author of *The War for Righteousness: The Progressive Clergy, the Great War, and the Rise of Messianic Nation* (ISI Books, 2003) and editor of *The Great Tradition: Classic Readings on What It Means to Be an Educated Human Being* (ISI Books, 2008).

**D. G. HART** teaches history at Hillsdale College and is the author of several books on the history of Christianity in the United States, including most recently *From Billy Graham to Sarah Palin: Evangelicals and the Betrayal of American Conservatism* (2011) and *Between the Times: the Orthodox Presbyterian Church in Transition, 1945 to 1990* (2011).

**MARK MITCHELL** teaches political theory at Patrick Henry College, where he is the chair of the government department. His first book, *Michael Polanyi: The Art of Knowing*, was published in 2006 by ISI Books. He is the co-founder and editor-in-chief of the web-zine Front Porch Republic. He lives in West Virginia with his wife and three sons.

JASON PETERS is professor of English at Augustana College (Illinois). His work has appeared in *Sewanee Review, South Atlantic Quarterly, Orion,* and *Journal of Religion and Society,* among other places. He is the editor of *Wendell Berry: Life and Work* (The University Press of Kentucky, 2007).

LUKE SCHLUETER holds a Ph.D. in English from Kent State University, where he wrote his dissertation on the poetry of Wendell Berry and Gary Snyder. He is a Lecturer in English at Cuyahoga Community College in Cleveland, Ohio, where he lives with his wife and three children. He is currently developing a comprehensive Great Books literature curriculum for the Institute of Reading Development. Luke also writes extensively on contemporary poetry, and is a published poet himself. His work has appeared in *Blueline, Slant, Arsenic Lobster,* and *Asphodel.*

NATHAN SCHLUETER received his Ph.D. in Politics at the University of Dallas. He is an associate professor of philosophy at Hillsdale College, where he teaches courses in political theory, English literature, and philosophy. He is the author of *One Dream or Two? Justice in America and in the Thought of Martin Luther King, Jr.* (Lexington Books). His published essays, treating subjects ranging from Plato to Shakespeare to abortion and the fourteenth amendment, have appeared in *First Things, Touchstone, Logos,* and *The Catholic Social Science Review.* When not teaching and writing, he keeps busy helping his wife Elizabeth homeschool their six children.

MARK SHIFFMAN is assistant professor in the Humanities Department and the Classical Studies Program at Villanova University, where he also teaches courses in political theory. He earned his B.A. from St. John's College, Annapolis, and his M.A. and Ph.D. from the University of Chicago's Committee on Social Thought. He has published articles and essays on Aristotle, Plutarch, Virgil, Augustine, Ralph Ellison, and Rémi Brague, and has translated Aristotle's *De Anima* (*On the Soul*) for Focus Press. He lives in the Mt. Airy neighborhood of Philadelphia with his wife and two sons.

CALEB STEGALL is the former District Attorney of Jefferson County, Kansas and current Chief Counsel to Governor Sam Brownback. He was the founder and editor of the late, great web journal The New Pantagruel. He lives on a small farm with his wife and their five sons in Perry, Kansas.

MICHAEL STEVENS is a professor of English in the Humanities Division at Cornerstone University (Grand Rapids, MI), where he has taught since 1997. He teaches a range of courses in literature, creative writing, and philosophy, and also directs the university's Honors Program. He received his Ph.D. in Literature from the Institute of Philosophic Studies at the University of Dallas. He is the co-author with Matt Bonzo of *Wendell Berry and the Cultivation of Life* (Brazos Press) and the author of several articles on T. S. Eliot's socio-political ideas. He and his wife Linda live in Grand Rapids with their three children, Ethan, Julia, and Gabriel.

# Index

Abbey, Edward, 2, 52, 58, 93
*Abolition of Man, The*, 214
abortion, x, 21–22
"Abstraction," 199
Adam, 8, 139, 217, 231
*Advancement of Learning, The*, 67
"Against the War in Vietnam," 108, 110
Agar, Herbert, 194–95
agrarian mind, 99–100, 180–81
agrarian standard, 46–47, 52–64
"Agrarian Standard, The," 62
agrarianism, x–xi, 144–45, 151, 167, 179–81, 197–200
agrarians, 20–21, 46, 52, 99, 126, 134–38, 194–97, 284
agricultural ideals, 250–52
agricultural policies, 141, 154, 161, 199
agricultural practices, 40–49, 58, 60, 119–20, 145, 150–51, 160–62
agriculture
    appreciation of, x–xi
    environment and, 62–63, 284–85
    industrial agriculture, x–xi, 46–48, 52, 107, 113–14, 179–82
    land use and, xi, 5, 59–64, 179
    support for, 40–41, 74, 284–85
Altieri, Charles, 237
*American Review*, 194
*Andy Catlett: Early Travels*, 48, 227
*Another Turn of the Crank*, 23, 55
anthropology, 65–68, 77–80, 203
Anti-Federalists, 85–86
"Appeal from the New to the Old Whigs," 278–79
Aquinas, St. Thomas, 205
Aristotle, 68–72, 78, 83–87, 147–53, 156–59, 162, 166, 193, 206, 214
art
    of farming, 150–51, 198
    literary art, 161–62, 239–40, 244
    power of, 220–21
    science and, 129, 206–7, 211, 213–14, 217, 222
autonomy. *See also* self-control; self-governance; self-sufficiency
    of communities, x

autonomy *(continued)*
  democracy and, 68, 85
  economic autonomy, 277
  quest for, 225–26, 245
  self-control and, 216
  sexual autonomy, 277
Ayres, Milton, 19

Babbitt, Irving, 229
Bacevich, Andrew, 279
Bacon, Francis, 66–67
Bailey, Liberty Hyde, 52
*Band of Brothers*, 106, 120
*Becoming Native to This Place*, 37
Belloc, Hilaire, 172–74, 180–81,
  187–88, 192–94, 199–200, 206–8
Benedict Option, 283, 286
Berry, Tanya, ix, 6, 7, 244
Berryman, John, 3
Bible, 20, 41, 129–39, 204, 221
"Big Two-Hearted River," 6, 161–62
birth control, 23–26
Blake, William, 220
*Blessed Are the Peacemakers: Christ's
  Teachings about Love, Compassion
  and Forgiveness*, 118–19
"body and soul," 126–38, 218,
  227–28
"body, indolency of ," 67
Bonzo, Matt, 40
Borsodi, Ralph, 195
Bradford, William, 204
*Brave New World*, 211
British Distributists, 190–209
"Broken Ground, The," 25
*Broken Ground, The*, 240
"Burden of the Gospels, The," 119
Burke, Edmund, 278
Burleigh, Anne Husted, x, 7

capital punishment, 21–22
capitalism
  contemporary capitalism, 193–94

corporate capitalism, x, 167,
  170–73
  definition of, 172
  free market and, 167–68
  industrial capitalism, 172–74, 187
  laissez-faire capitalism, 172–73,
    196–97, 276
*Capitalism, Socialism and Democracy*,
  181–82
caretakers, 54, 81, 180
Carlson, Allan, 19, 199
*Catholic Worker, The*, 196
Catholicism, 193, 207
Caudill, Harry, 2, 52
*Centesimus Annus*, 193
Chain of Being, 222–25
*Challenging Nature*, 215
Chesterton, G. K., 172, 192–94, 200,
  205–7, 263
*Christian Century, The*, 118
Christianity, 124–46, 206, 231–32
*Christianity Today*, 124
"Citizen's Response to 'The National
  Security Strategy of the United
  States of America,'" 117–18
citizenship and "being ruled," 68–73
*Citizenship Papers*, 48, 99, 117, 170,
  198
*City of God*, 212, 267
Clinton, Bill, 276
Cobbett, William, 194
Cold War, 111, 194
Coleridge, Samuel Taylor, 194
college, 28–39, 50, 195, 215
communism, xii–xiii, 193–94, 196
communitarianism, xiii, 75, 157, 279
communities
  autonomy of, x
  defender of, 82–83
  leaving, 28–39
  marriage and, 10–11, 82–83
  priority of, 82–84
  schools and, 28–39

self-sufficiency and, 149, 166, 196–97, 282
competition, ideal of, 186–89
Conrad, Joseph, 2
conservation, x, 50–64, 145
"Conservation Is Good Work," 52
conservation movement, 51, 54, 56, 60
"Conservationist and Agrarian," 62
conservatism, x, xiii–xiv, 54, 124–46, 173, 193–99, 275–82
conservative Christianity, 124–46
contemporary capitalism, 193–94. *See also* capitalism
*Continuous Harmony, A*, 2, 114, 125
Coomaraswamy, Ananda, 52
corporate capitalism, x, 167, 170–73. *See also* capitalism
*Country of Marriage, The*, 114
*Courier-Journal*, 194
*Creative Intuition in Art and Poetry*, 244
*Criterion*, 196
*Crunchy Cons*, 281

Danielou, Jean, 269
Dante, xi–xii, 32, 221, 225, 255–74
Davenport, Guy, 52
Day, Dorothy, 194
D-Day, 106, 120
democracy
being ruled and, 68–73
definition of, 65, 68–69, 73, 85
nature and, 73–84
self-governance and, 65–88
self-sufficiency and, 71, 86
"tendencies" of, 74–75, 84–85
understanding, 65–73, 84–88
Democrats, 21–22, 276–78, 281
Deneen, Patrick J., 65
Descartes, Rene, 66
Diamond, Jared, 44
Dionysian writers, 4
Distributism
distinctions of, 199–202

fundamentals of, 197, 205
origins of, 192–97
theology behind, 204
distributist state, 172
Distributists, 190–209
*Divine Comedy*, 225, 257–59, 265–66
divorce, opposition to, x, 12
"domestic partnership," 22
Dreher, Rod, 275
*Dublin Review*, 196

economy
ethics and, 148–52
free market and, 167–89
Great Economy, 44, 48, 77, 133, 167, 178–82, 189
market economy, 166–68, 174–75, 182–88, 282
new economy, 152–56
Total Economy, 167–79, 188
education
community and, 28–39
higher education, 28–39, 50, 195, 215
for membership, 28–39
products of, 80–81
sex education, 22–23
Ehrenhalt, Alan, 278
"Elegy," 250
Eliot, T. S., xii, 196, 214, 218
elites, 81, 276
Emerson, Ralph Waldo, 3
environment
agriculture and, 62–63, 284–85
conservation and, 50–64
defending, 5, 21–22
"passing through" bodies, 53, 58–63
technology and, 58–59
"Envoy," 245
Esolen, Anthony, 255
ethics and economy, 148–52
evangelicalism, 124–26, 133–34, 142–44

Eve, 8, 217, 231
*Everlasting Man*, 206
*Eye Witness*, 196

*Fable of the Bees; Or, Private Vices,
    Publick Benefits*, 175
Fahey, William Edmund, 190
"Failure of War, The," 117
faithfulness, 9–10, 18
fallen condition, xii, 107, 120–23,
    140–41, 204, 230
fallen man, 140, 204, 226, 230
family farms, 45–47, 145, 190–91,
    199, 284. *See also* farming
farm animals, 20, 46
farming
    art of, 150–51, 198
    family farms, 45–47, 145, 190–91,
        199, 284
    importance of, 50–64
    satisfaction in, 40–46
    small farmers, 45–47, 108, 171,
        205–6, 282
*Farming: A Hand Book*, 108
farmlessness, 45–47
fascism, xii–xiii
"February 2, 1968," 119
"Feminism, the Body, and the
    Machine," 95, 244
fidelity, 8–18
"Fidelity," 103
*Fidelity: Five Stores*, 121
Flood, Owen, 250–53
food. *See also* agriculture
    gratitude for, 40–49
    growing, 40–49, 59–60
    responsibility for, 40–49, 59–60
    as weapon, 44–47, 161
    wholesomeness of, 2
"For the Hog Killing," 114
*Four Men, The*, 208
*Four Quartets, The*, 218
*Free America*, 196

free market, defense of, 167–89
freedom
    definition of, 69
    of mind, 4–5
    self-governance and, 88
    self-sufficiency and, 99, 101–3,
        181, 185
    technology and, 4–5, 99–102
Frost, Robert, 240

*G. K.'s Weekly*, 196
Gamble, Richard, 28
"Gathering, The," 246–48
"Gift of Good Land, The," 41, 97
Gioia, Dana, 236
*Given: New Poems*, 119
Goldberg, Jonah, 281
Gospels, 118–19, 134–36
Great Depression, 30, 175, 184
*Great Divorce, The*, 273
Great Economy, 44, 48, 77, 133, 167,
    178–82, 189. *See also* economy
*Guns, Germs, and Steel*, 44

*Hannah Coulter*, 12, 15, 26–27,
    30–31, 35–36, 122–23, 162–65,
    227
*Harper's*, 94, 95
Hart, D. G., 124
Hartz, Louis, 75
Hayek, F. A., 172
healthiness, 127–28. *See also* wholeness
Heidegger, Martin, 45, 159
Hemingway, Ernest, 6, 161–62, 213
Heraclitus, 237
*Hidden Wound, The*, 34
higher education, 28–39, 50, 195, 215
"Hind Tit, The," 195
Hobbes, Thomas, 66–67, 152–57, 213
Hollis Apple Festival, 190–209
*Home Economics*, 58, 77, 114, 158
homecoming, 28–31, 36–39
homelessness, 38, 45–48, 280

homemaking, 31, 37, 39, 151
Homer, 32, 221, 250
homeschooling, 38, 83, 284. *See also* education
hometowns, leaving, 28–30
homosexuality, 21–22
horse-drawn implements, 98–99
"Horses," 93
horses, and technology, 89–105
Howard, Albert, 52
Hubbard, Harlan, 52
*Huckleberry Finn*, 37
human, vision of, 234–54
*Humane Economy, A*, 174
humane vision, xi–xiv, 192, 211–12, 223–28, 235, 286–87
humanity and nature, 75–78, 161
husbandry, 26, 55, 119, 278
Huxley, Aldous, 211

ignorance, way of, xii, 48, 118, 218
*I'll Take My Stand*, 52
Illich, Ivan, 96–97, 99, 104
imagination
    Edenic imagination, 228–33
    humane vision and, 223–28
    integral imagination, 210–33
    reason and, 212–23
"In Distrust of Movements," 74
Incarnation, 13–15, 18, 206–7
individualism
    humanism of, 104
    ideology of, 276–77
    individuality and, xiii, 220
    metaphysical individualism, 155–60
    Miltonic individualism, 208
    religious individualism, 133–34
    romantic individualism, 31
    rugged individualism, 20–21, 73–74
    self-creation and, 225
individuality, xiii, 220

"indolency of the body," 67
industrial age, 31–32, 100
industrial agriculture, x–xi, 46–48, 52, 107, 113–14, 179–82. *See also* agriculture
industrial capitalism, 172–74, 187. *See also* capitalism
Industrial Revolution, 193
industrial tools, 97–103
industrialism
    agrarianism and, x–xi, 179–81, 198
    alternative to, 179–80
    Christianity and, 126, 133, 141–42
    evangelicalism and, 142–44
*Inferno*, 255, 269
intellectualism, xiii, 3
intimacy, 25, 246–47
*isms*, xiii, 51, 63, 213

Jackson, Wes, 37, 43, 52, 57
Jacobs, Alan, 124
Jarrell, Randall, 3
*Jayber Crow*, 30–35, 37, 203, 255–59
Jefferson, Thomas, x–xi, 52, 110, 182, 185, 188, 199
Jeffersonian tradition, x–xi, 196, 200
Jesus, 13, 118, 131–37, 204, 227–29, 258–59, 271
Jewett, Stephen, 190
John Paul II, Pope, 193, 229

Kant, Immanuel, 193
Kass, Leon, 213
Kemmis, Daniel, 21
"Kentucky barber," 255–74
Keynes, John Maynard, 175–76, 185
*King Lear*, 131–32, 139, 224, 258
King, Martin Luther, 112
Kipling, Rudyard, 55
Kirk, Russell, 196, 229
Knight, Frank, 177–78

laissez-faire capitalism, 172–73, 196–97, 276. *See also* capitalism
laws of nature, 76, 80, 282
*Leavings*, 240
Left, the, x, 20–21, 51, 80
Leo XIII, Pope, 194, 195
Leopold, Aldo, 52
*Letter Concerning Toleration, A*, 67
"Letter to Daniel Kemmis," 21
*Leviathan*, 152, 154
Lewis, C. S., 214, 215, 230, 273
liberal anthropology, 65–68, 77–79. *See also* anthropology
liberal democracy, 65–77. *See also* democracy
liberalism, x, xiii, 22, 65–77, 83–87, 149, 165, 187, 193, 283
libertarianism, xiii, 22, 155
*Life Is a Miracle*, 32, 35, 201, 215
Locke, John, 66–67, 154
*Long-Legged House, The*, 2, 112
*Lost City, The*, 278
love
  fidelity and, 8–18
  intimacy and, 25, 246–47
  marriage and, 7–10
  physical love, 25, 246–47
  sexual love, 19–27
  theology of, 269–74
Lytle, Andrew, 195–96

Machiavelli, Niccolò, 212–14
MacIntyre, Alasdair, 280–82
Maclean, Norman, 6, 161–62
"Mad Farmer Manifesto: The First Amendment," 89
"Mad Farmer's Love Song, The," 114
Madison, James, 199
"Making It Home," 121
Mandeville, Bernard, 175
Manning, Cardinal, 194
"March 22, 1968," 110
Maritain, Jacques, 244

market economy, 166–68, 174–75, 182–88, 282. *See also* economy
marriage
  community and, 10–11
  elements of, 8–10, 15–18
  fidelity and, 8–18
  garden of, 18
  love and, 7–10
  meaning of, 7–10
  membership and, 7–18
  same-sex marriage, 22
  vision of, 244–45
  as work of art, 18
Marxism, 193
materialism, 35, 192–97, 219, 260
Maurin, Peter, 194, 195
McNabb, Vincent, 192, 194–96, 206
"Membership," 230
membership. *See also* Port William membership
  education for, 28–39
  marriage and, 7–18
  wholeness and, 102–5
*Memory of Old Jack, The*, 48–49, 227
"meritocracy," 80
metaphysical individualism, 155–60. *See also* individualism
*Metaphysics*, 206
"Michael," 32
Michel, Virgil, 194
Milton, John, 221
Miltonic individualism, 208. *See also* individualism
Mitchell, Mark T., ix, 167
Montesquieu, 86
moral vision, 285–87
More, Thomas, xiii
Morton, Thomas, 204
movements, distrust of, xiii, 50–58, 63, 73–74, 213
Muir, John, 52

Nabhan, Gary, 52
*Nathan Coulter*, 2
"Native Hill, A," 200–201
nature
    democracy and, 73–84
    humanity and, 75–78, 161
    laws of, 76, 80, 282
    state of, 67–70, 79
    work and, 243–44
*New Age, The*, 196
new economy, 152–56. *See also*
    economy
*New Witness, The*, 196
*New York Times*, 279
Newman, Henry, 194
Nietzsche, Friedrich, 158
"Notes: Unspecializing Poetry," 238,
    245

Obama, Barack, 276
"Of Man," 67
*Of Plimouth Plantation*, 204
*Oikonomia*, rediscovery of, 147–66
*Old Man and the Sea, The*, 213
*Openings*, 110, 111
*Orate–Fratres*, 196
orchards, 91, 190–91
Orwell, George, 55
Osteen, Joel, 146
"Our Children, Coming of Age,"
    248–49
*Outline of Sanity*, 207
"overpopulation," 26

pacifism, x, 106–23
*Paradise Lost*, 202
*Paradise Lost*, 215
*Part, A*, 114
Patriot Act, 117–18
patriotism, 117–18, 155, 228
"Peace of Wild Things, The," 111, 243
peacemaking, 106–23
Percy, Walker, 214

Peters, Jason, 50
Peterson, Eugene, 124–25, 134
piety, xiii, 118, 137, 142
Pius XII, Pope, 205
place, free to know, 35
place, of poetry, 234–54
*Place on Earth, A*, 2, 122
place, respect for, 2–3
"placed Creation," 203–8
"placed person," ix, 1–6
Plath, Sylvia, 3
Plato, 68, 148, 156, 159, 165, 212,
    214
*Playboy*, 20, 22
"Pleasures of Eating, The," 2
"Poetry and Marriage," 237
poetry, place of, 234–54
Polanyi, Karl, 166, 170, 172–73, 187
political movement, 275–80
*Politics*, 68, 149
"Politics, Philosophy and the Com-
    mon Good," 281
Pope, Alexander, 52, 221
Port William membership, 11–12,
    16–17, 32–37, 89–90, 103,
    162–63, 256, 259
practical philosophy, 148–49, 152, 166
Pratt, Don, 112
"Pray Without Ceasing," 9
*Prince, The*, 212–13
private property, x, 20, 167–68,
    180–86
procreation, 19–27
*Progressive*, 55
promiscuity, x
propriety, restoration of, 190–209
prosthetics, 89–90, 97, 102
Protestantism, 126, 133–34, 141–45

Ransom, John Crowe, 52
Reagan, Ronald, 276
reason and imagination, 212–23
reductionism, 178, 219

religious individualism, 133–34. *See also* individualism

*Remaking Eden*, 215

"Remarks on the Southern Religion," 94

*Remembering*, 15, 28–31, 89–90, 92, 160, 225–27, 232

reproductivity, 23–24. *See also* procreation

*Republic*, 212, 214

Republicans, 21, 199, 275–78, 281

*Rerum Novarum*, 193

Richards, I. A., 157

Right, the, 20–21, 27, 51, 80, 146

"right to life," 21–22

"River Runs Through It, A," 6, 161–62

romantic individualism, 31. *See also* individualism

romanticism, xi, 213–18, 221, 227, 230, 237

Roosevelt administration, 196

Röpke, Wilhelm, 174, 182–83, 187–88, 196–97

"rugged individualism," 20–21, 73–74. *See also* individualism

"ruling and being ruled," 68–73

Ruskin, John, 194

"Sabbath," 10

"Sabbath IV, 1983," 115

St. Augustine, xii, 205, 212, 267, 273

St. Benedict, 275–87

St. Bonaventure, 205

same-sex marriage, 22

Sandburg, Carl, 240

Santayana, George, 86–87

"Satisfaction of the Mad Farmer, The," 40–41

Schlueter, Luke, 234

Schlueter, Nathan, ix, 210

schools and community, 28–39. *See also* communities; education

Schumacher, E. F., 52, 196

Schumpeter, Joseph, 181–83

Schwartz, Delmore, 3

science and art, 211–17, 222

scientific method, 195, 219

scientism, x, xi, 214

self-control, 26, 82, 174–75, 184, 205

self-governance, 65–88

self-sufficiency
  community and, 149, 166, 196–97, 282
  democracy and, 71, 86
  freedom and, 99, 101–3, 181, 185
  local self-sufficiency, 117
  technology and, 90

September 11 bombings, 107, 115–16

*Servile State, The*, 172

servitude, 44, 100–101

"Sex, Economy, Freedom, and Community," 11, 13, 22, 276

*Sex, Economy, Freedom, and Community*, 114

sex education, 22–23

sexual liberation, 24

sexual love, 19–27

sexual privacy, 23–24

sexual responsibility, 22–23

Shakespeare, William, 52, 224

Shaw, Nate, 2

Sherrard, Philip, 52

Shiffman, Mark, 147

Silver, Lee, 215

small farmer, 45–47, 108, 171, 205–6, 282. *See also* farming

Smith, Adam, 154

Smith, J. Russell, 52

Smith, Kimberly K., 278

Snyder, Gary, 239, 240

*Social Justice Review*, 196

social vision, 197–98

socialism, 172, 182, 194, 196

"Some Thoughts on Citizenship and Conscience in Honor of Don Pratt," 112

"Specialization of Poetry," 236
Spenser, Edmund, 52, 76
Spinoza, Baruch, 66
spiritual health, 127–28, 138, 140–41
standard of living, 55–59, 184
*Standing by Words*, 9, 211, 215–16, 238
"Standing Ground, A," 105
state of nature, 67–70, 79
"Statement Against the War in Vietnam, A," 108, 111
"Statement of Principles," 52
Stegall, Caleb, 89
Stegner, Wallace, ix, xiii–xiv, 1, 6, 52
sterilization, 23, 25–26
Stevens, Michael R., 106
stewardship
    discovering, 284–85
    ethic of, 278
    importance of, 5, 16, 196
    irresponsibility of, 276
    responsibility of, 54, 80, 203–4
    shared stewardship, 146
"Stones, The," 241, 242

*Tablet*, 196
Tate, Alan, 94
"technological multipliers," 26
technology
    environment and, 58–59
    freedom and, 4–5, 99–102
    horses and, 89–105
    self-sufficiency and, 90
    wariness of, 89–94
    of wholeness, 89–105
Tennyson, Alfred, 32
terrorist attacks, 107, 115–16
thanks, giving, 40–49
*Theology of the Body, The*, 229
Thoreau, Henry David, 3, 5, 52, 132, 204, 287
"Thoughts in the Presence of Fear," 116

*Timbered Choir: The Sabbath Poems 1979–1997*, 115
"To a Siberian Woodsman," 111
"To My Children, Fearing for Them," 110
Todd, John, 52
tools, 94–103
*Tools for Conviviality*, 96–97
Total Economy, 167–79, 188. *See also* economy
totalitarianism, xii–xiii, 77, 236
transcendentalism, xi, 3, 204
Twain, Mark, 37
"2002, I," 119
"2004, III," 120

"Ulysses," 32
*Unsettling of America, The*, 2, 51, 53, 59–63, 114, 125–27, 139, 141, 143, 151, 177, 198
"urban conservationists," 58–61
utility, 94–103
utopianism, xii–xiii, 173, 225

Vietnam War, 106–23
Virgil, 52, 205–6, 240, 250, 266
virtues, cultivation of, 167, 178–79, 182–86
vision
    of human, 234–54
    humane vision, xi–xiv, 192, 211–12, 223–28, 235, 286–87
    of marriage, 244–45
    moral vision, 285–87
    restoring, 160–66
    social vision, 197–98
von Mises, Ludwig, 178

*Waiting for God*, 159
Walker, Graham, 194
"Want of Peace, The," 111
war
    Cold War, 111, 194

war *(continued)*
  narratives of, 120–23
  opposition to, 21–22, 108–11
  shadow of, 106–23
  on terror, 107, 115–16
  Vietnam War, 106–23
  World War II, 11, 15, 106–7,
    120–22, 196
Warren, Rick, 146
*Way of Ignorance, The,* 48, 118, 218
Weaver, Richard, 196
*Weekly World News,* 19, 27
Weil, Simone, 159
welfare state, hostility to, x
*What Are People For?,* 1, 2, 4, 92, 114
Whitefield, George, 142
Whitman, Walt, 240
*Who Owns America?,* 196
"Whole Horse, The," 145
wholeness
  grasping, xi–xii

  health and, 127–28
  integral wholeness, xi, 211–12, 231
  membership and, 102–5
  restoring, 139–44
  state of, 89–105
  technology and, 89–105
"Why I am Not Going to Buy a Com-
    puter," 58, 94
"Wild Birds, The," 225
Williams, William Carlos, 239, 240
Winters, Dick, 106, 120
Worcester, Samuel T., 190
Wordsworth, William, 32, 220, 237
"Work of Local Culture, The," 31,
    280
World War II, 11, 15, 106–7, 120–22,
    196
Worster, Donald, 52
"Writer and Region," 2

Xenophon, 148